D1154052

THE COMMODIFICATION

OF ACADEMIC RESEARCH

The Commodification
of Academic Research

SCIENCE

AND THE

MODERN

UNIVERSITY

Edited by Hans Radder

University of Pittsburgh Press

(CLD)
Q
180.55
.E25
C66
2010

Published by the University of Pittsburgh Press, Pittsburgh, Pa., 15260
Copyright © 2010, University of Pittsburgh Press
All rights reserved
Manufactured in the United States of America
Printed on acid-free paper
10 9 8 7 6 5 4 3 2 1

Library of Congress Cataloging-in-Publication Data

The commodification of academic research : science and the modern university / edited by Hans Radder.
    p. cm.
  Revised and expanded papers from an international workshop held in June 2007 at the Faculty of Philosophy, VU University Amsterdam.
  Includes bibliographcal references and index.
  ISBN 13: 978-0-8229-4396-9 (cloth : alk. paper)
  ISBN 10: 0-8229-4396-4 (cloth : alk. paper)
  1. Research—Economic aspects. 2. Science—Philosophy. 3. Science—Moral ethical aspects.
I. Radder, Hans.
    Q180.55.E25C66 2010
    306.4'5—dc22

                    2010011539

LOYOLA UNIVERSITY LIBRARY
WITHDRAWN

Contents

Preface   vii

1. The Commodification of Academic Research   1

    Hans Radder

2. The Commercialization of Academic Culture and the Future
of the University   24

    Daniel Lee Kleinman

3. Knowledge Transfer from Academia to Industry through
Patenting and Licensing: Rhetoric and Reality   44

    Sigrid Sterckx

4. Financial Interests and the Norms of Academic Science   65

    David B. Resnik

5. One-Shot Science   90

    James Robert Brown

6. The Business of Drug Research: A Mixed Blessing   110

    Albert W. Musschenga, Wim J. van der Steen, and Vincent K. Y. Ho

7. The Commodification of Knowledge Exchange: Governing the
Circulation of Biological Data   132

    Sabina Leonelli

8. Research under Pressure: Methodological Features of
Commercialized Science   158

    Martin Carrier

9. Robert Merton, Intellectual Property, and Open Science:
A Sociological History for Our Times   187

    Henk van den Belt

Contents

10. Mertonian Values, Scientific Norms, and the Commodification
of Academic Research   231

    Hans Radder

11. Coercion, Corruption, and Politics in the Commodification of
Academic Science   259

    Mark B. Brown

12. Capitalism and Knowledge: The University between
Commodification and Entrepreneurship   277

    Steve Fuller

13. Viable Alternatives for Commercialized Science: The Case
of Humanistics   307

    Harry Kunneman

List of Contributors   337
Index   341

Preface

WRITING THE PREFACE to a book is always a pleasure, since it means that a large and prolonged project almost has been completed. My first systematic engagement with the commodification of academic research was prompted by the reading of two illuminating books. The first was the 1997 edition of the volume *Biotechnology, Patents and Morality*, edited by Sigrid Sterckx; the second was the 1999 Dutch-language book *De onwelkome boodschap, of hoe de vrijheid van wetenschap bedreigd wordt* (*The Unwelcome Message, or How the Freedom of Science Is Being Jeopardized*), written by André Köbben and Henk Tromp. I felt that the issue of the commodification of scientific research, discussed in these and similar publications, constituted a deep and significant philosophical, political, and moral challenge.

To meet this challenge, we organized an international workshop on this topic, which was held in June 2007 at the Faculty of Philosophy of VU University Amsterdam. The workshop brought together scholars from different disciplines and backgrounds, in particular from philosophy of science, social and political philosophy, and research ethics. Funds for the workshop were made available by the Faculty of Philosophy and the Blaise Pascal Institute of VU University Amsterdam, by the Royal Netherlands Academy of Arts and Sciences, and by the Evert Willem Beth Foundation. I would like to thank these organizations for their financial support. I would also like to acknowledge the practical assistance provided by Anniek van der Schuit and Delene Engelbrecht.

This volume includes the revised and expanded papers from the workshop. Because of the comprehensiveness and complexity of our subject, working with a diverse range of prominent authors proved to be very rewarding. Furthermore, the high level of the comments by the discussants and, more generally, of their contributions to the entire workshop has certainly improved the quality of the chapters of this book. Hence many thanks should go to Justin Biddle, Frans Birrer, Kees Boersma, Bram Bos, Lieven Decock, Delene Engelbrecht, Kor Grit, Johan Heilbron, Marli Huijer, Peter Kirschenmann, Edwin Koster, Jeroen de Ridder, and Jan van der Stoep. In addition, the anonymous reviewers of the University of Pittsburgh Press provided encouraging and helpful review reports. Finally, completing and producing the book was greatly facilitated by the helpful suggestions of Sally Wyatt, the detailed copy editing of my own chapters by Neil Milne, and the professional assistance of the staff at the University of Pittsburgh Press.

THE COMMODIFICATION

OF ACADEMIC RESEARCH

CHAPTER 1

The Commodification
of Academic Research

Hans Radder

SINCE THE 1980s, most universities in the Western world have experienced sub-stantial changes as a consequence of an ongoing process of commodification. Commodification affects a variety of aspects of higher education, such as research, teaching, administration, and even such nonacademic activities as the intercolle-giate sports programs of U.S. universities. This book focuses on one of these as-pects, namely the commodification of academic research.[1]

The aim of the book is to describe, analyze, and evaluate the various facets of commodified academic research from a philosophical perspective; in addition, where appropriate, alternatives to commodified research will be proposed and discussed. More specifically, we will approach the subject from the perspective of philosophy of science, social and political philosophy, and research ethics. A com-prehensive discussion of the phenomenon of commodified science requires a view of the nature and justification of science as a whole, as well as an account of the nature and justification of specific research methods within particular sciences. Hence there is a central role for the philosophy of science. Simultaneously at issue is the question of the actual and desirable sociopolitical institutionalization and organization of science in modern societies. For this reason, the perspective of social and political philosophy is needed. Finally, commodification engenders far-reaching moral issues concerning appropriate conduct in academic research, which is the domain of research ethics. Given the multifaceted nature of the problem of the commodification of academic research, bringing together these different disciplines and approaches is important, and even necessary, for developing in-depth analyses, assessments, and alternatives.

Some good work on the commodification of science has been published recently, primarily by concerned journalists and by natural and social scientists. Moreover, several funding agencies and science policy organizations have issued relevant studies and policy papers on the subject. The contributions to this book use this and related work for the purpose of obtaining relevant empirical knowledge, detailed philosophical analyses and pertinent normative assessments of the commodification of academic research, as well as formulating sensible and practicable alternatives to commodified science.

Thus far, philosophers have hardly begun to explore this subject. Yet sustained and in-depth philosophical study of the commodification of academic research is badly needed. Because of a strong naturalistic tendency in recent accounts of science (both in cognitive and in social studies of science), the normative question of what should count as "good science" has shifted to the background. However, if we want to come to grips with the issue of the commodification of academic inquiry, this question should be center stage. By publishing this book we hope to provide the necessary stimulus for further philosophical research in this area.

The book aims to advance the subject by providing substantial research contributions. The chapters focus on various basic questions regarding the commodification of academic research. The contributions to the book are not, or not primarily, of a "case study" type; instead, they aim (more directly) to present and examine theoretical and philosophical analyses, discuss sociopolitical and moral assessments, and provide viable alternatives. Of course, such approaches need to be informed by the existing literature on the practices of commodified academic science. In addition, several of the chapters, including this one, show that the insiders' experiences of their authors as employees of academic institutions also inform their analyses and assessments in important ways.

This opening chapter introduces the subject of the commodification of academic research. It has two objectives. The first is to provide a conceptual map of the area. For this purpose, it presents and explains the pertinent concepts, cites the relevant empirical literature, discusses the major epistemic, ethical, and social problems, and reviews several proposed solutions. The second objective of this chapter is to place the other chapters of this volume on this map of the area. To this end, the approach taken in these chapters and their contribution to the research arena is sketched. This should not be taken to imply, however, that all contributors will endorse every single claim made in this chapter.

The guiding framework for this chapter is provided by seven *central research questions*. These questions constitute a comprehensive directory to the issue of the commodification of academic research.

1. *What, exactly, do we understand by "commodification of academic research"?* Answering this question includes addressing several more specific issues, such as: What are the historical roots of the notion of commodification? Is commodification limited to pecuniary matters? How does it differ from applying science? Is a private but nonprofit university an academic institution?

2. *Which forms of commodification of research can be distinguished?* Key notions in discussing this question include: commercialization, contract research, privatization, patenting, scientific productivity, publish-or-perish culture, marginalization of noncommodified research, and the demise of public interest science.

3. *How widespread and novel is the phenomenon of academic commodification?* Here, it is important to differentiate between present and past academic science, between different disciplines in present and past academic institutions, and between different national research systems.

4. *How should we assess the commodification of academic research?* From a theoretical perspective, the underlying question is what are, or should be, the basic ideas guiding the desirable behavior of academic researchers and the preferred institutionalization and organization of academic research? In particular, this question includes the meta-issue of the legitimacy of philosophical critique and normativity, and the nature (for instance, epistemological, political, or moral) of its assessment criteria.

5. *How to assess the actual practices of commodified research?* What are the pros and cons of the practices employed by this research? Addressing this question includes an analysis and evaluation of the impact of commodification on methodological procedures, epistemic appraisals, and public trust in scientific inquiry.

6. *Can the drawbacks of commodification be countered by regulation?* Here one should distinguish between external regulation by governmental agencies and self-regulation through ethical codes. A major issue is whether regulation can be effective in the case of structural patterns (rather than incidental instances) of commodification.

7. *What are the alternatives to commodified science?* Theoretically, we may distinguish between three ideal-typical models: commodified science and the alternatives of autonomous and public interest science. Do these models fully exclude one another? Are they compatible? Or can they even be combined in some way? And if alternatives to commodified science (for instance, autonomous or

public interest science) are seen to be preferable, how can they be practically institutionalized?

The subsequent sections briefly discuss several aspects of these central research questions.[2] Thus, these sections provide a conceptual map of the area of commodified academic research. Furthermore, they introduce the subsequent chapters by situating their basic approaches and main claims on this map. These chapters make a substantial contribution to the study of the central research questions, although it will be clear that they do not pretend to provide full and final answers to all aspects of these wide-ranging and difficult questions.

1. The Commodification of Academic Research

The commodification of academic research is a complex phenomenon that can be described in different ways. In a narrow sense commodification is identified with commercialization, that is, the pursuit of profit by academic institutions through selling the expertise of their researchers and the results of their inquiries. This definition evidently covers an important aspect of commodification, but it also overemphasizes the role of the academic institutions themselves. From a broader perspective, academic commodification is part of a comprehensive and long-term social development. This development is often described as the economization, or economic instrumentalization, of human activities and institutions, or even entire social subsystems. In this wider and more appropriate sense, academic commodification means that all kinds of scientific activities and their results are predominantly interpreted and assessed on the basis of economic criteria. Since real-world patterns are never a matter of all or nothing, it is important to keep in mind that commodification implies the dominance of economic criteria, and not their absolute prevalence.

To illustrate the claim that commodification is broader than straightforward commercialization, consider the following real-life story. In the course of 2007, the top administrators of my university, VU University Amsterdam, decided that its research should be clustered in a limited number (say fifteen) of big research institutes. Key characteristics of these institutes should be a clear focus on a specific theme, a substantial mass of senior researchers (one hundred or more), and a sizable participation from different disciplines. The faculty board of the Faculty of Philosophy complied with this plan and started a process of incorporating all philosophical research into two big interfaculty institutes. A letter detailing eight different arguments why this reorganization could not be expected to lead to an increase in the quality of the philosophical research—based on an analysis of what constitutes high-level, international research in philosophy—was completely overruled, or rather ignored, by the university board in favor of the claim that the proposed reorganization was the only way to acquire more external research funding. Although this claim is arguably questionable in the case of philosophy, the story perfectly illustrates the appropriateness and significance of the broad notion of commodified science introduced above. Major decisions that affect the organization and nature of university research are taken primarily on the basis of economic criteria, at the expense of more substantive arguments (such as those deriving from the nature of philosophical inquiry). Thus an important advantage of the broad construal of the notion of commodification is that it also covers those cases of commodification where there is no direct external funding by commercial firms, as is often the case in the social science and humanities disciplines.

What this definition of commodification also shows is that commodified research does not coincide with so-called applied science. If we take this term (for the sake of argument) to mean science used for purposes other than the development of science itself, then as yet nothing is implied about the nature of these purposes. Although it is true that, in our present-day "knowledge economy," the implicit or explicit identification of these purposes with economic purposes is pervasive, there is no necessity to do so. Science can be used, and still is being used, in the more general interests of the public.[3] Hence, fundamental philosophical thinking needs to avoid conflating applied and commodified science (as, for instance, Wise [2006, 1262–66] does). Put differently, commodification as economic instrumentalization needs to be distinguished from other forms of instrumentalization, in particular from technological instrumentalization.

The term "academic" also requires some explanation. A minimal construal of this term is to have it refer to those universities that are wholly or largely funded by public tax money. This minimal construal, however, is too narrow for the purpose of a comprehensive examination of the issues at hand. We should, at least, add basic research and scholarship in independent, publicly funded institutions, such as the Royal Netherlands Academy of Arts and Sciences or the Netherlands Environmental Assessment Agency, and their counterparts in other countries. In some countries, however, there are private, yet nonprofit universities. Hence one could argue that the relevant distinction for an academic institution is not being publicly or privately funded, but being a nonprofit or a for-profit institution. On this basis, Harvard University—which is a private, nonprofit research university—also counts as an academic institution, which certainly fits our common-sense understanding of academic institutions.

Several chapters of the book offer detailed analyses of the complex historical development and the conceptual intricacies of the notion of commodification. Through focusing on the idea of an academic culture, Daniel Kleinman unambiguously advocates a broad approach. From this perspective, he documents the profound transformation of this culture and the concomitant rise of an entrepreneurial ethos. Mark Brown similarly endorses a broad account of commodification. Drawing on a variety of studies in social and political philosophy, he emphasizes an often mentioned aspect of economic instrumentalization: commodification implies the expropriation of goods from the particular communities that produced them by reducing the intrinsic, community value of these goods to their pecuniary exchange value on an independent market. Further sociopolitical analyses of commodification, in particular the commodification of knowledge, are provided by Steve Fuller. He distinguishes, in chronological order, four levels of commodification: ideal-market, industrial, semiotic, and epistemic commodification. The last level pertains to the present and implies that present-day knowledge is not merely a means to commodification at the other three levels, but is itself the subject of pervasive processes of (epistemic) commodification. Another telling aspect of academic commodification is the large change in meaning of the related concept of intellectual property. As Henk van den Belt describes in detail, the present meaning of intellectual property as a kind of commercial monopoly strongly contrasts with its original sense as a form of immaterial recognition for outstanding scientific achievements.

In the discussion above I distinguish between commodified and applied, and between academic and nonacademic research. This does not imply, however, that the study of the commodification of academic research cannot benefit from analyses of industrial science or from investigations of knowledge in applied contexts. Thus Martin Carrier observes that recent academic and industrial research have converged in methodologically and epistemologically significant respects. Hence analyzing high-tech industrial science, he claims, may teach us important things about the future of academic inquiry. Harry Kunneman also points to the epistemological and methodological continuity between basic and applied science, but then goes on to argue for a noncommodified practice of applied research.

2. Analyzing Forms of Commodification

From the broad definition, different forms of commodification may be distinguished. Consider the following current practices. Frequently practiced these days is research contracted by an external, commercial firm. This research may be small-scale, for instance in the case of funding one doctoral dissertation project concerning a limited topic of direct interest to a particular firm. Or it may be large-scale, as in the case of so-called strategic alliances, in which a research group or entire department agrees on a five-year, or even ten-year, contract with a big corporation. In the case of such strategic alliances, the agreement involves that the corporation will provide extensive research funding on the condition that it will have the exclusive right to commercially exploit the research results. External funding may also come from noncommercial organizations. Quite a few academic research projects or programs are financed, partly or wholly, by specific governmental agencies or by other social organizations. If financial goals and interests acquire a predominant position in such projects or programs, they become commodified as well. Another frequent practice is the establishment at an academic institution of all kinds of special professorships or ordinary chairs paid for in part, or even wholly, by external companies. It will be clear that such practices may easily lead to commodification (even if it is not logically necessary). Finally, it is well known that the impact of scientometric indicators on the direction and content of academic research has increased dramatically. However, the fact that the major scientometric databases are compiled and exploited by private firms is either less well known or taken for granted. Hence, a comprehensive analysis of the commodification of academic research should include a detailed scrutiny of the possible influence of the commercial interests and policies of scientometric companies on the construction and uses of such databases. An intriguing question, for instance, concerns the impact of the procedure for the inclusion of journals in Thomson Reuters's influential citation indices, which is, in part, a "company secret" (Leydesdorff 2008, 282).

Thus far, it might seem that commodification is, as it were, externally imposed on the university. This is only one side of the coin, however. In fact, the universities themselves are also actively engaged in profit-seeking activities. The ever decreasing funding by public governmental agencies is often cited as the main reason for this type of commodification. One important form this phenomenon has taken is the acquisition and exploitation of patents on the results of scientific research. For example, the patenting of (parts of) organisms, such as genes, appears to be an accepted practice in academic departments in the biomedical sciences. More generally, it is not unusual anymore that acquired patents are acknowledged as legitimate academic achievements, and seen to be as valuable as journal articles.

It would be a mistake, however, to limit our analyses to exchanges of money. Economic instrumentalization of academic research also takes place through a variety of formal and informal personal ties. Increasingly, researchers who are employed by an academic institution are simultaneously running their own businesses. This is of course of particular significance if their research and their business are in the same area. Also, in the case of externally sponsored professorships and chairs, the significance of personal relationships may outweigh the import of the actual sums of money involved. Furthermore, as we have seen in the previous section, commodification is also realized through an increased corporate structure in university administrations. One way in which this is expressed is through a prevalence of economic vocabularies and metaphors. Thus, the University of Twente promotes itself as an "entrepreneurial" research university (although the original Dutch term—*ondernemende universiteit*—could just as well be translated as "enterprising" university!).

All of the subsequent chapters address one or more of these forms of commodification, but some of them examine particular forms in more detail. Thus, the chapters by James Brown and by Albert Musschenga, Wim van der Steen, and Vincent Ho analyze the issue of commercial funding of pharmaceutical research, with a special emphasis on randomized clinical trials in medical science. David Resnik's contribution discusses the impact of external financial interests in general, whether commercial or noncommercial. Sabina Leonelli provides an in-depth investigation of a more specific aspect of commodification, namely its impact on the nature of data exchange in contemporary biology and medicine. Harry Kunneman points to the state-controlled economic instrumentalization of science, in particular in modern China. The issue of academic patenting and licensing is examined in detail by Sigrid Sterckx, while it is used in my own later chapter as the main illustration of a proposed account of Mertonian values and scientific norms. Finally, the chapters by Daniel Kleinman and Mark Brown include explicit discussions of the commodification of university administration and the rise of entrepreneurial vocabularies and corporate metaphors.

3. How Widespread and Novel Is Academic Commodification?

Further study of these different forms of commodification should answer two important empirical questions: how widespread is academic commodification, and how novel is it? During the past five to ten years, several studies addressing these questions have become available.[4] As a matter of course, the chapters of this book both build upon this work and add to it. Although further empirical studies are very welcome, we may already conclude that, in recent times, the commodification of academic research is a substantial and significant phenomenon. The Dutch Advisory Council for Science and Technology Policy (Adviesraad voor het Wetenschaps- en Technologiebeleid) has provided some quantitative data. For instance, in 2001, 42 percent of all scientific research in the Netherlands took place in academic institutions, while 58 percent took place in companies. In countries like Finland, Japan, and the United States, the former figure is substantially lower and hence the latter substantially higher (AWT 2005, 55–56). Furthermore, in contrast to general state funding, between 1990 and 2001 funding for external contract research (excluding funding by national research councils) increased considerably, namely by 175 percent in the Netherlands, while the international average figure grew by 200 percent (AWT 2005, 45). Finally, between 1999 and 2001, commercial funding of university research in thirteen countries constituted, on average, 5.6 percent of their total research expenses (AWT 2005, 57).[5]

Of course, further differentiations are needed. Looking at different disciplines, we see that pervasive commodification occurs in the engineering, biological, and medical sciences, and, on a somewhat smaller scale, in the physical sciences.[6] But commodification can also be found in the social sciences, be it more often in the form of contract research funded by governmental institutions. Moreover, even humanities disciplines may be involved, for instance in the case of historians writing corporate history or of philosophers of management and organization involved in consultancy work. Furthermore, differences between countries and their distinct research systems and science policies need to be taken into account. The literature available thus far exhibits a strong focus on the Western world and, more specifically, on science as it is practiced in the United States (although the latter focus is not always made explicit). Hence further studies of commodification and its impacts on academic research in developing countries remain especially welcome. Finally, in studying the phenomenon of commodification it is important to distinguish between incidental and more structural cases of commodification. In this sense, several of the trends described in this and the previous sections go far beyond the incidental in suggesting the rise of a pervasive entrepreneurial ethos and a structurally commodified academic culture.

The question of the novelty of academic commodification has also been studied, and disputed. A cautious conclusion is that the commodification of academic research is not strictly novel but has substantially increased and intensified during the past thirty years. For the purpose of this book it is pertinent to keep in mind the following two points regarding the issue of novelty. First, the claim that academic commodification has significantly increased and intensified during the past three decades does not at all imply that earlier academic science was in some sense "pure" and unaffected by "social interests." The latter view has been rightly questioned by many studies in the sociology of science, which have documented the role of cultural, social, economic, and military factors throughout the development of the sciences. Second, whatever forms of commodification may be found in the sciences of the past, present-day academic commodification constitutes a significant phenomenon and an important challenge. If philosophers want their endeavors to be of relevance with respect to the major issues of their times, they should try to meet this challenge by proposing and debating detailed analyses and assessments of, and sensible and viable alternatives to, the commodification of academic research.

The issue of the spread and novelty of commodification is addressed in more detail in several chapters. Kleinman speaks of a pervasive transformation of academic culture, but emphasizes that this is a long-standing process of intensification rather than a sudden break occurring, say, around 1980. Sterckx focuses on the more recent period and concludes that academic patenting and licensing have strongly increased: in the United States since the 1980s and in Europe since the 1990s. The chapter by Fuller deals with the issue of novelty from a broader perspective. Fuller acknowledges the current existence of a new level of commodification (to wit, epistemic capitalism) but sees it as emerging from earlier stages of commodification already started in the eighteenth century.

As for differences between disciplines, some contributions focus on the strong commercialization of the biomedical sciences. The chapters by James Brown, Leonelli, Resnik, and Musschenga, van der Steen, and Ho review existing cases and/or add new examples. Carrier gives a particular twist to the emphasis on biomedical science by arguing that the commercialization of this area is exceptional and not typical of other commercially interesting research areas. Furthermore, while many debates on commodification focus on the physical and biomedical sciences, Kunneman's chapter explicitly addresses a wider range of scholarly inquiry, including research in the social sciences and humanities.

4. How to Assess the Commodification of Academic Research: Theoretical Issues

Given these forms of commodification of academic research and their substantial incidence, a natural question is how to assess these developments. This question has both theoretical and practical aspects. Theoretically, it concerns the issues of the legitimacy of critical assessment, and the nature and scope of the assessment criteria. A shared premise of the contributions to this book is that such critical analysis and assessment of commodified science are both legitimate and necessary. In this respect, they contrast with two other approaches.

First, certain types of social scientific studies of academic commodification explicitly limit themselves to empirical and conceptual issues (even if, in practice, they function to support or legitimize developments toward commodified science). This seems to be the case with the well-known mode-1/mode-2 approach (at least with those parts of this approach that pertain to the issue of commodification).[7] Although it is claimed that mode-2 knowledge production does not replace but *supplement* mode-1 and that its quality criteria are *additional* to mode-1 peer review standards (Gibbons et al. 1994, 14), the authors do not systematically examine the ways in which commodified science may, and does, *interfere* with mode-1 research and its quality criteria. In other cases, the new entrepreneurial ethos is explicitly endorsed as a somehow necessary historical phenomenon. In this vein, Henry Etzkowitz (2004, 69) claims that "the entrepreneurial university is an emergent phenomenon that is the result of the working out of an 'inner logic' of academic development that previously expanded the academic enterprise from a focus on teaching to a focus on research." From such a perspective, critically questioning the commodification of academic research, and thus going against the "inner logic" of scientific development, must necessarily be pointless and a waste of time. Philosophically, such a deterministic account of historical development is highly questionable, which makes it all the more remarkable that Etzkowitz does not provide any argument to support his Hegelian claim.

Second, critical analysis and assessment of commodified science is sometimes rejected because it would be based on the empirically inadequate idea of the purity of science in a bygone era. In this vein, Philip Mirowski and Esther-Mirjam Sent (2008, 635) accuse critics of commodification of "lamenting" and "bewailing" the loss of an academic "prelapsarian Garden." It is easy to see, however, that this sort of rhetoric—that pretends to disqualify an entire approach with one simple stroke—is inappropriate for two reasons. Firstly, the critics should have made the effort to provide explicit evidence for ascribing to specific authors a belief in an academic Fall; and secondly, as I emphasized in the preceding section, a critique of commodified science need not at all presuppose the existence of, and the wish to return to, a paradise lost. By way of comparison, Karl Marx's critique of capitalist manufacture was certainly not motivated by a wish to return to a feudal means of production.

Thus there is no reason to denounce, and therefore ignore, the question of how to assess the commodification of academic research.[8] Since we are obviously dealing with an evaluative and normative question, answering it presupposes some account of what constitutes good science. Such an account may be specified in different ways. One may attempt to provide a philosophical specification of methodological, epistemological, and perhaps even ontological values in science, and judge the commodification of academic research on this basis. Alternatively, one may argue for a normatively desirable position and function of science in and for society, and try to derive political or moral criteria that can be used in evaluating commodified research. Thirdly, one may argue that social or moral norms and methodological, epistemological, or ontological norms cannot or should not be separated, and hence the first two approaches need to be combined.[9]

In all three cases positions regarding the normative evaluation of commodified academic research may vary from quite strong to more moderate. Strong positions imply arguments for universal or noncontextual criteria, while moderate positions emphasize the pragmatic and situated character of their normative assessments. Finally, a point mentioned before is worth restating here. That point is that criticism of commodified science is not the same as criticizing any use of science for social purposes. Hence critique needs to be complemented by serious consideration of the alternatives to commodified science. This subject will be addressed in the final section of this chapter.

The subsequent chapters of this book address a variety of theoretical issues concerning the evaluation of commodified science. Van den Belt argues for the significance of a normative, Mertonian ethos of science and defends this approach against the claims of exclusively descriptive or explanatory accounts by economists and sociologists of scientific knowledge. Leonelli's analysis emphasizes the importance of key methodological values, such as equal access to resources, competition between different methods, and a long-term vision. Carrier employs methodological criteria (such as requirements for unification, causal analysis, and reciprocal control of prejudices) in his evaluation of the relation between epistemic and applied research. James Brown criticizes the lack of epistemic justifiability of what he dubs "one-shot science," of which commercialized, randomized clinical trials—that is, trials that are often called the gold standard of evidence-based medicine—are a prominent illustration. In addition to pointing out cases of methodological bias, Musschenga, van der Steen, and Ho question the ontological assumptions about the nature of human beings underlying psychiatric research that exclusively focuses on drugs.

From his analyses of neoliberalism and Marxism, Fuller concludes that commodification is "still evil even if necessary." Underlying his assessment of academic commodification is his normative sociopolitical vision of a republican university, a vision that is discussed in detail in Mark Brown's contribution. Brown also provides an extensive discussion and evaluation of the important distinction between "coercion" and "corruption" arguments against academic commodification: whereas coercion arguments focus on the structural effects of unequal power relationships, corruption arguments address the impact of commodification on the epistemic, social, and moral values of academic culture.

Mixed philosophical and sociological approaches can be found in Kunneman's proposal for a "mode-3" approach (a specific kind of humanized mode-2 social science, which consciously aims to advance both a critical academic culture and social responsibility) and in my own arguments for combining general moral or institutional values and more specific epistemic or methodological norms. Finally, an explicit mix of epistemic and ethical norms is advocated in Resnik's contribution.

5. How to Assess the Commodification of Academic Research: Practical Issues

In addition to the theoretical issue of the legitimacy of critical analysis and the nature and scope of its criteria, there is the issue of how to assess the actual practices of commodified academic research. Some emphasize its advantages. Universities become less dependent on the shrinking funding by government agencies. Commodification enables the orientation of academic research toward technological advancement and socioeconomic priorities. Research policies will be more flexible and more attuned to actual developments. Competition between public and private research will induce universities to seize opportunities for innovation more quickly. An underlying argument is that linear models of innovation are seen to be inadequate (see Grandin, Wormbs, and Widmalm 2004). In such models, innovation takes place in a fixed temporal order: from basic research to applied science, product development, marketing, production, and end-use. More recent accounts of innovation, however, emphasize the more-or-less permanent interactions and feedbacks among universities, industry, and government (Gibbons et al. 1994; Etzkowitz 2004; see also Carrier, this volume, chap. 8). From this perspective, it is only natural that industrial and governmental contractors be involved in academic research from an early stage and steer its direction and content in significant ways.

At the same time, these developments have evoked critical responses. Such critical voices have not only been raised by philosophical "outsiders," but at least as strongly by established scientists and academic administrators. It is a telling sign when a former president of Harvard University, Derek Bok (2003), publishes a fairly critical book about the commercialization of American universities. Equally significant is the fact that, since 2001, a large number of prominent biomedical journals require that their authors make public any ties to external funding bodies, and even demand them to sign a statement saying that, if such ties exist, the sponsors have not influenced the methods or contents of their research.

In assessing the commodification of academic research, the following subjects need to be taken into account. *First,* commercial interests may have an undesirable impact on research methods and their results. A consequence may be that, from a methodological or epistemological perspective, the research designs may be less than optimal, and the results of this research biased. *Second,* commercial motives may lead to a higher level of secrecy than would otherwise be the case, and thus could slow down the overall advance of science. This could, for instance, happen because of the specific requirements of the patenting system or because of the secrecy policies of private firms. *Third,* generally speaking, commodification will be detrimental to those areas of academic inquiry that are seen to be useless from the perspective of economic instrumentalization. This problem will be amplified in a situation of decreasing government funding. Here we should not just think of ancient history or medieval philosophy but, for example, also of those medical and health care approaches that do not focus on the use of drugs or other profitable technologies. *Fourth,* commodification tends to lead to a narrow orientation focused on short-term achievements and results. Hence it will be much more difficult to start and develop long-term projects, even if they might be more socially beneficial in the long run. *Fifth,* there is a variety of legal, moral, and philosophical questions about the patentability of the results of academic research. In particular, questions have been raised about the recent extension of patent law and practices to the "knowledge" generated by the biomedical sciences.[10] *Sixth,* there is the problem of potential abuse of public funds for private purposes. In the case of a researcher who simultaneously works for a public institute and runs his or her own business, the incidence of this kind of abuse seems to be more probable than not. A *seventh* important issue pertains to the measure of public trust in science. Commodification, in particular the highly publicized, dramatic cases of commercial abuse of science, may erode the public trust in science more generally. In view of the indispensability of science and science-based technology in present-day societies, the consequences of a waning of public trust in science may be considerable. The *eighth* and final point is the general issue of the justifiability of the privatization and economic instrumentalization of public knowledge. Is it just that private parties own and exclusively profit from scientific results that are in fact a collective achievement, built on an immense amount of publicly funded research results?

All chapters of this volume address one or more of these eight issues. The authors offer varying assessments of the merits and problems of commodified academic research. While none of them sees commodification, in an evaluative sense, as entirely unproblematic, or as more or less neutral, the interpretations of its problematic aspects differ. As we will see in the next two sections, these differences are reflected in different preferences for either regulation of, or alternatives to, commodified science.

The possible impact of commercial and financial interests on the epistemic quality and advance of science is a prime theme in the chapters by Resnik, James Brown, Musschenga, van der Steen, and Ho, Leonelli, and Carrier. Carrier also discusses the occurrence of secrecy in commercialized science and argues that it is being compensated for by counteracting mechanisms that favor openness (such as the need for cooperation with academic scientists in the application of public knowledge by commercial researchers). Musschenga, van der Steen, and Ho discuss and criticize the marginalization of ecological and nonbiological approaches to mental illness, a point that is addressed from a more general perspective in Kunneman's chapter. The issue of the short-term focus of commodified science is discussed in detail in Leonelli's contribution. She shows that private sponsorship encourages short-term, "product-driven" competition, while public sponsors tend to promote a longer-term, "resource-driven" competition, and she highlights the negative consequences of this type of commodification for the disclosure, circulation, and retrieval of data in the biomedical sciences. The practice of academic patenting and licensing is analyzed in detail by Sterckx. She discusses several undesirable and paradoxical consequences of patenting and licensing, and shows that the proposed economic justifications of this practice are more often than not based on rhetoric rather than reality. My own later chapter advocates a neo-Mertonian ethos of science, demonstrates that this ethos is often explicitly endorsed by established ethical codes of scientific conduct, argues that academic patenting goes against this ethos, and hence concludes that such patenting is unjustifiable. The private abuse of public research, the decrease of public trust in science, and the general justifiability of privatizing the fruits of academic research constitute important issues in the contributions by van den Belt and Fuller. Van den Belt argues for the lasting importance of the view of scientific knowledge as a "non-excludable and nonrival public good." In line with this, he advocates a revival of the Mertonian ethos of science, which is endangered both by the commodification of academic research and by proponents of reductionist and antinormative sociological approaches to scientific development. Finally, on the basis of subtle differences in the interpretation of the notion of commodification, Fuller explains and illustrates the harm done by commodification to the integrity of both knowledge producers and knowledge consumers. More generally, like Kleinman, Fuller perceives the mission of academic institutions as educating for citizenship instead of educating for the market.

6. Regulating Commodified Research

We may safely conclude that, at present, the problems of the commodification of academic research sketched in the previous section are broadly acknowledged. Yet, differences remain concerning the seriousness of these problems. Obviously, the urgency of looking for solutions and the extent to which advocated alternatives will deviate from the present situation will depend on whether commodification is seen to be a structural or a more incidental issue. In the latter case, solutions will primarily be sought through regulation.

For instance, in April 2008, Dutch newspapers carried a brief debate on the issue of special professorships and ordinary chairs financed by external organizations. In the Netherlands, a survey concluded, about 25 percent of all 5,481 university professors are paid by external organizations (see Persson and Rengers 2008). The major sponsors are commercial businesses (27 percent) and health care organizations (25 percent). One of the examples of commodification pertained to a professor at Wageningen University with an expertise in the area of dairy products. This agricultural scientist recently argued that drinking milk is beneficial to our health. Yet, what neither he nor his department made explicit is the fact that his chair is paid for by a national organization of dairy farmers and that he himself is one of the directors of a large dairy company. By many observers, the main problem was seen to be the lack of public information about the ties of such professorships to their sponsors. In the debate that followed, different views were taken about how to regulate this specific problem. The minister of education, for instance, suggested that making the information about the nature of the professorships public should be compulsory, while the Association of Universities in the Netherlands countered that this should be decided by the universities themselves.

More generally, public information and transparency about financial bonds is often seen as *the* solution to this kind of problem (Montgomery and Oliver 2009, 146–49). Yet, in a more comprehensive analysis, it proves to be questionable whether this is really the case.[11] Suppose you have been asked to review a paper for a journal and the author or authors (for instance, the above-mentioned dairy specialist) have properly declared their funding sources. The critical question, then, is what to make of this information? If you assess the paper's merits and problems in the usual way, the additional information about the authors makes no apparent difference. But if you decide that, because this information must have some significance, the paper requires a more scrupulous review and a more critical assessment, you effectively presuppose that, generally speaking, commodified science is more liable to bias. Furthermore, if the paper is published, its readers will find themselves in a similar predicament. Hence, in such cases, making financial ties public merely makes explicit, rather than solving, the problems in question. After all, the usual and more appropriate procedure in instances of a conflict of interests (for instance, in journalism, politics, and law) is to withdraw completely from the cases in which one is personally involved. It is hard to see why this should be different in science.

Apart from compulsory directives imposed through governmental policies, regulation may also be realized through devising and implementing ethical codes of good scientific conduct. In fact, during the past decades, a variety of such codes have been adopted or updated, in part for the purpose of coping with the issues of academic commodification (Kourany 2008; Montgomery and Oliver 2009). Usually, such codes consist of a number of principled statements, but frequently they also include a variety of mitigating qualifications of these statements. This means that these codes, depending on how the principles and qualifications are interpreted and used, may either function as instruments for regulating incidental problems of academic commodification or as vehicles for addressing its more structural problems. In the latter case, the basic ideas and criteria of the ethical codes should not merely be applied for sanctioning the behavior of individual scientists (as is the most common approach at present), but should also be structurally incorporated in the science policies of academic institutions and governmental agencies (see Radder 2009).

Most chapters of this book include or imply some suggestions for regulating the commodification of academic research, but some authors discuss or provide more extensive regulatory proposals. Sterckx, for example, concludes her analysis of academic patenting by suggesting a variety of regulatory measures that should be implemented at three different levels: an international, a national, and a university level. Similarly, Resnik offers a list of recommendations for counteracting the negative impact of financial interests on the norms of science. From a more general perspective, Carrier and Musschenga, van der Steen, and Ho argue that a substantial level of public funding is needed to compensate for the negative consequences of commercialized science. Finally, Mark Brown discusses several policy reforms that aim to correct the unequal distribution of power that often exists between academic researchers and dominant commercial contractors. The underlying idea is that researchers should be free, rather than coerced, to decide whether or not they will market their results.

7. Alternatives to Commodified Science

The last of our central research questions addresses the potential alternatives to commodified science. Which alternatives to commodified academic research are philosophically and socially justifiable and practically viable? Theoretically, we may distinguish between three ideal-typical models: commodified science and the alternatives of autonomous and public interest science.

A model of commodified science is provided by Etzkowitz's account of the entrepreneurial university, in particular by what he calls the "third mission" of this emerging type of university (Etzkowitz 1998, 2004). The core of this mission is the contribution to economic growth or the "capitalization of knowledge." Important elements are the external exploitation of university research through protected intellectual property, the incorporation of commercial firms within a university, and the creation of new university-industry research centers. A related account has been developed by John Ziman, who speaks of postacademic, or industrialized, science. According to Ziman (2000), postacademic science aims for proprietary knowledge; it focuses on local, technical problems; it is performed under managerial authority and commissioned for practical purposes; and it employs experts in the sense of specialized problem solvers.

In view of the structural problems of commodification described in the preceding sections, consideration of alternatives becomes a pertinent challenge. Is there a preferable model for performing academic research, both from a methodological or epistemological and from a social or ethical perspective? If so, what are, or should be, the alternative ideas guiding the desirable behavior of academic researchers and the preferred institutionalization and organization of academic research? In response to these questions, I will briefly consider the models of autonomous and public interest science.

The model of autonomous science is often associated with the name of Robert K. Merton, who proposed an influential account of an independent scientific community characterized by universal social-epistemological criteria, common ownership of research methods and results, disinterested review procedures, and a critical attitude toward all scientific claims (Merton 1973/1942). Of course, proponents of such a model may and do add certain qualifications, for instance that the model should be seen as an ideal-type or that it is intended to be partly normative. In view of such qualifications, "autonomy" should not be taken in an absolute sense, and "autonomous science" not as an empirical reality. For this reason, more cautious characterizations may be preferable, for example the idea of a "self-governing science" (Polanyi 1962) or even the notion of a nonneutral, "self-interested science" (Pels 2003).

The basic idea of the model of public interest science is that science should, primarily, contribute to a lessening of human suffering and an increase in human well-being. Under present circumstances, however, there is a major, structural divide between those who do, and those who do not, benefit from the fruits of academic research. An exemplary case is the contrast between the vast resources spent on medical research into relatively minor or rare complaints in Western countries compared with the small efforts devoted to studies of frequent and serious diseases in developing countries. For this reason, the task of public interest science is to acknowledge a much wider array of social problems and to contribute toward relieving or solving these problems. Thus, public interest science differs from autonomous science by incorporating social goals, at least institutionally but sometimes also methodologically, and it differs from commodified science in embracing a much broader range of social goals than merely economic ones. Some proponents of public interest science (e.g., Krimsky 2003) take the notion of a public interest to be more or less clear or focus on issues that are generally (or at least widely) agreed to be of public interest. More sophisticated approaches include procedures to find out which types of issues legitimately count as "of public interest." These approaches are often based on principles of equality, democracy, and justice. Examples include Philip Kitcher's arguments for combining the search for (significant) truth with the claims of democracy (Kitcher 2001) and Steve Fuller's plea for a republican science in an open society (Fuller 2000). Fuller's concept of a republican science, with its emphasis on democratization and its leveling of expert and lay contributions, represents a radical public interest approach. A detailed discussion and evaluation of the political philosophy of republicanism and its application to the problems of the governance of science can be found in Mark Brown's contribution to this volume.

As is illustrated by the case of Kitcher, the models of science advocated by specific authors may also be hybrids that include elements of the distinct ideal-types explained thus far. And indeed, this makes sense if we agree (as I think most authors of this volume do) that academic research does possess specific characteristics that deserve to be fostered and protected, that contributions of science to economic development are in principle legitimate, and that science ought to be used for battling human suffering and promoting the well-being of humanity. The challenge, then, is to make explicit the extent to which, and the conditions under which, elements of each of these models legitimately apply.

Several of the chapters of the book try to meet this challenge. Inspired by Merton's ideas of autonomous science, van den Belt advocates a truly meritocratic but open science, which aims at improving and expanding a commons of knowledge. In arguing for a structural incorporation of a deflationary, neo-Mertonian ethos in academic institutions and science policies, my own later chapter develops a congenial approach, but also intends to make a connection to the model of public interest science. Kunneman's mode-3 approach similarly insists on the value of academic criteria but simultaneously includes elements of the public interest model.

NOTES

1. For analyses of teaching and administration, see Bok (2003); Slaughter and Rhoades (2004), and Lorenz (2008); the first two books also discuss the U.S. university sports programs.

2. In part, my discussion draws on material published in Radder (2003).

3. Note also that the definition of commodification in principle allows for the occurrence of "noncommodified industrial research," namely in those cases where industrial research is not dominated by economic interests. For instance, in the period between 1947 and 1972, industrial researchers at Philips electronic laboratories were relatively free from direct commercial pressures (de Vries 2005).

4. As for books and edited volumes, see Köbben and Tromp (1999); Shulman (1999); Sterckx (2000); Grit (2000); Bok (2003); Kleinman (2003); Krimsky (2003); Angell (2004); Grandin, Wormbs, and Widmalm (2004); Slaughter and Rhoades (2004); Healy (2006); May and Perry (2006); and Resnik (2007).

5. Further relevant data can be found in Slaughter and Rhoades (2004) and in the chapters by Kleinman, Sterckx, Resnik, and James Brown. As I emphasized before, we have to bear in mind that direct financing by commercial firms is only one of the many forms of commodification. It is also important to realize that, due to national differences in definitions of research categories and variations in research systems, the acquisition and interpretation of aggregated international data are far from straightforward.

6. For some recent case studies of microphysics, nanotechnology, medical science, and biological science, see, respectively, Mody (2006); Thurs (2007); Cooper (2009); and Sismondo (2009).

7. Very briefly, traditional or mode-1 research is claimed to be autonomous, academic, disciplinary, and methodological, while the more recent mode-2 knowledge is characterized by taking place in application contexts, by being commercialized and transdisciplinary, and

by essentially including social criteria of accountability and quality control. See Gibbons et al. (1994). For critical reviews and assessments, see Weingart (1997), and Hessels and van Lente (2008).

8. For detailed, positive arguments supporting the legitimacy of philosophical critique and normativity, see Radder (1996, chaps. 5 and 8) and Radder (2003, 21–24). See also Lock and Lorenz (2007, 413), who write, "If . . . the role of the university is to provide a sphere in which genuinely critical thinking, investigation and debate can take place, it would follow that university research cannot take the form of a mere response to 'societal demand,' nor university teaching that of 'textbook transmission.'"

9. For further discussion of the role of different kinds of values in science, see van der Steen (1995); Resnik (1998); and Carrier, Howard, and Kourany (2008).

10. In addition to their political and moral significance, the theory and practice of (academic) patenting constitutes a genuine gold mine for intellectually challenging research on basic philosophical issues (cf. Radder 2004; van den Belt 2009, section 3).

11. See also Schipper and Bojé (2008), who emphasize that transparency does not necessarily entail integrity.

REFERENCES

Angell, M. 2004. *The truth about the drug companies: How they deceive us and what to do about it*. New York: Random House.

AWT [Adviesraad voor het Wetenschaps- en Technologiebeleid]. 2005. *Een vermogen betalen: De financiering van universitair onderzoek*. Den Haag: AWT.

Bok, D. 2003. *Universities in the marketplace: The commercialization of higher education*. Princeton: Princeton University Press.

Carrier, M., D. Howard, and J. Kourany, eds. 2008. *The challenge of the social and the pressure of practice*. Pittsburgh: University of Pittsburgh Press.

Cooper, M. H. 2009. "Commercialization of the university and problem choice by academic biological scientists." *Science, Technology and Human Values* 34 (5): 629–53.

De Vries, M. J. 2005. *Eighty years of research at the Philips Natuurkundig Laboratorium (1914–1994)*. Amsterdam: Amsterdam University Press.

Etzkowitz, H. 1998. "The norms of entrepreneurial science: Cognitive effects of the new university-industry linkages." *Research Policy* 27 (8): 823–33.

———. 2004. "The triple helix and the rise of the entrepreneurial university." In *The science-industry nexus: History, policy, implications,* ed. K. Grandin, N. Wormbs, and S. Widmalm, 69–91. Sagamore Beach, MA: Science History Publications/USA.

Fuller, S. 2000. *The governance of science*. Buckingham, UK: Open University Press.

Gibbons, M., C. Limoges, H. Nowotny, S. Schwartzman, P. Scott, and M. Trow. 1994. *The new production of knowledge*. London: Sage.

Grandin, K., N. Wormbs, and S. Widmalm, eds. 2004. *The science-industry nexus: History, policy, implications*. Sagamore Beach, MA: Science History Publications/USA.

Grit, K. 2000. *Economisering als probleem: Een studie naar de bedrijfsmatige stad en de ondernemende universiteit*. Doctoral dissertation, Groningen University.

Healy, D. 2006. *Let them eat Prozac: The unhealthy relationship between the pharmaceutical industry and depression*. New York: New York University Press.

Hessels, L. K., and H. van Lente. 2008. "Re-thinking new knowledge production: A literature review and a research agenda." *Research Policy* 37 (4): 740–60.

Kitcher, P. 2001. *Science, truth, and democracy*. New York: Oxford.

Kleinman, D. L. 2003. *Impure cultures: University biology and the world of commerce*. Madison: University of Wisconsin Press.

Köbben, A. J. F., and H. Tromp. 1999. *De onwelkome boodschap, of Hoe de vrijheid van wetenschap bedreigd wordt*. Amsterdam: Mets.

Kourany, J. 2008. "Philosophy of science: A subject with a great future." *Philosophy of Science* 75 (5): 767–78.

Krimsky, S. 2003. *Science in the private interest*. Lanham, MD: Rowman and Littlefield.

Leydesdorff, L. 2008. "*Caveats* for the use of citation indicators in research and journal evaluations." *Journal of the American Society for Information Science and Technology* 59 (2): 278–87.

Lock, G., and C. Lorenz. 2007. "Revisiting the university front." *Studies in Philosophy of Education* 26 (5): 405–18.

Lorenz, C., ed. 2008. *If you're so smart, why aren't you rich? Universiteit, markt en management*. Amsterdam: Boom.

May, T., and P. Perry, eds. 2006. "Universities in the knowledge economy: Places of expectation/spaces for reflection?" Special issue of *Social Epistemology* 20 (3–4): 201–345.

Merton, R. K. 1973/1942. "The normative structure of science." In R. K. Merton, *The sociology of science*, ed. N. W. Storer, 267–78. Chicago: University of Chicago Press.

Mirowski, P., and E.-M. Sent. 2008. "The commercialization of science and the response of STS." In *The handbook of science and technology studies*, 3rd ed., ed. E. J. Hackett, O. Amsterdamska, M. Lynch, and J. Wajcman, 635–89. Cambridge, MA: MIT Press.

Mody, C. C. M. 2006. "Corporations, universities, and instrumental communities: Commercializing probe microscopy, 1981–1996." *Technology and Culture* 47 (1): 56–80.

Montgomery, K., and A. L. Oliver. 2009. "Shifts in guidelines for ethical scientific conduct: How public and private organizations create and change norms of research integrity." *Social Studies of Science* 39 (1): 137–55.

Pels, D. 2003. *Unhastening science: Autonomy and reflexivity in the social theory of knowledge*. Liverpool: Liverpool University Press.

Persson, M., and M. Rengers. 2008. "Een professor van WC-eend." *De Volkskrant*, April 12, Kennis, 1.

Polanyi, M. 1962. "The republic of science: Its political and economic theory." *Minerva* 1 (1): 54–73.

Radder, H. 1996. *In and about the world*. Albany: State University of New York Press.

———. 2003. *Wetenschap als koopwaar? Een filosofische kritiek*. Amsterdam: VU Boekhandel/Uitgeverij.

———. 2004. "Exploiting abstract possibilities: A critique of the concept and practice of product patenting." *Journal of Agricultural and Environmental Ethics* 17 (3): 275–91.

———. 2009. "Hoe herwin je 'de ziel van de wetenschap'? Academisch onderzoek en universitaire kenniseconomie." *Academische Boekengids* 75 (July): 8–13. Also available at http://www.academischeboekengids.nl/do.php?a=show_visitor_artikel&id=836.

Resnik, D. B. 1998. *The ethics of science*. London: Routledge.

———. 2007. *The price of truth: How money affects the norms of science*. New York: Oxford University Press.

Schipper, F., and D. M. Bojé. 2008. "Transparency, integrity and openness: The Nike example." In *Handbook of research on global citizenship,* ed. A. G. Scherer and G. Palazzo, 501–26. Cheltenham, UK: Edward Elgar.

Shulman, S. 1999. *Owning the future.* Boston: Houghton Mifflin.

Sismondo, S. 2009. "Ghosts in the machine: Publication planning in the medical sciences." *Social Studies of Science* 39 (2): 171–98.

Slaughter, S., and G. Rhoades. 2004. *Academic capitalism and the new economy: Markets, state, and higher education.* Baltimore: Johns Hopkins University Press.

Sterckx, S., ed. 2000. *Biotechnology, patents and morality.* 2nd ed. Aldershot: Ashgate.

Thurs, D. P. 2007. "No longer academic: Models of commercialization and the construction of a nanotech industry." *Science as Culture* 16 (2): 169–86.

van den Belt, H. 2009. "The philosophy of biotechnology." In *Philosophy of technology and engineering sciences,* ed. A. W. M. Meijers, 1301–40. Amsterdam: Elsevier.

van der Steen, W. J. 1995. *Facts, values, and methodology: A new approach to ethics.* Amsterdam: Rodopi.

Weingart, P. 1997. "From 'finalization' to 'mode 2': Old wine in new bottles?" *Social Science Information* 36 (4): 591–613.

Wise, M. N. 2006. "Thoughts on the politicization of science through commercialization." *Social Research* 73 (4): 1253–72.

Ziman, J. 2000. *Real science: What it is, and what it means.* Cambridge: Cambridge University Press.

CHAPTER 2

The Commercialization of Academic
Culture and the Future of the University

Daniel Lee Kleinman

IN THE SPRING of 2007, many professors at the University of California at Berkeley were distressed about that university's selection as the site for a $500 million research institute on biofuels to be funded by BP, the mega-energy corporation (Blumenstyk 2007). Their demand to institutionalize faculty oversight of this major academic-industry collaboration replays a controversy at Berkeley over its 1998 $25 million arrangement with Novartis (Rudy et al. 2007). And yet while these partnerships may be emblematic of the new age of the knowledge economy, such relationships are not especially widespread. Indeed, even adding these mega-initiatives to the smaller and more common university-industry collaborations, industry only supports in the neighborhood of 7 percent of all academic research in the United States (NSF 2006; Washburn 2005, 9). Of course, in some fields that figure is much larger—perhaps as high as 25 percent in the biotechnology area; yet industry funding, nevertheless, does not constitute the major source of support for scientific research in our universities, and university-industry relations (UIRs) do not dominate academia.

Despite the relatively small quantitative place industry funding and direct, formal university-industry research relationships play in the landscape of academic science in the United States, these matters receive a disproportionate amount of analytical attention among policy makers and critics of the commercialization of academia. In this chapter, I will examine and critique two prominent examples of this type of investigation and then consider two matters that I believe deserve more of our attention than they seem to receive and explain why. I will argue that we must be attentive to the processes of change in the character of the American university and that we should focus not primarily on *direct* university-industry relations and egregious violations of academic norms, but instead on subtle and pervasive changes underway in the *culture* of the academy.

1. A Threatened Ivory Tower?

With the development of the U.S. biotechnology industry in the late 1970s and 1980s, scholars, policy analysts, and activists directed their concern toward the university-industry research relationships fostered by this dynamic economic sector (e.g., American Association of University Professors 1983; Blumenthal et al. 1986a, 1986b; Kenney 1985; Shenk 1999). Sometimes implicitly and other times explicitly contrasting these arrangements with an insulated ivory tower, this work expressed concern about corporate influence on academic research agendas as well as marked increases in conflicts of interest, secrecy, and focus on research as proprietary. While much work since this early writing has posed different questions in exploring the place of the university in the new knowledge economy (e.g., Brint 2005; Owen-Smith and Powell 2003; Slaughter and Leslie 1997; Slaughter and Rhoades 2004), concerns about conflict of interest, secrecy, and the like retain a pivotal place in critical debate.

Indeed, these types of issues figured centrally in press coverage of the Berkeley-Novartis relationship in the late 1990s (see Rudy et al. 2007), and constitute the predominant focus of two important books: Jennifer Washburn's *University, Inc.* (2005) and Sheldon Krimsky's *Science in the Private Interest* (2003).

Troubled by what they see as the transformation of the university from an entity distinct from industry to a virtual arm of the private sector, authors like Washburn and Krimsky make their case, to a considerable extent, by highlighting egregious violations of academic norms—dramatic instances.

These authors and others consider many of the same cases. Thus, the Berkeley-Novartis deal I have mentioned figures prominently in the stories they tell (Krimsky 2003, 35, 36; Washburn 2005, 3–7, 9–23). The authors note that this deal meant Novartis supplied a third of a single department's budget and gave the company the right of first refusal to negotiate licenses for a third of the department's discoveries. From this case, they conclude that the university had been bought by industry.[1]

Another case Washburn and Krimsky highlight is that of Betty Dong, a University of California–San Francisco researcher studying the efficacy of a thyroid medicine (Washburn 2005, 19; Krimsky 2003, 14–18). In this episode, Boots Pharmaceutical, the funder of Dong's work and the manufacturer of Synthroid, engaged in a sustained campaign to prevent Dong from publishing results that showed that Boots's drug was no more effective than three cheaper, competing drugs.

Yet another instance reported by both authors concerns David Kern (Washburn 2005, 76; Krimsky 2003, 44, 45). Kern was an occupational health researcher at a Brown University–affiliated hospital, who was fired after finding that one of his institution's patrons was endangering its workers. In this case, Washburn and Krimsky suggest that corporate influence stifled Kern's research and ended his career at Memorial Hospital.

But how common are such cases? It isn't entirely clear, but as I noted at the outset of this chapter, industry funding certainly does not overwhelm the amount of research support universities receive from the federal government and other sources. I do not want to understate the problem reflected by these episodes; the concerns raised by authors like Krimsky and Washburn are real. There are surely cases of intellectual suppression, and there are, indeed, sectors of the academy where corporate sponsorship does directly shape the direction of research and research practices. However, I would suggest that focusing on dramatic cases of violations of academic norms draws attention away from understanding the deeper and more complicated issues of commercialization of academic culture.

Many analysts point to a move among academic scientists away from Merton-type norms of science (e.g., Shenk 1999 and Lewis and Anderson 1998). Indeed, both Krimsky (2003, 6, 7, 73ff) and Washburn (2005, 73ff) talk explicitly about three of the norms—communism, universalism, organized skepticism—highlighted by Robert K. Merton (1973/1942) and accept at face value that the world of science operated according to these norms before the biotechnology and associated commercialization revolution that began in the early 1980s.

But analysis of episodes before 1980 by such scholars as Mitroff (1974) and Mulkay (1980) suggests that science, even absent corporate pressures, often does not straightforwardly follow these norms (see also Radder, this volume, chap. 10). Mulkay argues that scientists have always engaged in interpreting norms, since norms do not have a single literal meaning. In his work on moon researchers, Mitroff found that for every Mertonian norm there was a counternorm. These existed in a state of dynamic tension, shaping scientific practice. Of course, these cases say nothing about the present moment.[2]

Krimsky, Washburn, and others suggest we face an epidemic of anti-Mertonian secrecy in academic science—secrecy induced by commercial pressures. They are right: secrecy in science is a problem. But a study by Campbell and his colleagues should lead us to question the idea that there is a simple and straightforward relationship between commercial pressures and secrecy in university science. Campbell and his colleagues surveyed geneticists in the United States. They found that 27 percent of respondents said they withheld information, data, or materials to honor the requirements of an industrial sponsor, and 21 percent explained their unwillingness to provide materials and/or data as stemming from the need to protect the commercial value of research results (Campbell et al. 2002).

But those percentages are low compared with some of the other explanations these geneticists gave for withholding information or materials. Eighty percent cited the efforts required to produce materials or information, 64 percent pointed to the need to protect a student's or colleague's ability to publish, 53 percent said they needed to protect their own ability to publish, and 45 percent cited cost as the reason they withheld data or materials (Campbell et al. 2002). Washburn explicitly acknowledges these kinds of reasons for secrecy in academic life, but downplays their importance in the political economy of academic science (2005, 75). Neither Washburn, Krimsky, nor any other author with whom I am familiar provides data on changes in secrecy practices over time. Consequently, we don't know whether academia is more secretive than it was in the past and if so why.

Again, I don't want to suggest that the university isn't in the midst of a transformation, that secrecy isn't a problem, or that corporate-university linkages do not inhibit the free flow of information in academia.[3] The question is whether the kind of approach Krimsky, Washburn, and others take best captures what is really going on.

Finally, another thing analysts of the neoliberal university worry about is the loss of "disinterested researchers."[4] Thus, Washburn asserts, "It would be hard to overstate the importance of preserving a space in our culture where the ideal of disinterested inquiry is preserved" (2005, xvi). She is looking for independent and impartial scholars (2005, 5). Broadly, however, I would say that scientists are always interested (see Bourdieu 1975). If the cases highlighted by Krimsky and Washburn are relatively exceptional, we still face the problem that disciplinary orientations, colleagues' reactions, and a host of other factors affect how scholars will speak to the public and what they (we) will say.

Relatedly, Krimsky argues that the growth of UIRs is associated with a decline in the public orientation of scientists (2003, 78). But Russell Jacoby (1987) provides a quite different explanation for this phenomenon. He focuses on the professionalization of scholarship, part of a process that certainly predates 1980. In a sense accepting Jacoby's conclusions, Michael Burawoy's (past president of the American Sociological Association) effort to promote *public sociology* is not an attempt to swim against commercializing pressures so much as a recognition that most scholars spend most of their time speaking to one another (2004). There are incentives for such behavior. At institutions like the one at which I work—major U.S. research universities—there are few incentives for doing research of public relevance. Such investigation certainly will not help you at tenure or salary adjustment time. And at my university, at least, such work is not as highly valued as work published in the top academic journals. Again, I would not want to suggest that we do not need scholars who seek to ascertain and promote the "public interest." However, I do not think that simply eliminating, or even carefully regulating, university-industry relations will lead to the (re)institutionalization of a space for publicly oriented scholars and scholarship.

2. The Transformation of the American University

Those authors whose work focuses on formal, concrete, and direct relationships between universities and firms as the mark of a transformed and commercialized university often point to several sharp and distinctive changes as prompting the move to university-industry relations. First, as I noted, many researchers highlight the advent of biotechnology in the late 1970s and 1980s, a new technoscience that blurred the boundaries between basic and applied science and the expertise for which was initially largely housed in universities (Kenney 1985; Krimsky 2003; Rudy et al. 2007). Second, authors emphasize a number of legislative milestones and court decisions from the 1980s. Particularly prominent among the legislative factors stressed is the Bayh-Dole Act (e.g., Rudy et al. 2007). This 1980 law permitted and facilitated the patenting of federally funded research undertaken in universities. In addition to Bayh-Dole, authors often point to the 1986 Federal Technology Transfer Act, which encouraged universities to stress the significance of industry collaboration. On the judicial front, *Diamond v. Chakrabarty* is seen as pivotal, since the Supreme Court's decision in this case permitted the patenting of life-forms, thus making intellectual property in the products of biotechnological research possible (see Kleinman 2003).

In the same way that I do not believe that formal direct relationships are the crux of the new American university, I am equally dubious of an explanation for the commercially oriented academy that focuses on individual events that prompted apparently abrupt change. To begin with, industry relationships with the American academy predate by more than a hundred years the supposed academic revolution of the late twentieth century. Indeed, more than twenty-five years before the U.S. Civil War, firms sometimes employed university scientists to do research (Noble 1977, 11). By the 1920s, some U.S. universities had established special organizations to supply "industry with applied research and development services" (Geiger 1993, 297). Thus, for example, Georgia Tech created its semi-autonomous Engineering Experiment Station in 1919 following a mandate from the state legislature (McMath et al. 1985, 189). And, indeed, Georgia Tech was intended to play a role in promoting economic development in the South (McMath et al. 1985, 35).

Despite these early developments, it is true that the struggle between the early 1940s until 1950 about the nature of the U.S. research policy-making establishment did lead to a victory for those who believed there needed to be a sharp division of labor between university science—which should be primarily fundamental or basic research, an effort to understand basic principles of nature—and industrial science—which should be applied and aim at the production of goods for sale (Kleinman 1995). But while the creation of Vannevar Bush's so-called contract for science, and with it the establishment of the National Science Foundation (NSF), did reflect a political pledge by the U.S. government to support basic research in university settings, this commitment was never especially deep. Bush's principal opponent in the battle that led to the genesis of the National Science Foundation, Senator Harley Kilgore, pushed for an institution that would support basic *and* applied research. By the mid-1960s, after over a decade of supporting basic research in university settings, the NSF confronted increasing pressure to show the practical value of its research support. In 1968, Congress passed the Daddario-Kennedy Amendment, which authorized the foundation to support applied research as well as basic science. By 1971, the NSF had added a directorate explicitly geared toward research applications, and unlike Bush and early leaders of the foundation, subsequent directors supported a central role for NSF in funding applied research (Kleinman and Solovey 1995, 135).

While the National Science Foundation and the federal government more broadly remain the most important supporters of basic research in university settings in the United States, the NSF today continues to promote commercially oriented science. In the waning years of George W. Bush's presidency, the foundation's direction was shaped by its inclusion as part of Bush's American Competitiveness Initiative. My own campus, the University of Wisconsin–Madison, is home to one of the foundation's Nanoscale Science and Engineering Centers, a multimillion-dollar effort to advance nanotechnology research and ultimately push it onto the market. Indeed, an early review of the university's program was criticized by external assessors for its failure to more fully and more quickly establish links with firms that might be interested in its NSF-funded research.

There are several observations to make from this brief historical discussion. First, formal connections between firms and universities are not new in the United States, at least. Second, these connections and, importantly and more broadly, the commercial orientation of American universities is not simply or only a reflection of changes that occurred in the 1970s and 1980s. Instead, they reflect several long-term trends. Significantly, in this context, the federal government since at least the late 1960s has promoted a commercial orientation among academic researchers. Finally, insofar as U.S. scientists' research takes on a commercial orientation or their practices reflect private sector values, this does not only echo financial support for university research from industry, it is also a sign of government policies that call on academic scientists to engage in practices traditionally associated with the commercial world in exchange for government patronage.

If we cannot see a sharp transformation as a result of the blurring of basic and applied science reflected in the biotechnology revolution, what about the transformative pressure of federal legislative initiatives? Again, the measure most often highlighted as the guiding light in facilitating university-industry relationships and a more commercial orientation on U.S. campuses is Bayh-Dole. However, as David Mowery and his collaborators have shown, university patenting was increasing many years before the passage of Bayh-Dole. These scholars have suggested, furthermore, that this piece of legislation cannot, by itself, explain the rise in academic patenting after 1980 (Mowery and Sampat 2001; Mowery et al. 2002; Mowery and Ziedonis 2000, 2002). University patenting was infrequent during the 1950s and 1960s. But between the 1960s and early 1970s, university patenting increased from around a hundred per year to more than double that (Mowery and Sampat 2001, 798; Berman 2008). In this context, Elizabeth Popp Berman elegantly shows that efforts by "federal bureaucrats [led by Norman Latker] and their interaction with an emerging community of university patent administrators helped increase and routinize patenting prior to 1980 as well as leading to the Bayh-Dole Act" (2008, 841).

For my argument, the implications of the work of Mowery and colleagues and Berman are clear. First, increased university patenting, as an indicator of a growing commercial orientation, predates the 1980s and is thus not a simple reflection of the biotechnology revolution or even the desire of university administrators to make up for budget shortfalls. The work of federal officials and university patent agents was changing the intellectual property landscape in U.S. academia well before 1980. Second, even without Bayh-Dole, the movement toward increased academic patenting would very likely have continued—it reflected an ongoing trend, not an abrupt change in environment and thus in policy. Finally, while the so-called crisis of U.S. competitiveness provided a propitious time for changing federal patent rules for academia, without the efforts of a coalition of federal and university officials, it is not clear that Bayh-Dole would have become law.

To say that the transformation of the American university—the increasing commercial orientation—was not abrupt and does not reflect some of the central causes authors use to explain the change is not to suggest that a transformation has not occurred, is not occurring, or is unimportant. Indeed, I agree that such an alteration has occurred and is happening. That change has taken place over a long time (for more on this, see below), and while it almost certainly has been accelerated by the so-called crisis of competitiveness of the late twentieth century and the scramble of academic leaders for research support, even these factors must be understood in a larger context. The U.S. academy, after all, exists within perhaps the most unabashedly capitalist economy in the world, and that socioeconomic orientation obviously predates the 1980s.

3. The Indirect Effects of Industry on Academic Science

One problem with focusing on direct formal university-industry relations is that attention is drawn away from more indirect but pervasive effects of industry on university science (Kleinman 1998). These indirect effects are harder than clear normative violations to measure and to regulate.

Many scholars have focused on how industry funding can alter the direction of research, shaping the agenda of researchers (Nelkin and Nelson 1987). But the ways in which direct funding from industry affects research practice really only captures a small piece of what is happening to academic science. A 2006 study by Rick Welsh and Leland Glenna (2006) vividly highlights the manner in which university research in one area has come to mirror private sector industry research. The Animal, Plant, and Inspection Service of the U.S. Department of Agriculture requires all organizations performing field research using transgenic crops to file notices of their intent. Welsh and Glenna used this information to explore the plants and traits studied in academic transgenic crop research. They were interested in assessing the extent to which the traits and plants field-tested by university scientists were the same as those studied by firms and whether there was a change over time (1993–2002) in the extent to which university research in this area mimicked industry investigations. Broadly speaking, industry has focused its transgenic crop research on a limited number of major crops, especially soybean, corn, and cotton, and on two traits, herbicide tolerance and insect resistance. Welsh and Glenna found that 57.6 percent—a quite substantial number—of notices filed by universities were also for these traits, while a larger 78.8 percent of industry notices of field tests were for these traits. Thus, although less than industry itself does, the majority of university transgenic research, by this indicator, focuses on research of concern to industry. As for crops studied, 73 percent of industry filings were for major crops, while only 32.6 percent of filings by universities were. More important, I would argue, however, is that over time the focus of the university research profile on transgenic crops, according to the indicators used by Welsh and Glenna, has come to look increasingly like that of industry. In their last time period (1999–2002), work by universities on major traits had increased to 73 percent from just 37 percent in the period between 1993 and 1995. Major crop work in universities had risen too, but much less substantially. To complicate this picture, Welsh and Glenna developed a commercial index, a composite measure that included both crop and trait types. Using this index, Welsh and Glenna found an increasing identity between corporate and university transgenic research over time.

Clearly, Welsh and Glenna's research shows that the practices of at least one variety of university research is increasingly isomorphic with corporate research. This is evidence of a university culture that bears traits of commercial culture. I would like to be able to argue that this transformation is entirely independent of funding of university research by corporations. Welsh and Glenna's data do not, however, allow such conclusions, since they lack information on funding source. That said, if transgenic research in university settings is typical of university science research in general, then only perhaps 7 percent of this transgenic university research is funded by industry, and still much of it mimics industry research in focus. This figure is almost certainly too low, since we know that university biotechnology research receives more corporate support than other areas (around 25 percent) and funding for agricultural research at land-grant universities receives lavish corporate support. That said, it still seems fair to say that a significant amount of university transgenic agricultural research on major traits and crops is *not* funded by industry, but nevertheless reflects the push of corporate norms and practices into university settings.

Welsh and Glenna do not document the mechanisms at work in pushing industry values into academia through the selection of research foci, but we can speculate on how corporate influence works here. Most obviously, academic scientists, especially in public universities, are increasingly pressured by university administrators, alumni, and taxpayers to undertake research with obvious economic development potential. Clearly aware of commercial trends in biotechnology, these scientists presumably believe, probably rightly, that the products currently pursued by industry are likely to be further developed in the future and that by undertaking research related to the products industry is currently promoting, their work is likely to have commercial relevance. More directly, university scientists may be encouraged to pursue this work by government officials and university leaders who learn of the work's importance to industry directly through their interactions with corporate representatives.

The indirect influence of the culture of commerce on research practice is less ambiguous in data from my ethnographic study of Professor Jo Handelsman's laboratory at the University of Wisconsin–Madison (2003). When I studied in the Handelsman lab in the mid-1990s, the central focus of researchers' work was biological control, in this case the use of microorganisms to control plant disease. More specifically, workers in the lab were doing research on a strain of *Bacillus cereus* that they called UW85, which their work showed is effective in controlling soil-borne diseases caused by a microorganism called *Phytophthora*. As it turns out, "effective" is a relative term, and, in the case of UW85, it must be defined in relationship to the chemical fungicide—metalaxyl—commonly recommended for treatment of the same diseases UW85 combats.

Here, the private sector indirectly shaped the research of work in the Handelsman lab. Since at least World War II, industry has dominated, and thus defined, agricultural disease control strategies. Much of the research on plant diseases was undertaken in industry, and thus the work on agrichemicals—the area of interest to industry—is considerably more advanced than the work on biocontrol agents, and the foundational research of agrichemical firms defines what counts as an effective fungus control agent and what tools are used to assess this efficacy.

To say that efficacy standards are defined by industry is to suggest that they are determined, in this case, by the disease control agents farmers will purchase. All else equal, farmers will select the disease control agent that most helps them to maximize their yields. As agrichemical industry analyst John Perkins notes in this context,

> To the farmer, of course, it matters little whether his yields are reduced in quantity or quality. In either case, his revenue is reduced and he is economically worse off. Moreover, no single farmer can decide unilaterally to abandon either

> quantitative or qualitative criteria in judging production methods. Competi-
> tion in capital-intensive agriculture encourages each individual grower to strive
> for maximum returns; those who don't risk losing their businesses. (1982, 268)

The "discipline of the market" first shapes the practices of industry and subsequently those of academic scientists conducting research on agricultural disease
control strategies that might compete with the existing approaches marketed by
industry.

In field tests of UW85, the biocontrol agent's effectiveness was measured
against various formulations of Ciba-Geigy's metalaxyl. Furthermore, past research on metalaxyl and the resulting knowledge of its target specificity makes the
chemical a useful research tool for scientists trying to understand biocontrol
agents like UW85. In sum, long-term domination of a research field has allowed
the agrichemical industry to influence university research without directly funding
university research.[5]

Of course, this is just one case, and I cannot say how common it is for the
historical dominance of a research field by industry to shape subsequent work in
that field in university settings. However, there are examples other than UW85.
Thus, in a related research area, as historian Richard Sawyer (1996) shows, the
measures of success of insect biocontrol agents studied by citrus researchers in
California in the mid-twentieth century were affected by cosmetic standards made
possible by industry development and citrus grower adoption of chemical pesticides to meet those standards.

Importantly, while the transgenic crop science investigated by Welsh and
Glenna suggests an increase in industry influence in precisely the period that critics of the UIRs point to, the impact of industry on biocontrol research in the case
of the Handelsman lab and in the area of citrus research suggests much earlier
influence. All three instances direct attention, at some level, however, to the effect
of commercial codes and practices on academic science, independent of direct
university-industry relations. In addition, the latter two cases point to the influence
of the world of commerce on the American university well before the 1980s.

4. The Culture of Academia

Beyond the indirect effects of industry on university research, we must look at the
way the culture of academia (its codes and practices) is being (re)shaped by industry, again, indirectly and independent of formal university-industry relations. To

make this case, I draw on earlier ethnographic work of my own (2003) as well as interview data from a study I undertook with Steven Vallas (Vallas and Kleinman 2008), documentary material I gathered recently, and the work of other scholars.

4.1. Promoting a Commercial Orientation among University Scientists

Let me begin with my own institution. The University of Wisconsin–Madison (UW) makes its role in the economy central to its strategic plan. The UW seeks to move "technological advances (ideas, products, and processes) into the private sector where they can be commercialized to produce new products and processes or used to improve existing ones" (University of Wisconsin 2001). This is not new for the University of Wisconsin. Since its establishment in 1925, the Wisconsin Alumni Research Foundation, the UW's patent agent, has served to administer the university's patents and licenses (Kleinman 2003, 133). The UW's Office of University-Industry Relations, recently reorganized and renamed the Office of Corporate Relations, was established in 1963 to promote technology transfer and foster university-industry relations.

These institutions have helped self-consciously transform the local culture. In 2001 and 2002, for example, along with Wisconsin's Graduate School, the Office of University-Industry Relations offered seminars (Wiley 2003) to at once alert faculty to the commercial potential of their work and provide them with market savvy. Among the courses was a five-session seminar entitled "High Tech Business Planning for Entrepreneurial Scientists and Engineers." The course taught participants how to write a business plan, market a product, develop financial and implementation plans, and walked "students" through the commercialization process.

Other courses offered through this initiative included "Introduction to Intellectual Property Management at the UW–Madison" and "Intellectual Property Issues in Sponsored Research." The former seminar provided information on such basic matters as how faculty-inventors should disclose inventions and seek patent protection. The latter taught participants about Bayh-Dole, royalty distribution for intellectual property created at the university, and related matters. In 2001 alone, these seminars were attended by nearly 800 faculty members and university staff (Wiley 2003).

So—the spread of norms and practices from the corporate world have, in recent years, at my university at least, moved into academia through traditional socialization mechanisms. Indeed, the new UW Office of Corporate Relations continues to offer education through an endowed seminar series. In addition, it provides expert assistance to faculty and students interested in starting private firms and publishes entrepreneurship guides for members of the UW community.

But such formal mechanisms are not the only way in which commercial values find their way into the university. Faculty and graduate students at the University of Wisconsin are bombarded with information about the importance of patenting potential inventions by the Wisconsin Alumni Research Foundation (WARF). WARF representatives were regular visitors at the laboratory I studied for my 2003 book, *Impure Cultures*. In these meetings, researchers from the laboratory of Professor Jo Handelsman provided WARF staff with updates about their research, and employees of the foundation in turn provided advice on how close to patentable this research was and what actions researchers needed to take to protect their intellectual property.

These kinds of interactions very likely reinforce faculty attitudes toward the virtues of intellectual property protection, but my research suggests that if there is an ideology of intellectual property—a set of taken-for-granted claims about the virtues of legal protections for inventions—members of the Handelsman lab had internalized it by the time I arrived in 1995. They made all of the arguments articulated regularly by university patent agents and corporate representatives (Kleinman 2003; Kleinman 2005). Centrally, Handelsman herself argued that without patent protection companies will not invest in university research: "If the invention is unlikely to be developed in the public sector, if it is not something that can just be used the way it is, but needs some major investment, then we tend to patent because it's the only way to ensure that a company or somebody will really take it and run with it commercially" (quoted in Kleinman 2003, 130). In addition, Handelsman researchers argued that patenting could provide much needed resources for the university and their work at a time of shrinking federal budgets. As one graduate student asserted, patenting is "good financially for the lab. . . . [T]he lab gets a certain percentage and then that can help fund other projects" (quoted in Kleinman 2003, 130). Finally, lab workers contended that having a patent would give the lab greater control over the transformation of their research into commercial products. As one member of the lab said, having a patent gives Handelsman the "ultimate freedom to do with that discovery whatever she wants" (quoted in Kleinman 2003, 130).

There is no question that this ideology is promoted formally by the University of Wisconsin through its publications, seminars for faculty and staff, and on its Web site. But I would suggest these beliefs are part of the broader culture. Students and faculty are exposed to them through newspapers and television as well as through talks by corporate representatives visiting campus, and they are reinforced in discussions with Wisconsin Alumni Research Foundation representatives (see Kleinman 2005).[6]

4.2. Commercialization and Everyday Academic Life

The spread of commercial norms and practices is not seen only in the context of making academic science commercially relevant. They appear to have infiltrated the administration of the university and everyday academic life. Universities are encouraged to use business as a model for their practice and appear to be doing so. Focus groups undertaken for a 2002 UW task force on university-business relations that were expected to report to the chancellor encouraged the UW to adopt a "business model approach" to the commercial role of the university, including developing a business plan, "benchmarking successful departments, schools, and colleges," and developing a marketing strategy (Wiley 2003). Steven Vallas and I found this kind of language used by some of the academic managers we interviewed.[7] In one instance, an administrator insisted that universities have remained sharply different from corporations, but ironically the model he used to describe university administration—one that likened faculty to a board of directors overseeing university administrators—was itself drawn from the corporate world.[8]

The use of corporate or commercial metaphors was common in the data Vallas and I collected. Describing institutional changes at his university, one dean spoke in terms of universities as sources for "the manufacture of capital goods." He said, "We manufacture minds, ideas, patents in some cases, and these are the capital goods that industries are built around" (quoted in Vallas and Kleinman 2008).

We see this business model approach elsewhere in the commercializing university. At Wisconsin, the university's strategic plan calls for the "consideration of entrepreneurial activities in tenure decisions" (University of Wisconsin 2001). In the biological sciences, UW tenure guidelines call on faculty members to include patents as part of their dossiers. This position has been advocated beyond Wisconsin, including in a 2004 op-ed in the *New York Times* by an engineer who is currently a dean at the Stevens Institute of Technology (Kunhardt 2004). Commercial activity in tenure decisions is a matter discussed by several of the administrators Vallas and I interviewed as part of our collaborative research. According to the dean of sciences at one prestigious Massachusetts university,

> *We are not given the privilege any longer of doing research just because we're curious about an answer. . . .* Because nowadays I think it's absolutely critical

that we justify the use of taxpayer money based upon the fact that it has some potential to have impact on people. I don't know whether or not the committees that are evaluating people for promotion and tenure are now beginning to understand that they must take into consideration numbers of patents, numbers of companies, the commercialization and the impact of that on the economy of the area. But I'm assuming that if we're going to encourage that, which I know we are, that that will start to become part of the equation, if it isn't already. (Quoted in Vallas and Kleinman 2008)

What I referred to as "business model" language is not found only at the University of Wisconsin. I came across it also at the University of Minnesota. In a talk at an academic leadership conference in the autumn of 2007 a high-level university official spoke of the value of running the university like a business. He talked of the importance of *protecting* university developed technology. He pointed to efforts on his campus to measure the *productivity* of faculty, and he described the necessity to increase the efficiency in the use of lab space. He told his audience that a campus measures and metrics task force had been set up to develop leading indicators.

Far away from practices directly related to commercializing university research, Vallas and I found an entrepreneurial ethos had intruded into academic life. Our interview data reveal a *"sharpening competition for professional distinction, combined with the entrepreneurial ethos driven by the scramble for scarce dollars, which has yielded increasingly potent barriers to the sharing of knowledge among scientists in the same or similar fields"* (Vallas and Kleinman 2008). Thus, one scientist commenting on secrecy suggested that "it's mostly self-protective and it doesn't have to do with financial interests. It has to do with credit, advancement, grants, prestige, all those things and that's why I think the simple answer is that the field has become highly competitive" (Vallas and Kleinman 2008).

If this entrepreneurial ethos and intensified competition has prompted secrecy among researchers, it has also led to an instrumental orientation toward scholarly collaboration. As one faculty member commented, "we sort of exchange reagents and so forth . . . but it's not, there's not . . . a whole lot of research done in the lab that is sort of directly feeding the collaboration" (Vallas and Kleinman 2008).

At my own university, the language of entrepreneurship has found its way into the humanities as well. In the autumn of 2007, the University of Wisconsin Humanities Center held a forum on entrepreneurship among humanities scholars. The session showcased the work of several people on campus who initiated innovative programs and used different mechanisms—fee for service, small donations, large corporate gifts—to obtain resources from private sources. What was interesting about the event was not the highlighting of innovative programs that have been successful in a difficult state budget climate, but that the behavior of the initiators of these interesting efforts was characterized as entrepreneurship. As a community, humanities scholars are a self-reflective bunch and the term "entrepreneurship" was not exactly taken for granted at the session, but the value of the term was justified by both the director of the Humanities Center, who noted that whether entrepreneurship was good or bad was a contingent matter, and a business professor, who asserted that not all entrepreneurship happens in the private sector. In the age of the neoliberal university, the commercial term "entrepreneurship"—from the French referring to a risk-taking business person—is spreading across campus, beyond business and science to the humanities.

5. Conclusions

My discussion here does not reflect a systematic historical analysis of the transformation of academic culture. Thus, I cannot be precise about the timing of changes and their ultimate depth and spread. My preliminary research suggests that the influence of industry on academia is longstanding, but there is significant variation across times, types of institutions of higher education, and regions of the globe. As always, more research is necessary to flesh out the picture I have sketched.

Still, I believe my arguments merit attention by all who are concerned about the future of the university. To reiterate, I made three central claims. First, I suggested that egregious violations of academic norms documented in popular and scholarly literature about the commercialization of the American university, while troubling, do not capture the deep transformation underway. Furthermore, focus on formal university-industry relations as the source of normative violations is equally misplaced, for while these relationships are often problematic, narrow attention on them fails to capture the deep and pervasive commercialization of university culture. Second, explanations for the transformation of the U.S. university that see this change as the product of recent and discrete factors oversimplify a complicated, uneven, and long-term process. Finally, what is more significant than formal university-industry relations are the indirect but pervasive impacts of commercial codes and practices on academic culture.

For those who see unambiguous virtue in increasing the role of the academy as part of a larger economic development engine, the emerging reality should be welcome. It means, I would think, that technology transfer and academic entrepreneurship will become increasingly easy and receive decreasing scrutiny. For those, like me, who imagine the university should have a distinctive noncommercial place in a capitalist society, the implications of the cultural transformation of American academia are less cheery. If we had hoped that the university would do those things the private sector cannot, we are likely to be increasingly disappointed. Instead of educating for citizenship, we will educate for the market. Already others have documented the advantage received by faculty whose work is "close to the market" over those whose work is apparently less commercially relevant (Slaughter and Leslie 1997). Furthermore, we increasingly hear about and are expected to treat students like consumers and not learners.

In a commercial university, we will have increasingly fewer critical voices. This won't, however, be because of the formal linkages the prospective critics have with industry, but because the virtues of commercial codes and practices will be increasingly taken for granted. Finally, research of broad social relevance, but of little commercial value, will get done with decreasing frequency, since it is work for which there will be decreasing recognition and few resources.

This situation is worse, I'm afraid, than what it would be if the real problem were formal university-industry relations. Those partnerships are discrete and identifiable. They can be monitored and regulated, and, as press coverage and scholarship suggests, they can be easily critiqued. Pinpointing subtle shifts in culture, especially when the virtues of that culture are taken for granted, is difficult, and establishing mechanisms for buffering the university from commercial culture will be tricky, indeed.

That said, the traditional norms of academia have always been and remain an important tool for those who wish to resist corporate pressures on the university. Those of us who want to see the university as a unique institution, relatively independent of the market, should draw on the prominence of traditional academic norms in the popular imagination to push policy makers and university officials to build institutions broadly in keeping with that image.

NOTES

This chapter was initially prepared for presentation at the workshop on the "Commodification of Academic Research," Amsterdam, June 21–23, 2007. In revising it, I benefited from the comments of workshop participants and especially from the reactions of Justin Biddle and Hans Radder. In addition, I received thoughtful comments from Claire Wendland. Research for this essay was supported, in part, by a Vilas Associateship from the University of Wisconsin–Madison and a Buttel-Sewell professorship from the Department of Community and Environmental Sociology at the University of Wisconsin.

1. The evidence appears to challenge this view. See Rudy et al. (2007).

2. For a discussion of the value of the normative structure of science, see Resnik, in this volume. On Mertonian norms and scientists' adherence to them, see Radder's and van den Belt's contributions to this collection.

3. Leonelli, in this volume, helpfully complicates the picture of why the free flow of information in science is important and how commodification affects the movement of information.

4. Disinterestedness is the fourth of Merton's norms of science.

5. We cannot say for certain what pest control agent use would look like had postwar research not been dominated by work on chemicals. However, if the extent of pest control offered by agrichemicals today was lower than it is, the level of control that would make biocontrol agents economically viable would also be lower. We might have a larger range of biocontrol agents in use and conceivably fewer hazardous substances running off from farm fields into watersheds. Of course, equally, with less research on agrichemicals and the way they work, such substances would be less valuable as tools for biocontrol researchers.

6. Sterckx's chapter, in this collection, appropriately points to the dangers of intellectual property protection for the development of science and new technology. In addition, Sterckx shows that, in fact, the profitability of university patenting is far less than the rosy ideology suggests. See also James Robert Brown's chapter in this volume.

7. We (actually, two graduate students working wth us at the time, Abby Kinchy and Raul Necochea) interviewed ninety-five scientists and managers, approximately half from biotechnology firms and the other half from universities in the California Bay Area and the Route 128/Cambridge area in Massachusetts. All universities—three in California and three in Massachusetts—fall under the Carnegie designation Research I.

8. In work currently in progress, my collaborators and I find that "codes of commerce" permeate the talk of academic administrators in the United States throughout the postwar period, although how these codes are drawn on varies with changes in the political economy of higher education (Kleinman, Habinek, and Vallas forthcoming).

REFERENCES

American Association of University Professors (AAUP). 1983. "Academic freedom and tenure: Corporate funding of academic research." *Academe* (November–December): 18a–23a.

Berman, Elizabeth Popp. 2008. "Why did universities start patenting?" *Social Studies of Science* 38 (6): 835–71.

Blumenstyk, Goldie. 2007. "Berkeley professors seek voice in research-institute deal with energy company." *Chronicle of Higher Education,* April 13, A33.

Blumenthal, David, Michael Gluck, K. Louis, and D. Wise. 1986a. "Industrial support of university research in biotechnology." *Science* 231:242–46.

Blumenthal, David, Michael Gluck, K. Louis, A. Stoto, and D. Wise. 1986b. "University-industry research relationships in biotechnology: Implications for the university." *Science* 232:1361–66.

Bourdieu, Pierre. 1975. "The specificity of the scientific field and the conditions for the progress of reason." *Social Science Information* 14 (5): 19–47.

Brint, Steven. 2005. "Creating the future: 'New directions' in American research universities." *Minerva* 43 (1): 23–50.

Burawoy, Michael. 2004. "Public sociologies: Contradictions, dilemmas, and possibilities." *Social Forces* 82 (4): 1603–18.

Campbell, Eric G., Brian R. Clarridge, Manjusha Gokhale, Lauren Birenbaum, Stephen Hilgartner, Neil Holtzman, and David Blumenthal. 2002. "Data withholding in academic genetics: Evidence from a national survey." *Journal of the American Medical Association* 287 (4): 473–80.

Geiger, Roger L. 1993. *Research and relevant knowledge: American research universities since World War II.* New York: Oxford University Press.

Jacoby, Russell. 1987. *The last intellectuals: American culture in the age of academe.* New York: Basic Books.

Kenney, Martin. 1985. *Biotechnology: The university-industrial complex.* New Haven, CT: Yale University Press.

Kleinman, Daniel Lee. 2003. *Impure cultures: University biology and the world of commerce.* Madison: University of Wisconsin Press.

———. 1998. "Pervasive influence: Intellectual property, industrial history, and university science." *Science and Public Policy* 25 (2): 95–102.

———. 1995. *Politics on the endless frontier: Postwar research policy in the United States.* Durham, NC: Duke University Press.

———. 2005. *Science and technology in society: From biotechnology to the Internet.* Malden, MA: Blackwell.

Kleinman, Daniel Lee, Jacob Habinek, and Steven P. Vallas. forthcoming. "Codes of commerce: Continuity and change in American academia." In *The American academic profession: Changing forms and functions,* ed. Joseph C. Hermanowicz. Baltimore: Johns Hopkins University Press.

Kleinman, Daniel Lee, and Mark Solovey. 1995. "Hot science/Cold war: The National Science Foundation after World War II." *Radical History Review* 63:110–39.

Krimsky, Sheldon. 2003. *Science in the private interest: Has the lure of profits corrupted biomedical research?* Lanham, MD: Rowman and Littlefield.

Kunhardt, Erich E. 2004. "Necessity as the mother of tenure?" *New York Times,* December 14. Available at http://www.poly.edu/events/newuniversity/KunhardtAnnouncement Feb2006.doc. Accessed April 24, 2007.

Lewis, Karen Seashore, and Melissa Anderson. 1998. "The changing context of science and university-industry relationships." In *Capitalizing knowledge,* ed. Henry Etzkowitz, Andrew Webster, and Peter Healy, 73–91. Albany: SUNY Press.

McMath, Robert C., Jr., Ronald H. Bayer, James E. Brittain, Lawrence Foster, August Giebelhaus, and Germaine M. Reed. 1985. *Engineering the new south: Georgia Tech, 1885–1995.* Athens: University of Georgia Press.

Merton, Robert K. 1973/1942. "The normative structure of science." In Robert K. Merton, *The sociology of science: Theoretical and empirical investigations,* ed. Norman W. Storer, 267–78. Chicago: University of Chicago Press.

Mitroff, I. I. 1974. "Norms and counternorms in a select group of Apollo moon scientists: A case study of the ambivalence of scientists." *American Sociological Review* 39:579–95.

Mowery, David C., and Bhaven N. Sampat. 2001. "University patents and patent policy debates in the USA, 1925–1980." *Industrial & Corporate Change* 10:781–814.

Mowery, David C., Bhaven N. Sampat, and Arvids A. Ziedonis. 2002. "Learning to patent: institutional experience, learning, and the characteristics of U.S. university patents after the Bayh-Dole Act, 1981–1992." *Management Science* 48:73–89.

Mowery, David C., and Arvids A. Ziedonis. 2000. "Numbers, quality, and entry: How has the Bayh-Dole Act affected U.S. university patenting and licensing?" *NBER Innovation Policy & the Economy* 1:187–220.

———. 2002. "Academic patent quality and quantity before and after the Bayh-Dole Act in the United States." *Research Policy* 31:399–418.

Mulkay, Michael. 1980. "Interpretation and the use of rules: The case of norms in science." In *Science and social structure: A festschrift for Robert K. Merton,* ed. Thomas Gieryn, 111–25. New York: New York Academy of Sciences.

National Science Foundation (NSF). 2006. "Industry funding of campus research declines for third straight year." May 4. Available at www.nsf.gov/news. Accessed April 15, 2007.

Nelkin, Dorothy, and Richard Nelson. 1987. "Commentary: University-industry alliances." *Science, Technology, and Human Values* 12 (1): 65–74.

Noble, David. 1977. *America by design: Science, technology, and the rise of corporate capitalism.* New York: Oxford University Press.

Owen-Smith, Jason, and Walter W. Powell. 2003. "The expanding role of university patenting in the life sciences: Assessing the importance of experience and connectivity." *Research Policy* 32 (9): 1695–1711.

Perkins, John H. 1982. *Insects, experts, and the insecticide crisis: The quest for new pesticide management strategies.* New York: Plenum.

Rudy, Alan P., Dawn Coppin, Jason Konefal, Bradley T. Shaw, Toby Ten Eyck, Craig Harris, and Lawrence Busch. 2007. *Universities in the age of corporate science: The UC Berkeley-Novartis controversy.* Philadelphia: Temple University Press.

Sawyer, Richard. 1996. *To make a spotless orange: Biological control in California.* Ames: Iowa State University Press.

Shenk, David. 1999. "Money + science = ethics problems on campus." *The Nation* (March 22): 11–18.

Slaughter, Sheila, and Larry Leslie. 1997. *Academic capitalism: Politics, policies, and the entrepreneurial university.* Baltimore: The Johns Hopkins University Press.

Slaughter, Sheila, and Gary Rhoades. 2004. *Academic capitalism and the new economy: Markets, state, and higher education.* Baltimore: The Johns Hopkins University Press.

University of Wisconsin. 2001. "Amplify the Wisconsin idea—Technology transfer." Available at www.chancellor.wisc.edu/stategicplant/view.php?get=amptech. Accessed April 15, 2007.

Vallas, Steve P., and Daniel Lee Kleinman. 2008. "Contradiction, convergence, and the knowledge economy: The confluence of academic and commercial biotechnology." *Socio-Economic Review* 6 (2): 283–311.

Washburn, Jennifer. 2005. *University, Inc.: The corporate corruption of higher education.* New York: Basic Books.

Welsh, Rick, and Leland Glenna. 2006. "Considering the role of the university in conducting research on agri-biotechnologies." *Social Studies of Science* 36 (6): 929–42.

Wiley, John D. 2003. "Report of the chancellor's task force on university-business relations." April 21. Available at www.chancellor.wisc.edu/businessrelations.html. Accessed April 15, 2007.

CHAPTER 3

Knowledge Transfer from Academia to Industry through Patenting and Licensing

RHETORIC AND REALITY

Sigrid Sterckx

1. Introduction

THIS CHAPTER ADDRESSES one aspect of the question of the actual versus desirable sociopolitical organization of academic science in modern societies—the aspect of patenting and licensing activities of universities. Academic patenting and licensing activities have massively increased since the 1980s in the United States and the 1990s in Europe. As this trend is clearly impacting the dissemination of and access to academic knowledge, the question arises whether the current encouragement of academic patenting and licensing is indeed generating the main benefit that policy makers at both the university and the government level claim it is achieving, namely, the commercial development of academic knowledge. This chapter will discuss empirical evidence on the practical effects of the current trend as well as on the role of university patents and licenses in the process of academia-to-industry knowledge transfer. As we shall see, academic patenting and licensing are much less critical for commercialization of academic knowledge than is claimed. The "prevailing wisdom"—that *the* key to promoting knowledge transfer is academic patenting and licensing—fails to recognize the undesirable and paradoxical consequences of these activities. This chapter argues that current policy making is based on empirically weak premises and concludes with suggestions to improve policy making in this field.

2. Trends in Academic Patenting and Licensing

The 1980s saw an explosion of patent filings by U.S. universities. This seems to be related to three factors in particular: the biotechnology revolution; the U.S. Supreme Court decision in *Diamond v. Chakrabarty;*[1] and the passage of the Bayh-Dole Act. While there had been a generally increasing trend in patent filings by U.S. universities before the 1980s, a significant increase then occurred. Although many factors contributed, the above-mentioned three are particularly striking. Firstly, in the field of biochemistry, previously very much an academic preserve, developments occurred that made this look to be a potential gold mine for industry. An explosive growth of the new biotech industry occurred with many start-up companies being formed out of or with close links to the universities. Secondly, a landmark decision was issued by the U.S. Supreme Court on what was proper subject matter for patent protection, encouraging companies and patent attorneys to push for still further expansion of the scope of patentable subject matter in the United States. Notably, this decision, *Diamond v. Chakrabarty,* was in the biotechnology field, relating specifically to the patentability of microorganisms. Thirdly, U.S. law was amended by the Bayh-Dole Act (1980; see below section 5.4) to allow, and indeed to encourage, U.S. universities to patent and license inventions made with federal funding. Since then, and in Europe since the 1990s, the number of academic patents and licenses has risen immensely, especially in biomedical sciences and some areas of engineering. In 2004, U.S. universities and research institutions entered 3,928 new license agreements, obtained more than 3,600 U.S. patents, and amassed more than $1 billion in patent licensing income (Bagley 2006, 217, with reference to AUTM 2005). In 2005, 4,932 new licenses were signed, 3,278 U.S. patents were obtained, 628 spin-off companies were created, and $1.3 billion in licensing income was collected (AUTM 2006). In 2006, the most recent year for which figures are available, 4,963 new license agreements were signed, 3,255 U.S. patents were obtained, and 553 spin-off companies were launched (AUTM 2007).[2]

Figures for Europe are available that show the same trend of a very rapid increase in the number of academic patents and licenses (ProTon Europe 2007).[3] In

2005, 2,310 patent applications were lodged,[4] 731 licenses were signed, €94 million was generated in licensing income, and 434 spin-off companies were set up. These figures may still be significantly lower than the above-mentioned U.S. figures, but the numbers are rising fast, as shown by ProTon Europe's comparison with 2004 (ibid.).

3. Undesirable and Paradoxical Consequences

Several commentators rightly note that academic patenting and licensing amount to double taxation—as "[t]axpayers usually help fund the initial research through government grants, then must pay again in the form of higher product prices that reflect the cost of royalty payments to universities" (Wysocki 2004, A1). The pro-intellectual property culture which has become so widespread in academia also leads to numerous other, more concrete problems such as reorientation of research, "patent-friendly" presentation of research results, erosion of norms regarding sharing of results, diminishing social return of academic research as a result of exclusive licensing, and patent infringement suits against universities.

3.1. Reorientation of Research

The orientation of academic research, e.g., the selection of research topics, is susceptible to being influenced by university policies on patenting and licensing.[5] These may cause research funding as well as research efforts to be redirected from fundamental to applied research as well as from research in the arts and humanities to research in the "hard" sciences. Moreover, as a result of the "push" toward patenting and licensing, academic research efforts may diminish in socially important fields which are typically neglected by researchers in the private/for-profit sector. If researchers in universities or other public research institutions decide that research in certain areas would be insufficiently acknowledged by their employers because of lack of potential for commercialization, these areas risk becoming virtually completely neglected. Research into rare and tropical diseases is a pertinent example in this context (Sterckx 2004b).

3.2. "Patent-Friendly" Presentation of Research Results

Another problematic effect of the increasing pressure to commercialize is that it may encourage academic researchers to present their results in a "patent-friendly" format, which is almost invariably selective. The following statement by a person working for a technology transfer office of a university is illustrative in this regard:

> What the patent attorney's trying to do is establish that there's no mechanism, [that] you couldn't have foreseen this [because one of the legal requirements for patentability is "nonobviousness"]. Which is the exact opposite of the faculty inventor who's trying to establish that their understanding of the mechanism and predictability led to this discovery. . . . That scares patent attorneys to death. People could say "Wait a minute, you mean anybody could have formed this hypothesis based on what Professor Joe Schmoe said in this paper and that all you did was test [that idea]?" (McSherry 2001, 174)

3.3. Erosion of Norms Regarding the Sharing of Results

A further important problem with the growth of the pro-intellectual property culture in academia lies in the undesirable effects it may have on the sharing of research results among academics (e.g., Blumenthal et al. 1997; Campbell et al. 2002; Washburn 2005).

Patent laws provide that patents are only granted for inventions which are new. The precise "novelty" requirement varies from country to country, but in most places outside the United States the requirement is essentially that there must not have been any nonconfidential disclosure of the invention before the application to patent it is filed. Under U.S. law, a patent may still be granted when the inventor has made a nonconfidential disclosure as long as the U.S. patent application is filed within one year of the disclosure.[6] Nonconfidential disclosures—discussions in the cafeteria, presentation of papers at symposia or posters at conferences, and so on—are, or at least were, central to academic life; however, if academic inventions are to be patented, then confidentiality must be maintained and this is being communicated to the researchers by their university technology transfer offices. Thus, the "novelty requirement" results in the technology transfer offices and the industry sponsors of academic research instructing university researchers to delay publishing and presenting their results until after a patent application has been filed, so as not to jeopardize potential patent rights.

As Margo Bagley remarks, "While not amenable to precise quantification, the stifling of discourse and the erosion in the norms of sharing and colloquy historically associated with the scholarly enterprise are costs that must be balanced against the technology transfer gains" (Bagley 2006, 2–3). A closely related problem lies in the increasing involvement of academic scientists with material transfer agreements, or MTAs (Streitz and Bennett 2003). Academic scientists frequently wish to carry out experiments using materials or organisms developed or isolated by other research groups (whether industrial or academic) and which are not commercially available. The reason may be simple scientific curiosity; however, it may be that a commercial possibility has been identified. In keeping with the "openness" and "sharing" norms of academic science, it was traditional simply to ask for a sample of the material or organism. With the increased awareness by the technology transfer offices of the commercial potential of such materials, it has now become routine for the source university either to refuse such requests or to require the recipient university to enter an MTA, which defines the conditions under which the sample will be provided. These conditions may be straightforward and reasonable, for example that any excess sample be returned or destroyed, that the sample only be used for the agreed purpose, and that any resulting publication should acknowledge the source of the sample. Frequently, however, insidious conditions are placed on the recipient, for example that no publication may be submitted without prior review or even consent by the donor, that any publication should list the donor scientist as a coauthor, that there should be a profit share from any resulting patentable inventions, or even to the extreme that any resulting patentable inventions should belong to the donor.[7]

3.4. Diminishing Social Return of Academic Research as a Result of Exclusive Licensing

The extent to which academic research can yield benefits to society at large does not only depend on the way governments and universities design academic patenting policies, but also on their *licensing* policies.

A patent license is a contract in which the patent holder agrees not to invoke her patent rights against the licensee, and in return the licensee agrees to pay the patent holder a royalty or some other consideration. Licenses can be nonexclusive, sole, or exclusive, with respectively the patent holder being free to license others, not being free to license others but being free to exploit the invention herself, and being neither free to license others nor to exploit the invention herself.

Where an invention is created within a university using *public* funding, the difference between having *any* interested party free to use it as long as he pays an appropriate royalty to the university and having *no one* other than the exclusive licensee free to use it should be clear.

Analyzing survey data from the (U.S.) Association of University Technology Managers as well as data from two surveys they have conducted themselves,[8] economists Thursby and Thursby (2003) have found that more than a quarter (27 percent) of licenses issued by universities and research institutes are reported to include clauses allowing the industry partner to *delete* information from research papers before they get submitted for publication, while almost half (44 percent) allow the industry partner to insist on *delaying* publication (Thursby and Thursby 2003, 6).

Research by Stanford law professor Mark Lemley has revealed that the vast majority of licenses granted under university patents are exclusive (Lemley 2007). Such exclusive licenses have advantages and drawbacks for both the university at issue and society as a whole. First, exclusive licenses usually restrict access to technology to a larger extent than nonexclusive licenses, so the greater the social utility of a technology the stronger the case is for broad access. Secondly, staff at technology transfer offices of universities have a tendency to think that exclusive licenses are beneficial because they generate more money, but this is not necessarily so. If a technology is an "enabling technology"—a technology on the basis of which other, improved, technologies can be built—only nonexclusive licensing is likely to produce the optimum outcome, i.e., the highest number of developments/improvements of the technology. Moreover, as Lemley notes, "exclusive licenses can block any development of a technology if the licensee doesn't deliver" (Lemley 2007, 6).

Where a key technology is licensed nonexclusively and for a reasonable royalty, the take-up rate can be high and the revenue to the university significant. The Cohen-Boyer patent on recombinant DNA technology is a fine example of this.

3.5. Patent Infringement Suits against Universities

Another problem raised by current university policies concerns the risk of patent infringement suits against universities in countries that do not have a (sufficiently broad) "research exemption" or "experimental use exception" in their patent law.[9] In this regard, the decision by the U.S. Court of Appeals for the Federal Circuit (CAFC) in the case *Madey v. Duke* was a real "wake up call." The case law on the extent to which "experimental use" of patented inventions is exempt from normal rules regarding patent infringement shows that, in the United States, the exemption has traditionally been construed narrowly. As the famous Justice Story argued in *Whittemore v. Cutter* (1813), "[I]t could never have been the intention of the legislature to punish a man, who constructed . . . a machine merely for philosophical experiments, or for the purpose of ascertaining the sufficiency of the machine to produce its described effects."[10] In *Gayler v. Wilder* (1850) the court decided that patent holders cannot sue for infringement: a person whose "use is for experiments for the sole purposes of gratifying a philosophical taste or curiosity or for instruction and amusement."[11]

However, the question is to what extent is this an accurate description of what academics do, and how does the current trend of commercialization of academic research impact the applicability of the exemption? As Jaffe and Lerner observe, the CAFC's decision in *Madey v. Duke* has made it crystal clear that there is little reason to be hopeful for U.S. academics:

> A recent CAFC decision has sent ripples of fear through the general counsel's offices at universities. In a case between Duke University and a former faculty member named John Madey, the experimental use exception was construed so narrowly that whatever fig leaf it may previously have provided university activities may have shriveled to the point of irrelevance. (Jaffe and Lerner 2004, 65)

This decision overruled an earlier decision by a district court in favor of Duke University. The district court had construed the exception broadly as covering activities "solely for research, academic or experimental purposes."[12] According to the CAFC, this construction of the exemption was much broader than the traditional test (are the activities at issue "for amusement, to satisfy idle curiosity, or for strictly philosophical inquiry"?).

The CAFC concluded that,

> [R]egardless of whether a particular institution or entity is engaged in an endeavor for commercial gain, so long as the act is in furtherance of the alleged infringer's legitimate business and is not solely for amusement, to satisfy idle curiosity, or for strictly philosophical inquiry, the act does not qualify for the very narrow and strictly limited experimental use defense.[13]

In June 2003 the U.S. Supreme Court refused to hear an appeal of the CAFC decision.

Following the CAFC's interpretation of the experimental use exception, most basic research will *not* be considered as exempted from patent infringement suits in the United States. This situation is highly disturbing since much basic research depends on access to technologies and materials. If academics are obliged to ask for licenses before beginning their research, that research may be delayed, reduced, or may never take place.

Shortly after the CAFC decision in *Madey v. Duke,* the experimental use defense once again was before the CAFC in the case *Integra v. Merck.*[14] Here, in a dissenting opinion, Judge Newman argued that the law had not been developed in a way that was correct or socially desirable:

This case raises a question of the nature and application of the common law research exemption. . . . Its correct treatment can affect research institutions, research-dependent industry, and scientific progress. The question is whether, and to what extent, the patentee's permission is required in order to study that which is patented. [Here the panel holds that all the relevant activity] . . . was "discovery-based research" and that there is no right to conduct such research, under either the common law research exemption or the statutory immunity established in 35 U.S.C. §271(e)(1). However, neither law nor policy requires that conclusion, and both law and policy have long required a different conclusion in implementation of the purpose of the patent system.[15]

Judge Newman considered that the purpose of the patent system was not only to provide a financial incentive to innovate but also to add to the body of published knowledge. In this regard she argued,

The right to conduct research to achieve such knowledge need not, and should not, await expiration of the patent. That is not the law. . . . Yet today the court disapproves and essentially eliminates the common law research exemption. This change of law is ill-suited to today's research-founded, technology-based economy.[16]

Regarding the court's earlier decision in *Madey v. Duke,* Judge Newman commented, "I do not disagree with that decision on its facts; I disagree only with its sweeping dictum, and its failure to distinguish between investigation into patented things, as has always been permitted, and investigation using patented things, as has never been permitted."[17] This comment arose in the context of patents for "research tools"—patents that the majority in *Integra v. Merck* considered would be rendered ineffective by the research exemption. Judge Newman stated that this was a misconception, as there is a fundamental difference between researching *into,* and research *using,* patented technology.

Interestingly, at the Supreme Court level, the CAFC majority decision in *Integra v. Merck* was reversed, but the question of the research exemption was not addressed.

4. Tragedy of the Anticommons

The above-mentioned negative effects of academic patenting and licensing are exacerbated by the fact that universities as well as university spin-off companies increasingly apply for and obtain patents for the results of "upstream" research, especially in biomedical areas and nanotechnology.

If we think of the things that might be perceived by the public as inventions, these might include mechanical or electrical devices in day-to-day use—a telephone, a light bulb, a can opener—or a material which through its chemical properties helps us—penicillin, polythene, etc. Nonetheless, the development of such products may involve many stages the results of which we do not see. Drug development can involve identifying genetic susceptibilities to disease, biochemical pathways, and so on, all of which ultimately lead to the identification of candidate compounds for human trials. Many developments within academic research contribute to the successful performance of these stages, which may be far "upstream" of the final commercial product. Where these are patented, the patents are often referred to as "upstream" or "research tool" patents.

Since the *direct* product of the use of the research tool is not itself put on the market, there is a tendency by the research tool patent holder to demand a royalty on the final commercial product as well as on the use of the research tool.

As product development involves many stages, there is a risk of these royalties stacking up. A moment's thought will reveal that if each research tool patentee demands a royalty of 10 percent of the sale price of the end product, then with ten research tool patents in the way a product will very likely never be developed.

A proliferation of "upstream" patents can stifle "downstream" research and development (Heller and Eisenberg 1998; Eisenberg 1996; Rai and Eisenberg 2003; Rai 1999). The more people who must consent to a project in order for it to proceed, the more likely it is that negotiations will fail or that transaction costs will become excessive. *Too few* property rights may lead to an *overuse* of resources in a "tragedy of the commons," but *too many* property rights may result in an *underuse* of resources in a "tragedy of the anticommons."

5. Reasons Given by Policy Makers to Justify Academic Patenting and Licensing

Despite all the potential and real problems discussed above, governments and university policy makers strongly defend academic patenting and licensing as *the* way to promote "knowledge transfer" or "technology transfer" from academia to industry. Are these negative effects the price we must pay for technology transfer, which is vital to our economies? Various empirical studies suggest that academic patenting and licensing are *not* the main channels for such transfer (Mansfield 1991; Levin et al. 1987; Cohen et al. 2002). So why is the pro-patent culture in universities intensifying rather than being readjusted to take into account the above-mentioned problems? What reasons are put forward by policy makers to justify academic patenting and licensing? The four main reasons appear to be strengthening the regional economy, generating more money for universities, providing an incentive to invent, and creating an incentive to innovate.

5.1. Strengthening the Regional Economy

In policy documents of international bodies, governments, and universities (e.g., OECD 2002), it is argued increasingly frequently that academic patenting and licensing can support the regional economy, e.g., by creating products and jobs. Indeed, encouraging academics to generate things that are valuable to the community can be a laudable thing, but this can be done without universities getting involved with patenting and licensing and thus avoiding the undesirable consequences discussed above in section 3.

5.2. Generating More Money for Universities

It is often argued that, via patenting and licensing, universities may generate income for themselves, which is necessary in view of the reduction of state funding of universities. Nonetheless, even though universities may well have a legitimate claim to more funding, the patenting and licensing of results of academic research is not necessarily the best way to obtain this goal—especially given the above-mentioned disadvantages of the current trend.[18]

Moreover, for most universities, patenting and licensing activities are unmistakably *unprofitable*. Even the revenues of universities that have considerable experience with patenting and licensing are dominated by a very small number of outstandingly successful inventions (mostly in the biomedical area) (Powell and Owen-Smith 2002, 108–15). Thursby and Thursby conclude from empirical research that "[F]ew technologies and even fewer universities earn substantial sums of money [from licensing]. Most technologies earn small (and frequently zero) license income" (Thursby and Thursby 2003, 8). However, the wish to generate income seems to be the main reason universities get involved with patenting and licensing. Studies by Jensen, Thursby, and Thursby, surveying university technology transfer officers, found that 70.5 percent of them rated revenue ("royalties/license fees generated") as "extremely important," making it the most important objective of technology transfer offices according to this category of respondents (Thursby and Thursby 2003, 4; see also Jensen and Thursby 2001 and Thursby, Jensen, and Thursby 2001).[19]

5.3. Providing an Incentive to Invent

A major part of the utilitarian defense of the patent system is that it offers a necessary incentive to invent (Sterckx 2004a). It is sometimes claimed that this incentive effect may be real in the context of industry but has little relevance for universities, since academic researchers are paid to invent and therefore don't require any extra encouragement. Still, the argument does have some force: paying academics to do research does not necessarily imply that they will make inventions. Admittedly, it implies that they will produce *information* from research, but that is not the same thing as creating *inventions*.

The pressure on the academic to publish new knowledge revealed by her research is not the same as the pressure to contemplate possible ways in which that knowledge might be exploited commercially. Since it is the *originality* of research/ knowledge that has traditionally been valued among academic scientists, there has been little incentive to examine the suitability of that knowledge for commercial end-uses. When pushed by their university employers to seek patents, academics feel pressure to think about how to turn the new knowledge into a patentable invention.

5.4. Creating an Incentive to Innovate

The most commonly invoked argument for academic patenting and licensing is that this is vital for "innovation," i.e., the process of transforming research results into new products or processes with market value. Proponents of this argument usually refer to Edmund Kitch's famous "prospect theory of patents" (Kitch 1977).[20] In a seminal article from 1977 Kitch notes that the delay between the granting of a patent and the commercialization of the invention in question is often long. He argues that it is *innovation* rather than *invention* which requires investment, and hence protection against competitors in the form of patents is vital.

Indeed, more frequently, "the receipt of the patent is not the last step in the process of innovation" (Abramowicz 2005, 3). Commercializing an invention may involve developing or perfecting technologies to manufacture the invention, conducting scientific tests, performing pre- and postmarketing research, and advertising the product or process, all of which necessitate investment.

The question at issue here is whether this "commercialization argument" is convincing in the context of *academic* inventions. Mowery, Nelson, Sampat, and Ziedonis have investigated this in great detail (Mowery et al. 2004) in the context of their analysis of the effects of the U.S. Bayh-Dole Act (1980), a law aimed at promoting the commercialization of federally funded inventions (including federally funded *academic* inventions).[21] One of the most significant findings of Mowery and his colleagues is that both before and after the entry into the enactment of the Bayh-Dole Act, a lot of technology transfer took (and takes) place *even in the absence of* patenting and licensing by universities.

It should be emphasized that the primary goal of the Bayh-Dole Act is to generate the greatest *public* benefit. To quote a few objectives mentioned in the preamble to the act: "to promote the utilization of inventions," "[for inventions to be] used in a manner to promote free competition and enterprise without unduly encumbering future research and discovery," to "promote commercialization and public availability of inventions," and to "protect the public against nonuse or unreasonable use of inventions." How these objectives can be achieved—and whether patenting and licensing by universities is necessary anyway—often depends on the field of technology and even the nature of the invention.[22]

The dominant view, namely, that academic patenting and licensing are vital to obtain commercial development of academic knowledge, clearly requires revision. Empirical research strongly suggests that academic patenting and licensing are much less essential for the commercialization of academic knowledge than is claimed by the popular view (Mansfield 1991; Levin et al. 1987; Cohen et al. 2002), while at the same time these activities produce various undesirable effects and paradoxical consequences, as discussed above.

The dominant view blatantly fails to see the real-world consequences of academic patenting and licensing. The weak pro-intellectual property arguments discussed earlier continue to play a major role in policy making, both at the university level and at the government level. What can be done to solve the problems? In the following and final section of this chapter I offer some suggestions as to how existing regulations and policies can be redesigned with a view to giving priority to the public interest. Obviously, there is insufficient space here to go into the specifics of required policy changes. Nevertheless, I will set out a number of proposals which deserve further consideration, as individually and together they address many of the failings of the current system.

6. Some Suggestions for the Reorientation of Current Patenting and Licensing Policies

Possible suggestions for reorienting the current policies can be divided into three categories: a first one which requires international agreement; a second one which necessitates amendment of national or regional law; and a third one which requires policy changes at the university level.[23]

6.1. Introduction of a Grace Period

A proposal that falls into the first category, although at first sight it might seem to fall instead into the second category, is the introduction of a grace period. Openness and willingness to share ideas, materials, and information are part of the Mertonian norms for academic science. Secretiveness and unwillingness to share without a signed material transfer agreement (MTA) are part of the commercial world of intellectual property. Secrecy is required if patents are to be obtained in most countries outside the United States since disclosure destroys novelty and renders an invention unpatentable. This need for secrecy could, however, be removed or at least relaxed, enabling academic researchers to interact more freely and openly, if the inventor's own disclosures were discounted as prior art for a given period, as is the case in the United States. In the United States, the period is one year—this gives time enough for the implications of an invention to be understood and for a patent application to be written and filed, and yet is short enough for competitors to have some certainty as to what patents they might encounter if they venture into the same field. Some safeguards would be required should a one-year grace period become the international norm (for example, the patent application should refer to the disclosure and should be published at the application stage), but such safeguards may be straightforward and easy to adopt.[24]

A word of caution is in order, however: the introduction of a one-year grace period in only one or two additional countries, rather than as an internationally agreed-upon norm, could in fact exacerbate the problems rather than reduce them, since more academics might mistakenly assume that they were free to disclose their ideas without harming the prospect of patent protection in important countries. While the current U.S. grace period is an oddity in global patent terms, most academics with any knowledge of the patent system are aware that premature disclosure is novelty-destructive for patent purposes outside the United States.

Some proposals that fall in the second category, i.e., requiring changes in national or regional law or in the practices of national or regional patent offices, are the following: strengthening research exemptions to liability for infringement, strengthening the exclusion from patentability of discoveries, aligning claim scope with "breadth" of disclosure, and integrating academic expertise into the patent examination procedure.

6.2. Strengthening Research Exemptions to Liability for Infringement

Researchers in universities carry out research funded by the state and by the private sector. Research funded by the state has often been "blue sky," i.e., without an immediate obvious commercial end. It is on such work that research with a commercial goal subsequently builds, and without state support it may not be accomplished. For any given country, funding blue sky research provides a skill and knowledge reservoir for future applied science, even though there is of course the risk that the applied science will be carried out and patented by foreign companies or institutions.

Given the development of skills and knowledge within the universities, it is frequently more efficient for companies to contract out research projects to academics rather than equip their own laboratories and hire skilled staff to carry out the research in-house. Contract work brings income into the universities and often exposes academics to knowledge and skills normally found only in commercial R&D departments. Thus it is in everyone's interest that such contract research, despite its above-mentioned drawbacks, can be carried out by universities. However, as discussed above, universities are not exempt from all patent infringement actions and are increasingly being sued. For this reason, I recommend that the research activities of not-for-profit research institutions in general, and universities and university hospitals in particular, should be excluded from being considered to represent patent infringement.

6.3. Strengthening the Exclusion from Patentability of Discoveries

Much of academic research is directed to the making of discoveries—the finding of new materials and phenomena, the elucidation of natural processes, etc. Such research does not always have obvious commercial implications but increasingly it is forming the basis for "prophetic" patenting by academics and nonacademics alike, and the rapid dissemination of such discoveries is of course frustrated by the current patent process.

European patent law forbids the patenting of discoveries (see Article 52 [2][a] of the European Patent Convention), yet the step from unpatentable discovery to patentable invention may be trivial: a compound as found in a plant or microorganism is a discovery, but the same compound isolated or in sterile form may be patented; a nucleic acid sequence as found in the DNA of a sick patient is a discovery, but the use of an assay for that sequence to provide a disease prognosis may be patented. This is made explicit in the Rules of the European Patent Convention, for example, where Rule 27(a) states, "Biotechnological inventions shall also be patentable if they concern . . . biological material which is isolated from its natural environment" (European Patent Office 2007). This means that such patents are more readily available for organizations with the funds to investigate nature and natural phenomena than for those without such funds, thereby creating an imbalance between the developed and the less developed countries. In addition to this utilitarian argument against such patents, one can add the principled position that what is there for us to find if we do but look should be free for all to exploit thereafter. Patents should require invention rather than serendipitous discovery and skilled wordplay. This recommendation should be implemented by amendment of national and regional patent laws and, more importantly, by the issuance of clear instructions to the national and regional patent offices to follow the will of the legislature.

6.4. Aligning Claim Scope with Disclosure

Patent attorneys, as usual acting in the "best interest of their clients," seek to obtain patent monopolies of as broad a scope as possible. Nonetheless, broad patents can block further development by other parties. In a well-established, slowly progressing field, such broad patents may pose little problem to the consumer, although they can have disastrous consequences for competition and hence to the interests of the state. In contrast, in new, rapidly developing fields, broad patents (which are relatively easy to obtain in new fields) can potentially block for decades further development by all other than the patentee.[25] To take a simple example, if the mobile phone had been patented as such, then the massive improvements that have been made seen since its arrival would not necessarily have been available to consumers—we might still be carrying phones the size of a brick.

If the goal of the patent system is to benefit the state and its citizens, then patent claims should be granted with a scope that encourages further development and thus of a scope commensurate with the invention as substantiated in the patent documents. In this context, the example of U.S. Patent No. 4528643 is instructive. On the basis of the broad language used in the patent claims, the patentee, E-Data, sought royalties from thousands of companies, including IBM.[26] This case is discussed at length in Bessen and Meurer's book *Patent Failure: How Judges, Bureaucrats, and Lawyers Put Innovators at Risk* (2008). As they introduce the case,

E-Data's patent was for a kiosk that produced digital audio tapes and the like in retail stores, but they interpreted this patent to cover a very broad swath of e-commerce. On the other hand, IBM holds hundreds of patents related to e-commerce, but this did not prevent E-Data from threatening to block IBM from marketing its own innovative e-commerce products. To market its own patented technologies, IBM was forced to pay E-Data for a license. (Bessen and Meurer 2008, 4–5)

Patents of this nature cannot help but be a discouragement to further research and development, both in academia and elsewhere. Therefore, patent offices should be instructed clearly by the legislature not to grant such broad claims.

6.5. Integrating Academic Expertise into Patent Examination Procedures

Patent applications are written by skilled patent attorneys with access to the resources their clients can afford. These applications are examined by patent office employees, who may in the past have been research scientists but no longer are. Nevertheless, the basis for judging inventiveness, and hence patentability, is the "person of ordinary skill in the art." Patent examiners must ask themselves whether the subject matter claimed in the patent application would have been considered obvious by a "person skilled in the art" at the time the patent application was filed. Where a patent application relates to a new technical field, the likelihood of the patent office examiner having any practical experience of that field is slim. To prevent patents from being granted when their subject matter would in fact have seemed obvious to someone skilled *and* working in the field, the patent office examiner should be able to call in the expertise of such a skilled person—for example, an academic. In the past in some countries patent applications were indeed assessed by members of distinguished scientific societies.[27]

As far as the *third category* of suggestions for policy change is concerned, i.e., policy changes by the universities themselves, I will here only make the following brief proposals, which are discussed further in Sterckx (2009).

1. Universities should not enter into agreements with industry that permit suppression or unreasonable delay of publication of research results by academics.

2. University policy should require all licenses granted to be nonexclusive unless exclusivity can be adequately justified to an independent body representing public interests, for example, including representatives of public research funding sources.

3. Universities should keep an open register of researchers' financial involvements and require faculty and staff to declare conflicts of interest in all submissions for funding, ethical approval, or publication in order to reduce fraud, misrepresentation, and avoid conflicts of interest.

4. University policy should require, as part of any license agreement granted, that the licensee agrees not to sue universities or university hospitals for infringement. This may reduce the risks of universities wasting resources in litigation and will increase academics' freedom to research. This parallels the proposal for strengthening the exemptions under national law made under heading 6.2 above.

NOTES

I am very grateful for the many comments and questions raised by the participants in the Amsterdam workshop. I would especially like to thank commentator Kor Grit for his comments, as well as Hans Radder and Julian Cockbain for their useful comments on an earlier draft of this chapter.

1. *Diamond v. Chakrabarty,* 447 U.S. 303, 1980. See http://caselaw.lp.findlaw.com/scripts/getcase.pl?court=us&vol=447&invol=303.

2. The report on the year 2006 does not mention total licensing income.

3. ProTon Europe is a European network of "knowledge transfer offices" and companies affiliated with universities or other public research organizations.

4. No information is given on the number of patents *obtained*.

5. Admittedly, Thursby and Thursby (2005), Colyvas et al. (2002), and Mowery et al. (2001) have not found a significant link between the extent of licensing by universities and the reorientation of research (toward applied research) by their faculty; however, these studies have only looked at particularly prestigious research universities. A significant effect on the orientation of research may be more likely to occur in "mainstream" universities (which form the majority of universities).

6. Actually, the position is slightly more complicated, as unprinted disclosures outside the United States cannot destroy novelty. Cf. section 102 of the U.S. patent law. See Cockbain (2007, 784).

7. It is, of course, possible for universities to take action to reduce the extent to which MTAs are a barrier to academic collaboration. Thus, for example, Stanford University has a sensible procedure for MTAs (see Stanford University Office of Technology Licensing, "Our Policy," available at http://otl.stanford.edu/inventors/policies.html): no MTA is required for academic or not-for-profit recipients, or even for industrial recipients where the donor scientist is certain that the material will only be used for research purposes; otherwise, an industrial recipient is required either to sign an MTA confirming that use will be for research purposes only or to negotiate with the technology transfer office.

8. A survey of 62 technology transfer offices of major U.S. universities and an "industry" survey of 112 licensing executives who regularly obtain licenses from universities.

9. National patent laws vary as to whether they include a research exemption, and how narrow or broad its scope is. See, e.g., Cook (2006).

10. *Whittemore v. Cutter,* 29 F. Cas. 1120 (C.C.D. Mass. 1813).

11. *Gayler v. Wilder,* 51 U.S. (10 How.) 477, 497 (1850).

12. *John M. J. Madey v. Duke University,* 307 F. 3d 1351 (Fed. Cir. 2002).

13. Ibid.

14. *Integra Lifesciences I, Ltd. et al. v. Merck KGaA et al.,* 340 F. 3d 860, 66 USPQ 2d 1865 (Fed. Cir. 2003), available at http://www.aipla.org/html/reports/2005/Integra.pdf.

15. Ibid., 20–21.

16. Ibid., 21.

17. Ibid., 30n.

18. This goal may better be achieved through a general tax (Lemley 2007, note 27).

19. The following quote from the announcement of the live audio conference, "Mining for Low-Tech Gold: Turning University Creative Works into New Licensing Dollars," aimed at staff of university technology transfer offices from all over the world (held on April 24, 2008), says it all:

> Dear Colleague:
>
> You are sitting on a potential gold mine. It's right under your nose, in the form of a mother lode of intellectual property created by your faculty that is ready for commercialization without further development, is relatively easy to license, brings a quick return in dollars to the university, and gives your tech transfer office a solid boost in performance. What's the secret? It lies in expanding your focus beyond strictly high-tech innovations to the realm of "creative works." Textbooks, software programs, education modules, courseware, web tools, databases, videos, and a host of other non-traditional forms of licensable IP too often go unnoticed and untapped in busy offices that are chasing the next high-tech "big winner." Let us show you how to mine this buried treasure, and add hundreds of thousands of dollars in new licensing revenues.

See http://www.technologytransfertactics.com/content/audio/ltg/.

20. For an interesting discussion of this theory, see Oddi (1996).

21. *The Universities and Small Business Patent Procedures Act,* Public Law 96-517, 96th Congress, 94 Stat. 3015 (1980), enacted as 35 U.S.C. §200, et seq. Prior to the enactment of this law, the U.S. federal government held title to inventions made in the context of federally funded research, and it made those inventions available to everyone on a nonexclusive basis. Via the mechanism of so-called Institutional Patent Agreements, exceptions to this principle could be decided on a case-by-case basis, but the procedure involved was burdensome. Under the Bayh-Dole Act, universities are allowed to retain title to and even exclusively license inventions resulting from federally funded research, provided that they file a patent application within a year of disclosure of the invention and work together with industry—preferably small businesses—to introduce the invention to the market in a timely fashion. If they fail to do the latter, the federal government can claim ownership of the invention.

22. In this context, one obviously needs to keep in mind the fact that "innovation" does not necessarily equal "public benefit," in spite of the rhetoric used by some commentators and policy makers.

23. This section has benefited significantly from my discussions with Julian Cockbain.

24. Reference to the inventor's earlier disclosure within the application text would allow third parties to be aware of its non-prior-art nature. Not all disclosures come with an

attached name and this way there would be no doubt what was excluded as prior art. At present in most countries patent applications are published eighteen months after the filing or priority date. Early publication, in contrast, would prevent long periods of investment and development by third parties being jeopardized by the sudden appearance of previously hidden patent rights. One of the worst offenders in this regard was Jerome Lemelson, whose "submarine" patents often surfaced after decades.

25. The problem of overly broad patents, including *inter alia* granted patents that cover virtually all genetically modified versions of particular plants such as cotton, soy, and coffee, is discussed further by, *inter alia,* van Wijk (1995) and Warner (2001).

26. Claim 1 of this patent reads as follows:

> A method for reproducing information in material objects utilizing information manufacturing machines located at point of sale locations, comprising the steps of: providing from a source remotely located with respect to the information manufacturing machine the information to be reproduced to the information manufacturing machine, each information being uniquely identified by a catalog code; providing a request reproduction code including a catalog code uniquely identifying the information to be reproduced to the information manufacturing machine requesting to reproduce certain information identified by the catalog code in a material object; providing an authorization code at the information manufacturing machine authorizing the reproduction of the information identified by the catalog code included in the request reproduction codes; and receiving the request reproduction code and the authorization code at the information manufacturing machine and reproducing in a material object the information identified by the catalog code included in the request reproduction code in response to the authorization code authorizing such reproduction.

27. In 1666 in France, for example, Jean-Baptiste Colbert founded the Académie des Sciences based on the Italian academies of the fifteenth and sixteenth century. In this period, the French king made it a rule to call upon scientific advisors when decisions had to be made concerning patent granting. The Académie des Sciences had to run the patent application through an examination procedure, the rules of which would later be written down in a royal decree of 1699. In 1791 a new French Patent Act came into effect which lifted this examination procedure and turned the patent system into a registration system. See Prager (1944).

REFERENCES

Abramowicz, M. 2005. *The problem of patent underdevelopment.* George Washington University Law School Public Law and Legal Theory Working Paper No. 179. Available at papers.ssrn.com/sol3/papers.cfm?abstract_id=873473.

AUTM (Association of University Technology Managers). 2005. *U.S. licensing survey: FY 2004.* Available at www.autm.net.

———. 2006. *U.S. licensing survey: FY 2005.* Available at www.autm.net.

———. 2007. *U.S. licensing activity survey: FY 2006.* Summary available at http://autm .net/events/file/AUTM_06_US%20LSS_FNL.pdf.

Bagley, M. 2006. "Academic discourse and proprietary rights: Putting patents in their proper place." *Boston College Law Review* 47 (1): 1–58.

Bessen, J., and M. Meurer. 2008. *Patent failure: How judges, bureaucrats, and lawyers put innovators at risk*. Princeton, NJ: Princeton University Press.

Blumenthal, D., E. Campbell, M. Anderson, N. Causino, and K. Louis. 1997. "Withholding research results in academic life science: Evidence from a national survey of faculty." *Journal of the American Medical Association* 277:1224.

Campbell, E. B. Clarridge, M. Gokhale, L. Birenbaum, S. Hilgartner, N. Holtzman, and D. Blumenthal. 2002. "Data withholding in academic genetics: Evidence from a national survey." *Journal of the American Medical Association* 287:473.

Cockbain, J. 2007. "Intellectual property rights and patents." In *Comprehensive medicinal chemistry II,* vol. 1, ed. J. Taylor and D. Triggle, 779. Oxford: Elsevier.

Cohen, W., R. Nelson, and J. Walsh. 2002. "Links and impacts: The influence of public research on industrial R&D." *Management Science* 48:1.

Colyvas, J., M. Crow, A. Gelijns, R. Mazzoleni, R. Nelson, N. Rosenberg, and B. Sampat. 2002. "How do university inventions get into practice?" *Management Science* 48 (1): 61.

Cook, T. 2006. *A European perspective as to the extent to which experimental use, and certain other, defences to patent infringement, apply to differing types of research*. London: Intellectual Property Institute.

Eisenberg, R. 1996. "Public research and private development: Patents and technology transfer in government-sponsored research." *Virginia Law Review* 82:1663.

European Patent Office. 2007. *Convention on the grant of European patents (European Patent Convention)*, 13th ed. Munich: European Patent Office.

Heller, M., and R. Eisenberg. 1998. "Can patents deter innovation? The anticommons in biomedical research." *Science* 280:298.

Jaffe, A., and J. Lerner. 2004. *Innovation and its discontents—How our broken patent system is endangering innovation and progress, and what to do about it*. Princeton, NJ: Princeton University Press.

Jensen, R., and M. Thursby. 2001. "Proofs and prototypes for sale: The licensing of university inventions." *American Economic Review* 91:240.

Kitch, E. 1977. "The nature and function of the patent system." *Journal of Law and Economics* 20:265.

Lemley, M. 2007. "Are universities patent trolls?" Stanford Public Law Working Paper. Draft available at papers.ssrn.com/sol3/papers.cfm?abstract_id=980776.

Levin, R., A. Klevorick, R. Nelson, and S. Winter. 1987. "Appropriating the returns from industrial research and development." *Brookings Papers on Economic Activity* 3:783.

Mansfield, E. 1991. "Academic research and industrial innovation." *Research Policy* 20:1.

McSherry, C. 2001. *Who owns academic work?* Cambridge, MA: Harvard University Press.

Mowery, D., R. Nelson, B. Sampat, and A. Ziedonis. 2001. "The growth of patenting and licensing by U.S. universities: An assessment of the effects of the Bayh-Dole Act of 1980." *Research Policy* 30:99.

———. 2004. *Ivory tower and industrial innovation—University-industry technology transfer before and after the Bayh-Dole Act*. Stanford: Stanford Business Books.

Oddi, S. 1996. "Un-unified economic theories of patents—The not-quite-holy grail." *Notre Dame Law Review* 71:267.

OECD. 2002. Draft final report on the strategic use of intellectual property by public research organizations in OECD countries. DSTI/STP (2002) 42/REV1. Paris: OECD.

Powell, W., and J. Owen-Smith. 2002. "The new world of knowledge production in the life sciences." In *The future of the city of intellect—The changing American university,* ed. S. Brint, 107–30. Stanford: Stanford University Press.

Prager, F. 1944. "A history of intellectual property from 1545 to 1787." *Journal of the Patent Office Society* 26:711.

ProTon Europe. 2007. "2005 annual survey report." Available at http://www.protoneurope .org/news/2007/Articles/2005AnnualSurveyReport.

Rai, A. 1999. "Regulating scientific research: Intellectual property rights and the norms of science." *Northwestern University Law Review* 94:77.

Rai, A., and R. Eisenberg. 2003. "Bayh-Dole reform and the progress of biomedicine." *Law and Contemporary Problems* 66:289.

Ritchie de Larena, L. 2007. "The price of progress: Are universities adding to the cost?" *Houston Law Review* 43:1373.

Sterckx, S. 2004a. "A critique of the utilitarian argument for the patent system." *Philosophy in the Contemporary World* 11:1.

———. 2004b. "Patents and access to essential drugs in developing countries: An ethical analysis." *Developing World Bioethics* 4 (1): 58.

———. 2009. "Patenting and licensing of university research: Promoting innovation or undermining academic values?" *Science and Engineering Ethics,* DOI: 10.1007/s11948-009-9168-8, published online September 19, 2009.

Streitz, W., and A. Bennett. 2003. "Material transfer agreements: A university perspective." *Plant Physiology* 133:10.

Thursby, J., R. Jensen, and M. Thursby. 2001. "Objectives, characteristics and outcomes of university licensing: A survey of major U.S. universities." *Journal of Technology Transfer* 26:59.

Thursby, J., and M. Thursby. 2003. *University licensing under Bayh-Dole: What are the issues and evidence?* Available at http://opensource.mit.edu/papers/Thursby.pdf.

———. 2005. *Are there real effects of licensing on academic research? A life cycle view.* Available at the Web site of the National Bureau of Economic Research, http://www .nber.org/confer/2005/ases05/thursby.pdf.

Van Wijk, J. 1995. "Broad biotechnology patents hamper innovation." *Biotechnology and Development Monitor* 25:15.

Warner, K. 2001. "Are life patents ethical? Conflict between Catholic social teaching and agricultural biotechnology's patent regime." *Journal of Agricultural and Environmental Ethics* 14:301.

Washburn, J. 2005. *University, Inc.: The corporate corruption of higher education.* New York: Basic Books.

Wysocki, B. 2004. "College try: Columbia's pursuit of patent riches angers companies." *Wall Street Journal,* December 21, A1.

CHAPTER 4

Financial Interests and the Norms of Academic Science

David B. Resnik

1. Introduction

MODERN SCIENCE IS a business: a big business. Every year, private corporations, government agencies, universities, and private foundations spend hundreds of billions of dollars on research and development (R&D). The amount of private money invested in science has risen steadily since the 1980s and has outpaced the amount of public money spent on science. Today, about 60 percent of the world's R&D is sponsored by industry, and about 35 percent is sponsored by governments. In 2004, the United States spent approximately $368 billion on R&D, $122.7 billion of which was federally funded R&D, and $245.4 billion of which was non-federally funded (mostly private). Though the United States is by far the world's leader in government R&D funding, other countries are catching up, including European nations like the United Kingdom, France, Germany, and the Netherlands, and Asian powers like Japan, China, India, and Singapore. Private companies invest in R&D in order to make a profit. Governments invest in R&D to stimulate scientific and technological innovation, which leads to economic growth and development. Advances in science and technology were responsible for the major economic changes in the last two hundred years, including the Industrial Revolution, computer revolution, and the biotechnology revolution (Resnik 2007).

Scientific research is not cheap. Gone are the days when an amateur scientist working out of his own laboratory could make a significant contribution to human knowledge. Today, most research projects cost anywhere from several hundred thousand dollars to several million dollars, and some projects cost much more than that. The Human Genome Project cost $3 billion over a ten year period, and the Space Station Freedom cost $30 billion. Pharmaceutical companies spend, on average, about $500 to discover, test, and develop a new drug.[1] The costs of defense-related R&D are even higher: since the 1980s, the United States has spent over $100 billion on national missile defense. Most research is conducted by professional scientists (principal investigators, postdoctoral fellows, graduate students, and technicians) working in university, industry, or government laboratories. All of these people require compensation for their time and effort. Although a career in science is not as lucrative as a career as a plastic surgeon or investment banker, many scientists reap handsome financial rewards from research, including salary from universities or other organizations, consulting fees from companies, stock and equity, honoraria, and revenue from licensing of intellectual property (Resnik 2007).

Even though scientific research could not take place without huge investments of public and private funds, money can have a corrupting effect on science. In the last two decades, many different scientists, scholars, consumer advocates, and political leaders have expressed strong concerns about the relationship between science and financial interests. Evidence is accumulating that financial interests can threaten the quality and integrity of scientific research (Krimsky 2003). Numerous studies have shown that industry-sponsored research tends to favor the company's products (Lexchin et al. 2003). For example, Friedberg et al. (1999) found that 95 percent of industry-sponsored articles on drugs used in cancer treatment reported positive results, as opposed to 62 percent for nonindustry-sponsored research. Ridker and Torres (2006) found that 67 percent of industry-sponsored studies of cardiovascular treatments favored the new treatment over the currently accepted treatment, as opposed to 49 percent of the studies sponsored by nonindustry sources. There are some well-documented cases of companies suppressing data, cooking or manipulating research data, intimidating researchers who want to report adverse results, and engaging in other practices that interfere with the quality and integrity of science. There also cases where scientists with financial interests related to their research have committed fraud, engaged in insider trading, failed to mention significant risks to human subjects, failed to report adverse events in clinical trials, or participated in other practices that violate ethical or legal duties (Resnik 2007).

Thus, money in science is like a double-edged sword: money is a necessary fuel for research, but it can also threaten the norms of science. In this chapter, I will explore the relationship between financial interests and the norms of academic science.[2] I will begin my inquiry by providing an account of science's epistemic and ethical norms. After briefly describing some of the financial interests related to research, I will explain how these interests can affect the norms of science. I will conclude by making some recommendations for dealing with financial interests in scientific research.

2. The Norms of Science

Science is a social activity governed by various norms (Kitcher 1993, 2001; Haack 2003). There are two very different senses of the term "norm" that pertain to the study of science. In the first sense, a norm is the normal behavior of a group of people. The norms of science, in this sense, simply describe scientific behavior. Sociologists of science, such as Robert Merton (1973) and Harriet Zuckerman (1984) have studied norms that govern scientific behavior.[3] Merton argued that four norms—communalism, universalism, disinterestedness, and organized skepticism—describe and explain a great deal of scientific behavior (Radder, this volume, chap. 10). In the second sense of "norm," a norm is an ideal standard for decision making and behavior. The norms of science, in this sense, prescribe scientific conduct. Many different philosophers of science, such as Kuhn (1977), Quine and Ullian (1978), Laudan (1986), Longino (1990), Thagard (1993), and Kitcher (1993) have developed prescriptive accounts of scientific norms. Although philosophers of science do not all agree on science's prescriptive norms, most accept the idea that science has norms. Philosophical accounts of scientific norms are based on a conceptual analysis of key scientific and ethical concepts, such as knowledge, justification, explanation, moral obligation, human value, and so on.

In this chapter, I will present my own version of academic science's norms, which I have defended elsewhere (Resnik 1998, 2007). My account is prescriptive, not descriptive. I happen to believe that most of the norms in my account also do a good job of describing scientific conduct, but I will not press that issue here. What is important, as far as I am concerned, is that the norms of academic science have social mechanisms of enforcement (Gibbard 2003). By that I mean that

(1) scientists recognize that they ought to obey norms, and they feel compelled to obey them; (2) scientists publicly defend norms; (3) scientists are rewarded for adhering to norms or punished for deviating from norms. Scientists who demonstrate originality, rigor, objectivity, and other normative ideals may receive forms of positive reinforcement, such as publication, career advancement, prizes, and so on. Scientists who deviate from norms without an explanation or excuse may be subject to criticism, disapprobation, or punishment. For example, honesty (discussed below) is one of science's most important norms. Scientists are honest most of the time, but they are not always honest: scientists, like all people, tell lies from time to time (and some scientists tell big lies!). However, since honesty is a norm, a scientist who is caught lying on a grant application or paper may be investigated for misconduct or even face criminal prosecution.[4] Science has mechanisms in place to enforce the norm of honesty.

My account of norms is also teleological: I hold that scientific norms are justified insofar as they promote the collective aims (or goals) of academic science.[5] Science has general epistemic goals, such as truth, knowledge, and explanation; and general practical goals, such as prediction, control, and problem solving. The norms of science promote the aims of science directly or indirectly. For example, honesty directly promotes the pursuit of truth, because the most effective way to obtain truth is to be honest. Truth may sometimes emerge at the end of a process involving lies and deceptions, but honesty is generally the best way of getting to the truth. Giving credit where credit is due in science (discussed below) promotes the goals of science indirectly by encouraging cooperation and trust among scientists, because scientists are not likely to collaborate if they believe they will not receive proper credit for their work. Social responsibility (discussed below) promotes the goals of science by helping to secure public support for science, because the public will not support research that it regards as dangerous and irresponsible.

One can think of scientific norms as a system of hypothetical imperatives: to achieve a goal, one should follow a rule (see fig. 4.1). For example, to bake a cake, one should follow a series of rules contained in the recipe. To be a good driver, one should obey the rules of the road. To do good science, one should adhere to various norms such as honesty, openness, precision, testability, etc. Some norms, such as honesty, objectivity, and testability, are common to all scientific disciplines. Others apply only to particular disciplines. For example, rules for controlled clinical trials apply to biomedical research, but not to physics or astronomy.

One of the criticisms of general norms of conduct is that they are too abstract to guide particular decisions (see Radder, this volume, chap. 10). One way

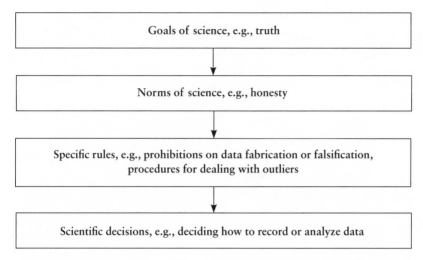

Fig. 4.1. Scientific Goals, Norms, Rules, and Decisions *(Arrows indicate direction of justification)*

to overcome this problem is to develop specific rules to implement general norms (Beauchamp and Childress 2001). Specific rules are more closely connected to particular decisions than general norms (see fig. 4.1). For example, there are a variety of methodological and ethical rules that help to implement honesty, such as prohibitions against data fabrication and falsification or procedures for dealing with data outliers. Individual scientists follow these more specific rules when they make decisions concerning the recording of data or data analysis.

Finally, my account of the norms of science fits within a movement in contemporary philosophy known as social epistemology (Goldman 1999; Solomon 2007). According to this perspective, knowledge development is inherently a social activity, and key epistemic concepts, such as justification, warrant, and truth, cannot be adequately understood without reference to a community of inquirers. The norms that guide knowledge development are rules that are necessary for the community to function well in achieving epistemic goals, such as truth, explanation, and so on. To function well, the community must have a high degree of trust and an effective division of epistemic labor among its members, as well as financial and legal support from the broader community, i.e., society (Resnik 1996). Though skepticism is important in developing new ideas and testing and confirming theories and hypotheses, science cannot move forward without support from society and a high degree of trust among people working within the same lab or university or collaborators at different institutions (Hull 1990; Radder, this volume, chap. 10).

So what are some of the norms of academic science? Science has epistemic norms, which apply to decisions concerning research design, testing and experimentation, data analysis and interpretation, and the acceptance of scientific theories and hypotheses. Other writers have called these norms by various names, such as criteria of theory-choice, epistemic values, theoretical virtues, and so on (Lycan 1990). Some of the most important ones are:

- Testability: Theories and hypotheses should be testable.
- Objectivity: Methods, theories, and hypotheses should minimize social, political, economic, personal, or other biases.
- Precision: Methods, theories, and hypotheses should be clearly defined and precise.
- Empirical support: Theories and hypotheses should be well supported by the empirical evidence.
- Reproducibility: Tests, procedures, observations, and experiments should be repeatable.
- Predictive accuracy: Theories and hypotheses should make accurate predictions.
- Explanatory power: Theories and hypotheses should be able to unify diverse phenomena into a coherent explanatory scheme.
- Conservatism: Theories and hypotheses should cohere with other well-established ideas, beliefs, or principles.
- Novelty: Theories and hypotheses should express original ideas.
- Simplicity: Theories and hypotheses should be simple, parsimonious, elegant.
- Fruitfulness: Theories and hypotheses should lead to new areas of investigation and inquiry.

Science also has ethical norms, which apply to many different decisions concerning interactions with other scientists and with society, such as research design, data analysis and interpretation, publication, peer review, collaboration, education, laboratory management, media interactions, and the treatment of research subjects. With some notable exceptions, e.g., Shrader-Frechette (1994), Resnik (1998), and Cranor (1993), philosophers of science have paid more attention to science's epistemic norms than to science's ethical norms. However, highly publicized scandals, ethical controversies, and concerns about the influence of money on science justify greater attention to the ethical norms of science from philosophers. Some of science's most important ethical norms include:

- Honesty: Don't lie or cheat in science; avoid deception.

- Openness: Share data, ideas, methods, tools, and results; be open to criticism and suggestions.

- Carefulness: Exhibit due care in experimental design, record keeping, data analysis, manuscript drafting and editing; avoid careless errors.

- Credit: Give credit where credit is due.

- Freedom: Allow scientists to explore and criticize ideas without fear of intimidation, censorship, or repression.

- Confidentiality: Protect confidential information related to personnel matters, human subjects in research, unpublished research, peer review, trade secrets, etc.

- Respect for persons and property: Treat colleagues, students, collaborators, and property with respect; do not exploit, harm, or harass people; do not destroy or steal property, including intellectual property.

- Respect for research subjects: Treat animal and human research subjects with appropriate care and concern; protect and promote human and animal welfare in research; protect the rights of human subjects in research.

- Respect for the law: Know and obey laws and regulations that pertain to research, such as human and animal research regulations, laboratory safety regulations, conflict of interest rules, etc.

- Social responsibility: Strive to benefit society and to prevent or avoid harm to society through research, public education, civic engagement, and advocacy.

Before concluding this section, I shall make a few additional comments about academic science's norms. First, the distinction I have drawn between ethical and epistemic norms is useful for the purposes of classification, pedagogy, and policy development, but it does not cut very deep. Since knowledge development is inherently social, even norms that most people would regard as ethical function to advance the epistemic goals. For example, fair credit allocation, which most people would classify as an ethical norm, helps to foster cooperation and trust among researchers, which helps to promote knowledge development. Though allocation of credit guides practical decisions made by scientists, it has an epistemic component as well.

Second, the norms sometimes conflict with each other. For example, the epistemic norms conservatism and novelty conflict when a new and impressive theory in particle physics conflicts with well-established theories, beliefs, and principles. The ethical norms openness and respect for research subjects conflict when an anthropologist must decide whether she will publish some research that could have an adverse impact on the community on which it is based. Sometimes scientists can settle a conflict among norms by appealing to the goals of science: when norms conflict, choose the option that best promotes the epistemic aims of science. However, because science has many different epistemic aims, which are incommensurable, there is no algorithm for settling conflicts among science's epistemic norms (Kuhn 1977; Lycan 1990; Resnik 1998).

Third, the norms sometimes conflict with broader social norms. For example, suppose a scientist has signed a confidentiality agreement with a company that requires her not to divulge company secrets. She has a legal duty, under the agreement, to keep company information confidential. Suppose she discovers, however, that the company is hiding important information about the risks of one of its drugs from the public. She may have to decide whether to obey the law (and maintain her loyalty to the company) or to prevent harm to the public. To resolve a conflict like this one, scientists must consider not only what is best for science but also what is best for society (Shrader-Frechette 1994; Resnik 1998).

Because the norms of academic science sometimes conflict with each other and with social norms, they are best understood as prima facie guides to epistemic or practical conduct, rather than as absolute rules. That is, other things being equal, scientists should adhere to the norms. Deviations from a particular norm can sometimes be justified by appealing to other norms.

3. Financial Interests in Scientific Research

Though I have already mentioned some of the financial interests in research, it will be useful to distinguish between some of the different types of interests. The first distinction is between the financial interests of individual scientists and the financial interests of organizations involved in research. The financial interests of scientists include: salary, consulting fees, honoraria, cash awards, stock or equity, and intellectual property (patents or copyrights). Usually, the best way that a scientist can promote his or her financial interests is to do good research. A scientist who is a successful researcher can advance his or her career, increase his or her salary, obtain lucrative deals with companies, speaking invitations, and so on (Krimsky 2003).

The second distinction is among the different types of organizations involved in research. These include private corporations, universities or colleges, hospitals or medical centers, government agencies, private foundations, and professional associations. The financial interests of private corporations include profit and financial strength. Private companies can promote these interests by sponsoring research that leads to successful products or services. The successfulness of a product or service depends on the size and strength of the market for the product or service. Pharmaceutical companies, for example, tend to shy away from developing drugs for markets where there are fewer than 300,000 patients (i.e., a rare disease), or markets where the patients don't have much money to buy drugs, such as markets for diseases that afflict the developing world (Resnik 2007).

Universities also have financial interests in research. In the last two decades, universities have become increasingly commercialized (Krimsky 2003). Universities receive funding from private companies to conduct research. Companies also provide significant gifts to universities, such as new buildings, endowed professorships, or new equipment. Universities own intellectual property and have technology transfer offices. Many universities own stock in companies involved in research, or they are associated with private foundations that own stock. Universities (or private foundations) help to provide capital for faculty start-up companies. Universities also have an interest in obtaining contracts or grants from funding agencies or private companies, and they reward faculty who bring in money from contacts or grants.

The financial interests of hospitals or medical centers include profit (if for-profit) or financial strength (if nonprofit). Hospitals and medical centers may own stock, have contracts with companies, or own patents. They may also use their involvement with research as a marketing tool to attract patients.

Even professional associations, such as the American Medical Association (AMA) or the American Chemical Society (ACS) may have financial interests. For example, professional societies have an interest in maintaining financial stability. To do this, they may accept money from companies to help support conferences or continuing education programs.

4. How Financial Interests Affect the Norms of Science

Are financial interests bad for academic science? Many people seem to think so (see M. Brown, Kleinman, Fuller, and van den Belt, this volume). While there is nothing inherently unethical or epistemologically problematic about having financial interests, trouble can occur when financial interests and the norms of science pull in opposite directions. Financial interests can cause people, companies, or institutions to deviate from epistemic and ethical norms. Deviations can occur intentionally, when people deliberately violate scientific norms to achieve a financial goal. For example, a scientist who lies on a grant application to strengthen his grant proposal would be intentionally violating the norm of honesty. Though intentional violations of norms probably happen on a regular basis, it is likely that many (perhaps most) of the deviations from norms caused by financial interests are unintentional. For example, a scientist who owns stock in a drug company that is sponsoring her research may overestimate the benefits of the company's drug or underestimate its risks, because the financial interest clouds her judgment. The effect of the financial interest would be subconscious: she might not even be aware of how her judgment has been affected. Though money can cause scientists to deviate from science's descriptive norms, this does not mean that money also affects science's prescriptive norms. Norms can still function as prescriptive ideals even when people fail to meet them (Resnik 2007).

While it is possible for scientists to continue to hold some types of norms in high regard even when many of their peers deviate from them, the corrosive effect of money could eventually undermine academic science's prescriptive norms by changing the culture of academic science (see Kleinman, M. Brown, van den Belt, this volume). The actual practice of science would deviate so far from the prescriptive norms that these norms would lose any substantial influence. For example, many sports have been transformed from amateur activities to professional ones as a result of the influence of money. This transformation has, in many cases, come at the expense of norms associated with amateur sports, such as fair play and good sportsmanship. Though it is conceivable that academic science could be changed in the same way that some sports have been transformed, I am not yet convinced that this will happen, provided that universities, policy makers, and scientists take appropriate steps to protect the academy from the influence of financial interests. At the conclusion of this article, I will make some recommendations for keeping these corrupting influences at bay.

To explain how money can have an impact on scientists' adherence to epistemic and ethical norms, I will use a model of the steps of scientific research that should be familiar to most readers. The steps are: (1) problem selection, (2) literature review, (3) hypothesis generation, (4) experimental design and protocol development, (5) observation/testing, (6) recording data, (7) analyzing data, (8) interpreting data, (9) peer review, (10) publication of research, (11) replication of research, and (12) acceptance by the scientific community. The model combines the account of scientific reasoning developed by philosophers, such as Hempel (1966) and Giere (2005), with the description of scientific practice provided by scientist/scholars, such as Ziman (2000). The model is an idealization, of course, because scientists often deviate from it. They sometimes skip some steps, add other steps, or do steps out of sequence. Nevertheless, the model is still a useful way of representing, analyzing, and discussing the process of scientific research. I will refer to some of the steps in the model when discussing the impact of money on science.

There is not sufficient space or time in this chapter to explore all of the different ways that financial interests can impact the process of research. I refer the reader to Resnik (2007) and Krimsky (2003) for more on this. I would like to briefly discuss how financial interests can affect scientists' adherence to norms.

4.1. Skewing the Publication Record

There are many different ways to skew the publication record. One of those ways is to control the problems that are studied. Because research is so expensive, those who provide funding (the sponsors) determine what will be studied. Although many studies have shown a strong connection between the source of funding and the outcome of research, the reason for this connection is best explained by factors other than the money itself, which will be discussed below. While the source of funding does not necessarily bias the outcome of a particular study, it can bias the research record (i.e., the sum of published results) by setting the agenda. For example, if a pharmaceutical company decides to develop Drug X, it can invest money in sponsoring ten studies of Drug X. If the company had not made this decision, then there may have been no studies of Drug X. Thus, in this trivial way the company can affect the research record. To reduce the imbalance of funding favoring a company's drug or treatment, the government should fund studies that compare different drugs (or treatments) to the company's drug.

A more serious concern is that the company might decide to publish only the studies that favor its drug, which can violate objectivity, honesty, credit, and other norms (Resnik 2007). There are some notable cases where this has occurred, such as Merck's decision to delay publication of studies showing that its drug Vioxx increased the risk of cardiovascular problems. Though companies are required to submit their data to regulatory agencies, they are not required to publish their research. Thus, a company could skew the research record by suppressing research that does not favor its product(s) and by publishing research that does. A company can take other steps to skew the record, such as publishing the same favorable study twice (i.e., duplicate publication) or breaking a large favorable study into several articles for the purposes of publication (i.e., salami science). An expert who reviews the literature pertaining to the company's drug or conducts a meta-analysis will be misled by the research record. It will appear that the

Table 4.1. Skewing the Publication Record

Study	Result	Published	Notes
1	Negative	No	
2	Positive	Yes	Published twice
3	Negative	No	
4	Positive	Yes	Divided into 3 publications
5	Negative	No	
6	Positive	Yes	Published twice
7	Negative	No	
8	Negative	No	
9	Positive	Yes	Published once
10	Positive	Yes	Published once

Total positive publications: 9

published studies conclude that the drug is safe and effective, when, in fact, an equal number of unpublished studies draw the opposite conclusion (table 4.1).

One of the ironies of modern research is that if someone used this tactic with data points in a research article, they would have committed a type of fraud/misconduct known as data falsification. When you conduct a study, you should publish all of the data, not just the data that support your hypothesis. Private companies can get away with deception, however, because society has not yet adopted laws or regulations forcing them to publish all of their research. However, time may be running out for companies that try to suppress negative results, since most biomedical journals now require that clinical trials be registered in a public database known as a clinical trial registry (DeAngelis et al. 2004). If a company wants to publish a study that favors its drug, the study must come from a registered clinical trial. A clinical trial registry contains important information concerning the trial, such as the drug (or the biological or medical device) under investigation, the sponsor, experimental design, the population being studied, research sites, when the trial begins, and when it closes. Unfortunately, most trial registries do not include crucial items of information, such as the data and results, which researchers need to assess the safety and efficacy of the product under investigation. To counteract attempts to distort the research record, and also to promote honesty, openness, and objectivity, clinical trial registries should include data and results. Moreover, companies should be required to register all clinical trials to obtain approval for their products (Resnik 2007).

4.2. Cooking the Data

Cooking the data occurs when one designs an experiment to achieve a predetermined outcome. The experiment is not a true test, but one that is used to bolster the hypothesis. Cooking the data undermines adherence to many different epistemic norms, such as objectivity and testability, as well as some ethical norms, such as honesty and openness. One way of cooking the data is to deliberately ignore a particular outcome in one's experimental design. It is a truism of common-sense epistemology that if you don't look for something, you are not likely to find it. In scientific epistemology this occurs when a test is not designed well enough to detect a particular effect. The mere fact that you don't find an effect does not prove that the effect does not exist: absence of evidence is not the same as evidence of absence. For example, suppose that a company designs a clinical trial to measure a variety of health-related outcomes such as blood pressure, heart rate, blood sugar levels, nausea, headaches, kidney function, liver function, and so on, but the company deliberately fails to include an important variable, such as the drug's effect on muscle function, because animal studies indicate this might be a problem with the drug. When the trial is complete, it will not produce any evidence that the drug has an effect on muscle function, because this type of evidence was not sought. The data generated by the company may be sufficient to convince regulators and physicians that the drug is safe, when, in fact, the drug may not be safe. The biomedical research community may eventually obtain evidence that the drug impairs muscle function from adverse event reports or comparative clinical trials. In the meantime, many patients may suffer adverse effects from the drug unnecessarily while the company profits (Resnik 2007).

   This problem can also occur when someone designs a study so that it lacks sufficient statistical power to detect an effect. In hypothesis testing, this particular problem is known as a type II error (failure to reject the null hypothesis when the null hypothesis is false). For example, suppose that a pesticide company has decided to generate some data on the effect of its chemical on human subjects to convince a regulatory agency to loosen the restrictions on the pesticide. The company's goal is to demonstrate that the pesticide has no adverse effect on human beings at a particular level of exposure. Suppose, also, that the company measures all relevant adverse effects but that the sample size is not large enough to demonstrate that some of these potential effects are statistically significant. Although this strategy may allow the company to achieve its corporate goals, it would commit the same type of methodological blunder that occurs when one fails to measure a particular effect (Lockwood 2004).

To prevent research sponsors from cooking the data, or committing other methodological (and ethical) transgressions, it is important for independent scientists (i.e., scientists without financial relationships to the company) to have meaningful input into research design. Research design must be thoroughly reviewed by regulatory agencies, institutional review boards for human subjects research (IRBs), and other independent parties with an obligation to assess the quality of the research. Companies should make their research plans and protocols available to the public before research begins and after it is complete. Research sponsors should disclose and justify changes in research plans or protocols. These steps will help to promote adherence to epistemic and ethical norms.

4.3. Misconduct and Fraud

Financial interests can also affect scientific research by causing researchers not just to cook the data, but to commit misconduct, which can also lead to charges of fraud.[6] The U.S. government defines misconduct in research as data fabrication or falsification or plagiarism. Fabrication is defined as "making up data or results and recording or reporting them"; falsification is defined as "manipulating research materials, equipment, or processes, or changing or omitting data or results such that the research is not accurately represented in the research record"; and plagiarism is defined as "the appropriation of another person's ideas, processes, results, or words without giving appropriate credit" (Office of Science and Technology Policy 2000). Misconduct does not include honest errors or differences of opinion.[7] The rate of misconduct in research is thought to be low. Using confirmed cases of misconduct, Steneck (2000) estimated that the rate of misconduct on federal grants is 1 per 100,000 researchers per year. This method probably underestimates the rate of misconduct because many cases are not reported or investigated. In a survey of over 3,000 scientists by Martinson et al. (2005), 0.3 percent of respondents admitted to committing misconduct in the last three years (1 per 1,000 per year). The survey may also underestimate the rate of misconduct because people who commit misconduct may not be willing to confess to it on a survey.

Even if the rate of misconduct is very low, misconduct is still a very serious problem when it occurs. Misconduct in science can have a negative impact on the research record, journals, collaborators, institutions, entire research fields, and the public. Consider the wide-ranging effects of the fraud committed by Seoul University stem cell researcher Woo Suk Hwang. Some of Hwang's colleagues began to have suspicions about a paper Hwang and collaborators published in *Science* in May 2005 on therapeutic cloning. The results of the paper, if correct, would have represented a tremendous breakthrough in human embryonic stem cell research and would have put South Korea on the map as a center of stem cell research. Soon after the paper was published, Hwang became a national hero. Hwang's colleagues tipped off some journalists and the editors of *Science* about problems with the May 2005 paper, and the university began an investigation. The investigation of Hwang's research revealed that Hwang had also fabricated data on another stem cell paper published in *Science* in 2004, and that he had violated ethical standards for authorship and informed consent for egg donation for the experiments. In May 2006, Hwang and five collaborators were indicted on charges of fraud and embezzlement. Due to the importance of Hwang's research, the case made headlines around the world. This misconduct case had adverse effects on people associated with Hwang, Seoul University, the journal *Science,* and the field of stem cell research. In addition, many people in South Korea felt betrayed and ashamed (Resnik et al. 2006).

What is the relationship between financial interests and misconduct? While there is no direct evidence that unchecked financial interests cause misconduct, there are good reasons to believe that financial interests are a risk factor for misconduct (Resnik 2007). Since virtually all researchers have financial interests, one of the keys to discouraging misconduct is to ensure that the appropriate checks and balances are in place in the institutional settings in which science is conducted. Since the research environment can encourage or discourage deviation from scientific norms, it is important to understand how that environment affects conduct.

In academic research, there is tremendous pressure on investigators to obtain government grants or contracts, since investigators usually cannot do research, or may lose their job, if they do not secure funding from outside sponsors. To obtain grants and renew grants, researchers must generate data. Researchers often need preliminary data to convince reviewers that their proposal is worth funding, and they also need data to convince reviewers that their funding should be renewed. This pressure to produce data affects people at all levels, from laboratory directors, to principal investigators, to junior researchers, to postdoctoral fellows, down to graduate students and technicians. Many of the researchers who have committed misconduct involving federal grants or contracts have admitted to succumbing to the pressure to produce results (Shamoo and Resnik 2009). The pressure to produce becomes even more intense if the research involves intellectual property, trade secrets, or company funding, or has the potential to launch a scientist's career.

Financial pressures exist in industrial science as well (see Carrier, this volume). Industrial scientists also desire to produce results to keep their job, earn money or a promotion, and so on. Company executives often make decisions that promote profits but compromise scientific integrity (Ziman 2000). However, much less is known about industrial science than academic science due to the secrecy that pervades this environment. Businesses treat information about their operations as propriety, and take full advantage of trade secrecy laws (Resnik 2007). Though I will focus on academic science in this chapter, it is important to realize that a great deal of research occurs not on university campuses but in private laboratories.

Preventing misconduct is not easy, since people who sincerely desire to cheat the system will always figure out ways to do it. Fortunately, genuine scoundrels are very rare in science. Most cases of misconduct probably occur when ordinary researchers succumb to temptations or pressures. The best way to prevent ordinary researchers from committing misconduct is for research institutions to promote ethical conduct through education, training, and policy development. Institutions should take steps to help relax some of the pressures in the research environment and to help researchers cope with the stress of competition for career advancement and scarce resources, such as basing personnel decisions on factors other than the quantity of publications or amount of money generated. Other strategies for preventing misconduct include random audits of data, the use of electronic record-keeping systems, and access to ethics consultation for researchers (Shamoo and Resnik 2009).

4.4. Spinning the Data

"Spin" is a pejorative term for putting a particular slant, twist, or bias on something, such as a newsworthy event or a government report. The term emerged in the 1990s to describe how politicians and public relations officials would try to present information in a light most favorable to their interest. Spinning can occur in science during the analysis and interpretation of data. Spinning is contrary to several norms of science, including objectivity, honesty, social responsibility, carefulness, and accuracy.

After a study is complete, scientists analyze and interpret the data. Although most laypeople think of data analysis as objective, it often is not. There may be more than one way to analyze the data, and different statistical methods may yield different results. A research sponsor may choose a method of data analysis that is most favorable to its product. In one well-known case relating to data analysis, Boots Pharmaceuticals sponsored a study comparing its thyroid medication to other generic versions of the medication. The investigator leading the study, Betty Dong, concluded that the company's drug was more expensive but not better than competing drugs. The company tried to prevent Dong from publishing these results, claiming that her analysis of the data was flawed. The company conducted its own analysis of the data, which showed that its drug was superior to the other drugs. Dong eventually published her analysis, despite the company's objections (Bok 2003; Krimsky 2003; Resnik 2007).

Data interpretation can be even more problematic than data analysis. An interpretation of data is a claim about the scientific and practical significance (or meaning) of the data. What do the data prove, disprove, or fail to prove or disprove? What do the data suggest or imply? Philosophers of science frame data interpretation problems as questions concerning the relationship between the observation and theory.[8] This way of thinking about data interpretation leads to a well-known conundrum in the philosophy of science developed by W. V. Quine and Pierre Duhem known as the Quine-Duhem thesis (aka the underdetermination of theories): there are indefinitely many theories that are logically consistent with the evidence produced by scientific experiments (Quine 1986). Thus, the evidence never proves only one theory is correct, since another theory may also be consistent with the evidence. The Quine-Duhem thesis is more than a mere philosophical problem, because real scientists often have disputes about data interpretation (Ziman 2000). Scientists who agree on the details of a particular experiment and regard the data as valid (i.e., legitimate, credible) may still subscribe to different interpretations of the data.

Data interpretation becomes even more problematic when one moves from scientific to practical significance, because one adds practical indeterminacy to the scientific indeterminacy. The practical significance of data depends on its potential impact on different human values, such as health, safety, the economy, etc. People may disagree about the practical significance of research results because they disagree about how the results will impact human values, or they disagree about the relative importance of different values. Suppose, for example, that a company has sponsored a study on a new blood pressure medication, and the study shows that the medication is more effective than other medications at lowering blood pressure, but that the medication also has a variety of side effects such as headaches, dizziness, fatigue, and decreased sexual function. People may disagree about the significance of this new drug if they have different opinions about the drug's side effects. For example, one person might consider the new drug to be safe, while another might regard the drug as unsafe because of its effects on sexual function. The drug's effects on sexuality might be important to one person but not another. Because people have different understandings of "harm," "benefit," "risk," and "safety," they may disagree about the significance of new drugs.

Companies can take advantage of the uncertainty of data interpretation to present their products in the most favorable way possible. In the blood pressure example discussed above, a company might claim that its drug is the best available treatment for high blood pressure, when the evidence shows, at best, that its drug has a variety of different benefits and risks. Now there is nothing inherently wrong with a company trying to interpret the data in a light most favorable to its product. Companies are in business to sell their products, and a little marketing is acceptable. However, companies (and scientists with financial interests in companies) often go way beyond putting a positive face on the data and engage in exaggeration and hyperbole. A salient example of this type of problem occurred when a panel convened by the National Institutes of Health (NIH) reviewed the literature on cholesterol-lowering drugs known as statins and recommended that the threshold for prescribing statins be lowered from 130 mg/dl of low density lipoprotein (LDL) to 100 mg/dl for patients without heart disease, and from 100 mg/dl to 70 mg/dl for patients with heart disease. This recommendation, if followed, would greatly increase the number of people taking statins and would result in increased profits for pharmaceutical companies. Eight out of the nine members of the panel had undisclosed financial relationships with companies that manufacture statins. Researchers and physicians argued that the benefits of lowering the threshold for prescribing statins were questionable. Consumer groups and ethicists objected that conflicts of interest had biased the panel's decision making (Lenzer 2004).

In some ways, making exaggerated claims about a product is less dangerous than cooking the data or skewing the research record, because these claims are often easy for experts to spot: experts often cannot tell whether data have been fabricated or cooked. An expert (or educated reader) usually will be able to see through a company's spin tactics and assess the true benefits and risks of a product. However, ordinary consumers usually lack these skills. To help ordinary consumers and experts, journal editors and reviewers should be on the watch for exaggerated claims. They should require authors, especially authors with conflicts of interest, to carefully substantiate claims concerning the practical significance of their research. Journal editors should also publish editorials, critiques, or commentaries to counterbalance overstated claims by company-sponsored researchers.

4.5. Inappropriate Authorship

Financial interests can also have an impact on authorship practices and undermine adherence to norms, such as credit, honesty, and objectivity. Authorship is a key part of science's reward system, and the quest for authorship motivates most researchers (Merton 1973; Hull 1990). The quality and quantity of one's published research is usually the decisive factor in decisions concerning hiring, promotion, and tenure in science. People who publish often are more likely to succeed in science than those who do not. Authorship should be granted on the basis of one's contribution to the research. Responsibility and credit should go hand-in-hand: a person who is responsible for conducting the research should receive credit for his or her work; conversely, a person who is not responsible for the research should not receive credit for doing it (Shamoo and Resnik 2009). Responsibility should be the basis for authorship for two reasons. First, it is unfair to grant authorship to people who do not deserve it, or to fail to grant authorship to people who do deserve it. Second, if there are problems with the research, such as errors or suspected fraud, it is important to know who can be held accountable for addressing the problems. There have been numerous cases of suspected research misconduct where authors have tried to evade responsibility by claiming that they had nothing to do with the problematic part of the research. To avoid this problem, all authors should at least know all of the other authors as well as their roles in the research. Authors do not need to be familiar with the details of work that they have not done, but they should at least understand how the different parts of the research fit together (Shamoo and Resnik 2009).

Many journals have adopted authorship guidelines that they display in the information for authors. The International Committee for Medical Journal Editors (ICMJE), an organization representing six hundred biomedical science journals, has adopted the following guideline for authorship:

> Authorship credit should be based on 1) substantial contributions to conception and design, or acquisition of data, or analysis and interpretation of data; 2) drafting the article or revising it critically for important intellectual content; and 3) final approval of the version to be published. Authors should meet conditions 1, 2, and 3. . . . Acquisition of funding, collection of data, or general supervision of the research group, alone, does not justify authorship. All persons designated as authors should qualify for authorship, and all those who qualify should be listed. Each author should have participated sufficiently in the work to take public responsibility for appropriate portions of the content. (ICMJE 2007)

The ICMJE also recommends that people who make contributions to an article but do not qualify as authors be listed as "contributors" at the end of the article, and that the article clearly states the responsibilities of different authors. For example, if a person made a substantial contribution by helping to design the experiment(s), then this should be indicated in the article; if a person drafted the article, this should be indicated, and so on (ICMJE 2007).

Because authorship has such great value among scientists, it is often the source of controversy and foul play. There are two main problems related to authorship in science: (1) granting authorship to people who have not made significant intellectual contributions to the research, i.e., honorary authorship, and (2) failing to name people as authors who have made significant contributions, i.e., ghost authorship (Shamoo and Resnik 2009). Honorary authorship often happens because people want, expect, or demand to be named as authors even though they have not made significant contributions. Honorary authorship might be granted to help a colleague in his or her quest for tenure or promotion, to thank a collaborator for providing data, reagents, or tissue samples, or to appease a lab director who expects to be named as an author on all articles coming out of his lab (Shamoo and Resnik 2009).

One of the main reasons ghost authorship occurs is that pharmaceutical companies use this tactic to publish articles. For an article to receive widespread recognition, it is important for it to be associated with a prestigious researcher at a university or academic medical center. Pharmaceutical companies have paid academic researchers money to sign their names on articles that they have scarcely read, much less written. All of the work has been done by company scientists, whose names may not be mentioned at all. The academic researcher is an author in name only, when the real authors are invisible "ghosts." Companies want to hide the ghost authors so that they will not have to disclose the company scientists' conflicts of interest and so the article won't appear to be biased (Hargreaves 2007).

There is a straightforward way to deal with these authorship problems: journals should develop and strictly enforce authorship policies. As noted earlier, many biomedical journals have adopted authorship policies. Journals that have not stated their authorship policies should do so immediately. In addition, journals should develop some way to enforce their policies, such as random audits to verify authorship, and penalties for violations.

5. Conclusion and Recommendations

In this chapter, I have explored some of the ways that financial interests can affect the norms of academic science. I have explained how financial interests can undermine scientists' adherence to honesty, openness, carefulness, credit, objectivity, and other epistemic and ethical norms. Like other authors who have contributed to this volume (e.g., J. Brown, M. Brown, Kleinman, Radder, Fuller), I hold that financial interests can corrupt the norms of academic science. This conclusion is painfully obvious to most people who are familiar with contemporary scientific research. What is not so obvious is how scientists and society should respond to financial and commercial influences in the academy. This is a difficult problem with no simple solutions. There are no simple solutions because it is not possible to remove financial interests from science. Research costs a great deal of money, and someone must pay this bill. Some have suggested that since private money is the source of most of the problems related to financial interests in research, the solution is to decrease or eliminate the amount of private funding of academic science (Brown 2000; J. Brown, this volume; Krimsky 2003).

I am not convinced that keeping private money out of the academy would be a very useful or workable solution. First, government-funded research has its own problems related to financial interests. Government-funded scientists will still compete for grants, jobs, prestige, and intellectual property. Indeed, most of the major misconduct scandals (that we know about) have involved government-funded research, not private research (Shamoo and Resnik 2009). Second, it is doubtful that private money can be eliminated from universities without causing major disruptions to research programs, university budgets, graduate education, and academic-industry collaborations. Private industry funds more than 10 percent of all research conducted at academic institutions in the United States, many government-funded research projects involve collaborations with private industry, and private companies give numerous gifts to universities (Bok 2003). To maintain universities at their current level of funding and research activity, governments would need to replace the billions of dollars that would be lost if private money were eliminated or drastically reduced. It is unlikely that the public will be willing to pay for this bill.

Since money—even private money—is an indispensable part of modern academic science, the only realistic way of dealing with financial interests in research is to live with them as best as we can. Scientists and society should adopt strategies for managing financial interests and minimizing their impact on the norms of academic science. Some of these are as follows:

- Disclosure of financial interests to all relevant parties (journals, research institutions, etc.)
- Use of independent committees to manage financial interests that pose difficult problems for research
- Prohibition of financial relationships that are too problematic to manage

- Promotion of education, training, and mentoring in research ethics for scientists, research staff, and students
- Development of research ethics policies at institutions, funding agencies, journals, private companies, and other organizations involved in research, such as authorship and publication standards, misconduct definitions and procedures, conflict of interest rules, etc.
- Requiring all clinical trials to be registered with a clinical trial registry; incorporating all the information about the trial one would need to evaluate it, including data and results
- Government funding of clinical trials that compare different medications or treatments to offset data generated by private companies
- Publishing editorials and commentaries to counterbalance research claims made by industry
- Refining intellectual property laws and policies to manage the proper balance of private versus public control of intellectual property (cf. Radder, this volume, chap. 10)
- Strengthening the research exemption in patent law
- Auditing research records
- Easing some of the pressures to produce data
- Supporting committees and other organizations that are responsible for overseeing scientific research, such as institutional review boards, animal care and use committees, biosafety committees, and so on
- Assessment of clinical trial research design by independent scientists
- Careful review of research contracts with pharmaceutical companies to avoid suppression of publication or unreasonable delays of publication

Adopting these strategies will not prevent financial interests from having an adverse impact on the norms of academic science, but they should help to preserve it in its current form and stop the slide toward Gomorrah.

NOTES

This research was sponsored by the intramural program of the NIEHS/NIH. It does not represent the views of the NIEHS/NIH. I would like to thank Hans Radder for helpful comments.

1. This number is disputable. According to industry estimates, it costs $800 million, on average, to bring a single new drug to the market (Pharmaceutical Research and Manufacturers Association 2007). Some scholars have challenged this figure, however, arguing that the costs are closer to $200 million (Goozner 2004). I am simply splitting the difference with my $500 million estimate.

2. By "academic science" I mean science as practiced by people in an academic setting, such as a university. Most science scholars focus on academic science, but it is worth noting that there are different types of science that do not share the academic ethos, such as industrial science and military science (Ziman 2000).

3. I recognize that Merton is regarded as passé by many contemporary sociologists of science. Latour and Woolgar (1986), Jasanoff (1998), Collins and Pinch (1998), and many other scholars eschew talk of "norms" in favor of "interests." Though Merton has fallen out of favor in current sociology of science, he has admirers in the philosophy of science, such as Hull (1990), Kitcher (1993), and Haack (2003). Call me old-fashioned, but I still regard talk of norms as fruitful and insightful. See also Radder, this volume, chap. 10.

4. Some of the more infamous cases of research misconduct in the last few years include South Korean stem cell scientist Woo Suk Hwang's fabrication of digital images and data in support of articles on therapeutic cloning on human embryos, University of Vermont clinical researcher Eric Poehlman's fabrication and falsification of data on numerous grant applications and publications pertaining to research on female hormones, and Bell Laboratories physicist Jan Hendrick Schön's fabrication and falsification in dozens of articles (Shamoo and Resnik 2009).

5. Individual scientists also have goals, but these are not the goals of science (Kitcher 1993). Individual scientists may pursue scientific goals, such as truth or explanation, but they may also pursue personal goals, such as career advancement or prestige.

6. "Fraud" has different senses in the research ethics literature. In the informal sense, "fraud" simply means dishonesty or deception. In the technical, legal sense, "fraud" is an illegal act of deception. Scientists who are found to have committed misconduct may also face fraud charges (Resnik 2003).

7. Some governments, universities, and organizations use definitions of "misconduct" that go beyond fabrication, falsification, or plagiarism, and include acts such as interfering with a misconduct investigation or wanton violations of human or animal research rules (Resnik 2003).

8. The difference between observations and data is that data are recorded observations. There are also different types of data: primary data, secondary data, and even tertiary data. The primary (rough, original) data are the recorded output of a test or experiment. In some sciences, such as astronomy or genomics, the primary data are so large and complex that they must be reduced to something more manageable. The goal of data reduction is to reduce the amount of data without losing significant informational content. But the reduced (or secondary) data may still be reduced or analyzed even more, which leads to tertiary data.

REFERENCES

Beauchamp, T., and J. Childress. 2001. *Principles of biomedical ethics,* 5th ed. New York: Oxford University Press.

Bok, D. 2003. *Universities in the marketplace.* Princeton: Princeton University Press.

Brown, J. 2000. "Privatizing the university—the new tragedy of the commons." *Science* 290:1701–2.

Collins, H. M., and T. Pinch. 1998. *The golem: What you should know about science.* Cambridge: Cambridge University Press.

Cranor, C. 1993. *Regulating toxic substances*. New York: Oxford University Press.

DeAngelis, C., J. Drazen, F. Frizelle, C. Haug, J. Hoey, R. Horton, S. Kotzin, C. Laine, A. Marusic, A. Overbeke, T. Schroeder, H. Sox, and M. Van Der Weyden; International Committee of Medical Journal Editors. 2004. "Clinical trial registration: a statement from the International Committee of Medical Journal Editors." *Annals of Internal Medicine* 141:477–78.

Friedberg, M., B. Saffran, T. Stinson, W. Nelson, and C. Bennett. 1999. "Evaluation of conflict of interest in new drugs used in oncology." *Journal of the American Medical Association* 282:1453–57.

Gibbard, A. 2003. *Wise choices, apt feelings*. 2nd ed. Cambridge, MA: Harvard University Press.

Giere, R. 2005. *Understanding scientific reasoning*. 5th ed. Belmont, CA: Wadsworth.

Goldman, A. 1999. *Knowledge in a social world*. New York: Oxford University Press.

Goozner, M. 2004. *The $800 million pill*. Berkeley: University of California Press.

Haack, S. 2003. *Defending science within reason*. New York: Prometheus Books.

Hargreaves, S. 2007. "Ghost authorship of industry funded drug trials is common, say researchers." *British Medical Journal* 334:223.

Hempel, C. 1966. *Philosophy of natural science*. Englewood Cliffs, NJ: Prentice-Hall.

Hull, D. 1990. *Science as a process*. Chicago: University of Chicago Press.

ICMJE. 2007. "Authorship and contribution." Available at http://www.icmje.org/#author. Accessed March 27, 2009.

Jasanoff, S. 1998. *The fifth branch: Science advisors as policy makers*. Cambridge, MA: Harvard University Press.

Kitcher, P. 1993. *The advancement of science*. New York: Oxford University Press.

———. 2001. *Science, truth, and democracy*. New York: Oxford University Press.

Krimsky, S. 2003. *Science in the private interest*. Lanham, MD: Rowman and Littlefield.

Kuhn, T. 1977. *The essential tension*. Chicago: University of Chicago Press.

Latour, B., and S. Woolgar. 1986. *Laboratory life: The construction of facts*. Princeton, NJ: Princeton University Press.

Laudan, L. 1986. *Science and values*. Berkeley and Los Angeles: University of California Press.

Lenzer, J. 2004. "U.S. consumer body calls for review of cholesterol guidelines." *British Medical Journal* 329:759.

Lexchin, J., L. Bero, B. Djulbegovic, and O. Clark. 2003. "Pharmaceutical industry sponsorship and research outcome and quality: A systematic review." *British Medical Journal* 326:1167–70.

Lockwood, A. 2004. "Human testing of pesticides: Scientific and ethical considerations." *American Journal of Public Health* 94:1908–16.

Longino, H. 1990. *Science as social knowledge*. Princeton, NJ: Princeton University Press.

Lycan, W. 1990. *Judgment and justification*. Cambridge: Cambridge University Press.

Martinson, B., M. Anderson, and R. de Vries. 2005. "Scientists behaving badly." *Nature* 435:737–38.

Merton, R. 1973. *The sociology of science*. Chicago: University of Chicago Press.

Office of Science and Technology Policy. 2000. "Federal research misconduct policy." Available at http://ori.dhhs.gov/policies/fed_research_misconduct.shtml. Accessed February 1, 2007.

Pharmaceutical Research and Manufacturers Association. 2007. "Innovation." Available at http://www.phrma.org/innovation/. Accessed December 13, 2007.

Quine, W. 1986. *Theories and things.* Cambridge, MA: Harvard University Press.

Quine, W., and J. Ullian. 1978. *The web of belief.* New York: Random House.

Resnik, D. 1996. "Social epistemology and the ethics of research." *Studies in History and Philosophy of Science* 27:566–86.

———. 1998. *The ethics of science.* New York: Routledge.

———. 2003. "From Baltimore to Bell Labs: Reflections on two decades of debate about scientific misconduct." *Accountability in Research* 10:123–35.

———. 2007. *The price of truth: How money affects the norms of science.* New York: Oxford University Press.

Resnik, D., A. Shamoo, and S. Krimsky. 2006. "Fraudulent human embryonic stem cell research in South Korea: Lesson learned." *Accountability in Research* 13:101–9.

Ridker, P., and J. Torres. 2006. "Reported outcomes in major cardiovascular clinical trials funded by for-profit and not-for-profit organizations: 2000–2005." *Journal of the American Medical Association* 295:2270–74.

Shamoo, A., and D. Resnik. 2009. *Responsible conduct of research.* 2nd ed. New York: Oxford University Press.

Shrader-Frechette, K. 1994. *Ethics of scientific research.* Lanham, MD: Rowman and Littlefield.

Solomon, M. 2007. *Social empiricism.* Cambridge, MA: MIT Press.

Steneck, N. 2000. "Assessing the integrity of publicly funded research: A background report for the November 2000 ORI Research Conference on Research Integrity." Available at http://ori.hhs.gov/documents/proceedings_rri.pdf. Accessed February 1, 2007.

Thagard, P. 1993. *Computational philosophy of science.* Cambridge, MA: MIT Press.

Ziman, J. 2000. *Real science.* Cambridge: Cambridge University Press.

Zuckerman, H. 1984. "Norms and deviant behavior in science." *Science, Technology & Human Values* 9 (Winter): 7–13.

CHAPTER 5

One-Shot Science

James Robert Brown

1. Introduction

PEOPLE OFTEN FAIL to worry about commercial sources of research funding. Perhaps this is because they take it to be part of the "discovery" side of science. That is, commercial interests are seen as the source and motivation of new ideas, nothing more. The real testing and justification of such ideas is independent of their noble or unsavory origins. The discovery-justification distinction is old and perhaps even a part of common sense. Indeed, the so-called genetic fallacy is part of common wisdom. The distinction has occasionally been rightly criticized, but some weak form of it is surely correct and that is enough for my purposes here. It will, for instance, be acknowledged by all that for-profit research in medicine and elsewhere is not disinterested. But these worries are often mollified in most minds by the additional belief that the process of justification, the rigorous testing of any proposal, will filter out harmful influences that go into the discovery process. This common attitude fails to address two major concerns, especially in the realm of medical research.

First, only a limited class of theories, ones that lead to intellectual property rights, will be "discovered." For instance, patentable drug solutions to health problems will be proposed while nonpatentable, but possibly superior, food, exercise, and environmental solutions will go underexplored. Even though this issue is of prime importance, I will only briefly discuss it near the end.

Second, the methods of justification that are open to us will often not allow the kind of independent justification that is typically taken for granted. An idea for a proof of the Poincaré conjecture, for instance, might come to a mathematician while in a drunken stupor or while dreaming of winning the $1,000,000 Millennium Prize. However, we needn't worry how it came, since any appropriately trained mathematician can check the proof to see if it is correct. This sort of easy check is not open to us when justification takes the form of an enormously complex computer proof or of a randomized clinical trial (RCT) costing hundreds of millions of dollars. The one who pays for the trial is the one who will enjoy considerable royalties, if the drug turns out to be a success. This fact makes current ways of testing in commercialized medical research highly problematic.

I will develop these points, especially the second, and offer some suggestions for dealing with them, including a pair of proposals: (1) that medical trials be conducted only by public institutions and (2) that intellectual property rights in medical research be greatly weakened, if not outright eliminated. This may seem drastic, but theory justification in such cases may be possible no other way, if it hopes to be objective and reliable.

2. Discovery versus Justification

For a very long time, philosophers of science have dismissed worries about motivations, ideology, and so on in the creation of scientific theories, for the simple reason that the bad stuff will come out in the wash. At least, that is what they think. Reichenbach famously introduced the terms "context of discovery" and "context of justification" to mark an important difference. Discovery has to do with the subjective source of ideas, anything from an apple falling on Newton's head to gross racist bigotry. These are sources of ideas—they can come from anywhere and we can have no rational method for generating them. Justification, by contrast, comes through careful, objective testing of those ideas. It is the latter that matters to epistemology; the former is of concern to psychology. What matters is the evidence for a theory, not its genesis.

There are from time to time objections to the distinction; some will defend the existence of a logic of discovery, that is, a rational method of having good ideas. For the most part, however, Reichenbach's distinction is accepted. Not only is it standard logical empiricist gospel, but Karl Popper championed it, too. (It is an amusing paradox that Popper's most famous book, *The Logic of Scientific Discovery*, denies there could be anything answering to its title.)

It seems so obvious a distinction that we might wonder when and by whom it was not thought so. Was there ever a time when a logic of discovery was thought to be obtainable? The answer is yes. Discovery has long been an ideal. Bacon, Descartes, and Newton all had the great hope of finding a method to generate knowledge. Newton's "hypothesis non fingo" was part of this outlook. The general idea was simply this: *theory T is justified if and only if T is discovered by a correct method*. Find the correct method and great discoveries will follow.

What happened? Why was the hope of a logic of discovery discarded? The answer has to do with the methodological development of science itself. Much of the work after Newton had exactly the features he disavowed—it offered hypotheses. Invisible atoms, the aether, phlogiston, caloric, and so on were obvious conjectures. Some of these conjectures worked well and some did not. Clearly these were hypotheses, good guesses at best, and just as clearly there would have been no method of reliably generating the right ones. Needless to say, guessing is not a reliable method. If these theories were to be evaluated, it would have to be on the basis of something other than upon the way they were generated. And so, the much hoped for logic of discovery was abandoned (see Laudan 1981).

Evaluation of hypotheses would have to be based on their consequences. What sorts of consequences? Many were and continue to be suggested: novel predictions, unification of diverse phenomena, accuracy, and several others, including various aesthetic features. Though the relative merits for theory evaluation of different kinds of consequences are a subject of ongoing debate, the general view today is widely accepted; indeed, it is completely dominant. According to the general consensus, all that matters in testing a belief is its consequences, not its origin. And it explains why so many are not too worried, at least not in principle, about the motivations of drug companies and their scientific researchers. If their proposals are bad ones, we can catch them out when we put their claims to the test in randomized clinical trials (RCTs).

I should add a qualification, since I may have overstated the lack of interest in heuristics. Thomas Nickles, Herbert Simon, and Hans Radder, for instance, have contributed recently to this project. I should also mention some early dissident views about the discovery-justification distinction. Russell Hanson (1958) tries to uphold a logic of discovery, but has had few followers. Imre Lakatos's *Proofs and Refutations* (1976) is another of the very few contemporary works to take issue with it. He claims there is a (fallible) logic of discovery in mathematics, and he spells it out with wonderful illustrations from the history of thinking about polyhedra. The point of these authors is that discovery is more like justification, in being rational, after all. Later, I will argue that (at least in the case of some examples), justification is more like discovery, in being less rational than normally thought. Kathleen Okruhlik (1994) accepts the discovery-justification distinction, but notes that justification is comparative, that is, depends to a large extent on rival theories. This means that if rival theories are discovered in a similar way, then any bias in discovery will not be filtered out in justification. The upshot, according to her, is that a sensible community will ensure as diverse a range of theorizers as possible.

3. Mathematical Examples

With the introduction of hypotheses as a dominant method of doing science, it is clear that the dream of a logic of discovery has disappeared. But were we too quick to throw it out? What was meant by a method of discovery, anyway? For some it meant an algorithm, a more or less infallible method of generating the truth. This notion of discovery is gone, at least in most cases, though not in all. There are weaker notions, such as heuristic methods. And this, though not fully acknowledged or appreciated, is still with us. After all, if it were not, then we couldn't make much sense of practices such as awarding research grants. We give them to promising projects; we do not pass them out at random. PhD supervisors give their students problems to work on that they think can be solved, using methods that they recognize. If there were no logic of discovery of any form whatsoever, then all of this would be hopeless nonsense.

The current conception of the discovery-justification distinction puts far too much emphasis on the latter, ignoring the lingering features of the former. (I mentioned Hanson and Lakatos as exceptions to this; it would be useful to keep them in mind.) There are simple examples where the logic of discovery is crucially important. What is the product of 2,374 and 9,281? The answer is 22,033,094. How do we know? There is a method of discovery, the method we learn as schoolchildren, namely, multiplication. That's how we discover the answer. How do we justify the answer? Exactly the same way. We simply point out that the answer was arrived at by the method of multiplication. The logic of discovery in this case is the same as the logic of justification. It might be thought that mathematical examples are irrelevant, since the discovery-justification issue is concerned with induction, while mathematical reasoning is largely (if not entirely) deductive. Set that consideration aside for now, since I'm using mathematical examples mainly for the purpose of motivation.

Not all mathematical problems are so simple as multiplication. What are the roots of $x^5 - 15x^4 + 85x^3 - 225x^2 + 274x - 120 = 0$? I would have to guess. For a start I might try 17. To check this guess I let $x = 17$ in the equation and see if the left side turns out to be 0. It does not. So, I try again, this time guessing $x = 3$. Now it works, so 3 is a root. Similar trial and error will, I hope, lead to the other four roots. There is no algorithm for this, unlike for quadratic equations or for simple multiplication, though experience can be a big help.

Now to a third example. Lam et al. (1989) used several thousand hours of Cray supercomputer time to prove the nonexistence of finite projective planes of order ten. (It is not important to know what this is. For those interested, a brief account can be found at http://mathworld.wolfram.com/ProjectivePlane.html.) Their work, obviously, would have been quite costly. The team worked long and hard on several aspects of the project, including time spent begging for a few hours here and there of precious Cray time, when various machines were not being used by others. The evaluation of the theorem was anything but easy, quite the opposite of checking a typical proof of a page or two in a journal.

The computation required the examination of 10^{14} cases, which allowed plenty of scope for problems. In their paper, Lam et al. (1989) note the possibility of error. Interestingly, they note several types. One source of error stems from human mistakes in entering data. This is, perhaps, akin to regular calculation mistakes that are often made. A second source stems from software problems. As we all know from regular commercial software, eliminating bugs is no easy matter. In writing a program there are many levels of software to worry about: the operating system such as DOS or UNIX, the programming language such as PASCAL or FORTRAN, a compiler, and, of course, the particular software created to do the specialty computation. There are numerous opportunities for problems to enter. And with so few users, specialty software, in contrast to popular commercial programs (with thousands of so-called beta testers), has fewer opportunities to have its problems revealed through use.

Third, one of the most interesting sources of error stems from hardware problems. With normal PC use hardware problems are usually obvious when they happen—a power failure, for instance. But some mistakes are random and possibly undetectable. In the case of Cray computers, mistakes are made on average about once per thousand hours. These are quite random, perhaps due to cosmic rays. What Lam et al. do is (in brief) note the frequency of this type of error, the total time elapsed, and the number of cases that had to be examined; they then calculate the chance that an error was made when the computer was examining a case that was actually an instance of a projective plane of order 10. They conclude that this probability is very small, and when some special considerations concerning the nature of the search are considered, the probability of a misleading error is "infinitesimal" (Lam et al. 1989, 1122). Small, yes, but not zero. In describing what he takes to be the philosophical upshot of this work, Lam at one point says he is tempted to "avoid using the word 'proof' and prefer[s] to use the phrase 'computed result' instead" (1990, 8).

There is an important moral to this last of our three mathematical examples. Evidence for the theorem exists, but that evidence is not completely accessible to us. Instead, we must step back and examine the one thing that we can, namely, the software program that produced the proof, that is, that produced the evidence. Our three mathematical examples can be classified as follows:

1. Cases where the logic of discovery and the logic of justification coincide. The simple multiplication example fits this. More generally, any case involving a simple algorithm fits this pattern. Discovery and justification are both easy to carry out.

2. Cases where there is no logic of discovery, but there is a do-it-yourself logic of justification. Checking to see if a purported root of an equation is indeed a root. Discovery may be challenging, but justification is easy to carry out.

3. Cases where justification is a one-shot affair, since the expense of duplication is prohibitive. Justification is limited to examining the design and execution of a method of producing otherwise inaccessible evidence. Computer proofs requiring many hours of computation are in this class.

Some things are so much easier to check than others. But before expanding on this point, I first want to distinguish between cases where the criterion for evaluation is narrow and cases where it is broad. A mathematician asserts a theorem and offers a proof of it. The evidence for the theorem is the published proof. There is no other evidence for the theorem: no laboratory observations, no archival findings, no sampling of opinion, and so on. The criterion for evaluating the theorem is very narrow—the proof and nothing else. Contrast this with wanting to check, say, whether it rained in Moscow on June 15, 2006. There are numerous ways to do it. I could read old newspapers from the day before (which predicted rain) and the day after (which reported rain). Or I could ask Boris, who lives in Moscow and remembers well, since it was his birthday and his party was washed out by rain.

No doubt there are several other ways, too. The criterion for evaluating the claim "It rained in Moscow on June 15, 2006" is rather broad. Many different things count, unlike the mathematics case. Of course, there will be cases that are even narrower than the mathematics example and cases that involve more diversity than the weather example. And lots of cases in between. I merely want the differences to be recognized, even though they are differences of degree.

There is a second distinction I want to introduce, one that is more important. This is a distinction between low cost and high cost evaluation. The mathematics examples from above will nicely illustrate the difference. The multiplication example or determining the roots of a polynomial are both fairly easy. They are cases of do-it-yourself justification and take only a small amount of time and expense. Even in more serious cases, a published theorem with a one-page proof is quite easy to evaluate. Anyone with the appropriate background can simply read through the proof to see if it works. This is what the journal's referees do and it is what the reader typically does. This is low-cost evaluation.

Most mathematics is low cost, but not all. The evaluation of the theorem asserting the nonexistence of a projective plane of order 10 is of a very different sort. While it is logically possible to duplicate it, for all practical purposes it is done once and never again. This combination of factors—first, the computer proof is extremely expensive, and second, it is the one and only way to provide evidence for the theorem—means that this is a case of *one-shot science*.

4. EBM and RCT

Though it has obvious precursors, so-called evidence-based medicine (EBM) is a recent phenomenon. The term was coined in 1992 by researchers at McMaster University Medical School, who have been at the forefront of the EBM movement. The two-part idea is simple: the less contentious part says that medical practice should be based on the best evidence available, not on the individual observations and hunches of even quite experienced clinicians. The more contentious part is the claim that there is a hierarchy of evidential considerations, headed by the randomized clinical trial (RCT).

A typical RCT will start with a large number of patients with some condition, divide them at random into two groups, giving a treatment to one group (known as the treatment or study group) and a placebo (or perhaps a rival treatment) to the other (known as the control group). Participants will not know which group they are in, and those who administer the treatment and placebo will be similarly ignorant (hence, a "double-blind" trial). The resulting data will be subject to appropriate statistical analyses.

This is the common way of testing new drugs and is even used to test the effectiveness of some types of surgery, where the control group is given sham surgery (i.e., anaesthetized, cut open, stitched back together, but the relevant part of the operation is not performed). It has become so dominant in medical research that it is virtually impossible to be funded if one's methodology is along any lines other than those of EBM.

Within EBM the RCT is known as the "gold standard." It was thought by many to be the one and only thing that mattered. But things have somewhat relaxed and now a hierarchy of evidence is common, with RCTs at the top. Next in importance come trials that are not randomized. Then come so-called case-controlled studies, which often arise when an RCT would be out of the question, for instance when something like toxic poisoning is suspected in a group of people. At the bottom of this hierarchy is expert opinion. It counts for something, but placebo effects and various biases can easily cloud even an expert's judgment, so it is not trusted to any extent. Indeed, RCTs only began in the middle of the twentieth century at the same time as placebo effects were recognized as potential impediments to research.

The influence of EBM is remarkable. The *British Medical Journal* has listed it as one of the greatest medical innovations since that journal started in the early nineteenth century. There can be no doubt of its importance. But there have been criticisms. I'll mention a few, but only briefly, since my aims in this article lie elsewhere.

One problem is the unethicalness of subjecting people to nontreatment (including sham surgery) when something useful could be done. Another is the bias it introduces toward, say, pharmaceutical treatments of psychological problems, since so-called talking cures do not lend themselves to the RCT method. It also has the consequence of making treatments for extremely rare conditions largely unknowable, since we would not have sufficient numbers to run statistically significant tests.

In spite of problems, EBM is a dominant view in the epistemology of medicine and RCTs are at the core. Although many of the criticisms are perfectly justified, it is nevertheless reasonable to assume that RCTs do indeed provide good evidence for the safety and efficacy of any pharmaceutical product. I'm going to assume this for the balance of the discussion.

5. The Scandal of Current Medical Research

For the sake of the argument, I will take EBM and RCTs to be the proper way to do a wide range of medical research. Does the practice live up to the ideal? Alas, no, not by a long shot. In this section I will describe several of the shortcomings.

Vioxx is the brand name of rofecoxib, a so-called Cox-2 inhibitor, developed by the large American pharmaceutical company Merck. Vioxx was marketed for pain relief, especially for those with arthritis. The U.S. Food and Drug Administration (FDA) approved the drug as safe and effective in 1999. Eighty million people worldwide were prescribed this drug and annual sales were $2.5 billion.

Merck voluntarily withdrew Vioxx in 2004 because of increased risk of heart attacks and strokes. Speculation about the possible cause suggests Vioxx suppresses an anti-clotting agent, leading to clots and hence to heart attacks and strokes. The VIGOR study (Vioxx Gastrointestinal Outcomes Research) published in 2000 (Bombardier et al.) compared rofecoxib with naproxen and found a significant increase in heart attacks (which they claimed could be explained away), but otherwise no difference in the two drugs. Generally the VIGOR study was supportive of Vioxx.

It was subsequently revealed that Merck withheld data from their initial study. A *New England Journal of Medicine* editorial in 2006 bluntly said, "more than four months before the article was published, at least two of its authors were aware of critical data on an array of adverse cardiovascular events that were not included in the VIGOR article." A *Lancet* editorial in 2004 criticized Merck and the FDA, saying Vioxx should have been withdrawn in 2000. There are several lawsuits associated with Vioxx, some settled in Merck's favor, some against, many still pending.

There are numerous other cases, some of which I'll mention below. Indeed, the list is long. As well as dramatic individual cases, there have been systematic investigations, and they are very troubling. In particular, empirical work on the effects of commercialization of medical research has turned up results of the greatest importance.

Richard Davidson (1986), for instance, found that in his study of 107 published papers that compared rival drugs, the drug produced by the sponsor of the research was found to be superior in every single case. The Davidson study is typical; there are many like it coming to similar conclusions, though not quite so dramatically. Friedberg et al. (1999) found that only 5 percent of published reports on new drugs that were sponsored by the developing company gave unfavorable assessments. By contrast, 38 percent of published reports were not favorable when the investigation of the same drugs was sponsored by an independent source.

Stelfox et al. (1998) studied seventy articles on calcium-channel blockers, drugs that are used to treat high blood pressure. The articles in question were judged as *favorable, neutral,* or *critical.* Their finding was that 96 percent of the authors of favorable articles had financial ties with a manufacturer of calcium-channel blockers, 60 percent of the authors of neutral articles had such ties, and only 37 percent of authors of unfavorable articles had financial ties. Incidentally, in only two of the seventy published articles was the financial connection revealed.

Clearly, there is extensive corruption of medical research thanks to commercialization of the field, and we should be worried about who is funding the research. Let's look at a few more examples.

Celebrex, which is used in the treatment of arthritis, was the subject of a year-long study sponsored by its maker, Paramacia (now owned by Pfizer). The study purported to show that Celebrex caused fewer side effects than older arthritis drugs. The results were published in the *Journal of the American Medical Association* (*JAMA*) along with a favorable editorial. It later turned out that the encouraging results were based on the first six months of the study. When the whole study was considered, Celebrex held no advantage over older and cheaper drugs. On learning this, the author of the favorable editorial was furious and remarked on "a level of trust that was, perhaps, broken" (quoted in Angell 2004, 109).

Selective serotonin reuptake inhibitors, known simply as SSRIs, have been central in the new generation of antidepressants. Prozac is the most famous of these. There are several drugs in the SSRI class, including fluoxetine (Prozac), paroxetine (Paxil, Seroxat), sertraline (Zoloft), and others. They are often described as miracle drugs, bringing significant relief to millions of depressed people. The basis for the claim of miraculous results is a large number of clinical trials, but closer inspection tells a different story.

There are two related issues, both connected to nonreporting of evidence from clinical trials. Whittington et al. (2004) reviewed published and unpublished data on SSRIs and compared the results. To call the findings disturbing would be an understatement. The result was favorable to fluoxetine, but not to the others. They summarized their findings as follows:

> Data for two published trials suggest that fluoxetine has a favorable risk-benefit profile, and unpublished data lend support to this finding. Published results from one trial of paroxetine and two trials of sertraline suggest equivocal or weak positive risk-benefit profiles. However, in both cases, addition of unpublished data indicates that risks outweigh benefits. Data from unpublished trials of citalopram and venlafaxine show unfavorable risk-benefit profiles. (Whittington et al. 2004, 1341)

The related second point is illustrated in a GlaxoSmithKline internal document that was revealed in the *Canadian Medical Association Journal*. They were applying to regulatory authorities for a label change approving paroxetine (Seroxat) to treat pediatric depression. The document noted that the evidence from trials was "insufficiently robust," but further remarked: "It would be commercially unacceptable to include a statement that efficacy had not been demonstrated, as this would undermine the profile of paroxetine" (quoted in Kondro and Sibbald 2004, 783). They had lots to worry about from a commercial point of view, since annual sales of Seroxat at the time were close to $5 billion. In passing, I should also mention the high number of suicides associated with Prozac and other SSRIs. This was slow to come to light, but is well documented in Healy (2004).

A British newspaper, the *Observer,* reports a particularly shocking case of medical abuse involving a seventy-two-year-old woman in England who was being treated by her doctor for slightly elevated blood pressure (Barnett 2003). This was a few months after her husband had died; otherwise, she was in good health. Completely unknown to her, her doctor enrolled her in a clinical trial, gave her various pills that had serious side effects, and regularly took blood to the point that her arms were "black and blue." Some of the pills were given directly by the doctor, not through the usual process of taking a prescription to the pharmacy. Her suspicions were aroused, and after a particularly bad reaction to one pill she complained to health authorities. The subsequent investigation revealed that her doctor had been given £100,000 over the previous five years for enrolling patients in clinical trials at £1,000 each. The companies involved include AstraZeneca, GlaxoSmithKline, and Bayer. Many of the doctor's patients did not know they were being enrolled, many did not have any of the relevant symptoms to be included in the study in the first place, and many patients who did have relevant symptoms were given placebos, instead of the standard treatment they required.

One might hope that this culprit is just an isolated bad apple. But when we hear that in the U.K. more than three thousand general practitioners are enrolling patients in clinical trials at £1,000 each and that the pharmaceutical industry is spending more than £45 million for patient recruitment in the U.K., then it's not such a surprise to learn that there are dozens of examples of fraud. In the case of one general practitioner, the consent forms of twenty-five of the thirty-six patients he enrolled were forged. Another who collected £200,000 failed to notify patients of possible side effects. He was subsequently caught offering a bribe to one of those patients not to testify (Barnett 2003).

If this much corruption can be generated by a finder's fee of £1,000, imagine what might happen if the fee were tripled. In the United States in 2001 the average bounty was $7,000 per patient (Angell 2004, 31). Payment for recruiting is known as a "finder's fee," but the term is hardly ever used, since the idea is often thought to be unacceptable. The fee is usually hidden in so-called "administrative costs" or perhaps disguised in some other way for which compensation is considered acceptable, such as well-paid consultantships or invitations to conferences held in exotic and luxurious settings.

Next, consider research direction. Imagine two ways of approaching a health problem. One way involves the development of a new drug. The other way focuses on, say, diet and exercise. The second could well be a far superior treatment, both cheaper and more beneficial. But obviously it will not be funded by corporate sponsors, since there is not a penny to be made from the unpatentable research results. It should be just as obvious that a source of funding that does not have a stake in the outcome, but simply wants to know how best to treat a human ailment, would, in principle, fund either or both approaches, caring only to discover which is superior.

To get a sense of what is at issue here, consider a comparative trial carried out on patients who were at high risk of developing diabetes. Over a three-year period, 29 percent of the placebo group went on to develop diabetes; 22 percent who took the drug metformin developed diabetes; but only 14 percent of those who went on a diet and exercise program developed the disease (Angell 2004, 170). Clearly, the best result came from a treatment that is not patentable. This trial, by the way, was sponsored by the U.S. National Institute of Health, not by commercial interests.

The year 1980 saw a huge change in the way research was conducted. The Bayh-Dole Act and simultaneous legal rulings that allowed patents for biological organisms changed things dramatically. This act, passed by the U.S. Congress in 1980, promoted corporate medical research by allowing government money to be tied to intellectual property rights. Now university scientists could enter into partnerships with drug companies. The weak links of the past became strong bonds. Corporations could get much of their research costs covered by the public, and university scientists began to covet the profits that flowed from their work. Until then, governments and nonprofit foundations provided most of the research funding and, insofar as they set the research agenda, they did so with an eye to medical results, not profits.

The underlying ideology was the familiar one of providing monetary motives. The pharmaceutical industry in the United States now does well over $200 billion a year in business. Profit levels in the first decade of the new millennium are at a staggering 18 percent of sales, the highest of any U.S. industry listed in the Fortune 500. (The median of that group has profits of less than 4 percent of sales.) How can we account for this extraordinary success? Does it have something to do with the 11 percent of the $200 billion that goes into research? That's certainly a lot of money. Or does it have more to do with the 36 percent that goes into marketing? That's more than triple the research budget.

In 2002 the U.S. Food and Drug Administration (FDA) approved 78 new drugs. Only 7 were classified as improvements over older drugs. The rest are copies, so-called "me too" drugs. Not one of these seven was produced by a major U.S. drug company. There is nothing special about the year 2002. During the period 1998–2002 the FDA approved 415 new drugs and classified them as follows (relevant information can be found at the FDA website, www.fda.gov/cder/rdmt/pstable.htm):

14 percent were new innovations,

9 percent were significantly improved old drugs,

77 percent were no better than existing drugs.

The last of these are the "me too drugs." They are copies of existing drugs (not exact copies, since they have to be different enough to be patentable). By U.S. law the FDA must grant approval so long as a new drug is thought to be safe and effective (where being effective just means it does better than a placebo in a clinical trial). Once approved, marketing takes over and monstrous profits can be made. A cheaper and better generic alternative won't be similarly promoted, since there is no hope of stupendous earnings.

Not surprisingly, there are calls for clinical tests to compare new drugs with the best existing alternative, not just with placebos. The importance of such comparative testing is illustrated by a massive comparative study on various types of blood-pressure medication. It was carried by the National Heart, Lung, and Blood Institute (part of NIH) and almost completely publicly funded. The result was striking: the best medication turned out to be an old diuretic ("water pill"); it worked as well as or better than the others, had considerably fewer side effects, and cost about thirty-seven dollars per year, compared with several hundred dollars annually for each of the others (Angell 2004, 95).

It is clear that licensing of any new drug should then be based on relative performance. This is the sort of problem that could be obviously and easily controlled with proper regulation. It is hard to imagine a more poorly constructed regulatory system than the current one in place in the United States. It leads one to think that U.S. lawmakers are either a pack of fools or as corrupt as the pharmaceutical companies who lavishly lobby them. There is ample evidence for either conclusion.

Where does genuine innovation come from? Consider the case of Taxol (paclitaxel). It's a very important drug, widely used to treat various forms of cancer.

It was derived from the bark of the Pacific yew tree in the 1960s. The cost of this research was $183 million. It was paid for by taxpayers through the National Cancer Institute (NCI). However, in 1991 Bristol-Myers Squibb signed an agreement with NCI. The upshot is that they, not taxpayers, make several millions in royalties each year on annual sales of up to $2 billion (Angell 2004, 58f). This is a common pattern: risk and innovation come from the public; profits are privatized. How profitable can this be? When Taxol was brought to market, the cost of a year's treatment was $10,000 to $20,000—a ten-fold increase over the cost of production (Angell 2004, 66). It's hard to know whether we should respond with outrage or admiration. Imagine getting the public to pay extravagantly, not once, but twice for this research.

After looking at the actual practice of medical research, we might fall into a deep depression, utterly convinced that the situation is hopeless. On the other hand, from the point of view of the discovery-justification distinction, we might hold out hope for rigorous testing that would eliminate harmful and corrupt research and needlessly expensive medicines. The big problem with this line of thinking is that, so far, RCTs have not delivered good results. We need now to take a much closer look at RCTs, the method of justification.

6. RCT and the Cost of Justification

Although mathematics and medical research seem to be very different activities, there is one striking similarity that should by now be evident. Large-scale computer proofs and randomized clinical trials are both very expensive to run. The cost of evaluation is so enormous that for all practical purposes they can only be done once. But they are typically aimed at establishing facts that can be determined in only this way, which means they also fall into the narrow criterion of evidence category, as I characterized it earlier. Of course, other means of establishing those facts may be discovered in the future, but at the time of the activity, they are generally the one and only way, and that way is very expensive. They are both cases of one-shot science.

Table 5.1 indicates the situation. For our purposes, it is the top row that matters. The focus is on the difference between low-cost and high-cost methods of evaluation. Computer proofs and RCTs are both high-cost. The drug companies claim that it costs $800 million to bring the average drug to market. This is a gross exaggeration, but even the more reasonable estimates of $100 to $200 million is still a huge amount.

Table 5.1: Cost and criteria of evaluation		
	Low-cost evaluation	*High-cost evaluation*
Narrow criterion of evidence	"104,729 is a prime number."	"There is no projective plane of order 10." "Vioxx does not increase the risk of heart attacks."
Broad criterion of evidence	"It rained in Moscow on June 15, 2006."	"There is life on Mars."

Let me repeat what I said above. In the low cost of evaluation cases, anyone competent can do it with minimal resources. This is why the discovery-justification distinction seems right and useful. Who cares if Hitler asserts or George Bush denies "104,729 is a prime." We can easily check to see if either is right. But this easy option is not open to us in the high-cost cases. For all practical purposes, the evaluation process happens only once, if at all. None of us has the money needed to run a major RCT a second time.

People often recommend an adversarial process in science. Every conjecture gets put to a ruthless process of testing. This is the Popperian ideal. An adversarial account works well, perhaps, in the easy to evaluate cases. But we must cooperate in the expensive cases where independent tests are out of the question.

Nonsurveyable proofs in mathematics are like clinical trials—the way the proof is created or the way the trial is designed becomes all important. We cannot check the computer proof itself, but we can check the software that produced the proof. Similarly, we cannot reproduce the clinical trial ourselves, but we can ensure that the trial design and execution is the best possible. This may seem an obvious point, but it is only because we are used to seeing the software for things like the four-color theorem made public. Mathematicians and computer scientists examine it carefully. We will not find a flaw in the proof, since it is not accessible to humans. But we might find a flaw in the software that generated the proof.

7. Public Control of RCTs and Its Benefits

If we could not examine the software, we would have no confidence in a computer-generated proof. Confidence in the result depends on confidence in the method of getting the result. Exactly the same can be said about RCTs.

Here are a few of the problems with the current practice of medical research and some of the proposals to deal with them.

Data withheld. I mentioned the Vioxx and the Celebrex cases above. In the Celebrex study, only six months of a twelve-month study were reported. In the Vioxx study, some heart attacks were not reported. The *New England Journal of Medicine* angrily complained about this. Merck replied that these were after their cut-off date, so not included in the data. The journal countered by pointing out that there was no mention of a cut-off date in Merck's report.

Some trials that find negative results for a new drug or that learn of harmful effects of existing drugs are quietly set aside. The information is not revealed, since, after all, no one is obliged to publish.

ICMJE (International Committee of Medical Journal Editors) has instituted a new rule that requires all trials to be registered at the outset, if they are ever to be considered for publication (DeAngelis 2004). This partly addresses some problems.

Corporate interpretation of data. Large RCTs are often carried out at several locations by several participants. The data are collected by the corporate sponsor and interpreted by them. Publications are written by ghost authors. The names of researchers are on the paper, but often they have not had access to the whole body of data, just to their own contribution. ICMJE has instituted a policy of requiring that all authors of any article published in their journals must be allowed full access to all data and be permitted to participate in the interpretation of that data. Whether participating researchers pursue this remains to be seen. Rocking the boat may harm future partnerships.

Selective publication. Many studies are published in supplementary issues of regular journals. These issues are paid for by corporate sponsors and are little more than advertising outlets, yet they look like regular journal issues. Journals are aware of this problem, but financial needs make them reluctant to act.

JAMA reserves the right to subject the data in any study submitted to them for publication to their own independent statistical analysis. The editor reports hearing that sponsors of some reports have told their authors not to submit to *JAMA* because of this policy.

Recruitment. Subjects in RCTs don't come out of thin air. They need to be found. This is an expensive and costly process. Recruitment can be so profitable that one family practice organization in the United States placed an ad on the Internet:

> Looking for Trials! We are a large family practice office. . . . We have two full time coordinators and a computerized patient data base of 40,000 patients. . . . We are looking for Phase 2–Phase 4 trials as well as postmarketing studies. We

can actively recruit patients for any study that can be conducted in the Family Practice setting. (Quoted in Lemmens and Miller 2003)

Here are some of the methodological problems that arise from paying large fees to recruit patients for studies:

- It is increasingly difficult to find test subjects for government-sponsored research, since typically they do not pay a finder's fee. This means that it is increasingly difficult to do research that is relatively independent of economic interests.

- Incompetence. This arises when general practitioners, for instance, become involved in clinical trials; they have no particular skill or training in research.

- Improper inclusion. The criteria for inclusion are improperly expanded so as to make it easier to recruit test subjects. This weakens the reliability of experimental results.

Bias, corruption, and theory-ladenness. With so much money involved, we should certainly expect bias to prevail. Some will be outright, conscious corruption.

These are just a few of the many serious problems that arise from having trials in the hands of corporate sponsors. The conclusion we naturally draw from the problems with RCTs is that they should be in the hands of a neutral party. It is a conclusion that dovetails with the same view we naturally hold about software for computer proofs. We can only trust the result when we can trust the method that produces the result. And in the case of RCTs, we need to control that process in all its many details.

This means *the design, the execution, and the interpretation of the data must be in public hands.* There are simply too many influences to put a good test off the track when the testing process is funded, designed, executed, and interpreted by the sponsors who stand to gain or lose so much. In short, the evidential component of medical research must be in public hands.

There are two huge benefits that come from the public control of medical research testing. The first of these is a significant increase in the objectivity of testing when complex and expensive methods such as RCTs are required.

The second benefit is financial. It might be thought that the public benefits enormously by putting the cost of medical research in private hands. The usual argument runs: They have deep pockets and are willing take risks. We all benefit when their gambles pay off.

What nonsense. How anyone can believe this for a moment is almost beyond comprehension. The public is going to pay either way. It can do so through taxes or it can do so through royalties. Anyone who thinks the latter would be better might also be interested in some snake oil I have for sale—it must be good, because I charge a lot for it.

8. Conclusion

The first conclusion I would like to draw is that it is time to resurrect the logic of discovery, or at least one crucial aspect of it—justification comes from using the right method of discovery. From the software that produces computer proofs to RCTs that produce significant medical discoveries, there are interesting and important cases that deserve analysis along discovery-justification lines. Of course, this will be a more modest logic of discovery than earlier aspirations envisaged, but it could be of some significance.

The second conclusion is directly relevant to the theme of the conference that gave rise to this volume, namely the commercialization of research. Theory testing, thanks to the enormous cost and complexity, must pass into independent hands. We simply cannot trust those in control of RCTs to produce objective results. The only neutral hands to take this on are, of course, public hands (presumably, returned to university researchers, but this is something to be decided when working out the details).

This is all I will argue for here, but I actually wish to urge something even stronger. I would like to see the whole of medical research put into public hands and all intellectual property rights eliminated (see Brown 2008). Public control of RCTs would then be an important component of a more general public control of all medical research.

NOTES

Note added in proof. More bad news about SSRIs continues to come out. Jay C. Fournier, et al. 2010, "Antidepressant Drug Effects and Depression Severity: A Patient-Level Meta-analysis." *JAMA* 303(1): 47–53, shows that for patients with mild or moderate depression (i.e., most cases), SSRIs are no more effective than placebos. Only in severe cases is drug treatment effective.

I am very grateful for the many comments from the audience at the Amsterdam conference. In particular, I would like to thank Lieven Decock for his commentary, "Buying the Language," and Hans Radder for his careful reading of an early draft and his many useful suggestions.

REFERENCES

Angell, Marcia. 2004. *The truth about the drug companies: How they deceive us and what to do about it.* New York: Random House.

Barnett, A. 2003. "Patients used as drug 'guinea pigs.'" *Observer,* Sunday, February 9, 2003 (available at www.observer.co.uk/politics/story/0,6903,891938,00.html).

Bombardier, C., et al. 2000. "Comparison of upper gastrointestinal toxicity of rofecoxib and naproxen in patients with rheumatoid arthritis. *New England Journal of Medicine* 343 (21): 1520–28.

Brown, James Robert. 2008. "The Community of Science®." In *The challenge of the social and the pressure of practice: Science and values revisited,* ed. M. Carrier, D. Howard, and J. Kourany, 189–216. Pittsburgh: University of Pittsburgh Press.

Curfman, G. D., S. Morrissey, and J. M. Drazen. 2006. "Expression of concern reaffirmed." *New England Journal of Medicine* 354 (11): 1193.

Davidson, R. 1986. "Sources of funding and outcome of clinical trials." *Journal of General Internal Medicine* 12 (3): 155–58.

DeAngelis, Catherine, et al. 2004. "Clinical trial registration: A statement from the International Committee of Medical Journal Editors." *Journal of the American Medical Association* 292:1363–64.

Dickersin, Kay, and Rennie Drummond. 2003. "Registering clinical trials." *Journal of the American Medical Association* 290:516–23.

Drazen, J. M., and G. D. Curfman. 2002. "Editorial." *New England Journal of Medicine* 346 (24): 1901–2.

Drummond, Rennie. 2004. "Trial registration." *Journal of the American Medical Association* 292: 1359–62.

Dunn, A., et al. 2005. "Exercise treatment for depression: Efficacy and dose response." *American Journal of Preventive Medicine* 28 (1): 1–8.

Friedberg, M., et al. 1999. "Evaluation of conflict of interest in new drugs used in oncology." *Journal of the American Medical Association* 282:1453–57.

Friedman, L. S., B. A. Elihu, and D. Richter. 2004. "Relationship between conflicts of interest and research results." *Journal of General Internal Medicine* 19 (1): 51.

Guyatt, G., et al. [Evidence-Based Medicine Working Group] 1992. "Evidence-based medicine: A new approach to teaching the practice of medicine." *Journal of the American Medical Association* 268:2420–25.

Hanson, N. R. 1958. *Patterns of discovery.* Cambridge: Cambridge University Press.

Healy, David. 2001. *The Creation of psychopharmacology.* Cambridge, MA: Harvard University Press.

———. 2004. *Let them eat prozac: The unhealthy relationship between the pharmaceutical industry and depression.* New York: New York University Press.

Jüni, P., L. Nartey, S. Reichenbach, R. Sterchi, P. A. Dieppe, and M. Egger. 2004. "Risk of cardiovascular events and rofecoxib: Cumulative meta-analysis." *Lancet* (published online).

Kondro, Wayne, and Barbara Sibbald. 2004. "Drug company experts advised staff to withhold data about SSRI use in children." *Canadian Medical Association Journal* 170 (5): 783.

Krimsky, Sheldon. 2003. *Science in the private interest.* Malden, MD: Rowman and Littlefield.

Lakatos, I. 1976. *Proofs and refutations: The logic of mathematical discovery*. Cambridge: Cambridge University Press.

Lam, C. W. H. 1990. "How reliable is a computer-based proof?" *Mathematical Intelligencer* 12:8–12.

———. 1991. "The search for a finite projective plane of order 10." *American Mathematical monthly* 98:305–18.

Lam, C. W. H., L. Thiel, and S. Swiercz. 1989. "The non-existence of finite projective planes of order 10." *Canadian Journal of Mathematics* 41 (6): 1117–23.

Laudan, Larry. 1968. "Theories of scientific method from Plato to Mach: A bibliographic review." *History of Science* 7:1–63.

———. 1981. *Science and hypothesis*. Dordrecht: Reidel.

Lemmens, Trudo, and P. B. Miller. 2003. "The human subjects trade: Ethical and legal issues surrounding recruitment incentives." *Journal of Law, Medicine and Ethics* 31 (3): 398–418.

Okruhlik, K. 1994. "Gender and the biological sciences." *Canadian Journal of Philosophy,* supp. vol. 20: 21–42. Reprinted in Curd and Cover, eds. *Readings in the philosophy of science*. New York: Norton, 1998.

Stelfox, H. T., et al. 1998. "Conflict of interest in the debate over calcium-channel antagonists." *New England Journal of Medicine* 338 (2): 101–6.

Whittington, Craig, et al. 2004. "Selective serotonin reuptake inhibitors in childhood depression: Systematic review of published versus unpublished data." *Lancet* 363 (April 24): 1341–45.

CHAPTER 6

The Business of Drug Research

A MIXED BLESSING

Albert W. Musschenga, Wim J. van der Steen,

and Vincent K. Y. Ho

1. Introduction

DECADES AGO, in the 1970s and 1980s, the idea that science should be "socially relevant" had broad support, also among (university) scientists. Scientists should leave their ivory tower, stop doing science only for the sake of science, become aware of the impact of their research on society, and let the needs of society determine their research agenda. Critical scientists worked together, for example, with trade unions and environmental groups, but rarely with business corporations, which were assumed to act for their own interests rather than the interests of society. They held that socially relevant research (or public interest research) should be financed by the state. This view was based on two arguments (O'Neill 1998). First, as argued by leading economists, knowledge would be inappropriate as an object for exchange on the market because it represents a public good. The provision of public goods cannot be left to the market for risk of underprovision. Therefore it is a central task of the state (Arrow 1962; Dasgupta and David 1994).

Second, property relations appropriate to the market would undermine good scientific practice. O'Neill mentions three further arguments supporting this claim. First, market mechanisms are incompatible with the open communication in science, which is a necessary condition for the growth of knowledge. Second, the market as an institutional framework for science dissociates the external rewards assigned to a contributor to science from the value of his or her contribution to the development of science. Third, private property in science is at odds with the practice of science (O'Neill 1998, 151ff). In the view that the state should finance universities and their scientific research, ideological and economical arguments converge. It implies that science and knowledge are a public interest and also a public good. Therefore, their provision should not be left to the market.

Nowadays the ideological and the economical arguments are not taken for granted anymore. The idea of socially relevant research is still invoked, but the interpretation of social relevance has changed. Research is now (also) regarded as socially relevant when an organization—a business corporation, a public institution such as a ministry, or a nongovernmental organization—is willing to pay for it. In this view social relevance is (co-)determined by the market. The private interests of business corporations and nonprofit organizations on the one hand, and science and knowledge as a public interest on the other hand are no longer seen as mutually exclusive.

Business corporations are willing to finance research if they expect that the results directly or indirectly lead to profitable products. Governmental and other nonprofit organizations commission research when they expect that its results may serve their goals and policies. Libertarian economists believe that the public good argument for state financing is no longer valid for sectors of research where the results can be protected by intellectual property rights (Cowen 1988).

Although we are sympathetic to Sheldon Krimsky's idea of the university as the place for public interest science (Krimsky 2003), we would not maintain that the market should never play a role in determining what socially relevant science is. However, two serious problems with contract research loom large. First, legitimate doubts exist about the scientific integrity of procedures and people involved in contract research. Second, sectors where researchers depend to a large extent on external funding do not bode well for basic research and research into social and cultural problems beyond the interest of market parties.

We will illustrate these problems through a case study that concerns the role of pharmaceutical companies in medical research, especially research into drugs for the treatment of mental illness. Pharmaceutical companies finance about

60 percent of medical research. They exert pressure on individual scientists, research groups, and universities to provide results that serve their interests. In some cases this results in violations of scientific integrity. To increase the demand for their products, pharmaceutical companies also attempt to influence the prescriptions by doctors, the expectations of patients, and treatment guidelines. These attempts, at least those by pharmaceutical companies in the United States, are well documented. We review them in section 2.

The influence of contractors on the results of research does not necessarily lead to overt violations of scientific integrity. It may also cause a more covert research bias. A lot of material exists on biases in medical research financed by pharmaceutical companies. We summarize the material in section 3.

Pharmaceutical companies aim to develop profitable drugs, understandably with much emphasis on drug treatments of diseases that are common in affluent societies. Thus, research on medical treatments for rare diseases and treatments that do not involve drugs may not receive the attention they deserve for lack of funds. However, the fact that pharmaceutical companies finance the greater part of medical research need not imply that they determine the research agenda in harmful ways in the areas covered. In section 4, we argue that the situation is more complicated.

Considering psychiatry, we regard drugs as a salient problem. Traditionally, a controversy exists between adherents of a biological approach to mental illness who promote treatment with medication and those inspired by psychology, anthropology, and sociology, who promote psychotherapy.

In the last few decades, the biological approach to mental disease has won much ground. The biological approach—the so-called medical model—in psychiatry does privilege biology over other disciplines. We are indeed getting too much biology. In a different way, though, we are getting too little of it. The areas of biology assimilated by psychiatry and medicine generally have a limited scope. The influence of nutrients, infections, and biological rhythms in mental illness, for example, is undervalued. Hence, drugs and psychotherapy are by no means the only feasible options in the treatment of the illnesses.

In the last section we discuss what can be done to counter the influence of pharmaceutical companies on medical research. A change in the system of financing medical research seems imperative. But what system should replace the present one? Even if medical research became completely deprivatized, the dominance of the biomedical model would not necessarily disappear. What policy and what structures are needed so that other approaches receive evenhanded attention in medical research? These are the questions we ultimately attempt to answer.

2. The Influence of Pharmaceutical Industries on Medical Practice

Many medical treatments consist of using drugs. According to some authors we are living in an era of massive overmedication (van der Steen and Ho 2001; van der Steen 2003; Angell 2004). The large majority of drugs are both developed and produced by profit-seeking pharmaceutical companies. Before drugs are allowed to be introduced on the market, research has to be done into their safety, efficacy, and (cost-)effectiveness. This kind of research is often contracted to university research groups.

Whether a drug becomes profitable depends on several factors and actors which pharmaceutical companies will try to control. It is evident that pharmaceutical companies are not indifferent to the outcome of evaluation research of drugs, which they developed at great costs. Thus, they will try to influence research and researchers. If a drug is finally approved, it has to be prescribed on a large scale in order to become profitable. Pharmaceutical companies will, of course, try to induce doctors to prescribe the drugs. The best thing that can happen to the companies is that the drug is recommended as a standard treatment in a clinical guideline. Thus, they will also try to influence such guidelines. In some cases at least, this may be actually or potentially illegitimate. In this section the focus is on examples concerning the sales promotion of approved drugs, with particular emphasis on psychotropic drugs.

First, doctors visited by medical representatives of the industry are provided with free samples of drugs, and presents on top of this, which does influence their prescription behavior. Also, medical professionals are enabled to attend conferences in expensive settings provided by the industry, where they are told about all the benefits of drugs marketed by funding companies. This is all well documented (Angell 2004; Bouma 2006; Brody 2007). Moreover, advertising on a grand scale seduces the general public to aim at drug treatments for illnesses such as depression, real or imagined (Medawar and Hardon 2004; Moynihan and Cassells 2005).

Second, guidelines concerning diagnoses and treatments, and also guidelines concerning risk factors, are mostly set up by medical opinion leaders paid for by the industry. An excellent survey of the process is to be found in Moynihan and Cassells (2005). Here is an example from their book. According to official guidelines of the National Institutes of Health in the United States in the 1990s, some thirteen million Americans should be eligible for treatment with statines, cholesterol-lowering drugs. In 2001, guidelines were changed so that, all of a sudden, the number rose to thirty-seven million. Almost all the medical professionals involved in the decision making were receiving money from the pharmaceutical industry. This suggests that arguments on the part of these professionals may reflect vested interests rather than new scientific insights into the impact of cholesterol. Concerning psychiatry, depression would be a prime example of a similar trend. Official estimates of the prevalence of depression have been rising over the years, due in part to biased questionnaires helpfully concocted by the industry. The estimates suggest that, at the very least, a quarter of the general population is suffering from depression. This is a clear example of medicalization, ordinary problems of living being marketed as psychopathology. "Depression" is now commonly treated with SSRIs, selective serotonin reuptake inhibitors, the idea being that a shortage of serotonin is responsible for the depression. However, this idea was discredited long ago (for sources, see Healy 2004).

Third, a high percentage of articles on drug treatments in medical journals are now being written by ghostwriters paid by the industry (Krimsky 2003; Healy 2004). In many cases, the official authors have not even seen the original data. This enhances a biased, positive view of the treatments. An analysis by Sismondo suggests that between 18 percent and 40 percent of the literature published between 1998 and 2000 on the antidepressant drug sertraline was ghost-managed by a single medical education and communication company acting on behalf of the drug's manufacturer (Sismondo 2007).

Fourth, the industry has managed to sell general theories of illness that help to promote diagnoses fostering drug treatments. Views of schizophrenia are a telling example (Healy 2002, 265–70). On a common theory, schizophrenia is characterized by positive symptoms such as delusions and hallucinations and negative symptoms such as withdrawal and incoherence of language and action. In the 1970s, tests run with a new drug, clozapine, appeared to have a beneficial effect on the negative features, which was heralded as a great success by the industry. However, something else was really happening. Clozapine had been compared with chlorpromazine, an older drug applied in megadoses. The megadose therapy had been responsible to a large extent for the negative features and the success of clozapine merely represented the use of less poisonous medications. Thus the industry was now promoting a kind of "negative" schizophrenia it had first helped to create, while later providing drugs to do away with its own creation.

Fifth, also illuminating is the history of catatonia as described by Healy (2002, 270–75). Catatonia is a serious condition in some schizophrenia patients characterized by almost total unresponsiveness. Many psychiatrists have assumed until recently that the condition had almost disappeared due to the use of antipsychotics. But this is not true at all. The presence of catatonia came to be ignored for lack of interest on the part of the industry after the patent on lorazepam, an effective medication, ran out. Hence, an important motive for recognizing and treating catatonia ceased to exist. Indeed, the condition resembles neuroleptic malignant syndrome (NMS), a serious disorder caused by the older antipsychotics.

Sixth, the industry also took part in the development of successive versions of the *DSM*, the *Diagnostic and Statistic Manual of Mental Disorders*. The later versions of the manual came to conceptualize the disorders as distinct entities even though all sorts of transitions exist between them. This facilitated the use of medications with alleged benefits in homogeneous patient populations since routine prescriptions presuppose well-defined disease categories. In fact, the *DSM* categories are out of touch with the real world. The concept of schizophrenia, for example, stands for a highly heterogeneous collection of conditions (Boyle 2002).

3. Bias in Drug Research and Scientific Integrity

Pharmaceutical industries fund research done by academic scientists. This is not the only financial link between academic science and industry. Many medical scientists serve as advisors for pharmaceutical companies. Moreover, some medical specialists own or have an interest in a company that sells drugs they developed in their research at a university. Here we focus on the funding relation.

Financial links between academic scientists and industry may lead to conflicts of interest. According to Resnik, "A scientist has a conflict of interest if a) he is in a relationship with another scientist or member of the public requiring him to exercise judgment in that other's service and b) he has an interest tending to interfere with 1) the proper exercise of judgment in that relationship or 2) his ability to fulfil his obligations to that person in his role as a scientist" (Resnik 1998, 390). This definition emphasizes two components: the impairment of the judgment and the corruption of the will. In Resnik's view, either component may adversely affect scientific objectivity and trustworthiness. Well-documented cases exist of pharmaceutical companies putting illegitimate pressure on scientists, e.g., to adjust their research or not to publish unfavorable research results (Angell 2004; Krimsky 2003). This may amount to a neglect of duties to science and an impairment of scientific integrity caused by a desire to sustain a good relationship with the funding company.

Research funded by the pharmaceutical industry does lead to verdicts on the drugs investigated which are much more positive than those of independent researchers (Bekelman, Li, and Cross 2001). This suggests that research funded by pharmaceutical companies is biased. To help understand how financial interests can affect research, Resnik presents a model of the steps of scientific research. The first step is problem selection, and subsequent steps relate to developing and implementing a protocol, and the dissemination of research results, respectively (Resnik 2000, 266). It is easy to show that (financial) interests affect problem selection and dissemination of results in research. Financial interests also influence the development and implementation of research protocols. However, this need not imply that researchers violate methodological or ethical standards. As Resnik rightly remarks, biased research may still be scientifically sound. Referring to Longino (1990), he writes that research bias cannot simply be assessed by judging research results according to epistemic standards since external social, economic, and other factors influence the results (Resnik 2000, 259). (For critical comments on Longino, see van der Steen 1995.)

Research costs money. Irrespective of funding by the industry, the outcomes of research into drugs have an economic impact. Hence we cannot eliminate all financial interests that affect the design and the implementation of such research (Resnik 2000, 273). All research is subject to external influences. The impact of financial interests on research is not always visible. Researchers may have internalized the interests of their sponsors. This may influence professional decisions in diverse phases of research. For example, researchers paid by the industry may choose to investigate drug therapies while disregarding potential benefits of diet therapies. The ensuing bias of research agendas may seem to reflect investigator preferences even though agendas are in fact primarily set by the industry.

Although it cannot be eliminated, research bias can and should be reduced (Resnik 2000, 262ff). However, codes and guidelines for contract research that should protect researchers from open and direct intervention by funders into the research process cannot prevent unintended and covert research bias. Universities and authoritative scientific organizations such as the Royal Netherlands Academy of Arts and Sciences (KNAW) still think, naïvely so, that the dangers of contract research can be averted by clear codes and contracts. An example of this view is to be found in the KNAW report *Wetenschap op Bestelling* (*Science on Command*) of 2005, which reduces the dangers of contract research to violations of scientific integrity and disregards harmful unintended and covert bias in the wake of external funding.

4. The Alliance between Psychiatry and the Pharmaceutical Industry

On a naïve view, representatives of the pharmaceutical industry are villains who fund unwary medical scientists to conduct biased research and to succumb to biased interpretations of results favoring products they are paid to investigate. No such one-way traffic exists. Bias in current medical research results from two-way traffic between medicine and the industry, substantively and methodologically. Considering psychiatry in particular, we see several trends that have played right into the hands of the industry.

First, medicine never succeeded in bridging the gap between somatic and mental aspects of health and disease since we are still saddled with an unsolvable mind-body problem. Medicine has opted for purely somatic approaches, at best with marginal inputs from disciplines concerned with the mental. This puts psychiatry in a difficult position since it either had to become part of medical science, with undue emphasis on somatic aspects of mental disorders, or accept a position outside medical science. In the 1930s and 1940s, psychiatrists held to an eclectic mix of biological and psychological theorizing; in the 1950s and 1960s, psychoanalysts gained hegemonic influence within the profession, and by the late 1970s and early 1980s, biologically oriented psychiatrists started to dominate psychiatric theory, as they still do (Braslow 2000, 795).

According to Wyatt, to understand the rise of biological psychiatry, it is necessary to examine the changing public face of psychiatry in the last few decades (Wyatt 2006). From 1970 to 1980 the percentage of medical school graduates in the United States opting for careers in psychiatry had dropped from 11 percent to 5 percent. In an article in the *New York Times,* Nelson (1982) mentioned as causes the relatively low pay of psychiatrists and increasing interests in family practice rather than specialist practices. He also listed additional causes that foreshadowed a return to an increased emphasis upon biological explanations of mental problems.

Many medical school graduates thought that psychiatrists had become dinosaurs, mired in pits of psychoanalytic confusion. These graduates also did not like "alternative" treatments such as primal scream therapy. The article by Nelson describes the efforts of organized psychiatry to reverse the trend by doing two things. It held recruitment conferences, and it began to emphasize psychiatry's scientific character in order to advocate a return to biological explanations. These efforts were paralleled by the rise of biochemical and genetic explanations of abnormal behavior.

By the late 1990s and the early years of this millennium, biological psychiatry had gained a lot of ground among professionals (Wyatt 2006). Nowadays, the emphasis is overwhelmingly on biological psychiatry, which tends to relegate the mental to the domain of epiphenomena. The suggestion that the source of disorders such as schizophrenia, depression, anxiety, addiction, and several childhood disorders lies in the brain is heavily promoted by the pharmaceutical industry.

Biological causation, says Wyatt, is the theoretical mortar that has cemented the marriage between psychiatry and the pharmaceutical industry (Wyatt 2006). However, the evidence in support of biological causation of mental disorders, and biological treatment, appears to be less compelling than the adherents of biological psychiatry and the pharmaceutical industry want us to believe (van der Steen 1999; van der Steen, Ho, and Karmelk 2003; Joseph 2003; Lewis 2006).

In the last few decades both the dominance of the biological approach to mental disorders in psychiatry and the enormous publicity campaigns of the pharmaceutical industry led to a substantial increase in the sales of psychotropic drugs (van der Steen 2003; Moynihan and Cassells 2005). In the Netherlands, where antidepressants are prescribed by general practitioners as well as by psychiatrists, pharmacies supplied 746,000 persons with antidepressants in 2005. The costs amounted to €162 million. The alleged success of the new generation of antidepressants—particularly the selective serotonin reuptake inhibitors (SSRIs) and the serotonin-norepinephrine reuptake inhibitors (SNRIs)—has reinforced the belief that the biological approach is essentially sound. Unfortunately, the success of the treatment of depression with SSRIs and SNRIs is badly overstated. Their positive effects, if present at all, are minor, and psychotherapy is often a better option (Roth and Fonagy 2005). Moreover, the theory behind SSRIs and SNRIs, that is, the thesis that serotonin deficiencies are the cause of depression, is problematic from a scientific point of view (Healy 2002; Lacasse and Leo 2005).

It is true that psychosocial approaches also exist in medicine. In the previous century, a biopsychosocial model was defended by Engel in a number of seminal publications (Engel 1977, 1980). Many biological psychiatrists in theory affirm a biopsychosocial eclecticism, while focusing in practice on biological aspects of mental diseases. Indeed, biological/pharmacological approaches vastly outstrip psychosocial approaches both in research and in clinical practice (Ghaemi 2006). The fact that biological treatments can be protected with patents only reinforces this bias.

Furthermore, the "bio" part of Engel's model was unfortunately limited to somatic aspects of health and disease. This led to the identification of biological with internal factors and of psychosocial with external factors. However, there is more to biology than disciplines such as anatomy and physiology concerned with the internal workings of our bodies. The discipline of ecology falls by the wayside due to these identifications. For example, influences of diet, infections, and circadian rhythms on mental illnesses are mostly disregarded whereas they should be salient (van der Steen 2008). Recent texts on psychiatry by psychiatrists and scholars from other disciplines keep exhibiting this limitation, even though, in different ways, they are highly critical of existing one-sided biological approaches (Brendel 2006; Murphy 2006; Horwitz and Wakefield 2007; McLaren 2007; Szasz 2007).

5. The Role of Randomized Clinical Trials

The methodology of medical research also shows limitations that privilege drug treatments over other treatments, for example, psychotherapy. The dominant methodology adhered to by evidence-based medicine attributes evidential force especially to RCTs, randomized clinical trials, which are regarded as the golden standard par excellence. RCTs compare effects of drug treatments with effects of placebos, or alternative treatments, with the ideal double-blind set-up which ensures that neither doctors nor patients know who is receiving the target treatment.

RCTs became the ideal set-up after the disaster in the 1950s with thalidomide, a drug that unexpectedly caused birth defects. In the aftermath of the disaster, a dramatic change took place in U.S. health care (Healy 2002, 366–69). Drug therapies came to be regarded as risky, and RCTs became obligatory in 1962 with amendments correcting the 1938 Food and Drug Act. The introduction of RCTs, however well intended, has backfired in deplorable ways (see also J. Brown, this volume, chap. 5). It is indeed true that randomization ensures that a properly conducted RCT is unbiased in that the groups of patients compared differ only in the treatment studied. But this does not imply that other factors are irrelevant. For example, a sample of patients in a drug study from a population suffering from shortages of omega-3 fatty acids in their diets will reveal nothing whatsoever about the etiological role of the shortages (for details, see van der Steen, Ho, and Karmelk 2003).

This is deplorable since Western diets are now generally deficient in particular PUFAs, polyunsaturated fatty acids, omega-3 PUFAs (Simopoulos and Robinson 1999). The diets foster many diseases, psychiatric disorders among them (Parker et al. 2006; Kiecolt-Glaser et al. 2007; Ross 2007). This is easily understood: omega-3 PUFAs are important building blocks of brain tissue and are also a vital constituent of the blood-brain barrier. Indeed, positive effects with these fatty acids have been noticed in psychiatric disorders (van der Steen, Ho, and Karmelk 2003; Frangou, Lewis, and McCrone 2006; Freeman et al. 2006; Sontrop and Campbell 2006).

In addition to fatty acids, vitamins and amino acids are important in mental illnesses. Western diets often exhibit deficiencies not only in omega-3 fatty acids, but also in the vitamins B_{12} and folate, which leads to high concentrations of the amino acid homocysteine. Recent sources indicate that this has implications for the etiology and the treatment of mental illnesses (Bottiglieri 2005; Coppen and Bolander-Gouaille 2005; Sachdev et al. 2005; Abou-Saleh and Coppen 2006; Fraguas et al. 2006; Lerner et al. 2006; Muskiet and Kemperman 2006).

Infections are another area of biology that is sorely neglected in the study and the treatment of mental illnesses. Recent evidence indicates that all sorts of microorganisms and parasites are potentially implicated in the illnesses, for example *Toxoplasma* (Alvarado-Esquivel et al. 2006; Hinze-Selch et al. 2007; Torrey et al. 2007), *Parvovirus* (Hammond and Hobbs 2007), and several species of *Herpes* (Dickerson and Boronow et al. 2006; Dickerson and Kirkpatrick et al. 2006; Torrey et al. 2006; Kim et al. 2007; Prasad et al. 2007), and retroviruses embedded in our genome (Frank et al. 2005). Lyme disease has also been implicated (Fallon and Nields 1994). So has Borna disease virus infection (Bode and Ludwig 2003), but this is controversial (Wolff et al. 2006).

We would hypothesize that the factors of diet and infection, both sorely neglected in mainstream psychiatry, may well be interrelated in some cases, since the immune system is implicated in either case. Impairments of immunity observed in mental illness confirm this (Irwin and Miller 2007; Muller and Schwarz 2006; O'Brien et al. 2006; Strous and Shoenfeld 2006; for a survey, see van der Steen 2008).

To stay healthy, we need a balance between two major classes of cytokines, substances having to do with immunity, with pro-inflammatory and anti-inflammatory roles, respectively. Now omega-3 fatty acids stimulate the anti-inflammatory side of the equation. Hence the common omega-3 deficiencies promote inflammation to an undesirable extent (van der Steen, Ho, and Karmelk 2003). Infections work the same way. The effects of the two factors may thus be mutually reinforcing. Also, omega-3 deficiencies may promote mental illness by enhancing vulnerability to infection. Anyhow, excesses of pro-inflammatory substances have recently been demonstrated in mental illness (Anisman et al. 2005; Pucak and Kaplin 2005; Schiepers, Wichers, and Maes 2005). To our knowledge, potential interrelations among immunity, infection, and diet in mental illness have not been noted before.

In addition to all of this, the impact of biological rhythms, particularly circadian ones, has been sorely neglected in medical research (Halberg et al. 2003). A rhythm is called circadian if, under constant conditions, its period deviates somewhat from the twenty-four-hour period exhibited under normal conditions (for surveys, see Koukkari and Sothern 2006; Refinetti 2006; van der Steen 2008). Considering psychiatry, we note that disturbed circadian rhythms cause particular forms of depression associated with the short-day season. This has been known for centuries, and light therapy is nowadays a helpful treatment. However, few researchers appear to know that the quality of the light we are exposed to determines the ensuing phase shifts of circadian rhythms. To a large extent, the rhythms are generated by the hormone melatonin, which is produced in a particular area of the brain. This hormone is broken down by light at the blue end of the spectrum, if visually perceived by us, not by red light. During the night, melatonin levels increase provided that, if awake, we are exposed to darkness or red light. Now, in cultures in the West, light pollution is a potent source of circadian disruption. This fosters many illnesses, conceivably even cancer (Stevens 2006). Mental illness should also be affected thereby. Indeed, it is conceivable that the use during the night of spectacles using glass with a red tint is in some cases a better option than either medication or psychotherapy for the treatment of mental illnesses (for sources see Koukkari and Sothern 2006).

The impact of circadian rhythms on mental illness is confirmed by the finding that positive effects have been observed in experimental treatments with melatonin derivatives (Den Boer, Bosker, and Meesters 2006; Pandi-Perumal et al. 2006). The role of circadian rhythms is pervasive. Our entire physiology is subject to these rhythms. By implication, the positive and negative effects of all existing treatments depend on the time of the day. The results of experiments in medical science are also subject to time-dependent variations. For example, most parameters of the immune system exhibit such variations (van der Steen and Ho 2006).

Considering drug treatments, evidence indicates that medications ought to be administered at particular moments in recognition of circadian rhythms. In the treatment of cancers, for example, studies demonstrate enhanced effectiveness and reduced toxicity of chemotherapeutics using peak doses at particular times of the day compared with treatments with constant doses (for work on metastatic colorectal cancer, see Levi et al. 1999; Mormont and Levi 2003; additional examples are to be found in Koukkari and Sothern 2006; Refinetti 2006). Furthermore, administration of melatonin enhances cancer treatment outcomes considerably.

This adds to the limitations of RCTs already noted. If the time factor is disregarded in these trials, the results are context-dependent such that their reliability and validity are entirely unknown. Circadian rhythms thus affect medical research both substantively and methodologically, irrespective of funding matters. Intriguingly, the substantive and the methodological limitations of research disregarding the time factor have been charted in an excellent way by a volume published by the National Institute of Mental Health in 1970 (reprinted 2005). As research came to focus on allegedly more fundamental areas such as molecular biology, the old work came to face oblivion in spite of its vital importance for medicine and psychiatry. Now, it would be unreasonable to expect that the pharmaceutical industry pay attention to nutrition, infections, and biological rhythms. Hence, the primary responsibility lies with medical science, which should assimilate areas of elementary biology that have been sorely missing.

RCTs are mostly expensive. So they are generally funded by the industry, which leads to considerable bias. They do not allow for inferences from samples to individual patients (van Os 2005). Nor can they account for variability among patients. These limitations, and many others, have been documented in a recent study published by the American Psychological Association (APA), which subscribes to a highly sophisticated methodology (Goodheart, Kazdin, and Sternberg 2006). The other APA, the American Psychiatric Association, is still under the spell of the more old-fashioned methodology of evidence-based medicine. Unfortunately, both APAs disregard the importance of diet, infections, and circadian rhythms for our mental well-being.

In brief, we are dealing here with a complicated interplay between the substance and the methodology of medical research and agendas promoted by the industry. Substantively, medicine has assimilated a limited area of biology since ecology has mostly been outside the curriculum and outside the main areas of research. Thus food, infections, and biological rhythms have not received the attention these subjects deserve.

Methodologically, this trend is reinforced by the biopsychosocial model, which identifies external factors with psychosocial ones while overlooking the import of external biological factors. All this does play into the hands of the industry, which understandably privileges drug therapies over diet therapies, for example. Unfortunately, attempts to curtail risky impacts of the industry have backfired since they lead to ever more expensive RCTs that have to be financed by the industry.

6. What Should Be Done?

How are we to curb the dominance of drugs within medical treatments, especially of mental disorders, and the dominance of the pharmaceutical industry over medical research? As we have noted, we are dealing here with a complicated interplay between the substance and the methodology of medical research and agendas promoted by the industry. The pharmaceutical industry influences medical practice and medical research so as to promote undue emphasis on drugs in medicine. But apart from this, narrow approaches in medical research that disregard important areas of biology favor treatment with drugs as well. We start with the direct influence of pharmaceutical companies on medical practice.

(1) In section 2, we mentioned different ways in which pharmaceutical companies try to induce physicians to prescribe their drugs. Medical representatives visiting them provide information about new drugs, which should convince them that a particular drug is the best one for the treatment of some disorder (or at least as good as alternatives). The information obviously tends to be biased, and

doctors should know about this. That is why medical representatives will try to influence the views of doctors also in more indirect ways. The general aim would be to establish and maintain a positive reciprocal relationship between the doctor on the one side and the medical representative and his or her company on the other side. Seemingly insignificant gifts provided with free samples of drugs and documentation fit in with this aim, the ideal being that the doctor reciprocates by prescribing the company's drugs. There is sufficient evidence that such visits do influence doctors' prescriptions, even the prescriptions of doctors who are convinced that they make their decisions independently and autonomously (Brody 2007). Medical representatives, in our view, are entirely dispensable as a means to inform doctors about (new) drugs. Many other, more reliable sources of information do exist. We agree with Brody that doctors and their professional organizations should regard accepting small gifts from drug representatives as a violation of their professional integrity (Brody 2007).

Already during their education medical students receive gifts from pharmaceutical companies. Jerome Kassirer, a former editor of the *New England Journal of Medicine,* calls the environment within medical education that promotes the acceptance of representatives and their gifts a "culture of entitlement" (Kassirer 2000; Brody 2007). This may explain why many doctors still find it normal that pharmaceutical companies (co-)finance medical conferences and postacademic education, and, in exchange, have a dominant share in the program. We find it unacceptable that the industry has a dominant share in the program of such activities. Organizers of conferences and postacademic education should refuse a company's money if it demands a say in the program.

Pharmaceutical companies also directly approach the general public; in particular, they cooperate with patient groups. Many patient organizations are subsidized by pharmaceutical companies (Herxheimer 2003). We do not think that this is a good thing. Pharmaceutical companies may, e.g., subtly induce patient organizations to press health insurers for the reimbursement of new drugs that promise a more effective, often more costly, treatment for the health problem they represent. We also pointed to the influence of industry on the writing of guidelines and to the phenomenon of ghostwriters. It is evident that all financial relations between the industry and authors of journal articles or doctors involved in writing guidelines should be disclosed. The problem is that no airtight system exists to check whether information provided by the parties is correct and complete.

The industry also has marked effects on medical research and the medical research agenda. A study by Patsopoulos, Ioannidis, and Analatos (2006) shows that more than 50 percent of the most cited articles published between 1994 and 2003 were about research funded by industry. The percentage funded by industry increased while the amount of money spent by governments and other public institutions on medical research stayed the same. Of the 289 articles cited most, 77 reported on RCTs, 65 of them having been funded by the industry. The proportion of trials funded by the industry increased significantly. Thirty-one of 32 most frequently cited trials published after 1999 were funded by the industry, 18 of them exclusively so. Sixty of the 77 RCTs investigated drugs or biological agents and five considered medical devices and stents. Five trials investigated the efficacy of vitamins, four hormone replacement therapies, two lifestyle changes, and one a surgical intervention (Patsopoulos et al. 2006).

(2) In section 3 we showed that the dominant role of pharmaceutical industries within medical research inevitably leads to biases. (Financial) interests have an impact on problem selection, the dissemination of research results, and the development and implementation of protocols. The problem of unintended and covert research bias cannot be tackled by regulation and by promoting virtues of academic integrity. Here the limits of traditional research ethics become visible. What is needed is a change in the structure of the financing of medical research. We mention two proposals that are worth considering. We start with a proposal by Resnik that consists of two elements. First, government funding is needed to counterbalance private funding. If a pharmaceutical company sponsors a study on a new drug, the government should also sponsor research on that drug to help ensure a proper balance between positive and negative outcomes. Second, adequate scientific and public input should bear on government funding decisions. Public input is needed to ensure that the financial and professional interests of a small group of researchers do not dominate the entire funding process (Resnik 2000, 278; see also Resnik, this volume, chap. 4).

Resnik's proposal calls for a substantial increase of government funding of medical research. Some would hold that it is unrealistic to expect that governments will act in accordance with this. Indeed, existing trends appear to be in the opposite direction. However, more insight into the biological items we mentioned could lead to the recognition that the envisaged new treatments are less costly than drug treatments or psychotherapy. Thus, a (temporary) increase of public funds for medical research might result in a decrease of the costs of medical care for mentally ill persons.

The second proposal, by Soleto, involves the creation of a Collegiate Research Council (CRC) to be jointly appointed by leading academic institutions. This committee would be certified by the appropriate health authorities, such as, in the United States, the U.S. Food and Drug Administration, or equivalent authorities in other countries. The CRC would be the only recipient of a research protocol related to the clinical testing of a drug: the pharmaceutical company or contract research organization must submit the protocol to the CRC. The CRC would define the costs of the project, including the salaries of the scientific staff involved and appropriate compensation for the institutional review boards and for the CRC. The CRC would select the optimal investigators and institutions based on their expertise, prestige, and independence, and would offer, without the participation of the pharmaceutical company, to conduct the trial. In this way, the "sponsor" of the trial would be the CRC, not the pharmaceutical company (Soleto 2006).

The current discussion on the financing of medical research largely focuses on the system of financing drug research through patent monopolies. Some authors argue that the system of patent-based development of drugs is undesirable and inefficient (e.g., Baker 2004). Others hold that abolishing the system of patent monopolies does not provide the optimal solution for the problems surrounding the patent-based development of drugs. Barton and Emanuel (2005) plead for complementing the patent-based system with policies such as "tiered pricing" systems (having higher drug prices in developed countries and lower prices in developing countries), "buy-out" pricing systems whereby a company gets a cash bonus of public money for the estimated profits from monopoly prices, and targeted public funding of drugs that are of great societal value.

Several alternatives to the patent system are discussed in Baker (2004). We are not competent to judge whether a solution of the current problems requires abolishing or complementing the patent-based development of drugs. Above all, we want to stress that the importance of drug research is overrated by biological psychiatrists. Decisions about abolishing or complementing the system of patent-based development of drugs should be informed by a view on the financing of medical research as a whole, including the areas of biology that are still neglected.

The policies recommended by Resnik are relevant for countering biases within drug research, but not for overcoming the bias within medicine toward drug research. Risks of biases within drug research are only part of the problem. Additional bias is caused by narrow biological approaches that cannot be redressed by the industry. These approaches foster the erroneous view that drugs and psychotherapies represent an exhaustive dichotomy. We have indicated that many more possibilities exist, to wit: omega-3 fatty acids, particular vitamins, treatments boosting the immune system, and the use of proper light and other measures to redress circadian rhythms that are out of phase. These items are mostly disregarded now.

The dominance of biological approaches is also reflected in the education of psychiatrists. In the Netherlands, the Platform for Psychotherapy and Psychiatry, a section of the Dutch Society for Psychiatry and Neurology, holds that psychotherapeutic approaches are underrepresented in the training of psychiatrists. Still less attention exists for ecological factors such as food, infections, and circadian rhythms. The structure and the content of the training of psychiatrists are in need of revision. As we indicated, the existing emphasis is overmuch on biology, which leads to a morally problematic materialist and reductionist view of human nature and a suboptimal treatment of mental illness in the wake of this. At the same time, we need more biology as important areas of this science are virtually disregarded in psychiatry. Now, it is anything but easy to find out about disregarded areas. Unconnected literatures are common since nobody can oversee the huge amounts of literature produced. Indeed, more than two million articles are published yearly in medicine alone. No specialist is able to deal with this in an adequate way. Hence, it seems to us, we need to establish a curriculum aiming at the education of generalist researchers whose task would be the creation of bridges among existing disciplines rather than the addition of new data to knowledge within any particular discipline. Generalists should help us get acquainted, individually, with the gist of collective knowledge. This is a prerequisite for adequate problem selection in science, pure and applied.

Conclusion

We questioned the prominent role of drugs in the treatment of mental illnesses that is favored both by the influence of pharmaceutical industry within medicine and health care and the widespread currency among psychiatrists of unduly narrow biological approaches. Pharmaceutical companies continuously try to induce doctors to prescribe their drugs, and the public to ask for their drugs. They do so through advertisements at times at odds with science, visits to doctors, subsidies for medical conferences, postacademic educational activities for doctors, patient organizations, and so on.

The influence of the pharmaceutical industry on medical practice should be drastically curtailed. Its influence is also visible within medical research. Most of the drug research is funded by pharmaceutical companies. Even if the industry abstained from intentionally trying to influence research, research sponsored by pharmaceutical companies would unavoidably induce biases. To counter research bias, drug research should no longer be funded directly by the industry, or at least be counterbalanced by research funded by governments.

Undue emphasis on drugs is enhanced as well by medical and psychiatric research as such, due to its widespread but narrow biological approaches to mental illness. We plead that more public money be invested into research of neglected items from biology, such as treatments with omega-3 fatty acids and particular vitamins, treatments boosting the immune system, and the use of proper light and other measures to redress circadian rhythms that are out of phase. If these things were taken care of in integrative research, we could end up with a decreased need of public funding for medicine and health care. However, more is needed to arrive at truly integrative research. For integration to succeed, we need to know about areas in need of integration. This calls for generalist approaches in medical education and research.

REFERENCES

Abou-Saleh, M. T., and A. Coppen. 2006. "Folic acid and the treatment of depression." *Journal of Psychosomatic Research* 61 (3): 285–87.

Alvarado-Esquivel, C., O. P. Alanis-Quiñones, M. A. Arreola-Valenzuela, A. Rodríguez-Briones, L. J. Piedra-Nevarez, E. Duran-Morales, S. Estrada-Martínez, S. A. Martínez-García, and O. Liesenfeld. 2006. "Seroepidemiology of *Toxoplasma gondii* infection in psychiatric inpatients in a northern Mexican city." *BMC Infectious Diseases* 6:178.

Angell, M. 2004. *The truth about the drug companies: How they deceive us and what to do about it.* New York: Random House.

Anisman, H., Z. Merali, M. O. Poulter, and S. Hayley. 2005. "Cytokines as a precipitant of depressive illness: Animal and human studies." *Current Pharmaceutical Design* 11:963–72.

Arrow, K. 1962. "Economic welfare and the allocation of resources for intervention." In *The rate and direction of inventive activity: Economic and social factors,* ed. R. Nelson, 609–26. Princeton, NJ: Princeton University Press.

Baker, J. 2004. "Financing drugs research: What are the issues?" http://www.cepr.net/ publications/intellectual_property_2004_09.htm. Accessed on March 3, 2007.

Barton, J. H., and E. J. Emanuel. 2005. "The patents-based pharmaceutical development process: Rationale, problems, and potential reforms." *Journal of the American Medical Association* 294:2075–82.

Bekelman, J. E., Y. Li, and C. P. Cross. 2001. "Scope and impact of financial conflicts of interest in biomedical research: A systematic review." *Journal of the American Medical Association* 289:454–65.

Bode, L., and H. Ludwig. 2003. "Borna disease virus infection, a human mental-health risk." *Clinical Microbiology Reviews* 16:534–45.

Bottiglieri, T. 2005. "Homocysteine and folate metabolism in depression." *Progress in Neuropsychopharmacology and Biological Psychiatry* 29:1103–12.

Bouma, J. 2006. *Slikken: Hoe ziek is de farmaceutische industrie?* Amsterdam: L. J. Veen.

Boyle, M. 2002. *Schizophrenia: A scientific delusion?* Hove, East Sussex: Routledge (second print).

Braslow, J. T. 2000. "Therapeutics and the history of psychiatry." *Bulletin of the History of Medicine* 74:794–802.

Brendel, D. H. 2006. *Healing psychiatry: Bridging the science/humanism divide.* Cambridge, MA: MIT Press.

Brody, H. 2007. *Hooked: Ethics, the medical profession, and the pharmaceutical industry.* Lanham, MD: Rowman and Littlefield.

Coppen, A., and C. Bolander-Gouaille. 2005. "Treatment of depression: Time to consider folic acid and vitamin B$_{12}$." *Journal of Psychopharmacology* 19 (1): 59–65.

Cowen, T., ed. 1988. *The theory of market failure: A critical evaluation.* Fairfax, VA: George Mason University Press.

Dasgupta, D., and P. David. 1994. "Toward a new economy of science." *Policy Research* 23:478–521.

Den Boer, J. A., F. J. Bosker, and Y. Meesters. 2006. "Clinical efficacy of agomelatine in depression: The evidence." *International Clinical Psychopharmacology* 21, Supplement 1: S21–S24.

Dickerson, F. B., J. J. Boronow, C. Stallings, A. E. Origoni, S. Cole, F. Leister, B. Krivogorsky, and R. H. Yolken. 2006. "The catechol O-methyltransferase Val158Met polymorphism and herpes simplex virus type 1 infection are risk factors for cognitive impairment in bipolar disorder: Additive gene-environmental effects in a complex human psychiatric disorder." *Bipolar Disorder* 8 (2): 124–32.

Dickerson, F., B. Kirkpatrick, J. Boronow, C. Stallings, A. Origoni, and R. Yolken. 2006. "Deficit schizophrenia: Association with serum antibodies to cytomegalovirus." *Schizophrenia Bulletin* 32:396–400.

Engel, G. L. 1977. "The need for a new medical model: A challenge for biomedicine." *Science* 196:129–36.

———. 1980. "The clinical application of the biopsychosocial model." *American Journal of Psychiatry* 137 (6): 535–44.

Fallon, B. A., and J. A. Nields. 1994. "Lyme disease: A neuropsychiatric illness." *American Journal of Psychiatry* 151:1571–83.

Fraguas, R., Jr., G. I. Papakostas, D. Mischoulon, T. Bottiglieri, J. Alpert, and M. Fava. 2006. "Anger attacks in major depressive disorder and serum levels of homocysteine." *Biological Psychiatry* 60 (3): 270–74.

Frangou, S., M. Lewis, and P. McCrone. 2006. "Efficacy of ethyl-eicosapentaenoic acid in bipolar depression: Randomised double-blind placebo-controlled study." *British Journal of Psychiatry* 188:46–50.

Frank, O., M. Giehl, C. Zheng, R. Hehlmann, C. Leib-Mösch, and W. Seifarth. 2005. "Human endogenous retrovirus expression profiles in samples from brains of patients with schizophrenia and bipolar disorders." *Virology* 79:890–901.

Freeman, M. P., J. R. Hibbeln, K. L. Wisner, J. M. Davis, D. Mischoulon, M. Peet, P. E. Keck Jr., L. B. Marangell, A. J. Richardson, J. Lake, and A. L. Stoll. 2006. "Omega-3 fatty acids: Evidence basis for treatment and future research in psychiatry." *Journal of Clinical Psychiatry* 67:1954–67.

Ghaemi, S. N. 2006. "Paradigms of psychiatry: Eclecticism and its discontents." *Current Opinions in Psychiatry* 19:619–24.

Goodheart, C. D., A. E. Kazdin, and R. J. Sternberg, eds. 2006. *Evidence-based psychotherapy: Where practice and research meet.* Washington, DC: American Psychological Association.

Halberg, F., G. Cornélissen, G. Katinas, E. V. Syutkina, R. B. Sothern, R. Zaslavskaya,

F. Halberg, Y. Watanabe, O. Schwartzkopff, K. Otsuka, R. Tarquini, P. Frederico, and J. Siggelova. 2003. "Transdisciplinary unifying implications of circadian findings in the 1950s." *Journal of Circadian Rhythms* 1:2. http://www.JCircadianRhythms.com/content/1/1/2.

Hammond, C. J., and J. A. Hobbs. 2007. "Parvovirus B19 infection of brain: Possible role of gender in determining mental illness and autoimmune thyroid disorders." *Medical Hypotheses* 69 (1): 113–16.

Healy, D. 2002. *The creation of psychopharmacology.* Cambridge, MA: Harvard University Press.

———. 2004. *Let them eat Prozac: The unhealthy relationship between the pharmaceutical industry and depression.* New York: New York University Press.

Herxheimer, A. 2003. "Relationships between the pharmaceutical industry and patients' organisations." *British Medical Journal* 326:1208–10.

Hinze-Selch, D., W. Däubener, L. Eggert, S. Erdag, R. Stoltenberg, and S. Wilms. 2007. "A controlled prospective study of *Toxoplasma gondii* infection in individuals with schizophrenia: Beyond seroprevalence." *Schizophrenia Bulletin* 33:782–88.

Horwitz, A. V., and J. C. Wakefield. 2007. *The loss of sadness: How psychiatry transformed normal sorrow into depressive disorder.* Oxford: Oxford University Press.

Irwin, M. R., and A. H. Miller. 2007. "Depressive disorders and immunity: Twenty years of progress and discovery." *Brain, Behavior and Immunity* 21:374–83.

Joseph, J. 2003. *The gene illusion: Genetic research in psychiatry and psychology under the microscope.* Ross-on-Wye: PCCS Books.

Kassirer, J. P. 2000. "A piece of my mind: Financial indigestion." *Journal of the American Medical Association* 284:2156–57.

Kiecolt-Glaser, J. K., M. A. Belury, K. Porter, D. Q. Beversdorf, S. Lemeshow, and R. Glaser. 2007. "Depressive symptoms, omega-6: omega-3 fatty acids, and inflammation in older adults." *Psychosomatic Medicine* 69 (3): 217–24.

Kim, J. J., B. H. Shirts, M. Dayal, S. A. Bacanu, J. Wood, W. Xie, X. Zhang, K. V. Chowdari, R. Yolken, B. Devlin, and V. L. Nimgaonkar. 2007. "Are exposure to cytomegalovirus and genetic variation on chromosome 6p joint risk factors for schizophrenia?" *American Medicine* 39 (2): 145–53.

Koninklijke Nederlandse Akademie van Wetenschappen (Royal Dutch Academy of Arts and Sciences). 2005. *Wetenschap op bestelling: Over de omgang van wetenschappelijke onderzoekers met hun opdrachtgevers.* Amsterdam.

Koukkari, W. L., and R. B. Sothern. 2006. *Introducing biological rhythms.* New York: Springer.

Krimsky, S. 2003. *Science in the private interest: Has the lure of profits corrupted biomedical research?* Lanham, MD: Rowman and Littlefield.

Lacasse, J. R., and J. Leo. 2005. "Serotonin and depression: A disconnect between the advertisements and the scientific literature." *PloS Medicine* 2 (12). doi: 10.1371/journal.pmed.0020393.

Lerner, V., M. Kanevsky, T. Dwolatzky, R. Rouach, R. Kamin, and C. Miodownik. 2006. "Vitamin B$_{12}$ and folate serum levels in newly admitted psychiatric patients." *Clinical Nutrition* 25 (1): 60–67.

Levi, F., R. Zidani, S. Brienza, L. Dogliotti, B. Perpoint, M. Rotarski, Y. Letourneau, J. F. Llory, P. Chollet, A. Le Rol, C. Focan. 1999. "A multicenter evaluation of intensified, ambulatory, chronomodulated chemotherapy with oxaliplatin, 5-fluorouracil, and leucovorin as initial treatment of patients with metastatic colorectal carcinoma." International Organization for Cancer Chronotherapy. *Cancer* 85:2532–40.

Lewis, B. 2006. *Moving beyond Prozac, DSM, and the new psychiatry: The birth of post-psychiatry.* Michigan: The University of Michigan Press.

Longino, H. 1990. *Science as social knowledge.* Princeton, NJ: Princeton University Press.

McLaren, N. 2007. *Humanizing madness: Psychiatry and the cognitive neurosciences.* Ann Arbor, MI: Future Psychiatry Press (imprint of Loving Healing Press).

Medawar, C., and A. Hardon. 2004. *Medicines out of control? Antidepressants and the conspiracy of goodwill.* Amsterdam: Aksant.

Mormont, M. C., and F. Levi. 2003. "Cancer chronotherapy: Principles, applications, and perspectives." *Cancer* 97:155–69.

Moynihan, R., and A. Cassells. 2005. *Drug companies are turning us all into patients.* Crows Nest: Allen and Unwin.

Muller, N., and M. Schwarz. 2006. "Schizophrenia as an inflammation-mediated dysbalance of glutamatergic neurotransmission." *Neurotoxicity Research* 10 (2): 131–48.

Murphy, D. 2006. *Psychiatry in the scientific image.* Cambridge, MA: MIT Press.

Muskiet, F. A., and R. F. Kemperman. 2006. "Folate and long-chain polyunsaturated fatty acids in psychiatric disease." *Journal of Nutritional Biochemistry* 17:717–27.

National Institute of Mental Health. 2005. *Biological rhythms in psychiatry and medicine.* Honolulu: University Press of the Pacific (reprint, original edition 1970).

Nelson, B. 1982. "Psychiatry's anxious years: Decline in allure; as a career leads to its self-examination." *New York Times,* November 2, C1.

O'Brien, S. M., P. Scully, L. V. Scott, and T. G. Dinan. 2006. "Cytokine profiles in bipolar affective disorder: Focus on acutely ill patients." *Journal of Affective Disorders* 90 (2–3): 263–67.

O'Neill, J. 1998. *The market: Ethics, knowledge and politics.* London: Routledge.

Pandi-Perumal, S. R., V. Srinivasan, D. P. Cardinali, and M. J. Monti. 2006. "Could agomelatine be the ideal antidepressant?" *Expert Review of Neurotherapeutics* 6:1595–1608.

Parker, G., N. A. Gibson, H. Brotchie, G. Heruc, A. M. Rees, and D. Hadzi-Pavlovic. 2006. "Omega-3 fatty acids and mood disorders." *American Journal of Psychiatry* 163:969–78.

Patsopoulos, N. A., J. P. Ioannidis, and A. A. Analatos. 2006. "Origin and funding of the most frequently cited papers in medicine: A database analysis." *British Medical Journal* 332:1061–64.

Platform for Psychotherapy and Psychiatry. http://www.nvvp.net.

Prasad, K. M., B. H. Shirts, R. H. Yolken, M. S. Keshavan, and V. L. Nimgaonkar. 2007. "Brain morphological changes associated with exposure to HSV1 in first-episode schizophrenia." *Molecular Psychiatry* 12 (1): 105–13.

Pucak, M. L., and A. I. Kaplin. 2005. "Unkind cytokines: Current evidence for the potential role of cytokines in immune-mediated depression." *International Review of Psychiatry* 17:477–83.

Refinetti, R. 2006. *Circadian physiology.* 2nd ed. Boca Raton: CRC Press.

Resnik, D. B. 1998. "Conflicts of interest." *Perspectives on Science* 6:381–408.

———. 2000. "Financial interests and research bias." *Perspectives on Science* 8:255–85.

Ross, B. M. 2007. "Omega-3 fatty acid deficiency in major depressive disorder is caused by the interaction between diet and a genetically determined abnormality in phospholipid metabolism." *Medical Hypotheses* 68:515–24.

Roth, A., and P. Fonagy, eds. 2005. *What works for whom? A critical review of psychotherapy research.* 2nd ed. New York: The Guilford Press.

Sachdev, P. S., R. A. Parslow, O. Lux, C. Salonikas, W. Wen, D. Naidoo, H. Christensen, and A. F. Jorm. 2005. "Relationship of homocysteine, folic acid and vitamin B$_{12}$ with depression in a middle-aged community sample." *Psychological Medicine* 35:529–38.

Schiepers, O. J., M. C. Wichers, and M. Maes. 2005. "Cytokines and major depression." *Progress in Neuropsychopharmacology and Biological Psychiatry* 29:201–17.

Simopoulos, A. P., and J. Robinson. 1999. *The omega diet: The lifesaving nutritional program based on the diet of the island of Crete*. New York: HarperCollins.

Sismondo, S. 2007. "Ghost management: How much of the medical literature is shaped behind the scenes by the pharmaceutical industry." *PLoS Med* 4 (9). doi: 10.1371/journal.pmed.0040286.

Soleto, J. 2006. "Regulation of clinical research sponsored by pharmaceutical companies: A proposal." *PLoS Medicine* 3 (7). doi: 101371/journal.pmed.0030606.

Sontrop, J., and M. K. Campbell. 2006. "Omega-3 polyunsaturated fatty acids and depression: A review of the evidence and a methodological critique." *Preventive Medicine* 42 (1): 4–13.

Stevens, R. G. 2006. "Artificial lighting in the industrialized world: Circadian disruption and breast cancer." *Cancer Causes Control* 17:501–7.

Strous, R. D., and Y. Shoenfeld. 2006. "Schizophrenia, autoimmunity and immune system dysregulation: A comprehensive model updated and revisited." *Journal of Autoimmunity* 27 (2): 71–80.

Szasz, T. 2007. *Coercion as cure: A critical history of psychiatry*. New Brunswick, NJ: Transaction.

Torrey, E. F., M. F. Leweke, M. J. Schwarz, N. Mueller, S. Bachmann, J. Schroeder, F. Dickerson, and R. H. Yolken. 2006. "Cytomegalovirus and schizophrenia." *CNS Drugs* 20:879–85.

Torrey, E. F., J. J. Bartko, Z. R. Lun, and R. H. Yolken. 2007. "Antibodies to *Toxoplasma gondii* in patients with schizophrenia: A meta-analysis." *Schizophrenia Bulletin* 33:729–36.

van der Steen, W. J. 1995. *Facts, values, and methodology: A new approach to ethics*. Amsterdam: Rodopi.

———. 1999. "Bias in behavior genetics: An ecological perspective." *Acta Biotheoretica* 46:369–77.

———. 2003. "Assessing overmedication: Biology, philosophy and common sense." *Acta Biotheoretica* 51:151–71.

———. 2008. *Nieuwe wegen voor de geneeskunde*. Amsterdam: SWP.

van der Steen, W. J., and V. K. Y. Ho. 2001. "Drugs versus diets: Disillusions with Dutch health care." *Acta Biotheoretica* 49:125–40.

———. 2006. "Diets and circadian rhythms: Challenges from biology for medicine." *Acta Biotheoretica* 54:267–75.

van der Steen, W. J., V. K. Y. Ho, and F. J. Karmelk. 2003. *Beyond boundaries of biomedicine: Pragmatic perspectives on health and disease*. Amsterdam: Rodopi.

Van Os, J. 2005. "Verzamelen en interpreteren: De wetenschappelijke waarde van epidemiologisch onderzoek in de psychiatrie." In *Hoe wetenschappelijk is de psychiatrie?* ed. J. De Kroon, 49–65. Antwerpen: Garant.

Wolff, T., G. Heins, G. Pauli, R. Burger, and R. Kurth. 2006. "Failure to detect Borna disease virus antigen and RNA in human blood." *Journal of Clinical Virology* 36:309–11.

Wyatt, W. J. 2006. "Biological psychiatry: A practice in search of a science." *Behavior and Social Issues* 15:132–51.

CHAPTER 7

The Commodification of Knowledge Exchange

GOVERNING THE CIRCULATION OF BIOLOGICAL DATA

Sabina Leonelli

1. Introduction

PHILOSOPHERS OF SCIENCE tend to focus their attention on the conditions under which scientific knowledge is produced and applied. This chapter considers instead the conditions under which knowledge is *exchanged* in science, with particular attention to the boom in bioinformatic resources characterizing contemporary biology and medicine. I show how the ongoing commodification of the life sciences affects the ways in which data are circulated across research contexts. The necessity for scientists to develop ways to communicate with one another and build on one another's work constitutes a powerful argument against at least some forms of privatization of data for commercial purposes.

Science exists in its current form thanks largely to the modes of open communication and collaboration elaborated by scientists and their patrons (be they monarchs, churches, states, or private institutions) throughout the centuries. As "big science" research blossoms and expands,[1] the traditional modes through which scientific knowledge is shared are replaced by digital communication technologies, such as databases available through the Internet, that can cope with the increasing amounts and complexity of the data being exchanged, as well as with the uncertainty about the value of some types of data as evidence.[2] The regulation of data circulation across geographical locations and disciplines is in the hands of the private and public sponsors of these databases. My analysis focuses on the contrast between the strategies and values hitherto supported by the public and private sectors in governing data circulation. Both sectors have strong reasons to welcome the commodification of biology—more often referred to as "translation" —as a desirable development. However, they maintain different perspectives on the procedures best suited to achieving a commodified science. Ultimately, public institutions favor the development of tools for making data travel efficiently across the multifaceted community of life scientists, thus fostering the advancement of biological research. By contrast, the values endorsed by the private sector have hitherto proved harmful to the open exchange of knowledge that is vital to the development of future research. Science can only be enriched by the R&D efforts of private sponsors if data produced in that context are made accessible to any biologist that might need to consult them—a reality that biotech and pharmaceutical companies are slowly coming to terms with, but are not yet acting upon.

The structure of the chapter is as follows. I start by highlighting the importance of disseminating data in biology at a time when biological research is characterized by the massive production of data of various types. After introducing the field of bioinformatics and its role in creating tools to store and diffuse data, I consider the contrast between the regulatory policies for data circulation that are supported by private and public sponsors of databases, such as the corporate giant Monsanto on the one hand and the National Science Foundation on the other. I focus particularly on the regulatory tools characterizing the public governance of data exchange. In this context, regulation is geared toward what I call "resource-driven competition": competition used as a mechanism to create resources through which research methods and procedures can be improved. By contrast, private sponsors are driven by the need to obtain profitable products in the quickest and least collaborative way. Their management of data exchange, which I refer to as "product-driven competition," is geared toward the fast-track creation of new entities or processes by any means available. This instrumentalist approach is context specific and short term, and as a consequence there is no significant investment in tools or techniques that would enhance the usability of data *in the long run.*

With this analysis in mind, I consider the three stages through which data are shared: (1) *disclosure* by scientists who have produced the data; (2) *circulation* through digital databases; and (3) *retrieval* from databases by scientists seeking information relevant to their own research purposes. I discuss how each of these stages is affected by the private and public regulatory approaches to knowledge exchange. I conclude that the values and methodological criteria imposed by privately sponsored research have a disruptive impact on all three stages of data circulation. In the long term, the resulting inability of researchers to build on one another's work could be damaging to both science and society.

2. Disseminating Data in Biomedical Research

Even a committed Kuhnian will find it hard to deny that science is, at its heart, a cumulative process. This is particularly true when we focus not on the concepts and theories that scientists produce and sometimes discard, but on the results that they achieve in the course of their experiments. I am talking about *data,* that ultimate mark of the measurements undertaken in (and often also outside) the laboratory to document features and attributes of a natural process or entity. Bogen and Woodward have pointed to the relative independence of data production from claims about phenomena. As they put it, "we need to distinguish what theories explain (phenomena or facts about phenomena) from what is uncontroversially observable (data)" (1988, 314). In biology, typical examples of data are the measured positions of gene markers on a chromosome (fig. 7.1) and the scattered dots indicating gene expression levels in a microarray cluster (fig. 7.2).

My epistemological starting point here is the Duhemian intuition underlying Bogen and Woodward's view: data can be used as evidence for a variety of scientific claims, depending on a scientist's theoretical framework, expertise, commitments, and goals. For example, a geneticist working on fruit-fly metabolism can use measurements of the level of expression of specific genes in particular conditions (as in fig. 7.2) to inform claims such as "gene cluster X is expressed as an enzyme affecting the metabolic cycle of *Drosophila melanogaster*." Bogen and Woodward focus their discussion on the use of data as evidence for claims about phenomena. They stress the locality of data, that is, the extent to which they are idiosyncratic products of a specific experimental setting at a particular time.[3] While respecting the idea that the experimental context in which data are produced is crucial to their interpretation *as evidence for a new claim* (a point to which I will come back several times below), I wish to emphasize a different property of data that emerges when data are circulated across research contexts. This property is

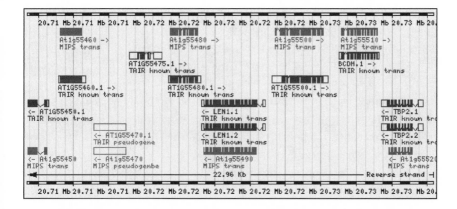

Fig. 7.1. The gene markers on a chromosome (represented by the dashed black lines at the top and bottom margins of the image), detected by various investigators. *Courtesy of the Munich Information Centre for Protein Sequence.*

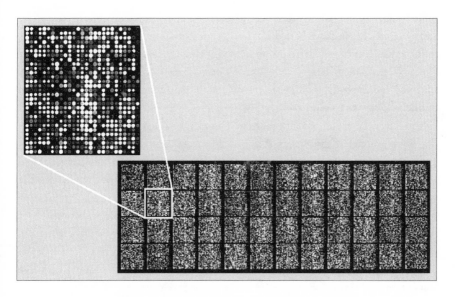

Fig. 7.2. The dots visible in the enlarged section of this microarray cluster represent the expression levels of specific genes in a particular region of a chromosome.

the relative independence of data from specific theoretical or even experimental frameworks, and it manifests itself in the context of data circulation rather than data production or use.

When researchers pass their data to one another, data are taken to speak for themselves. The results of measurements and observations are relied upon as incontrovertible facts, independent of their "local" origins. The quality and reliability of data, and thus the conditions under which they were produced, are critically scrutinized and possibly disputed only when data have already been appropriated by a new research context: that is, when they are used as evidence for new claims about phenomena. When data travel across scientific communities, it is their neutral value as "records" of phenomena that counts (and that makes them travel widely, so to speak).[4] In that context, data are everything but local. They can be and indeed are successfully transferred across different research contexts in biology. Indeed, experimental biologists tend to trust data more than they trust theories and models, and are, as a consequence, deeply concerned with finding ways to facilitate data circulation across disciplinary, institutional, and geographical boundaries.

There is no predicting the extent to which each available dataset might contribute to understanding the complex structure of living organisms. It is therefore of paramount importance that existing data can be put to as many uses in as many contexts as researchers deem necessary. Contemporary biologists are gathering massive amounts of data about organisms (including data about all their "omics": genomics, metabolomics, proteomics, transcriptomics, etc.). This is done through increasingly sophisticated instruments and techniques, such as shotgun sequencing for genomics, which allows the whole sequence of a relatively complex organism to be compiled in a matter of weeks; or microarray experiments, collecting hundreds of thousands of data points documenting gene expression levels in a specific cell culture (as in fig. 7.2). Further, the number of organisms studied to this level of detail is getting larger by the day. This richness of data is both the strength and the curse of contemporary life science. It is a strength insofar as it promises to inform hitherto unthinkable levels of understanding and control over living organisms. Biologists are succeeding in producing genetically engineered modifications of plants and animals at an astonishing rate; further, attempts to construct in silico organisms from scratch are under way and no longer look like the material of loony science fiction. Yet, these developments are only possible if biologists can take advantage of the ocean of data produced by the thousands of laboratories involved. This is where the curse emerges, for assembling tools and procedures through which all produced data can be stored and easily retrieved proves a daunting task.

For a start, there are considerable technical challenges. Consider the sheer size of the datasets being produced by researchers all over the globe about almost any aspect of the biology of organisms—billions of new data points every year. Further, there is the high variability in data types and formats, which makes it difficult to group them all together. And last but not least, there is the high degree of disunification characterizing biology as a whole. Philosophers of science have long been aware that biology is fragmented in countless subdisciplines and epistemic cultures, each of which endorses its own, project-specific combination of instruments, models, and background knowledge.[5] All these communities study the same small set of organisms, commonly referred to as "model organisms,"[6] so as to understand their complex biology. At the same time, what each community means by "understanding" depends on the specificity of its research interests and resources. Each group or individual in biology wants to be able to search other researchers' datasets in order to quickly discover whether data produced by others can be relevant to their own project.

This situation makes the search for tools to circulate data into the holy grail of contemporary biology. Researchers need efficient ways to exchange datasets with biologists working in other research contexts, without, however, losing time and focus on their own specific project and goals. Bioinformatics is the biological field devoted to tackling this need. The idea is to exploit developments in information and communication technologies so as to build *databases* "smart" enough to store data and transmit them through the Internet to whoever might need them. This strategy has hitherto been extremely successful, with databases steadily increasing their size, numbers, and popularity, and funding for bioinformatics acquiring priority over the development of other biological resources. Some of the most successful databases host data about specific model organisms. The Arabidopsis Information Resource (TAIR), for instance, brings thousands of different types of data gathered on the flowering plant *Arabidopsis thaliana* under the same virtual roof and facilitates access to that information through user-friendly search engines and apposite visualization tools. Other databases focus on data concerning the same level of organization of organisms (for example, Reactome gathers available data on biological pathways) and allow researchers to compare datasets derived from different organisms (the Munich Information Protein Service, or MIPS, enables comparisons between sequences of rice, *Arabidopsis,* maize, tomato, and various other plants; The Institute for Genomic Research, or TIGR, allows for cross-examinations of functional genomics data in humans, mice, and several species of plants, microbes, and fungi).[7]

I already remarked on the trust that researchers tend to grant to data as "indisputable facts." In fact, displaying trust in data coming from other research contexts is a matter of necessity. Within the competitive context of cutting-edge biology, short-term projects earn the highest rewards; researchers have quite literally no time to check on data produced by someone else unless this is made unavoidable by questions, problems, or discrepancies emerging in the course of applying those data to resolving new issues. Databases respond to this situation by incorporating some standards for format and quality control over data. In practice, this responsibility falls on the curators who develop and maintain databases. They are deciding on issues such as which datasets are circulated and which background information is included on their provenance (protocols, instruments, and materials used in producing them); the standards used to share data, such as the format used to publish and compare data of the same type; and the technical means (software, visualization tools) by which data are circulated.

3. Regulating Data Travels: The Public and the Private Sector

Before addressing these technical hurdles in more detail, it is important to note that resolving technical difficulties is not the only challenge faced by curators. Biologists devoting their efforts to facilitating data exchange need to confront the contemporary regulatory context for scientific collaboration, which is strongly affected by the need to translate the results of basic research into commodities of use to society at large. In its broadest sense, commodification is of course constitutive of scientific research. For science to remain a viable and socially relevant enterprise, the value of scientific discoveries needs to be evaluated not only through epistemic criteria, but also through social and economic ones. Using science toward the development of new commodities (or the bettering of old ones) is one important way in which scientific understanding informs our capability to interact with the world. The push to commodify research becomes problematic only when epistemic and social criteria are neglected in favor of purely economic considerations.

I hardly need to point out the commercial significance of constructing efficient means for distributing information across biology. Future developments in biomedical research depend heavily on how data are managed and on who controls the flow of information across research contexts. At stake is the future of "red" biotechnology (medical applications of biological research) as well as "green" bio-technology (production of genetically modified organisms for agricultural purposes). Both pharmaceutical companies and agricultural corporations have become heavily involved in basic research on model organisms, precisely because such research yields knowledge about how to intervene on plants and animals in ways seen as desirable to potential customers. These same industries have long sought to acquire exclusive control over the flow of data produced through their research and development efforts, in the hope to use those results to develop commercially interesting results faster than their competitors. Around 70 percent of green bio-technology research is officially in the hands of the private sector. Academic research is following in the same path, as it becomes increasingly tied to the private sector and driven by the necessity to produce marketable goods. The public sector is pushing biologists to pursue research with obvious biotechnological applications. Research projects aimed at acquiring knowledge of basic biological mechanisms are weeded out, as long as they do not guarantee to yield profitable applications within a short period of time.

One crucial factor in understanding the impact of profit-driven ambitions on biological research is the role played by the sponsors of such research in the governance of science. Both public and private agencies play a pivotal role in the regulation of the means through which data are distributed across research communities.[8] Not only do sponsors allocate the material resources necessary to the development of bioinformatics, but they also act as governing bodies over processes of data circulation. Their economic (and in the case of public institutions, political) power is taken to legitimize their role as legislators over goals, strategies, and rules adopted by databases. Database curators are not at liberty to decide who has the right to consult the database and use data therein stored. Nor can they determine the goals and procedures to be followed in storing and circulating data. Sponsors take upon themselves the responsibility of making those decisions.

Who are these sponsors? On the corporate side, we have giant industries such as Monsanto, Syngenta, GlaxoSmithKline, and giant biotechnology and pharmaceutical corporations with extensive R&D facilities. These companies maintain databases for all their research output. Further, there is a boom in smaller companies providing specialized services to data producers and curators. Affymetrix©, for instance, is the most popular company assisting the production of microarray data, which are now the main source of information about gene expression outside of the nucleus. As I already remarked, universities are now closely aligned with the interests of these various companies, since most of their staff is involved in contract research in some way or another.[9] Remarkably, this is one of the reasons universities do not play a decisive role in the regulation and development of bio-informatics efforts. This regulatory power is assigned either to the companies owning rights on the data being produced or to the government funding agencies that sponsor the development of databases.

The most active public institutions allocating funding to bioinformatics are the National Science Foundation (NSF) and the National Institute of Health (NIH) in the United States; the European Union (EU); and national funding agencies around the world such as the Biotechnology and Biological Sciences Research Council (BBSRC) in Britain, the German Federal Ministry of Education, Research, and Technology, and the Ministry of Education, Science, Sport, and Culture in Japan. The extent to which these agencies are committed to regulating international data traffic cannot be underestimated. Following over a decade of investments in this direction, the NSF just launched a funding program called Cyberinfrastructure, devolving 52 million dollars to the development of integrated bioinformatics tools. The EU has been almost equally generous with its Embrace program, set up to "improve access to biological information for scientists both inside and beyond the European border."[10] The funding program has run since February 2005 and involves seventeen institutes located in eleven European countries.

The reasons for the heavy involvement of government agencies in regulating and funding bioinformatics are illustrated by a brief reference to one of the best-known instances of the clash between private and public interests over this issue. This is the dispute surrounding the disclosure and circulation of data from the Human Genome Project (HGP). Officially running from 1990 to 2003, the HGP was a multinational project set up to sequence the whole human genome. Its resonant success in this task made it an exemplar for many other "big science" collaborations (such as the projects devoted to sequencing the worm *C. elegans,* the mouse *Mus musculus* and *Arabidopsis*).[11] The sequencing effort was funded by both the private and the public sectors. Research on the public side involved a multinational effort coordinated by Francis Collins. The main corporate investor was the Perkin-Elmer Corporation sponsoring the company Celera headed by Craig Venter, the creator of the shotgun sequencing techniques that effectively allowed the HGP to keep up with its completion schedule.

At the turn of the millennium, conflict erupted over the means through which data would be disclosed to the wider community. On the corporate side, Venter proposed to take over the remaining sequencing efforts from public funding and to create a database enabling access to both public and private data. In exchange for relieving government budgets of such expenses, Venter asked for the right to patent several hundreds of the genes mapped through the HGP, as well as the right to control access to the database for a period of at least five years, during which only researchers busy with nonprofit projects would be given permission to view and use data. Speaking for his publicly funded, multinational research group, Collins put forward a number of critiques of the terms set by Celera. First, he remarked, there is no unambiguous way to demarcate profitable from nonprofit research, as by now any project in basic biology might yield insights that can be commercially exploited at a later time. This meant that Venter's conditions effectively blocked the great majority of researchers from gaining access to the database. Collins also claimed that public agencies could grant Celera no longer than one year of unilateral control of the data. Five years of exclusive access would prevent the development of research that builds on the sequencing data, thus halting genomics in the most exciting moment of its history and barring biologists from exploring the significance of those data to other research fields, ranging from cell biology to ecology. Finally, Collins condemned Venter's requirements as an attempt to take over the results of investments by the public sector and exploit them for the commercial purposes of his company. Collins argued that accepting Venter's proposal meant fostering a monopoly over the access to and use of HGP data. Given the importance of such data to future biomedical research, sanctioning corporate claims of exclusivity would have been not only misguided, but also immoral—a judgment that was shared by other researchers working for public agencies.

Eventually, Celera gave in to most of Collins's demands and disclosed its data through publication in *Science* at the same time as the publicly funded researchers published in *Nature*. As discussed in detail by Bostanci (2004), however, the disagreements between private and public parties of the HGP remained, and the dispute over the means of data disclosure symbolized a deeper disagreement about the means and goals of research.[12] This is the point that I wish to emphasize in the next section.

4. Product-Driven versus Resource-Driven Competition

As evident in the HPG dispute, both public and private sponsors are susceptible to the demands of commodification and posit financial profit as an important goal of scientific research. However, they have different ways of specifying this minimal sketch of what commodification involves. Private sponsors see data as means to achieve marketable commodities. Data are in this view indispensable to acquiring the knowledge needed to develop new products. By contrast, public sponsors value data themselves as commodities with great potential for multiple uses: each dataset can potentially serve the development of a variety of ideas and products, which makes it a vital resource to whoever is involved in research. These two approaches encourage contrasting sets of criteria for what constitutes "good" science. As a consequence, public and private sponsors adopt diverging strategies toward regulating data distribution in biology.

Let us tackle private sponsors first. Corporations involved in scientific research have a strong preference for short-term efforts to produce immediately applicable results. Their assessment of the value of biological data is based on an estimate of the commercial value of products that are likely to be obtained from analyzing those data. Most importantly, products chosen as targets of a company's R&D efforts need to be developed and marketed before competitors in other industries or in the public sector reach the same result. The priority is to be the first to create a product of a specific type. As a consequence of such *product-driven competition* between companies, R&D departments are reluctant to share the data that they produce in-house, since the possession of unique datasets might constitute an advantage over competitors (and vice versa, data that are disclosed might end up helping competitors in their own quest). Data are not interesting in themselves, but rather as a means to achieve the scientific and technical knowledge that might allow for a commercially marketable discovery.

Thus, researchers working under private contracts take a short-term view on the quality and maintenance of data that are produced. Data quality is assessed in relation to the way in which data serve the creation of a viable product. Data are considered to be good when they guide biologists toward the realization of efficient means of intervention on an organism. Hence, privately sponsored research seldom adopts standards for data quality that do not depend on the specific research context; also, private sponsors are not interested in investing money toward the long-term maintenance of data produced in the course of a project, unless those data are thought to be potentially useful for in-house projects to come. As long as data are no longer of use to the company itself, no more time and money should be spent on them.

In practice, this set of values leads private sponsors to favor *project-directed databases,* i.e., databases that gather all available data that are relevant to exploring the specific problem tackled by researchers in a given period. These databases are quick to set up and yield results, since the range of data involved is very limited and there is little curation work involved. However, they are maintained only as long as they are useful to the production of the range of products of interest to the company. Data stored within those resources thus risk being lost, as the databases are discarded on completion of the project at hand. Also, since sharing data could enhance the chance of a competitor developing the same product in a shorter amount of time, project-based databases sponsored by private companies bar access and/or permission to use data to researchers who have no direct ties to their sponsors (note that they often give the option of building such ties as a way to gain admission to the database).

Public sponsors have a different view of both the role of data in science and the role of communication among researchers trying to transform data into products. The key value here is a long-term view on the possible developments in biology and the ways in which a strategic management of present knowledge might foster high returns in the future. Public sponsors invest large quantities of money in producing data and are interested in maximizing that investment by making sure that those results are used in as many ways and with as much impact as possible. This leads to a view of data as more than a means to the fast production of commodities: data are themselves seen as commodities whose potential utility is not yet clear and should be explored through appropriate resources. This standpoint is reinforced by the realization that, in practice, exploring the relevance of data is not compatible with retaining control on who can use data and when. In order to determine whether a given dataset might be relevant to their research, biologists need to be able to access it directly, compare it against all other available datasets and interpret it in the framework of their own research. Given the large amount of data whose relevance needs to be assessed, it is vital that biologists have unrestricted and quick access to all available datasets, thus increasing the possibility of finding datasets that suit their research interests. Ultimately, constructing tools facilitating data circulation to anyone interested is the most efficient way to yield profitable results out of the efforts involved in producing data in the first place. Data need to be made accessible and usable to any researcher interested in assessing their significance, no matter who funds them or what they are aiming to produce.

Public sponsors have therefore moved from an emphasis on product-driven competition to encouraging *resource-driven competition*. This kind of competition acts on two levels: between research groups and between databases themselves. Between research groups, sponsors exploit competitive forces to push researchers to donate their data to public databases. There is actually no consensus yet on what constitutes an appropriate reward for "data donors," since despite the efforts and time spent in disclosing data of good quality, data donation is not yet officially recognized as part of a researcher's curriculum vitae. Public agencies are acutely aware that this situation needs to be changed: research groups should be encouraged to compete not only for the number of publications or patents produced, but also for the number and quality of donations achieved. Strategies hitherto used to this end include context-specific rewards, such as the offer of specific services or materials in exchange for a donation to a database,[13] and disclosure obligations tied to publicly awarded grants, which imply that researchers sponsored by those grants disclose the resulting data to public repositories (this is a policy currently endorsed by the BBSRC, NIH, and NSF).

At the same time, government agencies encourage competition between databases for who provides the best service to their users. The success of a database, and thus decisions on its long-term survival through follow-up grants, is judged on the basis of the amount of users that it secures (as documented by surveys and Web site statistics).[14] This encourages database curators to put the interests and expectations of their users before their own. There is a constant trade-off between what the curators view as efficient ways to package data and what users from various contexts see as useful search parameters and forms of display. As a result of current public policy, curators need to be aware of what biologists expect to find on the database and how they will be handling the data, since user satisfaction will be the determinant factor for the survival of their database.

A further effect of governmental insistence on competition for user shares is the progressive diversification of databases seeking to please different needs. Curators have realized that there is no point for two databases to collect precisely the same type and amount of data in the same ways, as they would be competing for the attention of the same users, and one of them could eventually lose out. As a result of this insight, the landscape of existing databases is exhibiting more and more self-regulating division of labor—and at the same time, extensive networks of collaboration among databases are emerging (since, even if sponsored by different agencies, database curators can usefully exchange notes on how best to serve their user communities and how to boost one another's work by building links among databases).[15]

In all these different ways, resource-driven competition becomes a tool toward achieving an array of resources and methods facilitating all foreseeable types of research. This approach can certainly have unintended consequences that are potentially damaging to science. For instance, the division of labor occasioned by resource-based competition risks diminishing opportunities for dissent among database curators and pluralism among packaging strategies, as it reduces the chances to develop and test different packaging processes for the same data. Also, with databases building more and more of their work on one another's efforts, the chances of perpetuating errors and ultimately wrong approaches increase (although it should be noted that comparisons across databases can also highlight inconsistencies, thus signaling places where the quality and reliability of available data could be improved).[16] Last but not least, user interest alone is not enough to guarantee user satisfaction, as researchers might be consulting databases because they are the only source of information available, without, however, approving of the choices made by curators in packaging the data. To maximize the chance of data reuse across research contexts, public sponsors need to find better ways to assess what researchers wish to find in a database.[17]

These are surely only some of the possible complications involved in adopting resource-driven competition as a mechanism pushing data circulation. Their damaging effects may or may not be averted by improved policies and scientific practice. What I wish to emphasize here is that resource-driven competition does enforce the development of standards for producing and handling data that *do not* depend on the demands of one research context only.[18] This already constitutes a huge advance over the product-driven competition favored by private sponsors, as public institutions encourage the construction of databases aiming to serve biological research as a whole. This places careful maintenance and free circulation of data as important criteria for what constitutes "good science." Indeed, resource-driven competition has hitherto proved very productive from the scientific point of view. Within barely a decade, publicly sponsored databases have made enormous leaps in the quality of their services and of the data that they contain. Scientists note the increasing usefulness of databases in their research and are therefore becoming more aware of the advantages of contributing their data to these resources, which are seen as crucial services yielding high returns to whoever can afford a long-term view on the value of their data.

5. Data Travels in Commodified Science

I now turn to examine the three stages through which scientists actually use databases to distribute data. These three stages of data travel involve three sets of actors: database curators, scientists who produce data in the first place ("producers"), and users of data retrieved through databases ("users"). In each of these stages, a number of difficulties needs to be overcome for data to be shared across research communities in a manner that facilitates as much as possible the overall advancement of research. The contrasting values adopted by database sponsors have a strong impact on how producers, curators, and users deal with those technical difficulties. This analysis highlights how the product-driven competition encouraged by the private sector fails to reconcile the roles of bioinformatics as a research field and service to scientists with its role as an industry seeking to profit from available data.

5.1. Disclosure

There are no *general* rules in science about how researchers should treat the data that they produce. While in some cases the disclosure of data is policed by journal editors or funding agencies (see above and section 7 of J. Brown's chapter in this volume), the majority of researchers can still choose to discard specific datasets when they do not fit their interests or goals, so that no one will be able to see them again. Indeed, there are as yet no standard mechanisms within science regulating the selection of data to be disclosed from the wider pool of data produced by any one research project. This is partly because there is no consensus on what data are produced for. Clearly, data are produced as evidence for the hypotheses and beliefs characterizing a specific research context. It makes perfect sense, in this interpretation, to disclose only data of direct relevance to the questions investigated in that context. At the same time, however, data can be seen as a heritage to be shared among various researchers interested in different aspects of the same phenomenon. Making every bit of data produced in one's research accessible to others could prevent useless duplication of efforts, thus giving biologists more time to probe the significance of existing data and/or produce new ones.

This ambiguity in the goals of data production leaves scientific sponsors at liberty to impose their own values and regulations on the disclosure of data. As I pointed out in the previous section, private sponsors encourage scientists toward selecting data on the basis of their usefulness within the specific project in which they are produced. This is due to the instrumental constraints imposed by product-driven competition, in which there is simply no time to store and manage data that are not immediately relevant to the project at hand. In the private context, disclosure also depends on the level of control that sponsors wish to retain on the data. Producers are often asked to refrain from disclosing them for a specified time period, thus giving time to the sponsors to fully reap the commercial fruits of related discoveries. Alternatively, privately funded researchers may disclose data through various types of intellectual property rights (IPRs) granting exclusive legal ownership of the material being disclosed, including the power to control who gets to use data and under which conditions.

Researchers whose contract allows for public disclosure of (at least some of) their data have a choice between two means of disclosure. One is publication in a scientific journal. The incentives to disclose data through publications are very high for producers working in academia, where the number of one's publications constitutes the main indicator for the quality of one's research. Through publishing, producers earn academic recognition for their efforts and thus the right to apply for (or maintain) jobs in scientific institutions. The disadvantage with this method of disclosure is that it mirrors many of the values and methodological criteria underlying the product-driven competition fostered by private sponsors. Researchers disclosing data through publications tend to select those that directly support the specific claim made in their paper(s). This means again that the majority of data actually generated is never seen by other biologists. Also, because data are treated as the evidential means toward demonstrating one claim, little attention is paid to the format with which data are published. Journals seldom have rules on which format data should be reported in for publication, which means that researchers present data in the format that best fits their present purposes. This has two crucial implications. First, only biologists with a direct interest in the topic of the paper will access those data, regardless of the fact that the same data could be useful to investigating other biological questions. Second, without some expertise in the topic addressed by the paper, it can be very difficult to extract data from it.[19]

There is an alternative to this method for disclosure and to the assumption that data are only produced to provide evidence for one specific claim, no matter their potential relevance to other research projects. This is donation to public repositories, also referred to as "large-scale public databases" (Rhee, Dickerson, and Xu 2006).[20] Researchers can choose to donate all of their data to a repository (such as GenBank). This method of disclosure adheres quite closely to the resource-driven competition characterizing public governance of data sharing. Public repositories provide a platform for producers to contribute the results of their work so that database curators can use them to construct databases that the whole community (including the original producers) can enjoy. As I detail below in the circulation and retrieval stages, contribution to a public repository is the first indispensable step toward enabling efficient data sharing across biologists.

If the goal of producing data was solely to provide a legacy to biology as a whole, this form of disclosure would indisputably constitute the best option for everyone's benefit in this case. However, disclosure through public repository requires extra work on the side of producers, who have to format their data according to the minimal standards demanded by the repositories and have to take account of all the data that they produce, rather than simply the ones relevant to answering their own research question in a satisfactory way. Further, donation to public repositories is not yet fully recognized as a valuable contribution to science. It is certainly valued by individual scientists as a gesture of goodwill and openness, but it will not get people jobs or boost their curriculum vitae. These are big issues for researchers under strong pressure to move quickly from one project to the next and to maximize the recognition that they receive for each piece of research. Another stringent reason for researchers to prefer disclosure through publications over donations to repositories is the issue of ownership of data. Donation to public repositories requires producers to relinquish control of the data that they submit so that they can be freely accessed and used by other members of the community. This clause is in direct conflict with their sponsors' demand to retain control over the spread and use of the data. Thus, privatization drives researchers away from freely donating their data to public repositories.

5.2. Circulation

The mere disclosure of data through public repositories is not sufficient for biologists to be able to access and use those data in their own work. Due to both the amount and the diversity of data hosted by them, accessing data through repositories is not an easy task. There are no categories through which to search for specific sets of data; the formats in which data are presented are still rather heterogeneous, since each contributor of data tends to interpret and apply the standards imposed by the repository in his or her own way; and, most importantly, there are no tools through which users can visualize correlations among existing sets of data (such as, for instance, tools to assemble all data relevant to the sequence of genes on a chromosome, or models allowing one to view and compare all available data on a specific metabolic pathway).

These are the problems that the so-called "community databases," i.e., the entities that I hitherto referred to as databases, are funded to tackle. Their role is to extract data from either public repositories or other forms of disclosure (such as publications or even through direct interaction with data producers) and standardize those data in order to make them easily accessible to all biologists, no matter their specific expertise or location. Database curators are responsible for decisions concerning data selection (which data will be inserted in the database and which information on data source will be made available) and the "packaging" of data (the standard format in which data of the same type should be presented and the taxonomy through which data should be ordered in order to be easily retrieved by users).[21] Publications have tacit rather than formal rules as to what information—and what level of detail—should be inserted about protocols, instruments, and assumptions used in a study. Databases are much more exigent in their requirements, because, as I noted above, curators are responsible for verifying the quality and reliability of data hosted in their databases.

Notably, the role played by curators here is peculiar to resource-driven competition, and indeed these databases are sponsored almost exclusively by public agencies. These databases typically seek to serve the whole community of potential users by *making data usable for multiple purposes.* Efficiency, in the view of their curators, consists in enlarging the number of research contexts in which the same sets of data can be relevant. Product-directed databases are not interested in the outreach of data (which in fact they seek to control) as much as they are interested in their applicability to a specific context. In that context, there is neither time nor resources to curate data so that they are reusable in other contexts. This factor alone greatly limits the extent to which these data can be distributed, as users have to do a lot of work to retrieve them.

5.3. Retrieval

Users exercise two kinds of expertise to adequately retrieve data from databases. The first kind of expertise concerns the actual act of searching for data. Users need to be able to log into a database, move efficiently through the database interface, phrase their query in a way that is compatible with the parameters and visualization tools built into the database, and, finally, maneuver through the results displayed by the database until they obtain a visualization of data that is satisfactory to them. These are what I call "access skills." Without them, a user cannot hope to retrieve the data that he or she wishes to consult—which is why a lot of the curators' work consists in making these skills as easy to acquire as possible, thus minimizing the time that users have to spend in familiarizing themselves with the database and improving the chances that they get what they want from it.

The second kind of expertise needed by users is the ability to actually use the data acquired through the database within their own research. This implies an altogether different set of skills, which I call "expert skills" and which are acquired as part of biologists' own training and practice, rather than in direct connection to database use.[22] The exercise of expert skills requires a thorough knowledge of both the practices and the theoretical apparatus used within the disciplines dealing with the broad research question that is being asked.[23] It is on the basis of this background knowledge that biologists determine which sets of data could potentially inform their investigation of the research question. Through scrutiny of data accessed through a database, a biologist with adequate expert skills can substantially increase the precision of his or her research question as well as use the new information to design future research.

Consider the example of a biologist specialized in plant growth who wishes to study how a specific hormone influences the expression of a particular phenotypic trait. For a start, she might check whether there are any data already available on which gene clusters are affected by the hormone. If she discovers that there are indeed specific genes whose expression is strongly enhanced or inhibited by the hormone, she will have grounds to think that whichever phenotypic trait is controlled by those genes will be affected too. Again, she can check whether there are any data already available documenting the correlation between the gene cluster that she has identified and specific phenotypic traits in her model plant. If that is the case, she will be able to form a hypothesis about which traits are influenced by the hormone, and she will thus modify her research design in order to test her hypothesis.

Up to this point, the researcher has used her access to the database to identify possible causal links between the phenomena that she is interested in. This has helped her to construct a more detailed research question and experimental setting. To proceed with the investigation, the biologist might need to gather more information about the provenance of data so as to assess with more detail their quality and reliability with regard to her specific research context. This is where the information on data sources provided by curators becomes extremely useful. As I noted in my first section, "traveling" data are everything but local: their anonymity is a crucial factor in allowing them to circulate widely across research contexts. However, data become "local" again once they are adopted into a new context and used to pursue new research questions. In this phase, information about their provenance is often important to evaluating their role in the new domain (Leonelli 2009a).

A resource-directed database is constructed to minimize the skills needed to access the database and the information on data sources. The database is specifically built for consultation by any disciplinary background: as we have seen in the circulation stage, data are standardized and ordered so as to travel across disciplinary boundaries. Further, curators invest much effort in adding information about the provenance of data, which is not crucial to circulating the data, but is often very helpful to researchers wishing to use retrieved data in their projects. Researchers wishing to exercise their expert skills in using retrieved data have the needed information immediately at their disposal.

By contrast, project-driven databases serve the specific disciplinary interests informing the work of whoever produces the data. This implies that curators do not take time to standardize the data and the tools through which data are displayed to the user. The access skills needed to retrieve data from such a database are specific to the field in question, which makes them difficult to acquire for researchers working in other fields. This means that even if these databases were always freely accessible, the probability that a researcher will actually make the effort to retrieve data from them is very low. Further, project-driven databases do not invest effort into adding information about the local conditions where data were produced, as this would imply investing time and money in employing curators to do this work. The result is a list of anonymous data. These data can certainly be circulated if the access skills needed to retrieve them were easy enough to acquire. However, their usefulness within a new research context is severely compromised by the lack of information about their provenance.

6. Conclusion: Values in Data Circulation

My discussion of how the priorities of database sponsors affect the three stages of data travel brings me to the following conclusion. The privatization of research does not affect the dissemination of data solely by attempting to control it through the exercise of intellectual property rights, by distorting or spinning the data, or by affecting the research directions to which data are brought to bear (as illustrated, respectively, by Brown, Resnik, and Musschenga, van der Steen, and Ho in this volume). Private sponsors affect data circulation, and therefore the development of future research, by imposing criteria for what counts as data in science and how these data should be treated. These criteria are dictated by values such as speed and instrumentalism, which are in turn related to specific methodological procedures: product-driven competition and a preference for project-directed databases. Biologists are long discussing whether the insistence on seeking IPRs in contract research obstructs the community's *freedom to operate* on the basis of the data that are produced in that context (e.g., Delmer et al. 2003). I wish to add that the very values and temporal constraints that privatization currently imposes on scientific practices obstruct the development of future research.[24]

Science and technology are characterized by the ability of their practitioners to build new research projects on the insights acquired through old ones. The practices encouraged by product-driven competition force researchers to shy away from contributing to the bioinformatics effort toward improving existing resources for the circulation of data. As a result, they jeopardize current opportunities for an efficient transmission of knowledge. More specifically, *product-directed competition compromises the opportunity to use the same set of data for multiple scientific purposes.* This could be very damaging to science in the long term. Science and society at large seem to have everything to lose from the obstacles posed to data circulation by industries and, increasingly, universities.[25]

This situation is recognized by government agencies, which therefore support a resource-driven policy over a product-driven one. When it comes to determining procedures for data sharing, public agencies often act as gatekeepers for what Dick Pels calls "self-interested science"[26] by endorsing the following key values:

1. *equal access to resources:* especially in the context of biological research, where expertise is fragmented into specialized niches and division of labor is efficiently used to achieve common research goals, it is of paramount importance that researchers of any specialty have equal access to basic resources such as data;

2. *competition between different methods to achieve a common goal:* research groups are encouraged to compete on creating and improving resources and procedures useful to carrying out research (rather than competing purely on the quantity and quality of research results, i.e., number of publications);

3. *long-term vision:* investing time, as well as money and human resources, is of the essence in scientific research: "science is typically of the 'long breath,' depending on long-term cycles of investment in human and material resources, whereas politics expects quicker returns within a much shorter time-span" (Pels 2003, 32).

Adherence to these values allows public agencies to keep their commitment to the goals and means of commodified science without, however, losing sight of key methodological requirements for "good science," such as the need to share data freely and efficiently.[27] Providing means for adequate data circulation maximizes the usefulness of research that has already been done and paid for. In fact, it could be argued that it is just as important to maximize the flow of data across research contexts from a profit-driven perspective as it is from a Mertonian perspective. The construction of platforms through which data can be circulated and thus reused toward further research represents a great improvement in the efficient use of public research funds to serve the public interest, even if the latter is defined through appeal to the potential commodification of research.

In closing, I want to draw attention to the peculiar situation that allows publicly sponsored research to support the free exchange of scientific knowledge. If the advantages of this strategy are so great, why is it that private sponsors do not embrace them? For the same reasons as the ones motivating public sponsors, it would seem rational for them to pursue resource-driven competition rather than insisting on the short-sighted strategy of product-driven competition—a point that some of the main biotechnology and pharmaceuticals corporations are starting to take on board. At least a partial explanation for this difference is provided by the social roles and economic power characterizing private and public institutions. By its very nature, publicly sponsored research is at an advantage with respect to privately sponsored research. A government, at least among the majority of Western representative democracies, is a much more stable and durable entity than a company and can afford to invest capital in projects guaranteed to yield returns in the long term. Thus, public agencies can better afford to adopt resource-driven competition. Further, investing in facilitating data circulation has political as well as economic benefits. By encouraging cooperation among databases, resource-driven competition opens opportunities for international cooperation among countries involved in the same type of research, thus fostering diplomatic ties and political trust.

Individual companies, and particularly small businesses, do not enjoy these advantages. They need short-term profit to survive: a long-term vision on scientific research is difficult to maintain by an entity whose very existence depends on monthly revenues and the support of shareholders. As a consequence, they are more strictly bound to the market rules dominating international trade, which do not offer opportunities for long-term analysis. A fact that seemingly proves this point is that the only corporations willing to donate some of their data to publicly funded databases are giants like Monsanto. The company justifies this policy of disclosure by pointing out that public databases such as TAIR take better care of data on *Arabidopsis* than Monsanto itself would (as Monsanto does not intend to invest more money in maintaining the data). The underlying reality is that Monsanto can afford to make such a donation and reap its benefits in the long term. The same cannot be said of the hundreds of satellite companies specializing in one project at a time and producing much smaller and less organically compiled databases.

NOTES

This research was funded by the Leverhulme Trust (grant number F/07004/Z) and the ESRC as part of the project "How Well Do 'Facts' Travel?" at the Department of Economic History, London School of Economics. I am grateful to Bram Bos, Hans Radder, and Mary Morgan for their insightful comments on an earlier draft. I also benefited from discussions with the participants of the Amsterdam workshop held on June 21–23, 2007; with various biologists and database curators, particularly Sean May of NASC; and with my colleagues at the London School of Economics.

1. Scientific research, especially in biology, is increasingly financed and structured around large projects involving overt collaboration and sharing of resources among various institutions. The projects are typically interdisciplinary and, given the specificity of the topics at hand, they include researchers based in different locations, often widely distant from one another (as in the case of American-Japanese collaborations). Fuller (2000) reviews some of the issues involved in the governance of big science.

2. Especially in the case of genomics, it is impossible to determine the value of data as evidence for future discoveries: the more that is known about the complex regulatory role played by the genome, the more it will be possible to link specific genes to traits at other levels of organization of organisms.

3. "The characteristics of [data] are heavily dependent on the peculiarities of the particular experimental design, detection device, or data-gathering procedures an investigator employs" (Bogen and Woodward 1988, 317).

4. Indeed, it can be argued that data travel across communities precisely thanks to this temporary detachment from information about the local context in which they were produced. See Leonelli (2009a) and my discussion of the procedures through which data are standardized within publicly sponsored databases, below.

5. Dupré (1993) and Mitchell (2003) are among the many philosophical contributions to the discussion of disunity in biology. For a discussion of the notion of epistemic culture, see Knorr Cetina (1999).

6. For philosophical analyses of model organism research in biology, see Ankeny (2007) and Leonelli (2007).

7. For more details about how these databases operate, see the descriptions published by the team of curators responsible for each of them: for TAIR, Rhee et al. (2003); for Reactome, Vastrik et al. (2007); for MIPS, Spannagl et al. (2007); and finally for TIGR, Bammler et al. (2005).

8. In their excellent analysis of bioinformatic networks, Brown and Rappert (2000) have argued that the labels "public" and "private" only serve as "idealised codes to which various actors, whether they are universities or commercially funded initiatives, can appeal" (ibid., 444). While I agree that the notion of a public good and the related "philosophy of free access" is evoked by all participants in bioinformatics to fit their own agenda, I view the distinction between private and public as a valid and unambiguous tool to classify the sponsors of bioinformatic efforts. As noted by Brown and Rappert, there are of course bioinformatic institutes funded by both types of sponsors; yet, recognizing the difference in the values and commitments of those sponsors is necessary to make sense of the work carried out within these institutes.

9. Krimsky (2003) documents how contract research has been steadily displacing government funding toward most biomedical and genomic research in the last three decades.

10. From the mission statement on the EMBRACE home page, available at http://ec.europa.eu/research/health/genomics/newsletter/issue4/article04_en.htm.

11. For a general account of the HGP, see Sulston and Ferry (2002) and Bostanci (2004).

12. For documentation on this case, see also Marshall (2000, 2001).

13. The BBSRC-funded Nottingham Arabidopsis Information Centre, for instance, offers to perform microarray experiments at a low price in exchange for the permission to disclose all data obtained through this procedure to public repositories.

14. Again as an example, the Nottingham Arabidopsis Stock Centre was recently granted funds by the BBSRC on the grounds of user satisfaction surveys and statistics documenting how many researchers accessed and used their existing database.

15. Yet another interesting instance of competition in this context is the one existing between different funding agencies, such as the competition between NSF and NIH in the United States, or between American and European agencies. These agencies might be characterized as pushing different versions of resource-driven competition, insofar as some of them (e.g., the NSF) favor a centralized approach to database construction, with one group of "superexperts" responsible for a whole sector, while others (e.g., the BBSRC) prefer to decentralize funding into different curator pools. While interesting in themselves, these differences in regulatory policy do not impact my argument in this chapter, as all agencies agree on treating resource-driven competition as an efficient strategy to circulate data.

16. See Ruttenberg et al. (2007).

17. Another problematic issue, which is not directly related to resource-driven competition, however, is the lack of commitment of funding agencies to maintaining databases in the long term. Up to now, most government funding of bioinformatics is on a limited timescale, which encourages curators to constantly improve their services, but offers no secure support for the long-term storage of data.

18. This point was forcefully advocated by Olson and Green (1998) in the context of the HGP dispute.

19. The NSF-sponsored TAIR database has been searching for efficient ways to extract data from publications since. This process, aptly dubbed "text-mining" by bioinformaticians, is known to be both time-consuming and exceedingly subjective, as curators need to interpret the biological significance of the claims made in the paper in order to adequately export data from that context (Pan et al. 2006).

20. Hilgartner (1995) has put forward the idea of referring to journals and databases as two different *communication regimes*.

21. These taxonomies, which bioinformaticians refer to as "bio-ontologies," include precisely defined categories that allow users to search and compare data. On bio-ontologies, see Baclawski and Niu (2005).

22. A good example of the difference between access and expert skills is the difference between the skills exercised by myself and by a practicing biologist in accessing a database. Through my philosophical research on databases and biological knowledge, I have become reasonably skilled in accessing biological databases and getting some data out of them. However, I do not know how to use those data to pursue a specific research question in biology. This requires a commitment to goals that I do not share as well as a familiarity with cutting-edge techniques, methodologies, and concepts in specialized areas of research that I do not have.

23. A detailed analysis of how biologists coordinate embodied and theoretical knowledge of a phenomenon to acquire understanding of that phenomenon can be found in Leonelli (2009b).

24. Privatization is of course not the only mechanism imposing the values characterizing product-driven competition. The habit of assessing scientists' output through number of publications generates similar problems: a tendency to value the usability of data toward "minimally publishable units" rather than their usability in the long term.

25. Arguably, technologies such as databases provide opportunities for collaboration never before seen in biology or other sciences, because they free existing datasets from their disciplinary and geographical provenance. It is also true that the contemporary setting of "big science" differs so vastly from how science was conducted in earlier periods as to make comparisons almost impossible: the globalization of scientific education and research, as well as the invention of technologies gathering data of all types at increasing speed, make the question of data circulation more pressing than it has ever been in the history of science.

26. Pels introduces the idea of "self-interested" science as a useful way to overcome the problem that the current commodification of science is destined to completely erode the boundary between scientific and political or commercial activities (Pels 2003, 30). As Pels notes, science should work with a distinctive methodology and values compared to other human activities: the reasons for this have less to do with Enlightenment ideals, however, than with scientists' interest in safeguarding their own profession from excessive manipulations by "external" forces (such as the market or the state), which may compromise its functioning by distorting its methodology and procedures.

27. In this sense, these values constitute good examples of the "deflationary" Mertonian norms proposed by Radder in this volume, chap. 10.

REFERENCES

Ankeny, R. 2007. "Wormy logic: Model organisms as case-based reasoning." In *Science without laws: Model systems, cases, exemplary narratives,* ed. A. H. Creager, E. Lunbeck, and N. Wise, 46–58. Chapel Hill, NC: Duke University Press.

Baclawski, K., and T. Niu. 2005. *Ontologies for bioinformatics.* Cambridge, MA: MIT Press.

Bammler, T., R. P. Beyer, S. Bhattacharya, G. A. Boorman, A. Boyles, B. U. Bradford, R. E. Bumgarner, P. R. Bushel, K. Chaturvedi, D. Choi, M. L. Cunningham, S. Deng, H. K. Dressman, R. D. Fannin, F. M. Farin, J. H. Freedman, R. C. Fry, A. Harper, M. C. Humble, P. Hurban, T. J. Kavanagh, W. K. Kaufmann, K. F. Kerr, L. Jing, J. A. Lapidus, M. R. Lasarev, J. Li, Y. Li, E. K. Lobenhofer, X. Lu, R. L. Malek, S. Milton, S. R. Nagalla, J. P. O'Malley, V. S. Palmer, P. Pattee, R. S. Paules, C. M. Perou, K. Phillips, L. Qin, Y. Qiu, S. D. Quigley, M. Rodland, I. Rusyn, L. D. Samson, D. A. Schwartz, Y. Shi, J. Shin, S. O. Sieber, S. Slifer, M. C. Speer, P. S. Spencer, D. I. Sproles, J. A. Swenberg, W. A. Suk, R. C. Sullivan, R. Tian, R. W. Tennant, S. A. Todd, C. J. Tucker, B. Van Houten, B. K. Weis, S. Xuan, and H. Zarbl. 2005. "Standardizing global gene expression analysis between laboratories and across platforms." *Nature Methods* 2 (5): 351–56.

Bogen, J., and J. Woodward. 1988. "Saving the phenomena." *Philosophical Review* 97 (3): 303–52.

Bostanci, A. 2004. "Sequencing human genomes." In *From molecular genetics to genomics,* ed. J. P. Gaudilliere and H. J. Rheinberger, 158–79. New York: Routledge.

Brown, N., and B. Rappert. 2000. "Emerging bioinformatic networks: Contesting the public meaning of private and the private meaning of public." *Prometheus* 18 (4): 437–52.

Delmer, D. P., C. Nottenburg, G. D. Graff, and A. B. Bennett. 2003. "Intellectual property resources for international development in agriculture." *Plant Physiology* 133:1666–70.

Dupré, J. 1993. *The disorder of things.* Cambridge: Cambridge University Press.

Fuller, S. 2000. *The governance of science*. Philadelphia: Open University Press.

Hilgartner, S. 1995. "Biomolecular databases: New communication regimes for biology?" *Science Communication* 17:240–63.

Knorr Cetina, K. 1999. *Epistemic cultures*. Cambridge, MA: Harvard University Press.

Krimsky, S. 2003. *Science in the private interest*. Lanham, MD: Rowman and Littlefield.

Leonelli, S. 2007. *Weed for thought: Using Arabidopsis thaliana to understand plant biology*. Ph.D. diss., VU University Amsterdam. Available at http://hdl.handle.net/1871/10703.

———. 2009a. "On the locality of data and claims about phenomena." *Philosophy of Science* 76 (5): 737–49.

———. 2009b. "The impure nature of biological knowledge and the practice of understanding." In *Philosophical perspectives on scientific understanding,* ed. H. W. de Regt, S. Leonelli, and K. Eigner, 189–209. Pittsburgh: University of Pittsburgh Press.

Marshall, E. 2000. "Talks of public-private deal ends in acrimony." *Science* 287 (5459): 1723–25.

———. 2001 "Sharing the glory, not the credit." *Science* 291 (5507): 1189–93.

Mitchell, S. 2003. *Biological complexity and integrative pluralism*. Cambridge: Cambridge University Press.

Olson, M., and P. Green. 1998. "A 'quality-first' credo for the human genome project." *Genome Research* 8:414–15.

Pan, H., L. Zuo, R. Kanagasabai, Z. Zhang, V. Choudhary, B. Mohanty, S. Lam Tan, S. P. T. Krishnan, P. S. Veladandi, A. Meka, W. Keong Choy, S. Swarp, and V. B. Bajic. 2006. "Extracting information for meaningful function inference through text-mining." In *Discovering biomolecular mechanisms with computational biology,* ed. F. Eisenhauer, 57–73. Austin, TX: Landes Bioscience and Springer.

Pels, D. 2003. *Unhastening science*. Liverpool: Liverpool University Press.

Rhee, S. Y., W. Beavis, T. Z. Berardini, G. Chen, D. Dixon, A. Doyle, M. Garcia-Hernandez, E. Huala, G. Lander, M. Montoya, N. Miller, L. A. Mueller, S. Mundodi, L. Reiser, J. Tacklind, D. C. Weems, Y. Wu, I. Xu, D. Yoo, J. Yoon, and P. Zhang. 2003. "The Arabidopsis Information Resource (TAIR): A model organism database providing a centralised, curated gateway to Arabidopsis biology, research materials and community." *Nucleic Acids Research* 31 (1): 224–28.

Rhee, S. Y., J. Dickerson, and D. Xu. 2006. "Bioinformatics and its applications in plant biology." *Annual Review of Plant Biology* 57:335–60.

Ruttenberg, A., et al. 2007. "Advancing translational research with the semantic web." *BMC Bioinformatics* 8 (Suppl. 3), S2:1–16.

Spannagl, M., O. Noubibou, D. Haase, L. Yang, H. Gundlach, T. Hindemitt, K. Klee, G. Haberer, H. Schoof, and K. F. X. Mayer. 2007. "MIPSPlantsDB—Plant database resource for integrative and comparative plant genome research." *Nucleic Acids Research* 35, database issue.

Sulston, J., and G. Ferry. 2002. *The common thread: A story of science, politics, ethics and the human genome*. London: Bantam Press.

Vastrik, I., P. D'Eustachio, E. Schmidt, G. Joshi-Tope, G. Gopinath, D. Croft, B. de Bono, M. Gillespie, B. Jassal, S. Lewis, L. Matthews, G. Wu, E. Birney, and L. Stein. 2007. "Reactome: A knowledge base of biological pathways and processes." *Genome Biology* 8 (3): R39.

CHAPTER 8

Research under Pressure

METHODOLOGICAL FEATURES OF

COMMERCIALIZED SCIENCE

Martin Carrier

APPLICATION-DOMINATED INDUSTRIAL research is often claimed to suffer from superficial and biased judgments and to have lost its epistemic reputation. The commercialization process is said to lead to a biased research agenda, keep public science out of corporate laboratories, and induce methodological sloppiness. My thesis is that the impact of commercialization on the epistemic quality of scientific research is limited and that the remaining deficits can be remedied by an increased emphasis on publicly sponsored research. This conclusion is supposed to alleviate concerns associated with the commodification of academic research.

First, bias in topic selection is real in commercialized research but can be handled satisfactorily if mission-oriented research on problems of public relevance is underwritten by public funding.

Second, in order to ascertain privileged access to knowledge produced in an industrial company, research results tend be kept secret—a policy that violates Mertonian demands for open communication and unrestricted scrutiny. However, counteracting mechanisms push research toward openness, among them the benefits of cooperation or the wish to exploit the public academic sector.

Third, the relationship between scientific research and technology development is complex and multifaceted. I analyze various accounts of this relationship (among them the emergentist approach, the linear model, and the cascade model) and conclude that scientific understanding of the underlying natural processes is typically, although not exclusively, a precondition of technological innovation. This does not imply a unidirectional flow of knowledge from basic to applied research. By contrast, applied research projects or technological achievements often clarify issues of epistemic bearing. Although scientific theorizing is of limited impact on solving practical challenges, drawing on theory serves three important purposes: *identifying* relevant parameters, *generalizing* results, and *ascertaining the reliability* of the results in the face of distortions.

Epistemic and applied research are committed to shared objectives. Unified explanation and causal analysis codify what knowledge or understanding is all about. We understand a phenomenon when we are able to embed it in a nomological framework, and we grasp a causal relation when we can account for the process leading from the cause to the effect. Yet these same virtues are also essential for successful research on practical matters. Theoretical integration of a generalization or clarification of intermediate processes facilitate intervention. In virtue of these shared goals, successful application-dominated research will continue to incorporate essential epistemic commitments.

Finally, the impact of commercial bias on scientific objectivity can be kept in check. According to a pluralist notion of objectivity, as advocated, for instance, within social epistemology, objectivity should not be conceived as neutrality but as reciprocal control of prejudices. Competition in commercialized science might contribute to stimulating the plurality of contrasting approaches and thereby promote objectivity. The result constitutes an epistemic vindication, if limited, of industrial research, which suggests that the commodification of academic research does not necessarily degrade the epistemic dignity of research.

1. Science Operating in the Marketplace

Science was never pure. In spite of Aristotle's optimistic claim that humans by their nature desire to know (1998, *Metaphysics* 980a), organized production and systematic acquisition of knowledge was seldom done for its own sake. Only a tiny portion of scientific research was conducted out of pure intellectual curiosity and nothing else. In fact, the promise of the scientific revolution included at the same time the improvement of human understanding of nature and the betterment of the human condition. Bacon's slogan that knowledge is power meant that insights into nature's workings are suitable for creating an increased capacity for intervention. Knowledge was expected to further public utility and to serve economic interests right from the start.

It is true, the economic promise of science remained empty rhetoric for centuries and became more realistic only during the course of the nineteenth century. At the turn of the twenty-first century, this Baconian vision has come true—but is now regarded as a mixed blessing. Today, large amounts of research are financed by economic companies and conducted out of commercial interest. Underlying industrial funding of research is the idea that science is a primary source of technological development, which is in turn viewed as a driving force of economic growth. In fact, public funding of research is mostly due to the same motives. Financial support of academic and industrial research alike is widely understood as a kind of investment, the expected return of which is economic growth and, eventually, jobs. Research in the natural sciences has become a major economic factor and is viewed as a catalyst of industrial dynamics.

In terms of the goals pursued, university research in the sciences increasingly tends to resemble research in industrial laboratories. Public and private research institutions increasingly carry out applied projects; the scientific work done at a university institute and a company laboratory tend to become indistinguishable. This convergence is emphasized by strong institutional links. Universities found companies in order to market products based on their research. Companies buy themselves into universities or conclude large-scale contracts concerning joint projects. The commodification of academic research is one side of a process of reciprocal adaptation, the reverse side of which is the rise of industrial high-tech research. Given the importance of commercialized research, its methods and procedures can be expected to radiate into the whole of science. Therefore, examining methodological features of industrial research promises a look into the future of commodified academic research.

Worries about the detrimental impact of commercialization on the methodological dignity of science have been articulated frequently. These worries are based on the impression that the dominance of economic interests might narrow the agenda of research, encourage sloppy quality and tendentious judgments, and abandon the quest for truth that used to be the hallmark of the epistemic commitment of science. Scientists themselves sometimes articulate concerns to the effect that the commodification of research involves a reduction of the high methodological standards that used to characterize academic research. The new customers from politics and the economy are not willing to pay for advanced theorizing.

Epistemic challenges that transcend immediate practical needs might thus be ignored. The quick and dirty result, helpful but unsupported by theory, is more appreciated than the neat and elegant derivation that is a little beside the practical point at hand. Commercialization is feared to undermine the demanding test procedures inherent in respectable research. In this vein, the physicist Sylvan Schweber claims that "the demand for relevance . . . can easily become a source of corruption of the scientific process" and stresses the special role of "scientists engaged in fundamental physics" in that their community is committed to the vision of truth (Schweber 1993, 40). Analogously, the physicist John Ziman complained that science guided by material interests and commercial goals will lack objectivity, universality, creativity, and critical scrutiny. The epistemic commitment is threatened within "instrumental science," i.e., research pursued under the auspices of short-term material interests. Indications of corruption are widespread in instrumental science. They encompass withheld research data, censorship by sponsors, plagiarism and fraud, biased judgment, "antisocial projects," and excessive performance assessment (Ziman 2002, 399).

According to such voices, science in general, and academic research in particular, is likely to suffer in methodological respect from commodification. The apprehension is that a predominance of commercial incentives and a restriction to practical problem-solutions interfere with the epistemic standards that used to be the hallmark of scientific research. The judgments passed by scientists in commercialized research can be expected to be tainted with economic aspirations. Scientists are feared to lose their neutrality and objectivity and to adjust their research outcome to the expectations of the sponsor. In commodified research, commercial values tend to drive out the epistemic ones. This claimed epistemic decline is lamented in particular for academic research, since disinterested, unbiased inquiry also serves an important cultural function as a model of credibility and trustworthiness. In sum, according to the critics, commercialized science suffers from superficial and partisan assessment and runs the risk of losing its epistemic reputation.

Prima facie there are three elements characterizing commercialized science that are apt to fan such fears. First, the research agenda is set by economic goals, and such goals may differ from epistemic objectives and systematically diverge from the considered interests of society at large. Second, industrial research tends to be conducted behind closed doors. In contrast to epistemic science, commercial research and development is not committed to unrestricted access and comprehensive scrutiny. Third, proposals for practical solutions are assessed on purely pragmatic grounds. The sole criterion of success of a project in industrial research is that some device operates reliably and efficiently; no further epistemic ambitions are pursued. The worry is that a reduction of demanding standards of quality judgment might ensue. In sum, this commercialization process can be expected to lead to an imbalanced research agenda, keep public science out of corporate laboratories, and induce methodological sloppiness (Carrier 2008, 218). I will address these three worries and focus, in particular, on the latter fear of methodological decline. I will argue that industrial research is not substantially different from academic research in epistemic respect and that good reasons for this methodological convergence can be specified. The arguments amount to the thesis that the impact of commercialization on the quality of scientific research is limited and that the remaining deficits can be remedied by an increased emphasis on publicly sponsored research. This conclusion is suggested to alleviate concerns growing out of the commodification of academic research.

2. Biases in the Research Agenda

The primacy of the context of application produces a change in how the research agenda is set. Whereas problems in fundamental academic research arise from the smooth unfolding of the proper conceptual dynamics of a discipline (Kuhn 1962, 164; Lakatos 1970/1978, 50, 60–61), the emphasis on utility directs attention to practical challenges. As a result, the agenda of industrial research is shaped by commercial interests, the pursuit of which may benefit the customer but not everyone concerned. The most blatant examples for a biased agenda can be found in medical research. Ailments troubling the population of wealthy countries top the list of research items; third-world illnesses remain at the margins. Curing sleeping sickness is granted much lower urgency than treating breast cancer.

The most popular remedy offered for such a one-sided research agenda is the democratization of science. Participatory procedures, which are intended to include the stakeholders, are widely advertised as a means for forging a consensus on science policy. However, to the extent that such attempts at democratic inclusion are confined to the societies sponsoring the relevant research, as it applies to Philip Kitcher's ideal of a "well-ordered science,"[1] they can hardly be expected to produce the envisaged "fair" agenda. Citizens of the affluent countries of the West, even after having run through a Kitcherian process of mediation and tutoring, will probably not approve democratically to cover the health care cost of developing countries. Democratizing the setting of the research agenda cannot be assumed to affect significantly the uneven distribution of drug research allocations on a global scale.

An even deeper difficulty for the suggested public negotiation of the research agenda is that frequently no such agenda exists in advance—as studies of spin-off processes from university research have revealed. Many universities have offices that attempt to translate research outcome into ideas for marketable products which are then realized by start-up companies. The university supplies the patent and receives royalties in exchange in case of economic success. These offices operate by broadly surveying what ideas and options are cropping up in the laboratories and seek to assist their transformation into novel devices. No systematic agenda is issued by these offices. Rather, the initial step is that new effects are discovered and new capacities developed and explored. Only subsequently is it asked to which use they might be put or which functions can be performed with them. That is, new effects drive new functions, which in turn propel new technology. This is by no means an automatic process; it needs creativity and assistance. But basically the process of technological invention is driven from below. What can be accomplished technologically or which market niches exist are the salient questions, all of which are asked within a short-term perspective; no long-term ambitions are pursued. This is certainly different when big companies are brought into the scheme. Still, many technological novelties are introduced into the market by start-up firms, and in this field the dynamics proceeds bottom up. Setting up a systematic, over-arching research agenda for stepwise implementation is at odds with this anarchic, small-scale dynamics.[2]

What this analysis suggests, however, is that commercialized research proceeds with the customer in view. In market economies the expected commercial success will decide about the industrial research agenda, and the latter has a lot to do with being in resonance with the desires and aspirations of the broader public. A commercialized agenda tends to conform, broadly speaking, with the result of a democratic decision. This means that commercialized research operates with an eye on the needs and demands of the people—at least of those with money to spend. Still, even taking these qualifications into account, the orientation toward worldly needs would not be a matter of course if the agenda were set by the developmental logic of a discipline.

It is true, challenges that do not bear the promise of economic benefit tend to be disregarded by commercialized science. A challenge of this kind is the prevention or reduction of global warming which is, however, placed on top of the research agenda by political representatives and citizens alike. Problems of this sort are presently addressed by political regulations (like the EU regime of trading CO_2 licenses) or by state-funded research programs. That is, biases in the research agenda can be corrected by setting the incentives appropriately and by publicly funded research.

This means, all in all, that, first, the agenda of commercialized research is biased toward problem areas that bear economic prospects but that, second, this emphasis is not completely at odds with the desires of the people, and that, third, the best way to compensate the one-sidedness of commercialized research is by regulating the markets appropriately and by funding research projects through public allocations. Commercialized science needs to be complemented by science in the public interest, but the same applies to basic science or disciplinary research. The strategy should be to take advantage of the research done for the private benefit but at the same time to balance the results by differently oriented, publicly sponsored research endeavors. It is the usual practice of research authorities in Western countries or of political bodies like the European Union to underwrite mission-oriented research on problems of public relevance. Bias in topic selection is real in commercialized science but can be handled satisfactorily—if politics accepts its responsibility.

3. Commercial Research Performed Secretly

A charge frequently leveled against corporate research concerns its insistence on intellectual property rights, which is criticized as engendering a privatization of knowledge. Robert Merton codified a system of "cultural values" that is supposed to be constitutive of the "ethos of science"; among these values is "communalism" (or "communism"—as Merton put it), according to which scientific knowledge is and remains in public possession. It is an essential and indispensable part of the ethos of science that scientific findings are public property. Scientific knowledge, Merton argues, is the product of social collaboration and is owned by the community for this reason. This is linked with the imperative of "full and open communication." Merton demanded, consequently, that scientific knowledge should be accessible to everyone and suggested that the system of patenting is in conflict with this value (Merton 1942/1973, 273–75).

The commitment to openness of communication is claimed to be fundamental for epistemic science. By contrast, industrial research and development projects are intended to produce knowledge that can be put to exclusive use. After all, companies are not eager to finance research whose outcome can be used for free by a competitor (Dasgupta and David 1994, 495–98). As a result, important domains of scientific activity are constrained by industrial secrets or patents. The commercialization of research may thus go along with a privatization of science that compromises the public accessibility of knowledge (Rosenberg 1991, 340; Concar 2002, 15; Gibson, Baylis, and Lewis 2002). What is at stake here belongs to the essentials of scientific method: knowledge claims in science should be subject to everyone's scrutiny. The intersubjective nature of scientific method demands public tests and confirmation. Hypotheses developed behind closed doors are neither tested as critically as they would be if the claims or the pertinent evidence were more widely known, nor can the new information be employed in related research projects. From the epistemic point of view, such restrictions in the availability of knowledge constitute a worrisome feature.

However, there are counteracting mechanisms that tend to push commercial research toward openness. Indeed, some features of present-day industrial research and development practice bear witness to the recognition that keeping research outcomes classified could hurt a company. Chief among them is the realization that openness brings important benefits in its trains. This applies, first, to the cooperation among applied research groups that aim in similar directions. If two such groups each solved half of a given problem, sharing their knowledge may make them realize that they are done, whereas a lot of work would still be left to do if each one had proceeded in isolation. Conversely, without such cooperation, the same discovery may need to be made twice. Sequestration can be a costly impediment to commercially successful research outcomes, whereas cooperation may pay off economically (Carrier 2008, 220–21, 229–30).

In some fields, a division of labor emerges between academic and industrial research. Research projects that are not so closely tied to short-term applied goals or prospects are pursued in joint ventures with other companies or outsourced, as it were, to university departments, while the final steps in the development of a product are conducted behind closed doors. For instance, drug research typically involves two major steps: first, the identification of the relevant cell receptor, that is, the target protein whose activity or inactivity is part of the manifestation of a disease. Second, the identification of effective substances that are suited to affect the target appropriately. The first challenge is frequently handed over to university research and conducted in open labs, while the second phase is confined to industrial research sites.

This observation indicates that industrial research sometimes interacts with the academic sector, which provides another incentive for waiving restrictions on communication. One relevant effect is that taking advantage of the results produced by publicly funded fundamental research requires deeper understanding, which can be reached most conveniently by being locked into the pertinent research network. The reason is that part of the relevant know-how is tacit knowledge. It is hardly feasible to build a working device by relying on nothing but the knowledge published in research articles or laid down in the blueprints or patents that describe the operation of this device. Rather, research accomplishments achieved elsewhere are exploited most efficiently if one's own research laboratories have an advanced expertise in the relevant field—which they can best gain by conducting relevant research projects themselves. Yet being part of a research network demands making one's discoveries accessible to others (Rosenberg 1990, 171; Dasgupta and David 1994, 494; Nichols and Skooglund 1998).

The same desire to hook up with the academic research and education system translates via a different mechanism into public accessibility of findings of commercialized science. Companies regularly underwrite the work for diploma, master's, or Ph.D. theses. In exchange, they are granted the privileged use of the results. But this exclusive use expires after a limited time period (typically six to eighteen months), and the findings are published. After all, academic degrees are supposed to be conferred on their basis so that they need to be generally accessible.

In a similar vein, companies compete for the brightest brains and actively seek to produce an academia-like atmosphere in their research laboratories in order to attract them. Thus, industrial researchers are often allowed and encouraged to participate in conferences and publish in research journals. The guiding idea is that the simulation, as it were, of a university research lab contributes to strengthening the identification of the researchers with their company and to stimulating their creativity.[3]

Consequently, a plethora of mechanisms favor openness in commercialized research. In fact, a lot of industrial laboratories do publish their findings and seek recognition as scientifically reputable institutions. As a result, an exchange of ideas between academic and industrial research can be observed. It goes without saying that it would be better if all industrial research findings were publicly accessible from the outset. However, it would be worse if the knowledge had never been gained. It is not only the distribution of knowledge that counts but also its production. Given severe public budget restrictions, private funding contributes to securing academic research. Industrial sponsoring makes certain epistemic research projects feasible in the first place. Eventually, the conclusion is that secrecy in commercialized research raises problems, to be sure, but does not undermine the epistemic dignity of industrial research.

4. Application Pressure and the Emergentist View of Theory Structure

Applied research is faced with the charge of methodological decline. The tight epistemic demands that characterize epistemic research are said to be attenuated in commercialized science. Two reasons are adduced in support of this conclusion, namely, the pressure toward complexity and the pragmatic orientation of applied research. As to the first item, applied research has to deal with problems that are set from without, based on extrascientific considerations of an economic, social, or political nature. Accordingly, applied research cannot confine itself to areas in which effects appear without distortions, idealizations hold, and approximations work satisfactorily. The reason is that in order to be put to technological use reliably, phenomena and effects need to be known and controlled not only generically but also in their more remote properties and intricate aspects. The reason is that distortions and side effects are important in practical contexts; they cannot be neglected by focusing on the pure case—as it is well possible in epistemic science. As a result, applied research is driven toward the complex by specific causes that arise from the external selection of problems and are not equally operative in the whole of science.

Second, the principal goal of application-oriented inquiry is the search for the control of natural phenomena. Such projects strive for intervention in the first place, not for understanding (Polanyi 1962, 182–83). Due to its pragmatic attitude, applied research may appear to be committed to the production of short-term solutions and immediately useful results. Theoretical penetration is accepted only to the extent that is necessary to ascertain the proper functioning of some device. The pronounced pragmatism of application-dominated research is feared to translate into a restricted scope of theorizing and explaining so that applied scientists can be expected to resort to tentative epistemic strategies, which feature, for instance, local adaptations without theoretical integration and tend to cut off research from deeper epistemic aspirations. The commitment to immediate usefulness could prompt superficial judgments and eventually lead to trading the commitment to truth for the capacity of intervention.

In sum, the overtaxing of science by complexity might entail that applied research is at a loss to provide coherent theoretical accounts while the prevalent pragmatic attitude would make it appear superfluous to dig deeper for theoretical explanations. The goal to reach an understanding of natural phenomena is claimed to be abandoned in commercialized research (Bains 1997). Elucidating causal mechanisms or embedding the phenomena in the system of knowledge is said to be an epistemic luxury that industrial research cannot afford. As a result, commercialized science might comprise a heterogeneous collection of generalizations that are at best loosely tied to general theory and only weakly connected among themselves.

Nancy Cartwright has drawn attention to the failure of universal laws of nature to make it on their own all the way down to experience. Such laws and the highbrow theories of which they form a part are too abstract to capture the more subtle features of nature. They overgeneralize and thus lose touch with the richness of detail the phenomena exhibit. If the concrete experiences are supposed to be accounted for, generalizations of nontheoretical origin need to be part of the models (in addition to initial and boundary conditions). Rules of experience and specific assumptions bear the explanatory burden; tailor-made approaches are needed when the experiences are to be addressed in their full complexity. Descriptive adequacy only extends to small-scale accounts (Cartwright 1983, 45–50, 100–104; Cartwright 1996, 322–23).

Such an approach may be termed "emergentist." Emergentists feature the specific character of the phenomena at each level of organization and deny that insights into the theoretical principles that govern the constituents will have much impact on the clarification of the properties of organized wholes. The general laws that cover the undistorted behavior of the fundamental entities are not of much use for capturing the features of composites subject to the usual intersection of causal influences. Actually, this position squares well with Aristotelian views in the philosophy of nature. Aristotle insists on the basic nature of particulars and holds that they are prior to universals.[4] Emergentism can be taken to further accentuate this position and to hold that individual cases are always specific and unique if considered comprehensively. The differences among the particulars outweigh their shared features (Carrier 2006, 19).

The emergentist position does not refer to applied science in the first place but rather to "applying science" (a distinction due to Morrison 2006). The chief claim is that it is highly nontrivial to hook up theory with evidence and that the only way to get a grip on the phenomena is by making use of specific models that are tightly locked onto a particular problem. Still, emergentist approaches are tied up with a particular heuristic for applied research. Practical problems are to be confronted directly without taking a detour through fundamental research. Practical challenges should be addressed by doing research on precisely these practical challenges rather than directing research to the elucidation of the underlying principles and mechanisms. Fundamental truths only rarely produce technological spin-offs (Carrier 2004, 1–3, 9–14).

Emergentism in the methodology of applied research is buttressed by instances of technology development in which technological innovation was not accomplished by drawing on general principles but rather by recourse to experience with existing technology and by trial and error. Neither Thomas Edison's invention of the electric bulb or the phonograph nor Henry Ford's introduction of the assembly line owed anything to advanced theoretical penetration. The invention of the dishwasher was not prompted by a scientific breakthrough. A basic understanding of the matter, experience with technology, tinkering at the bench, and a good amount of ingenuity were needed instead. This applies equally to some more advanced technological innovations. The development of supersonic aircraft around 1950 proceeded largely independent of highbrow theory. Fluid dynamics had predicted at that time that air resistance or drag should soar for high subsonic speeds so that it appeared impossible to "break the sound barrier." The first supersonic aircraft was designed by ignoring fluid dynamics and by relying instead on practical knowledge and on experience with high speeds (Vincenti 1997, 822–23). Not one of these technological novelties was based on deeper scientific understanding of the universal properties of the constituents of the devices. The inventions were not based on a bottom-up analysis of the pertinent mode of operation, but rather on exploring the behavior of complex wholes by trial and error. Emergentism is not without support from the history of technology.

5. The Cascade Model: Control Based on Understanding

An alternative conception in stark contrast with this emergentist, mission-oriented account is the so-called linear model. This model involves the claim that fundamental research leads to applied research, which smoothly transforms into development and ends up with implementing the novelty. The four stages follow regularly upon each other (Stokes 1997, 3; Godin 2006, 639). According to the linear model, technological progress is achieved in a temporal sequence beginning with basic research, continuing with technological invention, moving on to development, and finishing with "innovation." At the origin, there is research performed without thought of practical ends, followed by investigations that are expected to have specific technological bearing or are concerned with translating scientific discoveries into products and procedures. Development involves the creation of new products on the basis of existing knowledge as well as the transfer of an invention from the lab to the manufacturing process. Finally, innovation has to do with bringing a technological novelty into commercial use, i.e., with the implementation and diffusion of an invention (Godin 2006, 639–57).

The linear model dominated science policy thinking throughout the twentieth century, and, in particular, during the first three decades after World War II. This preponderance was in considerable measure an effect of Vannevar Bush's report, *Science: The Endless Frontier* (Bush 1945), delivered in 1945 to the American president. The report provided arguments in favor of the linear model although it was not explicitly stated. The linear model had developed gradually over the previous century by the interaction of various communities—in accordance with Ludwik Fleck's ideas about the shaping of concepts. The model was produced *a motu sociali*—to use Fleck's apt phrase, that is, by sustained cross-reference of various social actors (Fleck 1936/1983, 92–96). The linear model is a social creation intended to track the organizational structure of science. Scientists from university and industry claimed that fundamental research is the source of technology, researchers from business schools brought in the development step, economists subsequently added the innovation phase. Eventually, the taxonomy survived and flourished because statisticians were in need of categories for structuring research expenditures (Godin 2006, 659).

The linear model is not tantamount to an approach that is much older and goes back to the scientific revolution. Francis Bacon suggested a then-revolutionary relationship between scientific knowledge and technological power, which is now sometimes called the "cascade model." The idea is that technological intervention relies on scientific understanding. Practical tasks are best solved by bringing to bear insights into the underlying processes. Controlling the course of nature demands uncovering nature's machinery; it requires studying the system of rods, gears, and cogwheels nature employs for the production of the phenomena (Bacon 1620/1990, I.§3, I.§110, I.§117, I.129). The pivot of the cascade model is logical or substantive dependence and only derivatively temporal sequence (which does make a difference; see below).

The philosophy of nature tied up with the cascade model is Platonism. Platonism in the philosophy of nature is committed to the rule of fundamental law; the universal is supposed to pervade the whole of nature. Whereas Aristotelianism emphasizes the variegated multiplicity of details that is part of each particular phenomenon, Platonism stresses the generic features of the phenomena that persist across changes in the relevant conditions and circumstances.

More specifically, the cascade model implies that subsuming a phenomenon under laws of nature or clarifying the causal processes by which it is connected to other phenomena constitute chief aspects of what it means to give a scientific explanation of the phenomenon. Accounting for a phenomenon in this fashion is an activity typical of epistemic science. Conversely, the theoretical integration and the causal explanation of an empirical regularity improve the prospect of bringing other factors to bear on the process at hand and to twist the latter so that it delivers more efficiently or more reliably what is demanded (Carrier 2004, 4–6). Consequently, the idea that the solution of practical problems is best achieved by theoretical penetration has not emerged from social interaction in the twentieth century. Rather, it was a revolutionary conception of the scientific revolution, advanced in addition to Bacon by Galileo Galilei and René Descartes, that technological intervention is best achieved by scientific understanding.

The cascade model refers at bottom to relations of entailment. It claims that technological development is dependent on scientific understanding, not necessar ily on recent scientific progress. By contrast, the linear model specifies the time sequence of epistemic research and technology development (and extends to development and innovation, which are left out of consideration by the cascade model) and implies that the best way to produce technological novelties is to sponsor fundamental research in a topically broad fashion. The linear model is now almost exclusively referred to with a critical intent. It is almost universally pronounced dead (Rosenberg 1991, 335; Stokes 1997, 84; Godin 2006, 639–40)—and rightly so. Yet the distinction between the linear model and the cascade model allows us to realize more clearly where the defect of the linear model lies and in which respect an element of truth is retained in it.

I mentioned examples from technological development that support the emergentist view, but there are contrasting instances in which technological achievements relied logically or with respect to their content on scientific understanding. Such instances are in harmony with the cascade model in that fundamental knowledge proved to be primary vis-à-vis practical utility and provided the basis for constructing useful devices. In such cases the practical solution involves the reorganization of knowledge elements known beforehand; such elements are combined in a novel fashion and entail hitherto unexpected consequences. The invention of gas discharge tubes or LEDs proceeded on the basis of insights into the interaction between electricity and matter; the invention of liquid crystal displays owed much to knowledge about the action of electric fields on liquid crystals and about the properties of polarized light. Likewise, the skyrocketing performance which research on computer hardware managed to accomplish over the past decades and the accompanying huge shrinking in size depended essentially on a thorough understanding of semiconductors at a microscopic level. This understanding was supplied by solid state physics, that is, epistemic science. Conversely, the failure of mission-oriented research can in some instances be attributed to insufficient basic knowledge. The lack of success of the American coordinated research program on fighting cancer in the 1970s, President Nixon's "war on cancer," is a case in point. The program was fashioned after the Apollo program and was intended to defeat cancer by pursuing targeted, application-driven research projects on a large scale. No tangible success came out of this endeavor; its major effect was a relabeling of research projects that were intended to be pursued for other reasons anyway. This failure is attributed with hindsight to insufficient basic knowledge about the disease (Hohlfeld 1979, 211–12).

In many cases, therefore, applied research really means bringing general principles to bear on specific, practical challenges—in accordance with the cascade model. Yet, in contrast to the linear model, these novelties did not in general emerge from recent findings in fundamental research. Some did, but others didn't, and the latter relied instead on established parts of the received system of knowledge. More often than not, the science invoked is of some age, yet it provided the basis for propelling new technologies. The body of scientific knowledge constitutes a huge reservoir of technological options that can be tapped at various locations, not only at the more recent additions (Rosenberg 1991, 337).

A second major fault of the linear model is that it confounds logical or substantive entailment of conceptions with the temporal order of their enunciation. Consider a pattern of technological development I call "application innovation." It involves the reversal of the linear model, that is, the emergence of theoretically significant novelties within the framework of use-oriented research projects. The typical pattern is that the solution of practical problems demands the clarification of some underlying process, and this challenge is addressed and eventually met within the applied research context (i.e., not by handing over the challenge to epistemic research). Innovative explanatory approaches that are relevant for basic research are formulated within mission-oriented research projects.

The first historical example of application innovation is Sadi Carnot's thermodynamic theory of the early nineteenth century. The theory grew out of the analysis of the steam engine and was designed to analyze and improve its workings. In order to accomplish this aim, Carnot introduced the seminal concepts of thermodynamic cycle and thermal efficiency. These concepts are of enduring theoretical significance up to the present day. A similar example is Louis Pasteur's microbiological theory, which was motivated by the desire to improve the quality of alcoholic fermentation. The pertinent industry suffered from some (at that time) mysterious problems and turned to Pasteur for helpful advice. Pasteur took on this practical challenge by inquiring into the causes underlying fermentation processes in wine, beer, vinegar, and others and found them in the action of microorganisms. In this vein, Pasteur created microbiology as a novel theoretical approach in contrast to the prevalent view, emphasized by Justus Liebig, that chemical, not biological processes were at the bottom of fermentation. Further, Carl Friedrich Gauß developed his groundbreaking contributions to mathematical statistics and probability theory as a means for coping with the problem of observational error. Faced with vacillating and divergent observation results, he devised a procedure for inferring the most probable true value from the collection of different observations.

The invention of "revolutionary technologies" arising from industrial research point in the same direction. The scanning tunneling microscope (STM) was conceived around 1980 at IBM in Zurich, that is, in an industrial laboratory. It was based on a new kind of scanning procedure and is now regarded as a major breakthrough and a first-rate technological achievement. The Nobel Prize awarded to Gerd Binnig and Heinrich Rohrer in 1986 bears witness to the scientific recognition of this novelty. The two researchers worked within a narrowly targeted research project on detecting inhomogeneities in thin films and looked for a method for identifying local changes in the atomic configuration. They turned to the tunnel effect, well known from quantum mechanics, in order to scan small regions of the sample surface. The physical basis is a dependence of the intensity of the tunnel current on distance. By moving an extremely sharp tip very closely over the surface in question, the local distortions of the atomic constellation translate into varying current intensity. Each such scan yields a narrow strip that can be added up and then represents a two-dimensional picture of the surface on which single atoms can be identified (Hon and Granek 2008). A mission-oriented, application-focused research project brought forth a device of fundamental importance and high scientific impact.

The same pattern is involved in the development of the polymerase chain reaction (PCR). The reaction was conceived and elaborated in a biotechnological company and is now one of the most important instruments in the whole area of microbiology (Mullis 1990). Similarly, the invention of so-called microarrays or DNA chips for high-speed automatic sequencing of gene strands originated in a start-up firm (founded by faculty members of various universities who wanted to explore practical opportunities offered by their scientific ideas). The microarrays have developed into a major platform of biomedical research (Lenoir and Giannella 2006).

These technologies are called "revolutionary" not because they were based on unprecedented principles and procedures. This is not the case; rather, they employed familiar approaches and combined them in a new way. Their revolutionary impact lies in their potential to provide answers to new questions and to be fruitful in various research contexts. The conceptual impact on academic research was indirect in that new surveying technologies opened up new areas of research. A more immediate conceptual impact is present in other use-oriented projects in the life sciences. The inquiry into the genetic and enzymatic processes that control cell division has generated knowledge about the foundations of cellular replication, but offers at the same time prospects of intervention if cell division gets out of hand. These studies were conducted in order to achieve a more effective cancer therapy (which practical interest is underscored by the fact that the Nobel Prize for medicine in 2001 was awarded to the corresponding scientists) (Fritsche 2001). Yet they also generated fundamental insights into the mechanism of cell division and thus had a direct theoretical impact.

The crucial point is that application innovation contradicts the linear model but is in conformity with the cascade model. It is at odds with the linear model since stimulation is directed from the applied to the basic realm; practical problems, not fundamental insights, mark the beginning of the inquiry. Conversely, the cascade model says that applied problem solutions are in their content based on fundamental knowledge. They need to take recourse to theoretical principles in meeting practical challenges, and this is made evident by the formulation of such principles in case they are missing in the system of knowledge. The logical relations are in agreement with the cascade model; the model explains in this way why the temporal development proceeds in the reverse direction. The cascade model accounts for the failure of the linear model.

Accordingly, the cascade model has a wider domain of application than the linear model. It includes exceptions to the latter. In addition to doing justice to application innovation, the cascade model also suggests that epistemic science is not always sufficient for producing technological novelties. Sometimes practical stimuli constitute an important catalyst for unveiling the underlying mechanisms and enunciating the pertinent principles that provide the basis for the technological innovation. In replacing the stress on time order by the emphasis on entailment, the cascade model reveals that it is a misunderstanding to believe that basic research automatically produces practical novelties. As a result, the transition from science to technology may need active support and institutional assistance (Etzkowitz 2006).

Yet the cascade model is also beset with important weaknesses. The first one is that its underlying Platonism needs to be qualified: the bearing of universal theories on explaining the phenomena is smaller than assumed within the cascade framework. It is among the chief insights of the so-called "model debate" from the mid-1990s onward that theories need models as "mediators" in order to bridge the gap between general principles and the subtleties of experience. The salient point is that the models typically used for applying theories are more complex than it was traditionally assumed in the philosophy of science. Such mediating models often do not only contain laws and boundary conditions but additional conceptual elements, such as generalizations from divergent theoretical sources or even without theoretical backing (that is, rules of experience), approximations and correction factors, or parameters that can only be evaluated empirically (that is, read off from the data). Consequently, such models cannot be derived from highbrow theory. They rather rely to a considerable extent on extratheoretical assumptions, and their construction may involve a highly creative process. The "articulation" of a theory, the procedure of bringing to bear theoretical principles on concrete evidence, does in no way resemble a deductive chain but needs to resort to additional empirical, conceptual, and mathematical resources (Morrison 1999; Winsberg 2003; see Carrier 2004, 6–13).

Consequently, the connection between the theoretical principles and their applications, that is, concrete accounts of the phenomena, is less tight than assumed within the cascade model. This creates room for a third mode of technology development. This "interactive" view of the relationship between theory and experience agrees with the cascade model in granting theory a key role in shaping the models. In contrast to the emergentist approach, models are not assumed to be constructed afresh and tailor-made to cope with particular challenges. Such phenomenological models are avoided in favor of models whose conceptual backbone is provided by theory while the details are filled in by recourse to observation. Yet the interactive approach agrees with emergentism in emphasizing the limitations of overarching theory to the generic features of a situation and the corresponding inclusion of local generalizations, correction factors, and a large amount of information about the specific conditions in question in the descriptive models. Comprehensive principles typically fail to capture the variegated subtleties of experience whose consideration is indispensable for constructing devices on a theoretical basis. This is why theoretical understanding may be of only limited help for technology development (as the examples given in section 4 reveal).

To recapitulate, there are three modes of interrelation between epistemic science and its applications. First, theoretical understanding produces technological progress. Second, technological improvements are based on existing technology as well as tinkering and handicraft. Third, practical problems induce research initiatives that bring about epistemic progress. The first and the third mode agree with the cascade model, whereas the second mode corresponds to the emergentist view and reveals that applied research has a life of its own (Stokes 1997, 87–88).

6. The Uses of Understanding in Commercialized Research

The challenge ahead is to clarify the reasons for the usefulness of theory in applied research, in spite of its limited grip on the phenomena, while highlighting at the same time the origins of these limitations. Why is it a good strategy to bring theory to bear on practical problems if theoretical understanding is often limited to the generic features of the situation while reliable intervention often needs to take the details into account? I wish to briefly expound three such reasons which have to do with the *identification* of relevant parameters, the *generalization* of the results, and with *ascertaining their reliability* in the face of distortions.

The first reason for drawing on theory is the crucial assistance it offers for the identification of the relevant quantities. Theoretical accounts serve to highlight the influential quantities and suggest relations among them. In this way they accomplish a figure–ground distinction, which is often a prerequisite of fruitful empirical investigation. Examples from the history of science provide ample testimony to the fact that relations which appear obvious in hindsight had escaped the notice of experimenters and were only identified after theoreticians had indicated what to look for. For instance, Brownian motion was studied intensively and unsuccessfully for decades in search of simple regularities. Only when Albert Einstein in 1905 managed to derive such regularities it became clear to the experimenters which quantities they should have attended to all along.

An example from applied research in pharmacology concerns the development of captopril, the first ACE-inhibitor. Captopril was identified in 1981; it lowers blood pressure by inhibiting the enzyme ACE (angiotensin converting enzyme). The substance had remained undetected by extensive schematic screening procedures and was not found until the research strategy switched to a so-called "rational" mode. That is, when the research was guided by a physiological hypothesis about the mechanism of the enzymatic action of ACE, captopril was eventually discovered. Investigating the phenomena without advance understanding, however tentative, of what are possibly relevant factors may thwart the discovery of empirical generalizations that appear highly plausible with hindsight (Adam 2005, 523–24; Adam, Carrier, and Wilholt 2006, 440–41).

Second, the generalization of theory-shaped models is much easier than the transfer of phenomenological models to new cases encountered. Phenomenological models are shaped conceptually by the demands of the problem-situation at hand. They are not necessarily completely independent of theory, but they contain comparatively few elements that transcend the particulars of the explanatory challenge addressed. As a result, each such problem needs to be approached on its own terms. For instance, the prediction of the tidal flow of a particular harbor is not based on the known causal mechanism underlying the phenomenon but is rather achieved by performing a Fourier analysis of the tidal oscillations observed in the past. The reason is that the influence of a multiplicity of factors relevant for the quantitative details of tidal flow (such as coastline, water depth, currents) can hardly be assessed on first principles so that the phenomenological analysis is more robust empirically (Sauer 2004). The drawback is that results gained in this phenomenological fashion cannot be transferred to different coastal areas; the latter needs to be addressed completely afresh. By contrast, theory-based models whose empirical shortcomings are rectified by parameter fitting and correction factors can be used for a whole class of phenomena. Without employing generic conceptions, each phenomenon had to be attacked without benefiting from the solution to the former.

An example of how theoretical accommodation facilitates generalization in applied research refers to a chemical reaction pattern called olefin metathesis. This pattern involves the exchange of carbon atoms between different compounds and provides a means for dissolving carbon double bonds which is difficult to achieve otherwise. However, the reaction was hard to control; it was not clear under which circumstances it proceeded and at what rate. The causal mechanism was discovered in the early 1970s and the role of metallic catalysts disclosed. Only after the mechanism was understood could the reaction pattern be applied reliably to óther cases not studied beforehand. The clarification of the mechanism, albeit incomplete and subject to further specification for the particular cases, made it possible to generalize the reaction pattern, anticipate the outcome of changed conditions, and develop more efficacious metallic catalysts. Olefin metathesis is now regarded as a revolution in organometallic chemistry; the Nobel Prize for chemistry of 2005 was awarded for its clarification (Groß 2005).

Third and finally, theories are of outstanding importance when the reliability of a device or procedure is to be secured in the face of distorting factors. Ascertaining robust operation typically demands elucidating the underlying causal mechanism. The history of pharmacological research is replete with examples of this sort. Statements about the therapeutic efficacy of a certain medical drug are initially phrased as contextualized causal relations. Such relations are restricted to typical or normal conditions and leave the pertinent causal processes out of consideration. "Penicillin cures bacterial infections" is a contextualized causal relation. It usually holds true but possesses exceptions for particular persons or conditions, and it contains nothing as to how the effect is brought about. Yet if the efficacy of a drug is to be improved or pernicious side effects are to be controlled, the mechanism of action needs to be cleared up. For instance, research on how to circumvent bacterial resistance against antibiotics proceeds from assumptions as to how the drug acts. Ciprofloxacin, an antibiotic drug released in 1982, resulted from a targeted inquiry into the causes of resistance to other antibiotics. The substance works by intervening in the spiraling and despiraling processes of bacterial DNA, thus inhibiting cell division. The research endeavor had focused on identifying lipophilic substances that could enter extravascular tissue and thus unfold their activity beyond the bloodstream. In sum, if perturbations intrude, upholding the desired operation of a procedure demands theoretical penetration.

Consequently, theoretical understanding is of chief importance for intervening reliably in natural processes. Limitations of bringing general theory to bear are not due to methodological sloppiness or an alleged inclination toward superficiality in applied research. For the greater part, such limitations are produced by the inherent complexity of practical problems. This complexity becomes salient if the details really matter, which is the case when technological challenges are on the agenda. By contrast, scientific understanding can often be based on the consideration of the pure or undistorted cases that can be captured by appeal to generic features only. In other words, limitations of the theoretical grip on the phenomena are due in some cases to the Aristotelian primacy of the particular or the wealth of subtle details inherent in the phenomena. Consequently certain lacunae or deficiencies of models are not to be blamed on the underlying theory. They do not represent anomalies, let alone refutations, that can be fixed by improved theorizing. Rather, some empirical shortcomings of the models betray general limitations of generic approaches in capturing the appearances without remainder. Such shortcomings can only be removed by filling in the interstices, left open by theory, by taking recourse to observation, adjustment, and correction. Although the conceptual backbone of the models is supplied by theory, the empirical content of these models needs to be specified by determining the missing pieces from the data and by fitting parameters to the particular cases.

However, we could not possibly drop generic approaches since it is only on their basis that we are able to understand.[5] We understand a phenomenon by placing it in the vicinity of a related one, by seeing both as different instances of the same kind. And we understand a phenomenon by tracing the causal chain of events leading from a certain type of cause up to a type of effect. Although generic approaches may be unable in principle to reach unrestricted accuracy, we have no choice but to adopt them in coming to grips with the phenomena. This is the human way of making sense of experience.

These same virtues of unification and causal analysis are also essential for successful research on practical matters. Theoretical integration of a generalization or clarification of intermediate processes facilitates intervention. Theoretically understood relations can be generalized more easily and applied to a wider range of conditions; causally reconstructed sequences can be altered specifically. Consequently, such relations are more useful in practical respects. It follows that industrial research or research in the context of application need not pose a threat to the epistemic dignity of science; neither theory structure nor confirmation procedures vary significantly between university institutes and industrial laboratories (Wilholt 2006, 81). Theoretical unification and causal analysis are inherent in both pure and applied research because such methodological virtues promote understanding and intervention at the same time.

7. Commercial Bias and a Pluralist Notion of Objectivity

The conclusion I wish to advance is that epistemic standards are not significantly undermined by economic interests. This conclusion might appear naïve in view of examples of obvious economic bias in judging claims. A particularly striking case is clinical trials in drug research. Surveys have revealed that results of tests of the comparative efficacy of new medical drugs comply to a high degree with the commercial interests of the sponsors of the pertinent study. In a survey of 107 comparative medical studies on competing drugs, not a single published paper was identified in which a drug produced by the sponsor of the study was found inferior to a product of a competitor. To all appearances, the prevalence of commercial interests does create an epistemic predicament in medical research (Davidson 1986; Lexchin et al. 2003; Brown 2008).

However, clinical drug trials are extraordinary in various respects and cannot be considered representative of commercialized research in general. Properly speaking, the critical case of so-called phase 3 clinical trials (to which the studies mentioned refer) does not even constitute research in the first place since nothing new is supposed to be found out. Rather, the expectation is that the earlier research outcome is confirmed. The standardized legal procedure for admitting new drugs comprises phase 1 studies, in which safety is tested; phase 2 inquiries, in which efficacy is examined; and phase 3 trials, in which the earlier findings are supposed to be confirmed with large patient groups. The latter trials are the most time-consuming and expensive part of the admission procedure.

The research process, properly so-called, precedes these phase 3 trials and is finished when the latter are set out. Such clinical trials are not exactly part of the research endeavor but of the legal procedure required for market access; they are obstacles to be overcome by pharmaceutical companies. The aim pursued here is not to generate new knowledge but to get supposed knowledge approved by the authorities in charge. Consequently, clinical trials are trivial in methodological respect; they involve nothing but routine procedures. No creativity, no novel perspectives are called for; the agenda involves no more than proceeding by the books. At the same time, the stakes involved are extremely high. Bringing out a new medication costs millions of euros so that the loss incurred upon failed trials may really hurt a company. Finally, the relevant effects are often small and subtle; they arise only with a low frequency within a framework of lots of other factors to which such effects might be attributed. This means companies can hope to get away with leaving ambivalent data out of consideration.

All these features are highly unusual and in no way typical of empirical tests in commercially relevant research. The exceptional factor is that no genuine epistemic interests exist among those who pay for the study. The sponsors don't want to know; rather, they believe they know and want to pass an inconvenient and economically risky examination quickly and without much ado. This is different in applied research proper, in which the sponsors of a study expect to receive new information and gain novel insights. Proprietary research ventures are launched because something as yet unknown is sought to be unveiled. Intruding in the research process from the business or administrative level can be expected to backfire. In fact, outside of the special realm of phase 3 clinical trials, in none of the known scandals about data manipulation has any outside interference on the part of the sponsors been identified.[6] And this is highly plausible in the first place since tampering with the outcome would be against the interests of the sponsors. What they pay for is reliable, robust results which stand the test of practice, not the approval of wishful thinking that would collapse under real-life conditions. Commercialized science does not enjoy the privilege of purely epistemic research to go wrong without thereby doing damage to the world outside of libraries and laboratories. In industrial research, unreliable performance or serious side effects may jeopardize a company. As a result, the standards of reliability are frequently placed at a level comparable to academic research.

There is a more fundamental or in-principle issue behind the question whether commercial interests induce a bias that is prone to generate one-sided and mistaken outcomes. According to the Baconian tradition, the objectivity of science is tantamount to the objectivity of scientists. They need to relinquish their prejudices and consider the problem-situation at hand from a detached point of view which includes all relevant perspectives. Conversely, no factors should intrude in the consideration that are merely subjective and do not represent factual elements of the situation at hand. Scientific objectivity is conceived as adequacy to the facts which is said to be rooted in the disinterestedness or neutrality of the individual scientists.

However, this individualist conception of objectivity has been shown to be unrealistic. Humans fail across the board to relinquish their prejudices. A contrasting, social notion of scientific objectivity was introduced by Karl Popper and

Imre Lakatos; it conceives of objectivity as a control of prejudices (rather than their abandonment) in a pluralist setting.[7] Scientists are allowed to be biased; different biases are supposed to keep each other in check. This approach suggests separating the objectivity of science from the objectivity of scientists. The individuals need not be disinterested; rather, in the large majority of instances, scientists pursue interests that transcend the research endeavor they perform. They may be eager to confirm or refute some assumption in order to promote their reputation or support some worldview—or they may aim at economic benefit. Such interests need in no way undermine the objectivity of science. In the pluralist understanding of objectivity, what matters is not to free scientists from all unfounded suppositions but rather to control judgments and interests by bringing to bear contrasting judgments and interests.

Competition among companies can contribute to stimulating such reciprocal control. As a rule, a number of corporations competitively struggle for a given novelty or innovation. Competition serves to provide a type of pluralism resembling the sort suggested by the social conception of objectivity. For instance, if research proceeds in a false direction in a company, there is a good chance that the involved scientists may be proven wrong by the more successful research product of a more fortunate competitor. If one company publishes fake research reports that give a false lead to their own product, the competitor will be glad to disclose the mistake. In conformity with the social notion of objectivity, competing interests serve to mutually rectify the defects of interest-guided research, and reliability is achieved by bringing contrasting voices to bear on a subject. The required pluralism can be expected to arise from the commercialization of research (Carrier 2008, 225–26).

However, objectivity does not emerge automatically within commercialized science. In a number of cases, pluralism is conspicuous in its absence—as the longstanding, unanimous denial of risks involved in smoking by the tobacco industry amply demonstrates. Biased results are not always challenged by a competitor who confronts them with differently biased outcomes. In areas relevant to the public, such as safety issues, such contrasting approaches need to be initiated by public sponsorship. Faced with an undisputed consensus, it's better to look twice and cast a fresh glance on the matter. Publicly funded institutions need to contribute to generating the plurality of approaches in case commercialization fails to maintain it. It is a continued challenge for research in the public interest to promote the openness of science and a plurality of approaches within science and to ascertain in this way the commitment of science to objectivity.

8. Conclusion

The assumption underlying the present inquiry is that one can gain worthwhile insights into the possible impact of commodification on academic research by studying the real impact of commercialization on industrial research. The upshot is that science centered on private interest need not suffer from a methodological decline and is in most cases not substantially different from publicly financed research. After all, interests of application are heavily emphasized in many publicly sponsored research endeavors, too. Rigging results does not serve this aim of discovering relations that could be put to commercial use. Rather, elucidating the causal context and the theoretical integration of an empirical generalization is the most promising way of ascertaining the validity and the relevance of this generalization and thus contributes to making a reliable technological use possible. Technological intervention is achieved best by relying on knowledge that has passed tough standards of quality control. This is the chief reason science can be expected to withstand the pressure of practice in methodological respect. Methodology represents a sort of safety cord that keeps commercialized science on the epistemic track.

Moreover, the commercialization of science has made a number of research projects possible in the first place. Large amounts of research in physics, chemistry, and biology would have never been undertaken if no economic interests were at stake. Regarding some fields of research, the alternative to commercialized science is not fundamental research, nor research directed at the common good, but rather no research at all. Presumably, in some such cases of undone research, the ensuing lack of knowledge would be detrimental to public welfare. The production of knowledge is an important asset and merits appreciation.

However, what remains worrisome regarding commercialized research is problem selection according to expected short-term economic benefit. A commercially biased research agenda serves its customers, to be sure, but humans are not mere customers, nor are all humans customers. I distinguished between fundamental research, commercialized research, and research in the public interest (see section 1). It deserves emphasis that the latter branch of research only thrives on public support. The pursuit of public interests is a matter of public concern in the first place. That is, the potential one-sidedness of the commercialized agenda should be counteracted by public efforts to redress the balance. It is not written in stone that medical research is almost completely handed over to pharmaceutical companies. Pursuing research projects complementary to those of the drug industry should be a primary commitment of public medical science. Uneven research expenditure of the sort outlined needs to be corrected by public intervention. The natural means to accomplish this sort of science in the public interest is non-commodified academic research.

NOTES

1. In well-ordered science, the research agenda is established on the basis of the preferences of the citizens of a society. Kitcher envisages a process of deliberation in which legitimate research topics are singled out by mediating the interests of the members of a society (Kitcher 2001, 117–23). The ideal of well-ordered science is supposed to represent a counterpoint to corporate research as it prevails presently. In commercialized science, the preferences of only a few members of a society are brought to bear on identifying research objectives. Research pursued under the pressure of market forces is likely to be shaped by the nonmediated interests of "the rich and powerful" (Kitcher 2002, 570).

2. This analysis is based on a talk by Kees Eijkel at the Bielefeld Center for Interdisciplinary Research (ZiF) on June 4, 2007. Eijkel is chief executive officer of Kennispark Twente, run (among others) by the University of Twente and responsible for its technology transfer activities and business development.

3. This information is based on an interview conducted with Rolf Krebs, former medical research director and chief executive officer of Boehringer Ingelheim, in Mainz, on April 21, 2007. The same policy of modeling an open, universitylike atmosphere is claimed to be pursued by the Walldorf-based software company SAP. The company advertises this policy (which includes the liberty of pursuing individual research goals) as a means for stimulating creativity.

4. At least this is how the ontology Aristotle outlines in the *Categories* is usually interpreted. A substance is characterized by its independent existence: substances can exist without presupposing the existence of other, more basic entities. Species and higher-order genera are not of this sort (in contrast to Plato's views); they are merely "secondary substances." Rather, the existence of species and genera presupposes the existence of individuals—which is why particular things are primary and basic whereas universals are derivative (Aristotle 1963, *Categories* 2ª 11ff; Rapp 2007, 147–48).

5. See Cartwright (1983, 57–61) for elaborating the tension between accuracy of representation and understanding, construed by her as a trade-off between truth and explanatory power.

6. The most striking cases of this sort in the past years were due to Friedhelm Herrmann and Marion Brach (Germany, 1997), Jan Hendrik Schön (U.S., 2002), and Hwang Woo Suk (South Korea, 2004).

7. Popper 1962/1971, 112; Lakatos 1970/1978, 68–69. "Disinterestedness" is also part of Merton's ethos of science. Yet Merton conceived of disinterestedness as an institutional feature, not a psychological factor, which becomes manifest (in a quite Popperian vein) in the scrutiny of the claims entertained by fellow scientists (Merton 1942/1973, 275–76). Social epistemology likewise conceives of objectivity in this pluralist, procedural sense (Longino 2002, 128–35).

REFERENCES

Adam, Matthias. 2005. "Integrating research and development: The emergence of rational drug design in the pharmaceutical industry." *Studies in History and Philosophy of Biological and Biomedical Sciences* 36:513–37.

Adam, Matthias, Martin Carrier, and Torsten Wilholt. 2006. "How to serve the customer and still be truthful: Methodological characteristics of applied research." *Science and Public Policy* 33:435–44.

Aristotle. 1963. *Aristotle's Categories and De interpretatione.* Ed. and trans. J. L. Ackrill. Oxford: Clarendon.

———. 1998. *Aristotle's Metaphysics.* Trans. H. Lawson-Tancred. Harmondsworth: Penguin Books.

Bacon, Francis. 1620/1990. *Neues organon I.* Ed. W. Krohn. Hamburg: Meiner.

Bains, William. 1997. "Should we hire an epistemologist?" *Nature Biotechnology* 15:396.

Brown, James R. 2008. "The community of science®." In *The challenge of the social and the pressure of practice: Science and values revisited,* ed. Martin Carrier, Don Howard, and Janet Kourany, 189–216. Pittsburgh: University of Pittsburgh Press.

Bush, Vannevar. 1945. *Science: The endless frontier: A report to the president.* Washington, DC: U.S. Government Printing Office; available at http://www.nsf.gov/od/lpa/nsf50/vbush1945.htm.

Carrier, Martin. 2004. "Knowledge gain and practical use: Models in pure and applied research." In *Laws and models in science,* ed. D. Gillies, 1–17. London: King's College Publications.

———. 2006. "The challenge of practice: Einstein, technological development, and conceptual innovation." In *Special relativity: Will it survive the next 101 years?,* ed. J. Ehlers and C. Lämmerzahl, 15–31. Heidelberg: Springer.

———. 2008. "Science in the grip of the economy: On the epistemic impact of the commercialization of research." In *The challenge of the social and the pressure of practice: Science and values revisited,* ed. Martin Carrier, Don Howard, and Janet Kourany, 217–34. Pittsburgh: University of Pittsburgh Press.

Carrier, Martin, Don Howard, and Janet Kourany, eds. 2008. *The challenge of the social and the pressure of practice: Science and values revisited.* Pittsburgh: University of Pittsburgh Press.

Cartwright, Nancy. 1983. *How the laws of physics lie.* Oxford: Clarendon Press.

———. 1996. "Fundamentalism versus the patchwork of laws." In *The philosophy of science,* ed. D. Papineau, 314–26. Oxford: Oxford University Press.

Concar, David. 2002. "Corporate science versus the right to know." *New Scientist* 173 (March 16): 14–16.

Dasgupta, Partha, and Paul A. David. 1994. "Toward a new economics of science." *Research Policy* 23:487–521.

Davidson, Richard. 1986. "Source of funding and outcome of clinical trials." *Journal of General Internal Medicine* 12 (3): 155–58.

Etzkowitz, Henry. 2006. "The new visible hand: An assisted linear model of science and innovation policy." *Science and Public Policy* 33:310–20.

Fleck, Ludwik. 1936/1983. "Das problem einer theorie des erkennens." In *Ludwik Fleck. Erfahrung und tatsache. Gesammelte aufsätze,* ed. L. Schäfer and T. Schnelle, 84–127. Frankfurt: Suhrkamp.

Fritsche, Olaf. 2001. "Geburtenkontrolle bei zellen." *Spektrum der Wissenschaft* 12:14–22.

Gibson, Elaine, Françoise Baylis, and Steven Lewis. 2002. "Dances with the pharmaceutical industry." *Canadian Medical Association Journal* 166:448–50.

Godin, Benoît. 2006. "The linear model of innovation: The historical construction of an analytical framework." *Science, Technology and Human Values* 31:639–67.

Groß, Michael. 2005. "Die olefin-metathese." *Spektrum der Wissenschaft* 12:23–25.

Hohlfeld, Rainer. 1979. "Strategien gegen Krebs—Die planung der Krebsforschung." In *Geplante forschung: Vergleichende studien über den einfluß politischer programme auf die wissenschaftsentwicklung*, ed. W. van den Daele, W. Krohn, and P. Weingart, 181–238. Frankfurt: Suhrkamp.

Hon, Giora, and Galina Granek. 2008. "Generating experimental knowledge: The invention and development of the scanning tunneling microscope." In *Generating experimental knowledge*, ed. U. Feest et al., 121–27. Max-Planck-Institute for the History of Science Preprint 340.

Kitcher, Philip. 2001. *Science, truth, and democracy*. Oxford: Oxford University Press.

———. 2002. "Reply to Helen Longino." *Philosophy of Science* 69:569–72.

Kuhn, Thomas S. 1962. *The structure of scientific revolutions*. Chicago: The University of Chicago Press, 1996.

Lakatos, Imre. 1970/1978. "Falsification and the methodology of scientific research programmes." In *The methodology of scientific research programmes*, Philosophical Papers, vol. 1, ed. J. Worrall and G. Currie, 8–101. Cambridge: Cambridge University Press.

Lenoir, Tim, and Eric Giannella. 2006. "The emergence and diffusion of DNA microarray technology." *Journal of Biomedical Discovery and Collaboration* 1 (11): 1–39.

Lexchin, Joel, et al. 2003. "Pharmaceutical industry sponsorship and research outcome and quality: Systematic review." *British Medical Journal* 326:1167–70.

Longino, Helen E. 2002. *The fate of knowledge*. Princeton, NJ: Princeton University Press.

Merton, Robert K. 1942/1973. "The normative structure of science." *The sociology of science: Theoretical and empirical investigations*, 267–78. Chicago: University of Chicago Press.

Morrison, Margaret. 1999. "Models as autonomous agents." In *Models as mediators: Perspectives on natural and social sciences*, ed. M. S. Morgan and M. Morrison, 38–65. Cambridge: Cambridge University Press.

———. 2006. "Applying science and applied science: What's the difference?" *International Studies in the Philosophy of Science* 20:81–91.

Mullis, Kary B. 1990. "The unusual origin of the polymerase chain reaction." *Scientific American* 262 (4): 56–61, 64–65.

Nichols, Steven P., and Carl M. Skooglund. 1998. "Friend or foe: A brief examination of the ethics of corporate sponsored research at universities." *Science and Engineering Ethics* 4:385–90.

Polanyi, Michael. 1962. *Personal knowledge: Towards a post-critical philosophy*. London: Routledge & Kegan Paul.

Popper, Karl R. 1962/1971. "Die logik der sozialwissenschaften." In *Der positivismusstreit in der deutschen soziologie*, 3rd ed., ed. T. W. Adorno et al., 103–23. Neuwied: Luchterhand.

Rapp, Christof. 2007. *Aristoteles zur einführung*. Hamburg: Junius.

Rosenberg, Nathan. 1990. "Why do firms do basic research (with their own money)?" *Research Policy* 19:165–74.

————. 1991. "Critical issues in science policy research." *Science and Public Policy* 18:335–46.

Sauer, Albrecht. 2004. "Im wandel der gezeiten." *Spektrum der Wissenschaft* (May): 56–59.

Schweber, Silvan S. 1993. "Physics, community and the crisis in physical theory." *Physics Today* (November): 34–40.

Stokes, Donald E. 1997. *Pasteur's quadrant: Basic science and technological innovation.* Washington, DC: Brookings Institution Press.

Vincenti, Walter G. 1997. "Engineering theory in the making: Aerodynamic calculation 'breaks the sound barrier.'" *Technology and Culture* 38:819–51

Wilholt, Torsten. 2006. "Design rules: Industrial research and epistemic merit." *Philosophy of Science* 75:66–89.

Winsberg, Eric. 2003. "Simulated experiments: Methodology for a virtual world." *Philosophy of Science* 70:105–25.

Ziman, John. 2002. "The continuing need for disinterested research." *Science and Engineering Ethics* 8:397–99.

CHAPTER 9

Robert Merton, Intellectual Property, and Open Science

A SOCIOLOGICAL HISTORY FOR OUR TIMES

Henk van den Belt

1. Introduction

LET US START with a remarkable letter from the famous chemist (and economist) Antoine-Laurent Lavoisier, written at a crucial juncture of the French Revolution when the Jacobins set out to reorganize or abolish the Academy of Sciences:

> SECOND LETTER TO MR. LAKANAL,
> DEPUTY AT THE CONVENTION,
> 18 July 1793
> *Citoyen,*
>
> As I am totally unacquainted with the plans that have been suggested for the suppression or reorganization of the Academy of Sciences, it might be possible that the remarks that I had the honor to address to you yesterday do not entirely correspond to your views.
>
> I hear, for instance, that one intends to make the Academy of Sciences into an association for sciences and arts. The motivation that inspires the scientists [*les savants*], if you allow me, differs completely from the motivation that inspires and that must inspire the craftsmen [*les artistes*]. The scientist works

only out of dedication to science and to enhance the reputation he enjoys. Once he has made a discovery, he will exert himself to publish it, and his aim has been achieved when he has secured his property, when it has become established that it is really his. The craftsman, by contrast, always aims to gain some benefit, either from his own investigations or from applying the discoveries of others; he publishes only what he cannot keep to himself; he tells only what he cannot hide.

Society benefits equally from the scientist's discovery and the craftsman's interested pursuits. They are both indispensable to the public good. But if you bring the craftsmen and the scientists together, they will both lose their characteristic spirit: the scientist will then become calculating, he will no longer work for fame nor for the advancement of human knowledge; it will appear more attractive to him to occupy himself with material gains, and from that very moment there will no longer be any academicians in the proper sense of the word.

Citoyen, this spirit of disinterestedness dominating the Academy of Sciences is a precious gift that is part of its tradition from the very beginning. The members of the Academy live in the midst of craftsmen; they are privy to their secrets. Each day offers opportunities for making a fortune, but no academician has ever entertained the idea to take advantage of them. Convert this simplicity of mores into a spirit of gainful pursuit [*esprit de spéculation*], and the most beautiful society that I know, the Academy of Sciences, where morality, simplicity and virtue reign to the fullest extent, will no longer exist. . . .

A. L. Lavoisier[1]

When Lavoisier wrote this letter to Lakanal he was the treasurer of the Paris Academy of Sciences. Joseph Lakanal was a prominent member of the Committee of Public Instruction of the National Convention, the legislative body that actually held executive power during the first three years of the French First Republic (from September 20, 1792, to October 26, 1795). Due to the turbulent political circumstances, Lavoisier had been the only permanent and active officer of the Academy of Sciences for the preceding year and a half (its secretary, the Marquis de Condorcet, had been too directly involved in parliamentary politics). It seemed a forgone conclusion that the convention was going to abolish Old Regime institutions like the Académie Française, the Academy of Painting and Sculpture, and the Academy of Architecture, but Lavoisier engaged in intensive lobbying to save the "temple of science" from a similar fate.

I reproduced such a large part of Lavoisier's letter because it has a special relevance for us today in that it combines a plea for "open" science with a particular conception of intellectual "property." The letter also neatly illustrates two main components of the so-called scientific ethos described by Robert K. Merton:

the norms of "communism" and "disinterestedness" of the famous CUDOS quartet (the other two being "universalism" and "organized skepticism"). Lavoisier captured what Merton refers to as the paradoxical or distinctive anomalous nature of "intellectual property" within the domain of science: "the more freely the scientist gives his intellectual property away, the more securely it becomes his property. . . . Only when he has published his ideas and findings has the scientist made his scientific *contribution* and only when he has thus made it part of the public domain of science can he truly lay claim to it as his" (Merton 1979, 47). It is also notable that Lavoisier's distinction between the characteristic motivations of *savants* and *artistes* prefigures the ideal-typical distinction between the realms of science and technology that economists Partha Dasgupta and Paul David introduced in 1994:

> It is the nature of the goals accepted as legitimate within the two communities of researchers, the norms of behavior especially in regard to the disclosure of knowledge, and the features of the reward systems that constitute the fundamental structural differences between the pursuit of knowledge undertaken in the realm of Technology and the conduct of essentially the same inquiries under the auspices of the Republic of Science. . . . [R]esearch undertaken with the intention of selling the fruits into secrecy belongs unambiguously to the realm of Technology. (Dasgupta and David 1994, 228)

Even more, it seems that Lavoisier already anticipated their economic argument that an institutional arrangement in which the two complementary spheres are clearly separated is most conducive to the advancement of knowledge and technology and thus to the general welfare (Dasgupta and David 1994, 239–40).[2]

At the risk of committing a grave anachronism, I would like to draw a further parallel with our own time. As we know, Lavoisier's solemn declarations on the moral virtues of the Académie des Sciences were to be to no avail, even though he spoke the language of the times. The radical Jacobins had no tolerance for what they considered an elitist institution that was still tainted with its previous role during the Old Regime, and on August 8, 1793, the academy was closed (see also Hahn 1971, 226–51). Lavoisier himself was beheaded on May 8, 1794, having been convicted on several charges, the revolutionary tribunal reputedly declaring, "The Republic has no need of scientists." Would it be too far-fetched to compare the Jacobins' attitude toward "academic" science with the views of a present-day detractor of "autonomous" science like Steve Fuller, who regards the Mertonian ethos as an ideological smokescreen for defending the narrow guild interests of the scientific elite (Fuller 1997; Fuller 2000a; Fuller 2000b)? Presumably, Fuller would also have opposed "the cult of merit" (Hahn 1971, 240) of the members of the Academy of Sciences, which the Jacobins considered incompatible with a democratic society.[3] Just as Fuller resents the arrogance of evolutionary biologists against popular creationism in the United States—"But what exactly would be wrong with teachers trying to render biological findings compatible with the Creationist commitments of most of their students?" (Fuller 2000b, 416)—the Jacobins took offense at the arrogance and mathematical pretensions of physical scientists thought to be insulting the virtuous simplicity of the craftsmen: "Theirs would be a science which, as to its technological aspect, would be a docile servant, and as to its conceptual, a simple extension of consciousness to nature, the seat of virtue, attainable by any instructed citizen through good will and moral insight. 'Let anyone be a savant who wishes,' is Cassini's summary of the Revolution" (Gillispie 1959, 681).[4] The latter phrase is echoed in the slogan of present-day advocates of intense public participation in science and technology policy: "we are all experts now" (Nowotny 2003, 156). I also can't help noting an uncanny resemblance to Fuller's avowedly republican program for the governance of science. After all, his "meta-theory" would "justify the participation of the *entire society* in the process of mutual criticism rather than just a self-selected community of experts" (Fuller 2000b, 400–401).

2. Discrepancies in the Conception of Intellectual Property

2.1. The Shifting Meanings of a Key Expression

Merton's use of the term "intellectual property" as the basic unit for recognition and reward within science may cause astonishment and perplexity as it is definitely at odds with the dominant use of the expression nowadays. At present, "intellectual property," often abbreviated to IP, is an umbrella term covering a range of legal instruments such as patents, copyright, designs, and trademarks. When the issue of IP is brought up today in connection with science, what usually comes first to mind is the patenting of scientific results (e.g., decoded DNA sequences) or the use of restrictive legal devices like material transfer agreements. It is most unlikely that the expression will currently still evoke the norm of "communism"— though it was precisely by adhering to that norm, according to Merton, that scientists established their private property by freely giving its substance away. So why, then, did Merton talk of "intellectual property rights" when he discussed questions of recognition and esteem within the domain of science, presumably knowing full well that the expression had quite different, even contrasting con-

notations in other spheres of life? This would seem to be a recipe for causing unnecessary confusion. Did Merton invent the concept all by himself? Did he make
it up out of thin air?

The norm of communism entails that the results of scientific research are
published within a reasonable time and assigned to the community: "Secrecy is
the antithesis of this norm; full and open communication its enactment" (Merton
1973, 274). The substantive findings of science constitute a common heritage;
they do not enter into the exclusive possession of the discoverer or his heirs. This
means that the rights of intellectual property are extremely curtailed: "[P]roperty
rights in science become whittled down to just this one: the recognition by others
of the scientist's distinctive part in having brought the result into being" (Merton
1973, 294–95). If one thinks about it, this is a very strange and curious notion of
"property"; it has indeed, as Merton himself notes, a "distinctive anomalous
character" (Merton 1979, 48). One might even wonder whether the term "property" is justifiably used at all in this context; wouldn't it be more appropriate to
speak of a right of recognition of "intellectual paternity" (or "intellectual mater-
nity" or, gender-neutrally, "intellectual parenthood") rather than of a right of
"intellectual property"? In a footnote Merton gives some examples of the language used by scientists in speaking of their work, to establish that "the notion of
property is part and parcel of the institution of science," but these examples are
not fully convincing.[5] True, they show that a property-*related* idiom is sometimes
used by scientists, but they do not demonstrate the presence of the notion of intellectual property in the precise, minimal sense in which he uses it.[6]

Nevertheless, Merton by no means invented the notion of intellectual property in this pregnant sense out of thin air. In fact, his employment of the term
reflects a fairly common usage within science, especially in Germany, throughout
the nineteenth and early twentieth century. To give just one example: the German
medical scientist and Nobel laureate Emil Behring wrote about the priority disputes in which he was involved in the following terms: "In that manner I tried only
to secure my intellectual property [*geistiges Eigentum*], albeit with all the ruth-
lessness I could muster" (quoted in Satter 1967, 20).[7]

As an umbrella term for patents, copyrights, trademarks, and several other
legal devices, by contrast, the expression "intellectual property" only started to
enter into common use after the founding of the World Intellectual Property Organization (WIPO) by the United Nations in 1968 (Lemley 2005). The economist
Frederic Scherer, who has been studying patent questions for more than half a
century, remarks that "the phrase 'intellectual property' was almost never heard
during the 1950s and 1960s" (Scherer 2007, 42). After the founding of WIPO, sev-

eral groups and organizations saw strategic advantages in this expression and set out to propagate its use. Thus the American Patent Law Association changed its name into American Intellectual Property Law Association. The new umbrella term lumps various legal devices together under one rubric and suggests that as different forms of "property" they can all be considered as analogous to ordinary physical property. In earlier times some European countries had used other generic terms like "industrial property" (*propriété industrielle*) to cover patents and trademarks as against "literary and artistic property" (*propriété litéraire et artistique*) to designate copyrights and the like. The expression "intellectual property" was rarely used in patent offices and courts. Sometimes, the term "industrial property" was even used to make a contrast with a Merton-like concept of intellectual property. Thus in December 1913 the Dutch Patent Office (*Octrooiraad*) rejected a patent application for a purely scientific finding with the following argument: "The elaboration of the problem that the applicant set himself does not lie in the domain of industry, because it resides not in the domain of industrial property but of intellectual property"[8] (de Reede 1937, 170). In this usage, patentable inventions did not belong to the realm of intellectual property but to that of industrial property. Intellectual property was reserved for the findings of "pure" science.

Such shifting meanings clearly underscore the need for a critical study in historical semantics (Williams 1983) in order to reconstruct the varying senses of key concepts and their mutual relations, not just in the allegedly confined domain of pure science, but also in related spheres like technology and literary writing. Merton himself gave an interesting hint in this direction in a footnote of his prewar monograph *Science, Technology and Society in Seventeenth-Century England*, without ever following up his own suggestion:

> The frequency of disputes concerning priority which, to my knowledge, first becomes marked in the sixteenth century, constitutes an interesting problem for further research. It implies a lofty estimation of "originality" and of competition; values which were very largely foreign to the medieval mind which commonly sought to cloak the truly original under the tradition of earlier periods. *The entire question is bound up with the rise of the concepts of plagiarism, patents, copy-rights and other institutional modes of regulating "intellectual property."* (Merton 1938, 169; my italics)[9]

Although Merton followed up the first part of this youthful suggestion with a delay of twenty years in his 1957 essay on "Priorities in Scientific Discovery" (Merton

1973, 286–324), he has never heeded the second part of it (italicized in the above quotation). Of course, priority is not just a concern in science, but also in technology and in the institutional realm of patent law, where novelty is established according to the "first-to-file" (Europe) or "first-to-invent" (U.S.) rule.

I think that his increasingly one-sided focus on the norms of "pure" science (rather than the relations between science and technology) has been responsible for this omission. While Merton had made his debut as a sociologist of science in 1938 with the publication of his reworked dissertation (Merton 1938), it was his essay from 1942 on the so-called "scientific ethos"—the normative framework for the conduct of science—which would provide the basic ingredient for what was to become the so-called Mertonian paradigm (Merton 1973), 267–78). Compared to his prewar work, in which he had analyzed the influence of Puritanism on seventeenth-century science and the relationship between science and technology, the focus was now much more on science as a relatively autonomous social institution, or in other words, on "pure" or "academic" science. The normative foundations of *this* kind of science were formulated as *the* "scientific ethos."[10] It took several more years before the outlines of the Mertonian paradigm became clearly visible. Important contributions were Merton's work on priority disputes (1957) and on "multiple" or simultaneous discoveries (1961) (see Merton 1973, 286–324, 343–70). These contributions constituted the heart of the Mertonian paradigm, because they forged a link between the normative structure of science (as described in the 1942 essay) and its reward system (to which later studies would be dedicated). Drawing the different threads together, Merton was finally able to offer a unified analysis of the functioning of science as a specific "social system," in line with the explanatory schemes of functionalist sociology in general. This advance in theoretical coherence, however, went *pari passu* with a marginalization of the older theme of the relations between science and technology. As so often is the case, there were both gains and losses.

2.2. Patents and the Science-Technology Distinction

Merton's essay from 1942 on the normative ethos of science contains a strong political statement, which is admirable for its candidness but which on closer inspection also betrays a theoretical difficulty for his treatment of science and technology: "The communism of the scientific ethos is incompatible with the definition of technology as 'private property' in a capitalistic economy" (Merton 1973, 275). It is indeed beyond dispute that publishing one's work without being directly recompensed for each publication constitutes an "anomaly" for a capitalistic society (Merton 1988, 623), but why should this institutional norm for science be "incompatible" with the arrangements that obtain in the (supposedly) separate sphere of technology? Perhaps Merton was vaguely aware that it is not so easy to demarcate science from technology (or "pure science" from "applied science," or "basic research" from "applied research"), so that technology may not be such a separate sphere after all. As Jerry Ravetz pointedly remarks in a related context, "Unfortunately, it is impossible to make a neat line of division between the two sectors, allowing one to serve Truth and the other Caesar" (Ravetz 1971, 23). Merton himself drew attention to a peculiar strategy regularly used by scientists to ensure that their work remains freely available: it consists in taking out patents on their findings and then immediately letting those patents lapse into the public domain. This preemptive measure presumes that there is no neat division between science and technology.[11] Merton listed the illustrious names of Einstein, Millikan, Compton, and Langmuir as scientists who have engaged in this practice; he could also have mentioned the prominent example of Pasteur, who was highly praised during his life for this form of self-effacing behavior.[12] Merton also indicated two other possible responses to the conflict situation, to wit, advocating socialism (as the British physicist John Desmond Bernal did) or encouraging scientists to become entrepreneurs (as Vannevar Bush did in 1934): "These proposals—both those which demand economic returns for scientific discoveries and those which demand a change in the social system to let science get on with the job—reflect discrepancies in the conception of intellectual property" (Merton 1973, 275).[13] In the postwar period, these "discrepancies" were solved or at least mitigated through unexpected government largesse for basic research, in conformity with the views set out in Vannevar Bush's famous report *Science: The Endless Frontier* (1945).[14] The option of "entrepreneurial science" temporarily receded from view, only to make a spectacular comeback after 1980.

In shifting his postwar theoretical interest toward purely academic science and away from its entanglements with technology, Merton moved in a direction that conformed to the thrust of American postwar science policy with its emphasis on so-called basic research (compare Fuller 2000a, 118). Indeed, some of Merton's critics regard this category and the implied distinctions with other forms of activity as no more than "an artifact of the Cold War regime" (Mirowski and Sent 2002, 22). Without wishing to take such a completely dismissive position, I have to admit that the somewhat blurred distinction between science and technology, or basic and applied research, constitutes a challenge to Merton's views of intellectual property.[15]

3. Intellectual Property and the French Revolution

3.1. The Enlightenment Debate: Diderot versus Condorcet

The period of the Enlightenment and the French Revolution would undoubtedly be a strategic research site for a historical-critical inquiry into the underlying discrepancies in the conception of intellectual property. Here is where we have to look to follow up the hint tucked away in the footnote of Merton's prewar monograph.

In prerevolutionary France, two leading intellectuals, Denis Diderot and the Marquis de Condorcet, had adopted diametrically opposed views with regard to copyright protection for books, with Diderot arguing in favor and Condorcet against such protection (Diderot 1763; Condorcet 1776). In his *Letter on the Book Trade,* which had been commissioned by the Paris Publishers and Printers Guild, Diderot argued that ideas represent the most inviolable form of property because they are the creation of the individual mind; they would thus ground a natural property right as the basis for an eternal copyright privilege on texts, which the author could transmit to his heirs (or his publisher). In comparison to property in ideas, Diderot held, property in land could only be a social convention that was not based on nature. Condorcet, by contrast, rejected *privilèges de librairie* or copyright on books on the grounds that such privileges would inhibit the diffusion of useful knowledge among the literate public and thereby the progress of "enlightenment" and the advance of happiness. He implicitly alluded to what nowadays would be characterized as the "public good" nature of knowledge. According to Condorcet, there could not be a relationship of exclusive ownership between a person and an idea, as there could between a person and a plot of land or a piece of furniture—the latter types of property derived from the natural order, but an exclusive right in ideas or works was just a privilege imposed by society, not a true right. As his exposition was oriented more to the writings of scientists than to poetical or dramatic works, we can interpret his argumentation against copyright as an early plea for the norm of communism in science:

> Indeed, let us assume that a book is useful; what makes it so is the truths it contains. Now, the privilege granted to the author does not extend so far as to prevent another person from expounding those same truths, to order them more intelligibly or offer better proofs, to develop them further or extend their consequences. Hence, the author of this useful book really has no privilege. . . . I can, if I like, publish a solution to the problem of the precession of equinoxes, set forth a general principle of mechanics, etc. etc. The author of these great and useful discoveries will have no cause for complaint: the glory will remain his. (Condorcet 1776, 57–58)

Thus, the only right reserved for a scientist is the recognition and fame (the "glory") others bestow on his discoveries, which of course presumes that his name remains connected to the discoveries he made. In this respect Condorcet's view agreed with that of his fellow academician Lavoisier.

Transplanted to a different plane, we can regard the contrasting views of Diderot and Condorcet as a variant of the recurrent opposition between the "heroic" theory of discovery and invention and the theory of the social determination of discovery and invention (on the regular alternation between these two theories, see Merton 1973, 352). Diderot's views on artistic creativity are also in conformity with romantic and idealistic conceptions of authorship which took shape in the later part of the eighteenth century and which were also used to justify legal protection of literary writings (see Woodmansee 1984).[16]

3.2. The Political Compromise of the French Revolution

During the French Revolution a new legal basis had to be sought to protect and regulate the rights of authors and inventors, as the royal "privileges" of the Old Regime were no longer acceptable. The question was whether Diderot's or Condorcet's views would prevail (Hesse 1990). At first sight it looks as if Diderot has won. The new legislation made rhetorical appeals to man's supposedly natural property rights in relation to his thoughts (Savignon 1989). Thus article 1 of the Patent Law of 1791 solemnly stated that every discovery or invention in all branches of industry was the property of its "author." The same principle was also adopted as the basis for the new copyright law of 1793 (regulating *le droit d'auteur*), which had been prepared by a committee that was presided by Joseph Lakanal (the same deputy of the convention to whom Lavoisier wrote his letter).[17] However, the new patent and copyright laws only granted rights that were limited in time, against Diderot's view that a natural property right would be of eternal duration. They were a political compromise between Diderot's and Condorcet's positions, not a philosophical resolution of the tension between the two. As Carla Hesse wrote about the new French copyright law,

> But the law did not resolve the epistemological tension between Condorcet and Diderot. Rather, it produced an unstable synthesis between the two positions. It drew upon Diderotist rhetoric of the sanctity of individual creativity as an inviolable right, but it did not rigorously respect the conclusions Diderot drew from this position. . . . [T]he law did not recognize the author's claim beyond his lifetime but consecrated the notion that the only true heir to an author's work was the nation as a whole. The notion of a "public domain," of

democratic access to a common cultural inheritance upon which no particular claim could be made, bore the traces, not of Diderot, but of Condorcet's faith that truths were given in nature and, though mediated through individual minds, ultimately belonged to all. Progress in human understanding depended not on private knowledge claims but rather on free and equal access to enlightenment. Authors' property rights were conceived as a recompense for the author's service as an agent of enlightenment through the publication of ideas. (Hesse 1990, 128–29)

The final legislative stages for the new copyright law coincided in time with the plans to abolish all academies, including the Academy of Sciences. When Lavoisier wrote his second letter to Lakanal, on July 18, 1793, he must have been aware of the views on property rights in ideas that circulated among the members of the National Convention, but as an academic scientist he only claimed "recognition" for his discoveries as his sole "property right"—asserting that the quest for reputation and fame rather than material gain was his overriding motive. We may infer that on this particular point Lavoisier's letter failed to impress Lakanal (assuming that it reached him in time), because on the very next day, July 19, 1793, the latter presented the draft for a new copyright law to the convention with the following words:

> Citizens, of all the forms of property, the least susceptible to contest, whose growth cannot harm republican equality, nor cast doubt on liberty, is property in the productions of the genius. . . . By what fatality is it necessary that the man of genius, who consecrates his efforts to the instruction of his fellow citizens, should have nothing to promise himself but a sterile glory and should be deprived of his claim to legitimate recompense for his noble labors? (Quoted in Hesse 1990, 128)

"Sterile glory" also sounds as a (probably unintended[18]) condemnation of the goals pursued by the distinguished savants of the Academy of Sciences.

3.3. Thomas Jefferson and the French Connection

Even before the First French Republic was to put the protection of the rights of authors and inventors on a new legal footing, the newly formed American republic across the Atlantic had already accomplished a similar task after its break with the English crown. The first result was article 1, section 8, clause 8 of the U.S. Constitution of 1787, also known as the Copyright and Patent Clause: "Congress shall have Power . . . to promote the Progress of Science and useful Arts, by securing for limited Times to Authors and Inventors the exclusive Right to their respective Writings and Discoveries." This clause in the Constitution was implemented in the U.S. copyright statute ("an Act for the encouragement of learning") and in the U.S. Patent Act of 1790. A notable difference with the French copyright and patent acts that would be passed a few years later is that the American legislation did not explicitly construe the exclusive rights to be granted as property rights. The American framers and legislators seem to have thought very much in terms of promoting the public interest. The decision to grant exclusive rights "for limited times" can accordingly be seen as the outcome of some rough utilitarian balancing with this aim in view. Legal historians disagree, however, about the question of whether notions of property rights had indeed been virtually absent in their considerations (for a dissenting view, see Mossoff 2007).

The similarities and differences in copyright and patent law of the two republics are part of a larger narrative on the historical confluence and divergence of the French and American Enlightenment. Recent historical scholarship has extensively documented the pervasive influence of Condorcet's thought on the socioeconomic and political views of two of the founding fathers of the United States, James Madison and Thomas Jefferson (McLean 2002; Schofield 2005). Unfortunately, the area of copyright and patent law has been a blind spot in the investigation of cross-Atlantic exchanges. I suspect that Condorcet's ideas may also have had a deep influence on Jefferson's views on patents. Jefferson, the principal author of the Declaration of Independence and a science enthusiast and inventor as well, was from 1785 to 1789 minister plenipotentiary (a kind of ambassador with the authority to conclude commercial treaties) in Paris, where Benjamin Franklin introduced him to the secretary of the Academy of Sciences, the marquis de Condorcet. Before long, he and Condorcet became "intellectual soulmates" (McLean 2002). Jefferson shared Condorcet's optimistic view on the perfectibility of human nature and his faith in the possibility of unlimited progress in science and technology. He was also much impressed by Condorcet's mathematical approach to the problems of social and political science, which anticipates modern social choice theory (e.g., the voting paradox, the jury theorem).

From Paris Jefferson criticized the Copyright and Patent Clause (as well as other parts) of the newly adopted U.S. Constitution. In a letter to his friend Madison he wrote that "the benefit even of limited monopolies is too doubtful to be opposed to that of their general suppression" (Jefferson 1788). Apparently, he would have preferred a general prohibition on monopolies without conceding an exception for patents and copyrights as temporary monopolies, because he was not too sure that their presumed effect on the encouragement of learning and the useful arts would be substantial enough to compensate for their disadvantages.

It is ironic that a person who entertained so many doubts about the advantages of patents was to become, as George Washington's secretary of state, directly in charge of the administration of the U.S. Patent Act of 1790. As one legal historian writes, "Jefferson was never enamored of the patent system and throughout his life displayed a marked ambivalence toward it" (Walterscheid 1999, 220). From 1790 to 1793, he was a member of the Board of Arts (together with the secretary of war and the attorney-general), which had to examine the applications filed by inventors and to decide on the issuance of patents (Meier 1990). It was a burdensome job from which he was only relieved when the new Patent Act of 1793 was passed and the existing examination system was replaced by a registration system. In his role as patent examiner Jefferson reputedly set the highest standards of patentability.

Jefferson's detailed views on the patent system can be drawn from a long letter that he wrote many years later, in 1813, to an inventor named Isaac McPherson (Jefferson 1813). The occasion was the attempt by another inventor, one Oliver Evans, to aggressively pursue his patent rights on the automatic gristmill against infringers (see also Meier 1990, 29ff). In his letter Jefferson cited various "anticipations" from the scientific and technological literature that called the novelty of the invention into question. But the letter is most famous for the passages exhibiting Jefferson's mature reflections on those peculiar characteristics of ideas that make them singularly unfit as objects of property rights. Here is a fairly long quote:

> If nature has made any one thing less susceptible than all others of exclusive property, it is the action of the thinking power called an idea, which an individual may exclusively possess as long as he keeps it to himself; but the moment it is divulged, it forces itself into the possession of every one, and the receiver cannot dispossess himself of it. Its peculiar character, too, is that no one possesses the less, because every other possesses the whole of it. He who receives an idea from me, receives instruction himself without lessening mine; as he who lights his taper at mine, receives light without darkening me. That ideas should freely spread from one to another over the globe, for the moral and mutual instruction of man, and improvement of his condition, seems to have been peculiarly and benevolently designed by nature, when she made them, like fire, expansible over all space, without lessening their density in any point, and like the air in which we breathe, move, and have our physical being, incapable of confinement or exclusive appropriation. (Jefferson 1813)

Here, in almost poetic language, Jefferson singles out the two key characteristics of a very peculiar "good" that economists would later designate as a (pure) "public good," to wit, *nonexcludability* ("the moment it is divulged, if forces itself into the possession of every one") and *nonrivalry* in consumption ("no one possesses the less, because every other possesses the whole of it"—"he who lights his taper at mine, receives light without darkening me"). It is perhaps no coincidence that Jefferson assigns these two attributes to "ideas." Indeed, modern economists are wont to mention knowledge and information as prime examples of public goods (Stiglitz 1999). My speculation is that Jefferson's view on the public-good nature of ideas has been derived from Condorcet, as the latter had already set out a quite similar view in his debate with Diderot on copyrights. The cosmopolitan perspective of the "mutual and moral instruction of man" on a global scale is also reminiscent of Condorcet's grand visions.

In edited collections Jefferson's letter to McPherson sometimes appears under the heading "No patents on ideas." The editors of his work may be forgiven for choosing such a catchy title, but this simple message is, strictly speaking, *not* the conclusion to be drawn from Jefferson's exposition of the public-good character of ideas. Just after the quoted passage, the letter continues: "Inventions then cannot, in nature, be a subject of property. Society may give an exclusive right to the profits arising from them, as an encouragement to men to pursue ideas which may produce utility, but this may or may not be done, according to the will and convenience of the society, without claim or complaint from any body" (Jefferson 1813). The point is thus that inventors do not have a natural property right to their inventions; society may decide to grant exclusive rights for a limited period as incentives for inventors on the basis of some utilitarian calculus of overall net benefit. The public-good nature of inventions does not as such militate against their being patented. Indeed, if inventions were naturally "excludable," it would not be necessary to seek a special "exclusive" right, that is, a legal right to exclude others from using the invention. However, as patent protection involves the serious drawback of preventing the use of the invention that otherwise could be allowed at no or only negligible additional cost (due to the nonrivalry attribute), it is clear that the benefits to be expected from introducing exclusive rights must be considerable to tilt the utilitarian balance in their favor. In the end, Jefferson was not convinced that a persuasive case for patents had been made.

3.4. A Legacy of Unresolved Issues

Emanating from revolutionary France, the new conception of intellectual property —or "property in the products of the mind," as Hegel referred to it in his *Rechtsphilosophie*—also gained currency in the rest of Europe, especially in Germany, where idealist philosophers like Fichte, Hegel, and Schopenhauer were particularly receptive to the new idea. The concept of *geistiges Eigentum* also percolated to German science, where it assumed an almost Mertonian shade of meaning. In one of his conversations with Eckermann, held on December 30, 1821, Johann Wolfgang Goethe touched upon the subject of priority disputes in science: "Questions of science are very frequently career questions. A single discovery may make a man famous and lay the foundation of his fortunes as a citizen. . . . Every newly observed phenomenon is a discovery, every discovery is property. Touch a man's property and his passions are immediately aroused" (Eckermann 1835, 22–23). This is a nice illustration of Merton's thesis that priority disputes in science turn about matters of intellectual property, the objective occasion for their occurrence being the fact that many discoveries in science are "multiple" discoveries (Goethe had been personally involved in at least two such "multiples," first with Félix Vicq d'Azyr in 1780 on the discovery of the intermaxilliary bone in the human skull, and later with Lorenz Oken on another discovery).

Outside the sphere of science, however, the very concept of intellectual property remained deeply controversial throughout most of the nineteenth century. The proponents of economic liberalism often considered copyright and patents as restrictive "privileges" characteristic of the Old Regime, no longer fit for the new era of free trade (Machlup and Penrose 1950). In the Netherlands such views even led to the abolition of the existing patent law in 1869. (Incidentally, the contrast with the economic liberalism at the end of the twentieth century is quite remarkable. Now the worldwide recognition of intellectual property rights is seen as the cornerstone of an international system of "free" trade—TRIPS is part of the WTO. Hence Mirowski and Sent use the phrase "globalized privatization regime" to designate the science funding regime after 1980.) It was only in the last quarter of the nineteenth century, when the free trade doctrine had been discredited by the Great Depression, that a general revaluation of patents and copyright set in. At the heyday of economic liberalism, however, the Dutch jurist Jan Heemskerk, who served as a minister in several Dutch cabinets, formulated his principled objections against "the inappropriateness of the designation *propriété intellectuelle"*: "What, after all, is property? Property is the right to have free enjoyment of a thing and to dispose of it in the most absolute manner. . . . Property without the possibility of exclusive possession is unthinkable; and the actual possession, which property presupposes, can only be thought of as a right to material objects" (Heemskerk 1856, 2–3). Similar voices can be heard in our own time. Thus Richard Stallman, the founder of the Free Software Foundation and a declared opponent of software patents, attacks the expression "intellectual property" as a "distorting and confusing term":

> It has become fashionable to toss copyright, patents, and trademarks—three separate and different entities involving three separate and different sets of law—into one pot and call it "intellectual property." . . . The term carries a bias that is not hard to see: it suggests thinking about copyright, patents and trademarks by analogy with property rights for physical objects. . . . These laws are in fact not much like physical property law, but use of this term leads legislators to change them to be more so. Since that is the change desired by the companies that exercise copyright, patent and trademark powers, the bias of "intellectual property" suits them. (Stallman 2006)

Stallman's claim is supported by the work of legal scholars like Mark Lemley, who interpret and criticize the dominant trend in patent, copyright, trademark, and related legislation and jurisprudence as one of increasing "propertization" (Lemley 2005).

4. Science as "Competitive Cooperation"

4.1. Cooperation, Teamwork, and the Quest for Personal Recognition

Merton was keenly aware that the scientific enterprise was not just cooperation but also competition. He coined the phrase "competitive co-operation" (Merton 1973, 273–74).[19] The competition is not so much, or not primarily, about the acquisition of monetary rewards, but turns on recognition and esteem, credit and reputation. Scientists cooperate to extend the frontiers of knowledge, but they compete with each other to be the first in making important discoveries. By publishing original contributions, they will earn recognition and esteem among their colleagues and the symbolic rewards that derive from these: *eponymy* (e.g., Boyle's Law, Condorcet paradox, Zeeman effect), medals, fellowships and membership of prestigious organizations, ennoblement (in the U.K.), and, of course, the Nobel Prize. A modern quantitative measure of "recognition and esteem" is provided by the Science Citation Index. The institution of science thus provides powerful incentives, albeit mainly of a nonmonetary character, for channeling individual efforts into the pursuit of collective aims.[20]

It is not always sufficiently recognized that the quest for personal fame plays such a prominent role in the scientific enterprise. Starting with Sir Francis Bacon, many writers have emphasized the collective nature of scientific work while simultaneously downplaying the importance of the quest for personal glory, sometimes to the point of dismissing such a motive as altogether inappropriate. Edgar Zilsel follows Bacon in this respect and contrasts the fame-hungry humanist *literati* of the Renaissance with the authentic scientists:

Essential to modern science is the idea that scientists must cooperate in order to bring about the progress of civilization. Neither disputing scholastics nor literati, greedy of glory, are scientists. Bacon's idea is substantially new and occurs neither in antiquity nor in the Renaissance. . . . As is generally known, Bacon's *Nova Atlantis* greatly influenced the foundation of learned societies. (Zilsel 1942, 557–58)

Zilsel, like Bacon, sees the cooperation but ignores the competition within science. The quest for personal fame, so prominent among humanist *literati,* is not absent among scientific researchers either. It is significant that already in the first decades of its existence the Royal Academy of Sciences in Paris, like the Royal Society in London one of those learned societies inspired by Baconian ideas, was forced to gradually abandon its policy of anonymous publication on which it had initially decided (Hahn 1971, 24–28).

Since the times of Bacon, as Merton notes, views on the progress of science and technology have also typically alternated between "collectivistic" theories centered on the social determination of scientific discovery and the "individualistic" or "heroic" theory centered on men of genius (Merton 1973, 352). Merton himself has tried to steer a careful middle course between these two extremes. I think there is real virtue in this attempt. One of its lasting merits is the recognition of frequently occurring conflicts over intellectual property (in the usual form of *priority disputes*) as a phenomenon that is characteristic of the institution of science and that should be seriously studied in its own right rather than politely ignored (as is often done by "individualistic" writers) or condemned as utterly futile (as is often done by "collectivistic" writers).

Interestingly, this issue was also brought up in one of the earliest critiques of Mertonian sociology of science from the nascent post-Kuhnian Edinburgh school. In 1970 Barry Barnes and Alex Dolby called into question the effective power of the scientific ethos to govern the behavior of scientists. They further claimed that "the possessibility of discoveries" represents a historically variable institutional form, which reached its zenith in the professionalized science of the nineteenth century (and even then did not operate ideally) and has declined in importance ever since. They emphasize the inherent difficulties in attributing a discovery to one person and point out that "discovery as a property right is not as clear and natural as has been thought" (Barnes and Dolby 1970, 21). (As if Merton had ever asserted anything of this kind! Why would there be priority disputes at all if the attribution of discoveries to persons were crystal clear?) They also refer to emerging new patterns: "The tendency for research to be done by whole teams, no one member of which can be called the discoverer of anything produced, has not caused the tension that might have been expected" (Barnes and Dolby 1970, 22). I think that this prediction of the impending demise of intellectual property may be somewhat premature. Barnes and Dolby risk treading in Zilsel's footsteps by assuming that the more scientists cooperate in teams the less reason they have to be concerned about their personal reputations. There is indeed a secular historical decline in the relative frequency of priority disputes, as has been established by Merton himself (Merton 1973, 365). Apart from that, however, it must be noted that there *are* cases in which team research has produced tensions with regard to intellectual property. Examples are disputes about the discovery of insulin in 1921–1922 (Bliss 1982), the discovery of streptomycin in 1943 (Mistiaen 2002; Kingston 2004), the discovery of pulsars in 1967 (Broad and Wade 1982, 143–49), the discovery or invention of the polymerase chain reaction or PCR in 1985 (Rabinow 1996), and the creation in 1996 of the first cloned mammal, Dolly the sheep (Sample 2006). The question requires at least more empirical investigation before such confident statements as asserted by Barnes and Dolby can be made with any assurance.

4.2. Merton versus Fleck

One illuminating case can be found in Ludwik Fleck's *Genesis and Development of a Scientific Fact* (Fleck 1935), which is generally considered to be a precursor not only of Thomas Kuhn's paradigm theory but also of modern varieties of social constructivism. Merton had been instrumental in having an English translation published and persuading Kuhn to write a foreword to it. Fleck makes some rather oblique allusions to the dispute over the intellectual ownership of the Wassermann reaction, which erupted in the aftermath of the development of this serological test for detecting syphilis (the main topic of Fleck's monograph)—as a bitter epilogue, so to speak.[21] In Fleck's collectivistic view, it was the serologists' collective or team led by August Wassermann that was the real "author" behind the development of the Wassermann reaction from initial irreproducible experiments along a veritable zigzag course toward what was eventually to become a clinically usable test. He claims that the principal actors in the drama (*die Heroen der Handlung*, as the German original ironically calls them) cannot tell us how it happened, "for they rationalize and idealize the development" (Fleck 1935, 76). He holds their defective epistemology, based on an individualistic point of view, responsible for this alleged inability. In Fleck's view, this defective epistemology lies also at the root of the fierce dispute over "authorship and contribution to the discovery of this extremely important reaction" (176n24) which erupted in 1921 between several of the protagonists, or "the lively polemics between, and personal protestations by, the various workers involved" (69). Fleck uses the occasion of this struggle over the *intellectual property* of the Wassermann reaction (for that is how we can describe it in Mertonian terms) to criticize each of the participants. He accuses them of using such "unscientific" notions as "lucky accident" or "the intuition of a genius" (76). If only they had adopted *his* superior sociological epistemology, Fleck seems to imply, then surely they never would have fought over such futile matters as the intellectual ownership of a scientific discovery. The sociological significance of such disputes, apparent from a Mertonian perspective, has completely eluded him. Paradoxically, the collectivistic bent of his sociological approach has led him to criticize the participants in this conflict rather than to treat such a dispute as a proper object for sociological analysis in its own right. In line with his approach, Fleck considers science as an exclusively *cooperative* venture, whereas the scientific enterprise is better seen as one of *competitive* cooperation.[22]

My claim is that the collectivistic thrust of Fleck's sociology of knowledge made him singularly ill-equipped to adequately deal with the struggle over the intellectual ownership of the Wassermann test—with dire consequences for his interpretation of the entire process of development. Only by putting on the spectacles provided by the Mertonian sociology of science, which takes a more balanced position between individualism and collectivism, is it possible to do justice to the intricacies of this dispute and to clear away the misunderstandings that block a proper understanding of the formation of the Wassermann reaction. The case also shows the subtle operation of Merton's "principle of cumulative advantage" (also known as the *Matthew effect* according to Matthew 25:29: "For unto every one that hath shall be given"), working especially in Wassermann's favor and to the detriment of his former collaborators. A more careful reading of the dispute helps to dispel many of the apparent riddles and mysteries that surround the development of the serodiagnosis of syphilis.[23] Or so I would argue (see van den Belt 1997 for a detailed elaboration).

5. Scientific Knowledge as a Public Good

5.1. Economics and the Sociology of Science

In her beautifully written review article on the economics of science, economist Paula Stephan credits Merton and his pupils with having provided a vital insight: "a priority-based reward system provides incentives for scientists to behave in socially beneficial ways. In particular, it can be demonstrated that the reward of priority encourages the *production* and *sharing* of knowledge and thus goes a long way toward solving the appropriability dilemma inherent in the creation of the public good knowledge" (Stephan 1996, 1229). The economic argument that the market would underinvest in the production of a "public good" like scientific knowledge (especially fundamental scientific knowledge) and that this provides a rationale for extensive government investment in (basic) scientific research, was most forcefully presented by Richard Nelson (1959) and Kenneth Arrow (1962). Briefly, the argument runs as follows. As a (pure) public good is characterized by "nonexcludability" and "nonrivalry," a private firm would generally not find it attractive to produce such a good because there would be no way to appropriate (a sufficient part of) the benefits to cover production expenses. Yet given the huge amount of benefits to be expected, it would be highly desirable from the viewpoint of the public interest to produce the good in sufficient quantity. Theoretically, it might be possible to solve the appropriability problem by devising suitable IP legislation. However, in the case of fundamental scientific knowledge, "patent laws would have to be unimaginably complex and subtle to permit such appropriation on a large scale" (Arrow 1962, 173).[24] In the end, then, it is appropriate for the government to step in and finance basic scientific research in order to ensure the optimal allocation of resources.[25]

We should guard against a possible misunderstanding of this economic rationale for government spending on basic research. It is sometimes assumed that establishing the public-good character of scientific knowledge suffices to make the case against patenting and for public funding. Thus, in a report on genomics and global health, the U.N. Genomics Working Group describes the SARS genome (or more exactly the knowledge about the sequence of the nearly 30,000 base-pairs that make up the SARS virus) as a public good, whereas it considers the diagnostic SARS gene chip that is marketed by the company Affymetrix a private good (Genomics Working Group 2004, 40–41). On these grounds, the working group argues against the patentability of the SARS genome (or any other genome, for that matter), while allowing patents on gene chips. This may be a sensible policy line, but the distinction on which it is based does not hold water. In economic terms, the gene chip (or rather, the knowledge needed to manufacture this diagnostic instrument) is just as well a public good. Affymetrix has taken out several patents on its gene chips precisely to tackle the appropriability problem that would otherwise result from their nonexcludability. By the same token, the public-good nature of genomic knowledge does not provide an effective barrier against patentability. Nowadays, patent offices prove quite willing to grant patents on DNA sequences and sometimes even on whole genomes. Like many others I consider such patents highly undesirable, but a robust *economic* argument against this patenting practice needs *more* than just pointing out that basic scientific knowledge constitutes a public good.[26] The argumentation should start with recognizing that government funding and patents are two possible answers to the problem of undersupply that would plague a nonexcludable good like scientific knowledge. It would then have to make the case that the first solution is in many circumstances superior to the second, for instance when research findings are to be used as inputs for further research.[27] In their classic papers Nelson and Arrow presented only a rudimentary sketch of the further chain of reasoning that would be needed to fully clinch the case for government funding. The reason is probably that around 1960 they could not possibly have foreseen the enormous expansion of the domain of patentable subject matter that would occur after 1980, well into areas that would then have appeared beyond the pale of the imaginable.

An objection that is sometimes also mounted against Nelson and Arrow's plea for public funding is that private companies are regularly engaged in fundamental research. This empirical fact can be readily admitted, but it does not affect the main point that *in the absence of (wide-ranging) intellectual property rights* (and/or compensatory government expenditures) a free market would grossly underinvest in the production of scientific knowledge. The extension of the domain of patentable subject matter since 1980 has undoubtedly encouraged private investments in such fields as biotechnology and genomics, but this in no way contradicts the thrust of the argument.

The economic analysis of Nelson and Arrow dovetails nicely with Merton's sociological account of the scientific ethos and the reward system in science. Indeed, as Arrow notes:

> The bulk of basic research has been carried on outside the industrial system, in universities, in the government and by private individuals. *One must recognize here the importance of non-pecuniary incentives,* both on the part of the investigators and on the part of the private individuals and governments that have supported research organizations and universities. (Arrow 1962, 179; my italics)

Merton highlighted, as we have seen, the importance of "recognition and esteem" among peers as a nonpecuniary incentive for scientists to engage in research and to publish their results as quickly as possible. He also recognized, implicitly and sometimes explicitly, the economic nature of scientific knowledge as a public good characterized by nonrivalry and nonexcludability.[28] On his part, Nelson also stressed the need for "free and wide communication of research results" (Nelson 1959, 158) in basic science and pointed out that natural laws and facts, which can be used as key inputs in new research projects, are not patentable. More recently, Dasgupta and David (1994) have deliberately combined insights from Mertonian sociology of science and from the neoclassical economic analysis of basic research to create their own "new economics of science." As Paula Stephan enthusiastically exclaims, "Surely this is interdisciplinary fertilization at its very best!" (Stephan 1996, 1230).

Not everyone is equally enthusiastic, however. Economists Philip Mirowski and Esther-Mirjam Sent and the French sociologist Michel Callon hold a much more jaundiced view. They reject both the synthesis and its sociological and economic building blocks.

5.2. Justifying the Cold War Regime?

According to Mirowski and Sent, postwar Mertonian sociology of science simply condemned itself to irrelevance by declining to engage with the issues of (military-dominated) funding and management of scientific research (Mirowski and Sent 2002, 36). Their exposition is in the format of a rather heavy-handed critique of ideology. The researcher, they claim, "could always take succor from the ethos of 'pure science' within the academy" (21), while the larger decisions about the research agenda were taken by the military.[29] It is precisely because of the (alleged) prominence of the latter in the postwar organization and funding of American science that Mirowski and Sent analyze the period from the Second World War until about 1980 under the rubric of the "cold war regime" (they focus on U.S. developments and ignore conditions elsewhere). However, Mirowski and Sent do not address the Latourian question of who was "enrolling" whom: did the military succeed in "enrolling" the academic scientists, or did the latter manage to get the best of the deal? After all, in terms of the language of economics, there would be an obvious "principal-agent" problem: the researchers were the "agents" of the military, but they may have betrayed the interests of their "principal" in various ways.[30] What is still left unexplained, in my opinion, is why the military was willing to buy this whole "ideology" of basic research.

In truly vulgar Marxist style Mirowski and Sent assert that each funding regime calls forth the version of the "economics of science" which justifies its particular arrangements (Mirowski and Sent 2002, 12). Thus, the analyses of Nelson and Arrow are considered (and dismissed) as justifications of the cold war regime of science policy. It is subtly noted that both were consultants to RAND when they wrote their classic papers (41). In these papers they even briefly commented that a large part of government funding of basic research was defense-oriented (although the same economic principles were deemed to hold for civilian research).[31]

For Mirowski and Sent, that is enough to conclude that these brief comments "reveal that the looming subtext of these debates was indeed the military reorganization of scientific research in the Cold War era." (41).[32] Here is the decoded message that they extract from Nelson's and Arrow's papers: "The thrust of this analysis was to portray 'basic' research as irreducibly opaque and uncertain and therefore requiring lavish government subsidy on welfare grounds, but simultaneously not being subjected to more conventional democratic structures of accountability that one might find in the more market-oriented 'downstream' applications" (42).

This is said to agree perfectly with how the military saw things. Moreover, it was also in the interest of military organization and funding of science policy that intellectual property rights were not strongly maintained and policed, so the "fact" of weak IP protection was also taken for granted in the economic analysis. Mirowski and Sent further dismiss the so-called linear model (from basic research to applied research to development to production) as a cold war artifact and repudiate the whole idea of a "public good."[33] They finally take issue with the treatment of knowledge as a thinglike "commodity" like every other that nevertheless possesses a number of very peculiar qualities. I am puzzled by Mirowski and Sent's exercise in debunking. It would seem to me that their vulgar Marxist approach invites the most blatant *tu quoque* reaction toward their own analysis.[34] If Nelson and Arrow are simply offering a justification of the cold war regime, why then would Mirowski and Sent be immune to the charge that they just provide a cleverly disguised legitimation for the global privatization regime? Reading Nelson and Arrow in a naïve way, I would say that their economic analysis seems to make a lot of sense. At first sight I would certainly not read their papers as pleas for the military funding of scientific research. Do I have to revise my opinion when I take the contextual information provided by Mirowski and Sent into consideration? Without being committed to a particular version of welfare economics (whether Samuelsonian or Walrasian or whatever), I would still buy the argument that investment in a public good like basic knowledge, when left to the market, would be "too low" in a crudely utilitarian sense. I also can think of many good reasons for a weak IP regime, so neither would I feel obliged to change my mind if I found out that the military happens to endorse the same view. Furthermore, I fully admit that the category of basic research cannot always be clearly delineated, but what is so problematic about the idea that knowledge and information are used as inputs in further research and that research outcomes are highly uncertain? Isn't that just common sense? And, finally, what is so terribly wrong with the notion of a public good, which at least to me seems intuitively clear enough?

Henk van den Belt

5.3. The Refutation of Callon's Criticism

For an answer to the last question, we might perhaps better turn to the French sociologist Michel Callon, who is well-known for his formulation, together with Bruno Latour, of Actor-Network Theory (ANT).[35] In 1993 he launched a frontal attack on the idea that scientific knowledge constitutes a public good (Callon 1994). Assuming that scientific knowledge (or information) is expressed (embodied) in the form of a (codified) statement, his surprisingly brief counter argument runs as follows:

> Economic theorists tell us that if A uses statement E, then the latter is not damaged by the fact that B also uses it. That is true, but only in exactly the same way as I can go out in my Ford Taurus, registration number BCD109876, without being inconvenienced by Mr. Brown going along in the same Ford Taurus, but this time with registration number BCD109877. A statement as used by A is neither more nor less similar to one used by B than one Ford Taurus is to another—or one tower of the World Trade Center to its twin. Two similar statements used in two different situations constitute two different goods, whose use and implementation presuppose specific investments. Science, even in its most codified forms, cannot therefore be considered a nonrival good. (Callon 1994, 403)

In a note, Callon tells us that this argument has met with much skepticism and failed to convince many of his economist colleagues. I do not find it convincing either. Callon's Ford Taurus and Mr. Brown's Ford Taurus are clearly two different cars. They may be of the same *design* or *type,* but as individual *copies* or *tokens* they are different. As individual vehicles they are characterized by rivalry in consumption or use. When Mr. Brown uses his Ford Taurus to drive from his office to his home, the same car cannot be used by Mrs. Brown to visit her sister in a nearby town. When talking about the "same" statement E used by A and B that apparently turns out to be two "different" statements after all, Callon should also have distinguished between *token* and *type.* As tokens, that is, as material inscriptions in A's and B's respective situations, the two "statements" are indeed different, but as a type there is (by assumption) only one statement E. Now when we talk about the nonrivalry of knowledge or information as a public good and we codify such knowledge or information in statements, we naturally refer to the *type*-level of statements. When B uses the information contained in statement E, this in no way detracts from A's use of the same information contained in this very statement. Callon reproaches economists for being too idealist when they deal with the issue of the nonrivalry of knowledge and information (Callon 1994, 402), but his own approach suffers from being crudely materialist. By equating information with its individual instantiations (the material inscriptions in concrete situations), he actually *defines away* the specific property of information that is responsible for its character as a public good.[36] Hence his whole argument is no more than a *petitio principii* and rightly fails to carry conviction.

Aware that his brief argument did not convince his economist colleagues, Callon also presents a more extended argument. He now addresses the view that a good need not be accessible at zero cost in order to be nonrival. Specifically, scientific knowledge or information may be a *local* public good insofar as it may be available to the members of a community of specialists who have made the required investments in skills, equipment, and complementary assets that are necessary to make use of the particular piece of knowledge or information. Or as Callon paraphrases this view, "For all those who have made the necessary investments, the statement is a nonrival good" (Callon 1994, 403). Callon inventories and elaborates on these various additional investments such as reproduction costs, investments in complementary assets, investments in maintaining skills, equipment and infrastructures and investments that are required to use the information as an input in new research or production processes, but after his detailed exposition he has still not succeeded in refuting the nonrival character of the statement in question as a local public good. The only thing he has shown is that there are many more costs incurred, sometimes very high investment costs, in making productive use of a particular statement than just the often negligible cost of reproducing the isolated statement. But that much had already been granted by his opponents from the outset and incorporated into the very definition of what constitutes a *local* public good.[37] Callon's criticism that the customary economic analysis introduces an "arbitrary" distinction between supply and demand (producers and users of information) and his lament that we should not concentrate on one particular link in the chain of costs (to wit, reproduction costs) are just repeating the same points and do not help to clinch his case either. Callon finally suggests that the theory of relativity too, like his Ford Taurus, is "a potentially privatizable good," and he claims to be capable of achieving its privatization by means of a very strict and strictly enforced "intellectual property system, extended to science" (Callon 1994, 407). It seems to me that invoking the use of such legal instruments is an inappropriate move in the debate on the public-good character of scientific knowledge and information.[38] After all, the purpose of such instruments is precisely to create artificial scarcity by turning the use of this peculiar good from nonexcludable into excludable, thereby annulling its character as a "public" good. By the way, the effective privatization of the theory of relativity would surely require a most draconic IP law.

6. Meritocratic Science between Elitism and Populism

6.1. Fuller's Neopopulist Challenge of "Autonomous" Science

While Mirowski and Sent, unlike Callon, seem to profoundly dislike the commercialization of scientific research that is currently occurring under the so-called global privatization regime, they agree with Callon that we cannot return to the good old days of a much less commercialized Mertonian science that still upheld the norms of communism and disinterestedness. Or even if we could, they hold, we would soon find out that those supposedly happy and innocent times were just the dark period of the cold war regime. So, for Mirowski and Sent as well as for Callon, there is no option but to accept the present commercialized regime of academic research, either cheerfully or with gnashing of teeth.

Steve Fuller, the *enfant terrible* of the STS community, adopts a much less resigned posture toward the contemporary modes of conducting and organizing academic research, but his primary objective is to increase popular control over the scientific enterprise rather than to combat the trend of increasing commercialization. His "neopopulist" (and I would also say "neo-Jacobin") position challenges the plea for an autonomous and professionalized science that is implied in Merton's account of the scientific ethos. If Fuller's criticism of Merton were indeed valid, it would make it so much more difficult to invoke the set of Mertonian norms as a critical yardstick for judging the "ethos of commercialism" in contemporary academic science (cf. Krimsky 2003). It is therefore clear that I have to confront Fuller's challenge.

In his masterly "philosophical history for our times" Fuller offers a broad historical panorama on the closing of the American and European mind that in his view accompanied the rise of professionalized "big" science in the postwar period (Fuller 2000b). Fuller's main culprit is "Saint" Thomas Kuhn, who followed the lead of his Harvard mentor James Bryant Conant, but an accessory role is reserved for Merton and his pupils. One of Merton's first contributions in this regard was his "successful deradicalization of Bernal's Marxist sociology of science" (Fuller 2000b, 164n).[39] Merton is also seen as a junior partner in the Harvard "conspiracy" led by Conant to resist a postwar New Deal approach in science policy and to opt instead for a more elitist approach in which peer review (not just of submitted articles but also and especially of research proposals) would be the cornerstone. Just like Mirowski and Sent, Fuller highlights the cold war context of these initiatives.

6.2. Fuller's Criticism of the Mertonian Norms

Fuller also emphasizes the "sinister side" of Merton's four norms (Fuller 2000b, 224n). To show that these norms can be read in a diabolical light, he resorts to the literary device of a group of Martian anthropologists visiting Earth who look at scientific practices from the outside. They shift the frame of reference from the scientific community to the larger society in which it is located, thereby putting a negative spin on each of the CUDOS norms. In this way the norm of universalism is understood as the norm of cultural imperialism, communism as mafiosism, disinterestedness as opportunism, and organized skepticism as collective irresponsibility (Fuller 1997, 64).

Let us look, by way of example, into how Fuller turns the norm of communism into the norm of mafiosism:

> Merton also held that scientists were normative *communists* in that they are committed to sharing data and credit, in contrast to the trade secrets kept by firms that are interested in science only as a means of making money. However, "sharing" means something a bit more proprietary than Merton's term implies. It is less a matter of assigning collective ownership for an empirical finding than of distributing ownership to others whom the scientist thinks (will think they) deserve it. To speak bluntly, "communal sharing" amounts to little more than insurance against risk. Although scientists are not, strictly speaking, coerced to share with their colleagues, they are really in no position to choose *not* to do so. (Fuller 1997, 65)

Elsewhere Fuller makes the same point more briefly: "'sharing' amounts to paying mafia-style protection money. Scientists cannot afford *not* to share with their colleagues. Otherwise, colleagues will not share with them, approve their grants, or hire their students" (Fuller 2000b, 224n).

Fuller is far from accurate in describing Merton's position here; he prefers to erect a straw-man that he can pull down more easily. For Merton, the norm of communism primarily refers to the requirement to publish research findings promptly and not so much to some vague sharing of data and credit.[40] Merton indeed holds that (the scientific ethos demands that) credit should be given where credit is due, but this is a matter of respecting the intellectual property (in the special Mertonian sense!) of other researchers on whose results you build (moreover, it is *giving* credit and not *sharing* credit). It is a matter of properly acknowledging your sources. Indeed, it is something Fuller himself does in his books. Or would he say that he is just "paying protection money" to his many colleagues and friends whose contributions to his own work he meticulously "acknowledges" by citing them or by inserting special thanks? It may be that when talking about the sharing of credit Fuller is also referring to other practices like granting honorary authorship (see also Biagioli 2002) to people who did not really contribute to the content of a scientific paper.[41] As he uses the term, "sharing" evokes the image of scientists acting according to the strategic adage: "I'll scratch your back if you scratch mine." At any rate, it seems rather unfair to blame questionable practices in attributing authorship and other abuses that have grown up in the conduct of scientific research on the norm of communism to which they are not directly related.

This is a more general pattern. Many of the abuses and perversions of modern academic life, or many of the customs and practices of contemporary science that Fuller considers objectionable, are laid at the door of Merton's sociology of science. For instance, Merton (together with his colleague Derek de Solla Price) is held personally responsible for the tyranny of citation counts under which researchers have to live nowadays:

> The most concrete symbol of their legacy is the *Science Citation Index (SCI)* and the attendant use of citation counts as indicators of quality, relevance or influence. Few scientists can completely escape from thinking in these terms. The urge to measure one's career in terms of the droppings left at the foot and end of other people's articles is near irresistible. (Fuller 1997, 69)

Fuller extensively details the modern abuses of citation counting, but he fails to mention that Merton himself already drew attention to the dangers of an unreflective use of the SCI and even went so far as to state that "to adopt the number of citations to a scientist's work as the exclusive, or even major, criterion simply represents conspicuous malpractice" (Merton 1979, 53).

6.3. The Principle of Cumulative Advantage and the Matthew Effect

Fuller also eagerly seizes upon Merton's so-called "principle of cumulative advantage" to rail against the supposedly unbridled elitist tendencies that are endemic in professionalized academic science. He calls this expression "one of [Merton's] classic euphemisms" (Fuller 1997, 73; cf. Fuller 2000a, 25). One wonders, however, what could be euphemistic about an expression that apparently serves Fuller's own critical purposes so well that it is cited each time an attack is mounted on the pernicious elitism of science. Moreover, the notion of "cumulative advantage" is usually mentioned in a single breath with the so-called *Matthew effect*, which primarily refers to inequities in the attribution of peer recognition for coauthored publications or other coproductions or similar achievements but which in a more general sense can be taken as synonymous with the principle of cumulative advantage. The biblical saying to which this designation alludes can by no stretch of the imagination be called a euphemism: "For unto every one that hath shall be given, and he shall have abundance: but from him that hath not shall be taken away even that which he hath" (Matthew 25:29). Indeed, this piece of ancient wisdom is often taken as a critical or cynical comment on the common experience that the rich are getting richer and the poor poorer (for the theological background of the quotation, Merton refers to the interpretations of the Dutch theologian Marinus de Jonge; see Merton 1988, 609n). The saying gives, as a correspondent to *Physics Today* observed, "a remarkably succinct characterization of the economic policies of George W. Bush" (Mermin 2005). Nowadays even Marxists use the term coined by Merton with good grace: "Today, we are witnessing an economic Matthew effect beyond what anybody could have imagined only a few decades earlier" (Perelman 2006).

How can "the principle of cumulative advantage" be called a euphemism if this expression immediately evokes the related term "Matthew effect," whose critical thrust is only too plain and straightforward? The probable reason is that Fuller wants us to believe that Merton actually approves and justifies the tendencies toward inequality within science that his terms aim to capture. He even makes the following incredible attribution: "Merton (1973) even went so far as to argue that if indeed genuine contributions to knowledge are likely to go unrecognized, disadvantaged scientists should try to get advantaged scientists to promote the findings as their own" (Fuller 2000a, 90).[42] Nowhere in *The Sociology of Science* can this particular advice to young scientists who have yet to make their mark be found. What we do find in this volume, in an included article on the Matthew effect first published in *Science* in 1968, is a discussion of a cruel dilemma often faced by eminent scientists. For them it can be a burning question whether or not to put their famous name on a paper reporting work largely done by a junior associate. As one of the Nobel laureates interviewed by Harriet Zuckerman explained, "if you don't [put your name on the paper], there's the possibility that the paper may go quite unrecognized. Nobody reads it. If you do, it might be recognized, but then the student doesn't get enough credit" (quoted in Merton 1973, 448). Merton agrees that there is a real danger that a paper to which no famous name is attached may not be read at all. This dilemma points to a deep tension in the social system of science:

[C]onsidered in its implications for the reward system, the Matthew effect is dysfunctional for the careers of individual scientists who are penalized in the early stages of their development, but considered in its implications for the communication system, the Matthew effect, in cases of collaboration and multiple discoveries, may operate to heighten the visibility of new scientific communications. (Merton 1973, 447)

So, rather than elevating the Matthew effect (and the principle of cumulative advantage) to the status of an "invisible hand" securing the optimal allocation of resources, as Fuller suggests (Fuller 2000a, 26, 108; Fuller 2000b, 384–85), Merton fully admits the presence of a tragic conflict in the heart of the scientific enterprise (Merton 1973, 448). Indeed, the normative ethos of science requires that credit be given where credit is due and that the recognition is commensurate with the contribution. Thus the Matthew effect involves a serious departure from these basic norms.[43] This is not something to be taken lightly, as is also illustrated by Merton's own painstaking efforts to set the record straight in a purported case of the operation of the Matthew effect—the attribution of the famous "Thomas theorem" in sociology to William I. Thomas only and not also to his coauthor Dorothy Swaine Thomas (Merton 1995).

The principle of cumulative advantage operates not only on the level of individual scientists but also on the level of scientific institutions and colleges, in mutual interaction. The "better" universities are able to attract, in addition to more facilities and material resources, the "better" students and "better" researchers, who by the quality of their work in turn enhance the reputation of their institutions. The net result may be a highly skewed distribution, especially under American conditions. Thus Merton reported some of the results obtained by Harriet Zuckerman in the late 1960s: "six universities (Harvard, Berkeley, Columbia, Princeton, the Johns Hopkins, and Chicago) which produced 24 percent of the doctorates in the physical and biological sciences produced fully 65 percent of the Ph.D.'s who later became Nobel laureates" (Merton 1973, 458; for additional data see also Merton 1988, 617). Such glaring figures showing a hugely skewed distribution are grist to Fuller's mill as they seem to cry out for immediate action (cf. Fuller 2000a, 120). His republican program for the governance of science precisely aims to radically counteract and diminish the "inertia" of cumulative advantage (Fuller 2000a, 112). What Fuller forgets, however, is that someone who is sincerely committed to the norms and values of the "scientific ethos" and the implied meritocratic ideals of equal opportunity and "careers open to talents" would also be embarrassed by the elitist tendencies resulting from the workings of cumulative advantage. It is surely misleading to portray Merton as the unrepentant apologist of these elitist tendencies, even if he would not be prone to advocate political activism. Already in 1942 Merton argued that persistent advantages might run counter to the norm of universalism as endorsed both by the ethos of science *and* by the ethos of democracy and hence call forth political correction:

> Democratization is tantamount to the progressive elimination of restraints upon the exercise and development of socially valued capacities. . . . Insofar as such restraints do persist, they are viewed as obstacles in the path of full democratization. Thus, insofar as laissez-faire democracy permits the accumulation of differential advantages for certain segments of the population, differentials that are not bound up with demonstrated differences in capacity, the democratic process leads to increasing regulation by political authority. Under changing conditions, new technical forms of organization must be introduced to preserve and extend equality of opportunity. The political apparatus may be required to put democratic values into practice and to maintain universalistic standards. (Merton 1973, 273)

That this passage was not just written under the impression of recent New Deal policies is proven by the fact that a similar passage recurs in Merton's later work.[44]

The big question is, of course, *how* to counteract the workings of cumulative advantage. As discussions about affirmative action have shown, crude measures such as introducing strict quota and timetables may cause all kinds of unintended and undesirable consequences and eventually provoke a strong backlash. A more cautious approach would look for specific "pressure points" on which to apply remedial action in order to enhance the chances of success. In fact, Mertonian sociologists have been active in detailed empirical research to uncover the various disadvantages and obstacles with which women scientists have to contend in their careers (Cole 1979; Zuckerman, Cole, and Bruer 1991). Similar detailed work may provide the empirical basis for a cautious and "piecemeal" approach to counteract other instances of cumulative advantage and disadvantage. Presumably, however, such work would be far too slow for Fuller. With his republican program for the governance of science, he offers an entire package for counteracting cumulative advantage in science wherever it is found. Some of his specific proposals (see Fuller 2000a, 120) definitely make sense, but we should not follow Fuller all the way. The problem is that he might see cumulative advantage everywhere, as in his approach "merit" is always considered an effect of clever networking (or even, as in Thomas Kuhn's case, of just "being there"). I fear that by adopting Fuller's program we will throw out the baby with the bathwater. It would spell the end of science as we know it.

7. Conclusions

The "sociological history for our times" that I recounted in the preceding sections is also a philosophical history in Steve Fuller's sense insofar as it necessarily carries a normative message for the present. Clearly, my political agenda differs from Fuller's agenda. My primary objective is not to democratize science, even (as some would have it) to the point of effacing the differences between experts and laypersons, but to decommercialize it. I think that Merton's classic formulation of the scientific ethos can be very helpful as a critical benchmark for judging the contemporary situation in science. My ideal image of the scientific endeavor is that of an autonomous and open, truly meritocratic profession engaged in steadily and cumulatively expanding the commons of knowledge. It is a worthy ideal that may claim a pedigree going at least as far back as the Condorcet-Jefferson tradition of the Enlightenment. As knowledge is in principle a nondepletable good, scientific research will result in a "comedy of the commons"—unless, of course, this happy outcome is disturbed by a proliferation of intellectual property rights that brings about a "tragedy of the anticommons."

It is important to infuse a whiff of realism into such an exalted view. This can be done by pointing out that scientists need not be pure altruists to make the comedy of the commons a reality. They may be in the game just for the fun of it, but also, as Merton emphasized, to earn recognition and esteem among their peers. The important point is that we do not have to view scientists as exclusively motivated by pecuniary incentives. I also felt it important to show that Merton's sociology of science is closely aligned with certain neoclassical approaches to the economics of science. The view of knowledge as a public good is an essential part of any conception of science as a cumulatively expanding commons. An "open" science is also economically viable. It is against this background that Merton's norm of communism makes sense at all. At this point my interpretation differs from the analysis of Hans Radder (this volume, chap. 10).

My ideal of open science may seem hopelessly out of touch with the dominant neoliberal spirit of the present time. In his contribution to this volume, Daniel Lee Kleinman notes that beyond the increasing number of formal university-industry relations a more subtle change in academic culture is also occurring inasmuch as the virtues of commercial codes and practices are increasingly taken for granted. He refers, among other things, to the courses and seminars on IP management for students and faculty at his own university, the University of Wisconsin–Madison, and to the propaganda by its allied organization WARF (Wisconsin Alumni Research Foundation) that relentlessly hammers on the importance of patenting potential inventions. These are indeed quite formidable forces, but the seemingly dry and rather technical subject of patents could also be the focus of a more critical scholarship. It is not too difficult to compile a critical history of intellectual property and patents with which to inoculate students and faculty against the most blatant propaganda. In the United States it would be convenient to discuss the views of Thomas Jefferson (who is sometimes, ironically enough, made out as the architect of the U.S. patent system) to plant the seed of doubt. In the Netherlands, the nineteenth-century economic liberals (mind you: liberals, not socialists) provide an extensive literature rich in arguments against patents and copyrights. One of the strongest indictments of the patent system can be read in the official business history of the Dutch Philips company, which is completely at odds with its present position on intellectual property (Heerding 1986).

It will indeed be difficult to reverse the commercialization of science. The trend may reach a point beyond which things simply cannot go. Or so it would seem. Thus in 2003 some dozen American universities engaging in agricultural research found out that many significant discoveries and technologies that had been generated by public funding, including important "enabling technologies," were no longer accessible even for themselves—they had actually been licensed out to several business firms by their own technology transfer offices (Atkinson et al. 2003). To regain their "freedom to operate," these universities had to pool their resources and set up PIPRA (Public Intellectual Property Resource for Agriculture), a collective management regime for handling their joint IP portfolio in such a way that the use of the patented discoveries and inventions in academic research would be secured, as well as their use for the development of subsistence and specialty crops in which private companies were not interested. Nowadays the cost and trouble of making special legal arrangements must be incurred to partly restore the traditional customs of open science that once came naturally. (The currently fashionable phrase "freedom to operate" is highly significant. It is something that cannot be taken for granted, but has to be obtained through "clearance.")

Patents may also become hot spots of contestation when NGOs target their campaigns at renowned universities. In early 2001 Yale University was approached by Doctors without Borders with the urgent request to allow the use of the AIDS medicine stavudine, on which it held a basic patent, as a generic drug in South Africa. The patent had actually been licensed to the pharmaceutical company Bristol-Myers Squibb. Under strong moral pressure, however, Yale agreed not to enforce its patent rights in South Africa and allowed production and sale of generics, drawing the pharmaceutical industry along in its wake (Kapczynski et al. 2005). The episode may provide a foretaste of things to come.

I further take courage from some remarkable initiatives that more directly challenge the legitimacy of patents and other forms of intellectual property. The relative success of the Free and Open Source Software (FOSS) movement belies the conventional wisdom that innovative products and services will only be generated when there is a prospect of strong IP protection. This movement has also been quite successful in undermining the respectability of software patents. Looking for the secret of the movement's economic success, scholars have come up with the idea that the open-software community practices a form of "commons-based peer production" (Benkler 2006). In several respects the moral underpinnings of this practice appear to be just a new incarnation of Merton's scientific ethos.

Researchers in the life sciences are currently trying to emulate the example of open-source software and have set up initiatives in open-source biology such as CAMBIA (agricultural biotechnology) and the BioBricks Foundation (synthetic biology). These attempts to create a relatively free space or commons beyond the reach of patents constitute an uphill struggle that will probably fairly soon be faced with unavoidable patent tangles. Yet even if they fail, these experiments may still be valuable as an object lesson on the stifling effects of our patent system. Moreover, the attempts as such show that the Mertonian spirit is still alive, against all odds.

NOTES

I would like to thank Edwin Koster and Hans Radder for their helpful comments on an earlier version of this chapter.

1. Antoine-Laurent de Lavoisier, *Oeuvres de Lavoisier*, vol. 4 (Paris, 1868), 623–24. The English translation is mine. I owe the reference to Lavoisier's letter to Boers et al. (1976). They rightly call attention to the significance and relevance of this letter for discussing the "Mertonian" norms of science.

2. One might be puzzled about Lavoisier's assertion that "the members of the Academy live in the midst of craftsmen; they are privy to their secrets." In fact, one of the traditional tasks of the Academy of Sciences, according to the *Règlement* of January 26, 1699, was to examine the novelty and utility of inventions for which inventors sought a royal privilege (patent). So the academy functioned also as a patent office *avant la lettre*. See Maindron (1888). The English Royal Society fulfilled a similar function (Weingart 1978, 261). The academy's role in judging the inventions of artisans created so much resentment among the latter that it would become a prime target for political attack during the most turbulent period of the revolution:

> the Revolution gave the artisans of Paris their opportunity for a decisive offensive aimed at reversing the aphorism by which science governs the arts. A revolt of technology was one among the many rebellions swelling into Revolution.

Specifically, the trouble went back to the Academy's responsibility for refereeing the monopolies and subsidies by which the State encouraged invention. This invidious role earned the Academy deep Gallic hatred among the artisans whose work it judged. These were not people whom it was safe to have offended, and the fall of the Academies set in train liquidation of the entire structure of French science. (Gillispie 1959, 680)

3. Roger Hahn's characterization of the political stakes that divided the proponents and opponents of the Academy of Sciences in the last decade of the eighteenth century could almost literally have been extracted from Fuller's polemics:

> On one side were the proponents of the academic system, who conceived of the advancement and propagation of learning as a national responsibility most efficiently carried out by a self-regulating and self-propagating body of talented intellectuals, free from political control and supported by government funds. On the other side were their antagonists, who rejected the bureaucratization of cultural elites because it would place a handful of "aristocrats" in control of matters that were ultimately not subject to human command. Knowledge of nature and discovery of truth were meant to be a public affair and not the exclusive province of an elite. In the political context of the anticorporate, democratic revolution of 1793, the victory of the anti-academic movement was inevitable. (Hahn 1971, 240)

4. "Let Everyman be a scientist," was also the motto of the popular romantic writer Bernardin de Saint-Pierre, a friend of Rousseau (Hahn 1971, 156).

5. Merton 1973, 294–95n19. Some of these examples may also raise doubts about the strictness of the norm of communism and about the alleged "minimal" character of property rights in science. In Merton's first example, Ramsay is asking Rayleigh's "permission to look into atmospheric nitrogen" on which Rayleigh had been working. If Rayleigh is still supposed to have the right for giving such permission, then clearly property rights in science are not as drastically curtailed as is suggested by Merton. In fact, this question points to the wider problem of "protection of exploitation rights" or "the principle of fairness in exploitation of results," which, according to Jerry Ravetz, "has received no mention in the classic literature on the sociology, or ethics, of science" (Ravetz 1971, 255–56).

6. Lavoisier's use of the term "property" in the above-quoted letter to Lakanal would have been a better example for Merton's purposes because it so perfectly illustrates the latter's intended meaning, although Lavoisier did not use the complete expression "intellectual property." In other parts of his work he also used the term "property" in an eminently Mertonian sense. An example is the following passage: "This theory [i.e., the theory of combustion] is therefore not, as has been declared, the theory of the French chemists, it is mine, and that is a property right that I claim vis-à-vis my contemporaries and posterity" (Lavoisier 1774, 104). See also in the same treatise: "I was young; I had just embarked upon a career in the sciences; I was hungry of fame; and I felt obliged to take some precautions to assure myself of the property of my discovery" (102–3). Lavoisier here refers to the sealed envelope containing a report of his discovery which he handed to the secretary of the Academy of Sciences on November 1, 1772, in order to ensure his priority. The envelope was opened on May 5, 1773. Lavoisier justified this action by pointing to the intense rivalry existing at the time between English and French chemists, "which sometimes led the writers of the one or other nation to contest the true author [of the new experiments]." On the use of sealed manuscripts, see also Merton 1973, 316, 364.

7. "So habe ich nur mein geistiges Eigentum zu wahren gesucht, das aber auch mit aller mir zu Gebote stehenden Rücksichtslosigkeit."

8. "Uitwerking van het probleem dat aanvrager heeft gesteld ligt niet op het gebied van de nijverheid, immers niet op het gebied van den industrieelen, maar op dat van den intellectueelen eigendom."

9. Interestingly, in this passage the young Merton used the expression "intellectual property" already as a broad umbrella term, albeit within quotation marks. The footnote may have been inspired by an incidental remark that Merton came across when reading Max Scheler's 1924 essay on the sociology of knowledge: "The juridical concepts of 'intellectual property,' of 'patent law' and analogous legal arrangements, are as foreign to the mode of knowledge of an organic community [*Lebensgemeinschaft*]—to any form of 'scholastics' [footnote]—as priority disputes in scientific polemics and criticism" (Scheler 1924, 104). The footnote says, "In scholastics, one tries to hide what is truly 'authentic' [*das wahrhaft 'Eigene'*] behind the tradition of earlier times." In fact, in the quoted passage Merton largely reiterates Scheler's point.

10. The different titles under which the 1942 essay were successively published indicate a significant change in focus. It originally appeared under the title "Science and Technology in a Democratic Order"; in the collection *Social Theory and Social Structure* it was republished as "Science and Democratic Social Structure"—thus the reference to technology had been deleted. In the collection *The Sociology of Science* it finally appeared under the title "The Normative Structure of Science"—now the allusion to the political dimension had also been omitted.

11. The reason for this seemingly pointless practice is that patent offices or legal courts did not always recognize the novelty-destroying effect of prior scientific "discoveries" on subsequent (alleged) technical "inventions" with the same or a similar content. Otherwise it would have sufficed to simply publish the findings.

12. Metlay (2006) shows that another major reason for university patenting in prewar America was the wish to control the quality and accessibility of the final commercial product (e.g., insulin, vitamin D), which apparently could not be entrusted to an unregulated and often unscrupulous business world.

13. Merton could also have pointed to the ill-fated attempts undertaken in France and other European countries during the 1920s to establish the concept of "scientific property" as yet another manifestation of underlying discrepancies in the conception of intellectual property. These attempts were aimed at changes in patent and copyright laws to ensure that scientific researchers would materially benefit from the practical applications that would ultimately derive from their discoveries and principles. For more on these initiatives, see Hermesdorf (1923), Ladas (1929), Merges (1996), and Verkade (1997).

14. In his contribution to this volume, Daniel Lee Kleinman remarks, however, that even in the first postwar decades the U.S. government's commitment to support basic research was less deep than the Bush report suggested.

15. In 1989, I analyzed the social creation of a boundary between science and technology in the course of patent disputes in the French dyestuff industry during the early 1860s (see van den Belt 1989). At a crucial stage in the legal proceedings, the English (German-born) chemist August Wilhelm Hofmann invented an ingenious distinction between "scientific discovery" and "industrial discovery" to save the French patent on aniline red held by the Renard brothers of Lyon from being invalidated due to lack of novelty. Using Thomas Gieryn's terminology, Hofmann's achievement could be described as "boundary-work."

16. Roger Hahn points out that in France the romantic concept of genius was actually forged to oppose the official role of the Academy of Sciences and was therefore bound to be rejected by the latter's members. See Hahn (1971, 140). Condorcet was appointed secretary of the Academy of Sciences in 1777.

17. Regulating *le droit d'auteur* was not only about granting author's rights but also about the responsibility of authors for seditious or libelous writings. To keep the story simple, I ignore this aspect. However, censorship issues were definitively important in this episode (see Hesse 1990). There is a clear parallel with concepts of authorship in earlier times. As Biagioli writes, "The author was not seen as a creative producer whose work deserved protection from piracy, but as the person upon whose door the police would knock if [his] texts were deemed subversive or heretical" (Biagioli 2002, 487).

18. Roger Hahn points out that Lakanal wanted to save the Academy of Sciences and for that purpose had asked Lavoisier to supply him with relevant materials and arguments that might convince the National Convention (see Hahn 1971, 236–37).

19. Compare David Hull: "Science is both a highly competitive *and* a highly cooperative affair" (Hull 1988, 286). Karl Popper has expressed a similar view.

20. Scientists also compete with each other to acquire research funds and to attract the best Ph.D. students and other "resources." This circumstance is emphasized by David Resnik in his contribution to this volume. Resnik notes that even without private money government-funded scientists would still compete for grants and jobs (in addition to their competition for prestige and intellectual property). Merton does not highlight *these* competitive relations between researchers, but his views on the working of the "principle of cumulative advantage" (discussed below in section 6.3) acknowledge their relevance by assuming that enhanced scientific reputations will be used to attract more funds and better students. In other words, scientific "credit" can be converted into financial "credit." To some extent, the contrary conversion is also possible, but there must presumably be rather strict limitations on this type of transformation if the integrity of the scientific enterprise and the quest for recognition and esteem is to be maintained.

21. In a lecture before the Berlin Medical Society, which triggered the whole controversy, Wassermann had claimed the serodiagnosis of syphilis as "my intellectual product and property" [*mein geistiges Produkt und Eigentum*] (Wassermann 1921, 197), while offering a theoretical interpretation of the nature of the reaction, the so-called auto-antibody theory, which had originally been developed by his erstwhile critic Eduard Weil. He did so in order to give the serological test a profile that would clearly distinguish it from Jules Bordet's complement fixation method, which had originally been the starting point for its development (in France and Belgium, during the first World War, the Wassermann reaction had been renamed the "Bordet-Wassermann reaction" for nationalistic reasons). Wassermann's "egocentric" approach provoked angry reactions from Weil and from his former collaborator Carl Bruck, among others. In the course of the dispute each of the protagonists presented accounts of the development of the Wassermann reaction that were destined to bolster their own claims to intellectual property or to deny the claims made by others. Fleck often naïvely takes their statements at face value to draw "epistemological" conclusions, without taking the strategic context in which they were made into account.

22. Fleck states that it is the democratic duty of every individual scientist to recede into the background, to "withdraw his own personality into the shadow . . . in the service of the common ideal" (Fleck 1935, 144). The editors of the English translation of Fleck's work (that is, presumably, Merton) have added the following critical comment on this: "Yet

scientists typically engage in competition, and priority disputes are not infrequent, which would suggest that Fleck's democracy of science remains incomplete" (163). Had Merton known the details about the dispute on the ownership of the Wassermann reaction, he would have been able to show how Fleck's "collectivism" (alias "democracy") ran afoul on the task of properly accounting for its salient features.

23. Recently the Swedish immunologist and historian of science, Eva Hedfors, published a reexamination of Fleck's work that is extremely critical in tone (Hedfors 2006). However, her own analysis is also marred with numerous misunderstandings. Just like Fleck, she fails to analyze the controversy about the serodiagnosis of syphilis as a strategic dispute over intellectual property and reads Wassermann's very provocative lecture which triggered the whole affair as if it were a neutral state-of-the-art report. In general, she uncritically takes sides with Wassermann as an unassailable authority in serology against his former collaborator Carl Bruck, whom she wrongly depicts as scientifically marginal. In this respect Bruck is compared with Fleck, whose "scientific marginality" is held responsible for several errors and mistakes in immunological science on which his relativist and constructivist approach is said to be based.

24. Compare: "it is quite likely that a firm will be unable to capture through patent rights the full economic value created in a basic-research project that it sponsors" (Nelson 1959, 158).

25. This line of reasoning follows mainstream neoclassical welfare economics: a "market failure" is identified and the government is called upon to remedy this failure. Economists of the Chicago school typically oppose this line of reasoning by downplaying "market failures" and emphasizing "government failures." For a Chicago response challenging Arrow's analysis, see Demsetz (1969).

26. Hans Radder (2006) offers arguments against gene patents (and other product patents) that are based on his work in the philosophy of science.

27. When patents are allowed to move "upstream" and to cover "research tools," this may evoke the well-known scenario of the "tragedy of the anticommons" first described by Michael Heller and Rebecca Eisenberg (1998). In her contribution to this volume, Sigrid Sterckx discusses this scenario and other disadvantages of the increase in academic patenting during the last few decades.

28. "[S]ince a fund of knowledge is not diminished through exceedingly intensive use by members of the scientific collectivity—indeed, it is presumably augmented—that virtually free and common good is not subject to what Garrett Hardin has aptly analyzed as the 'tragedy of the commons.' . . . In the commons of science it is structurally the case that the give and the take both work to enlarge the common resource of accessible knowledge" (Merton 1988, 620). See also Stephan (2004).

29. In a more recent publication, Mirowski and Sent elaborate on the illusion of "pure" science during the cold war regime:

> Hence, the American Cold War regime was largely structured as a concertedly nationalized system of science, but one whose ideological significance was so highly charged that it had to be presented as an autonomous and autarkic invisible college of stalwart stateless individuals who need pay no heed where the funding and institutional support for all their pure research was coming from. . . .
> It was only within the Cold War regime that "academic freedom" really seemed to possess sufficient *gravitas* to actually be used in an effective defense of aca-

demic tenure—something we can now appreciate in the era of its disappearance. The researcher had only to answer to his disciplinary peers, or in the last instance, to his individual conscience, and feel enlightened disdain for the hurly-burly of the marketplace—at least until the DARPA grants officer came to call. (Mirowski and Sent 2008, 654–55)

30. As historian of physics Helge Kragh notes, "The military's support was not limited to areas of direct—or even indirect—relevance to warfare, but covered all of physics, including areas that would seem to be utterly irrelevant to military interests" (Kragh 1999, 298). An example is the military funding of the research program in general relativity ("at the time an even more esoteric and useless branch of mathematical physics than it is today") from 1956 to 1970.

31. "But defense-oriented expenditure aside, the American political economy certainly treats basic research as an activity that creates marginal social value in excess of that collectable on the market" (Nelson 1959, 153).

32. Mirowski and Sent discount the explicit statements made by Nelson and Arrow: "But we need not accept their protestations that there was no difference between civilian and military support of research" (Mirowski and Sent 2002, 41–42).

33. The specific reasons for this repudiation are not entirely clear. In a more recent publication Mirowski and Sent write,

> There are plenty of reasons to think that the concept of the "public good" was never a very useful or effective tool with which to understand the economics of science in any era, much less the current one. Although it was often cited to justify the lavish public subsidies of scientific research in America during the Cold War, it mainly served to distract attention from the military and chauvinistic motives for science funding, not to mention the intricate ways in which corporate organization and academic science were intermeshed and imbricated. (Mirowski and Sent 2008, 666)

34. We can see the hermeneutics of suspicion at work in Mirowski's review of Steve Fuller's book about Thomas Kuhn:

> I have a sneaking suspicion that once Fuller's research agenda and policy prescriptions are fully spelled out . . . , his social epistemology will turn out to resemble nothing so much as the OR-inspired doctrines of the postwar period: in other words, it will be an "economics of science" not so very different from a cognitively inspired version of neoclassical economics. . . . Wouldn't it end up being the *SSR* [Structure of Scientific Revolutions] for the MTV generation, or more to the point, the era of fully global privatised science? (Mirowski 2003, 237–38)

35. Steve Fuller (2001) also takes issue with the idea of a public good. I will not deal with his arguments and objections.

36. Compare Norbert Wiener: "Information is information, not matter or energy. No materialism which does not admit this can survive at the present day" (Wiener 1948, 132). The way Callon treats codified knowledge and information by ignoring their situation-transcending aspect is a direct corollary of the characteristic suppression of the *nonlocal* meanings of concepts in Actor-Network Theory. For a criticism of this approach, see Radder (2006).

37. In the course of his argument Callon confuses the properties of "nonrivalry" and "nonexcludability." The need for additional investments may make a particular piece of knowledge less "accessible" and therefore more "excludable," but it does not affect its quality of "nonrivalry."

38. Callon's recourse to an "intellectual property system" in order to question the public-good nature of scientific knowledge is also problematic in another respect. Reasoning from Actor-Network Theory one might wonder how patents could be enforced at all, given the fact that "patent claims" of necessity intend to have a *nonlocal* meaning, aimed as they are at keeping potential infringers at bay. Following Callon's arguments, any counterfeiter could always counter an infringement charge by pointing out that his practices differ entirely from the patented invention.

39. According to Vidar Enebakk, the "deradicalization" may have been less than at first sight appears as far as Merton himself is concerned. It was largely the result of Bernard Barber's reformulation of Mertonian sociology of science during the early cold war years. It was Barber who suggested to translate the norm of "communism" into "communalism": "That change in terminology was proposed by Bernard Barber in the 1950s during the Joseph McCarthy period of political witch-hunting" (Merton, cited in Enebakk 2007, 234).

40. I am not sure whether the customary sharing of *materials* among scientists should be interpreted as an enactment of Merton's norm of "communism." In the modern life sciences this is certainly an important part of the practice of research, which moreover is increasingly burdened with MTAs (material transfer agreements) and other IP constraints. Sabina Leonelli's contribution to this collection demonstrates the importance of the sharing of data and materials for the research activities of modern life scientists.

41. See also David Resnik's chapter in this volume for a more extensive discussion of the norms of authorship.

42. The same attribution recurs elsewhere in Fuller's work. Sometimes he even has Merton appeal to the altruism of the young and still unknown scientists, urging them to give away their intellectual property: "Merton even suggests that truly selfless scientists would turn over their best ideas to the people who they think will most likely draw attention to them" (Fuller 1997, 74).

43. Michael Strevens denies that the Matthew effect compromises these norms. He holds that famous scientists contribute more than relatively unknown scientists to a new scientific finding, because they also add credibility or reliability to this fresh result. The fact that famous scientists receive more credit would therefore be in conformity with their higher "contribution" (see Strevens 2006). It is this "Panglossian" vision, rather than Merton's carefully balanced view, which would fully deserve Fuller's criticisms.

44. "As another countervailing process, populist and democratic values may be called into play in the wider society, external to academic institutions and to science, and lead governmental largesse to be more widely spread in a calculated effort to counteract cumulating advantage in the great centers of learning and research" (Merton 1988, 619).

REFERENCES

Arrow, Kenneth J. 1962. "Economic welfare and the allocation of resources for invention." In *Science bought and sold: Essays in the economics of science*, ed. Philip Mirowski and Esther-Mirjam Sent, 165–80. Chicago: University of Chicago Press, 2002.

Atkinson, Richard C., Roger N. Beachy, Gordon Conway, France A. Cordova, Marye Anne Fox, Karen A. Holbrook, Daniel F. Klessig, Richard L. McCormick, Peter M. McPherson, Hunter R. Rawlings III, Rip Rapson, Larry N. Vanderhoef, John D. Wiley, and Charles E. Young. 2003. "Public sector collaboration for agricultural IP management." *Science* 301:174–75.

Barnes, Barry, and Alex Dolby. 1970. "The scientific ethos: A deviant viewpoint." *Archives Européennes de Sociologie* 11:3–25.

Benkler, Yochai. 2006. *The wealth of networks: How social production transforms markets and freedom.* New Haven: Yale University Press.

Biagioli, Mario. 2002. "The instability of authorship: Credit and responsibility in contemporary biomedicine." In *Science bought and sold: Essays in the economics of science,* ed. Philip Mirowski and Esther-Mirjam Sent, 486–514. Chicago: University of Chicago Press.

Bliss, Michael. 1982. *The discovery of insulin.* London: Faber and Faber, 1988.

Boers, Chris, Herman Koningsveld, and Joost Mertens. 1976. *Natuurwetenschap in de samenleving.* Wageningen: Wageningen University.

Broad, William, and Nicholas Wade. 1982. *Betrayers of the truth.* Oxford: Oxford University Press, 1985.

Bush, Vannevar. 1945. *Science: The endless frontier.* Washington, DC: U.S. Government Printing Office.

Callon, Michel. 1994. "Is science a public good? Fifth Mullins Lecture, Virginia Polytechnic Institute, 23 March 1993." *Science, Technology and Human Values* 19 (4): 395–424.

Cole, Jonathan R. 1979. *Fair science: Women in the scientific community.* New York: The Free Press.

Condorcet, Marquis de. 1776. "Fragments concerning freedom of the press." *Daedalus* 131, no. 2 (2002): 57–59.

Dasgupta, Partha, and Paul A. David. 1994. "Toward a new economics of science." In *Science bought and sold: Essays in the economics of science,* ed. Philip Mirowski and Esther-Mirjam Sent, 219–48. Chicago: University of Chicago Press, 2002.

Demsetz, Harold. 1969. "Information and efficiency: Another viewpoint." In *Economics of information and knowledge,* ed. D. M. Lamberton, 160–86. Harmondsworth: Penguin Books, 1971.

Diderot, Denis. 1763. "Letter on the book trade." *Daedalus* 131, no. 2 (2002): 48–56.

Eckermann, J. P. 1835. *Gespräche mit Goethe.* Munich: Verlagshaus Bong & Co., 1949.

Enebakk, Vidar. 2007. "The three Merton theses." *Journal of Classical Sociology* 7 (2): 221–38.

Fleck, Ludwik. 1935. *Genesis and development of a scientific fact.* Chicago: University of Chicago Press, 1979.

Fuller, Steve. 1997. *Science.* Buckingham: Open University Press.

———. 2000a. *The governance of science.* Buckingham: Open University Press.

———. 2000b. *Thomas Kuhn: A philosophical history for our times.* Chicago: University of Chicago Press.

———. 2001. "A critical guide to knowledge society newspeak: Or, how not to take the great leap backward." *Current Sociology* 49:177–201.

Genomics Working Group of the Science and Technology Task Force, United Nations Millennium Project. 2004. *Genomics and global health.* Toronto: Report for the University of Toronto Joint Centre for Bioethics.

Gillispie, Charles Coulston. 1959. "Science in the French Revolution." *Proceedings of the National Academy of Science (PNAS)* 45:677–84.

Hackett, Edward J., Olga Amsterdamska, Michael Lynch, and Judy Wajcman. 2008. *The Handbook of science and technology studies*. 3rd ed. Cambridge, MA.: MIT Press.

Hahn, Roger. 1971. *Anatomy of a scientific institution: The Paris Academy of Sciences 1666–1803*. Berkeley and Los Angeles: University of California Press.

Hedfors, Eva. 2006. "The reading of Ludwik Fleck: Questions of sources and impetus." *Social Epistemology* 20 (2): 131–61.

Heemskerk Azn., Jan. 1856. *Voordrachten over den eigendom van voortbrengselen van den geest*. Haarlem: Kruseman, 1956.

Heerding, A. 1986. *The history of the N. V. Philips Gloeilampenfabrieken*. Vol. 1, *The origin of the Dutch incandescent industry*. Cambridge: Cambridge University Press.

Heller, M. A., and R. S. Eisenberg. 1998. "Can patents deter innovation? The anticommons in biomedical research." *Science* 280 (5364): 698–701.

Hermesdorf, Bernardus Hubertus Dominicus. 1923. "Wetenschappelijke eigendom." *Rechtsgeleerd Magazijn*, 411–27.

Hesse, Carla. 1990. "Enlightenment epistemology and the laws of authorship in revolutionary France, 1777–1793." *Representations* 30:109–37.

Hull, David. 1988. *Science as a process*. Chicago: University of Chicago Press.

Jefferson, Thomas. 1788. "Letter to James Madison, Paris, July 31, 1788." Available at http://teachingamericanhistory.org/library/index.asp?document=998.

———. 1813. "Letter to Isaac McPherson, Monticello, August 13, 1813." Available at http://odur.let.rug.nl/~usa/P/tj3/writings/brf/jefl220.htm.

Kapczynski, Amy, Samantha Chaifetz, Zachary Katz, and Yochai Benkler. 2005. "Addressing global health inequities: An open licensing approach for university innovations." *Berkeley Journal of Law and Technology* 20:1031–114.

Kingston, William. 2004. "Streptomycin, *Schatz v. Waksman*, and the balance of credit for discovery." *Journal of the History of Medicine and Allied Sciences* 59 (3): 441–62.

Kragh, Helge. 1999. *Quantum generations: A history of physics in the twentieth century*. Princeton, NJ: Princeton University Press.

Krimsky, Sheldon. 2003. *Science in the private interest*. Lanham, MD: Rowman and Littlefield.

Ladas, Stephen B. 1929. "The efforts for international protection of scientific property." *American Journal of International Law* 23 (3): 552–69.

Lavoisier, Antoine-Laurent. 1774. *Analyse du mémoire sur l'augmentation du poids par la calcination*. In *Oeuvres de Lavoisier*, vol. 2. Paris : Imprimerie Impériale, 1862.

Lemley, Mark. 2005. "Property, intellectual property, and free riding." *Texas Law Review* 83:1031–65.

Machlup, Fritz, and Edith Penrose. 1950. "The patent controversy in the nineteenth century." *Journal of Economic History* 10 (1): 1–29.

Maindron, Ernest. 1888. *L'Académie des Sciences*. Paris: F. Alcan.

McLean, Iain. 2002. "Thomas Jefferson, John Adams, and the Déclaration des Droits de l'Homme et du Citoyen." Available at www.nuffield.ox.ac.uk/Politics/papers/2002/w24/ddhc3.pdf.

Meier, Hugo A. 1990. "Thomas Jefferson and a democratic technology." In *Technology in America: A history of individuals and ideas*, ed. Carroll W. Pursell Jr., 17–33. Cambridge, MA: MIT Press.

Merges, Robert P. 1996. "Property rights theory and the commons: The case of scientific research." In *Scientific innovation, philosophy, and public policy*, ed. Ellen Frankel Paul, Fred D. Miller Jr., and Jeffrey Paul, 145–67. Cambridge: Cambridge University Press.

Mermin, N. David. 2005. "Proper citation of the Matthew effect." *Physics Today* 58 (4): 17.

Merton, Robert K. 1938. *Science, technology and society in seventeenth-century England.* New York: Harper and Row, 1970.

———. 1973. *The sociology of science: Theoretical and empirical investigations.* Chicago: University of Chicago Press.

———. 1979. *The sociology of science: An episodic memoir.* Carbondale: Southern Illinois University Press.

———. 1988. "The Matthew effect in science, II: Cumulative advantage and the symbolism of intellectual property." *Isis* 79:606–23.

———. 1995. "The Thomas theorem and the Matthew effect." *Social Forces* 74 (2): 379–424.

Metlay, Grischa. 2006. "Reconsidering renormalization: Stability and change in twentieth-century views on university patents." *Social Studies of Science* 36 (4): 565–97.

Mirowski, Philip E. 2003. "What's Kuhn got to do with it?" *Social Epistemology* 17 (2–3): 229–39.

Mirowski, Philip, and Esther-Mirjam Sent, eds. 2002. *Science bought and sold: Essays in the economics of science.* Chicago: University of Chicago Press.

———. 2008. "The commercialization of science and the response of STS." In *The handbook of science and technology studies*, 3rd ed., ed. Edward J. Hackett, Olga Amsterdamska, Michael Lynch, and Judy Wajcman, 635–89. Cambridge, MA.: MIT Press.

Mistiaen, Veronique. 2002. "Time, and the great healer." *The Guardian*, November 2.

Mossoff, Adam. 2007. "Who cares what Jefferson thought about patents? Reevaluating the patent 'privilege' in historical context." *Cornell Law Review* 25:953–1012.

Nelson, Richard R. 1959. "The Simple Economics of Basic Scientific Research." In *Science bought and sold: Essays in the economics of science*, ed. Philip Mirowski and Esther-Mirjam Sent, 151–64. Chicago: University of Chicago Press, 2002.

Nowotny, Helga. 2003. "Democratising expertise and socially robust knowledge." *Science and Public Policy* 30 (3): 151–56.

Perelman, Michael. 2006. "Some economics of class." *Monthly Review* (July–August).

Rabinow, Paul. 1996. *Making PCR: A story of biotechnology.* Chicago: University of Chicago Press.

Radder, Hans. 2006. *The world observed/The world conceived*, Pittsburgh: University of Pittsburgh Press.

Ravetz, Jerome R. 1971. *Scientific knowledge and its social problems.* Harmondsworth: Penguin Books, 1973.

Reede, J. J. de. 1937. "Uitvinding, nieuwheid en uitkomst op het gebied der nijverheid." In *Wat is een uitvinding en wat werd een kwart eeuw uitgevonden?*, ed. Octrooiraad, 104–77. The Hague: Zuid-Hollandsche Uitgevers Maatschappij.

Sample, Ian. 2006. "Who really made Dolly? Tale of British triumph descends into scientists' squabble." *The Guardian*, March 11.

Satter, Heinrich. 1967. *Emil von Behring.* Bad Godesberg: Inter Nationes.

Savignon, Francois. 1989. "The French Revolution and patents." *Industrial Property* 28:391–400.

Scheler, Max. 1924. "Probleme einer Soziologie des Wissens." In *Versuche zu einer Soziologie des Wissens*, ed. Max Scheler, 1–146. Munich: Duncker & Humblot.

Scherer, Frederic M. 2007. "The political economy of patent policy reform in the United States." KSG Working Paper No. RWP 07-042. Available at http://ssm.com/abstract= 963136.

Schofield, N. 2005. "The intellectual contribution of Condorcet to the founding of the U.S. republic 1785–1800." *Social Choice and Welfare* 25 (2–3): 303–18.

Stallman, Richard. 2006. "Did you say 'intellectual property'? It's a seductive mirage." Available at http://www.gnu.org/philosophy/not-ipr.xhtml.

Stephan, Paula E. 1996. "The economics of science." *Journal of Economic Literature* 36: 1199–1235.

———. 2004. "Robert K. Merton's perspective on priority and the provision of the public good knowledge." *Scientometrics* 60 (1): 81–87.

Stiglitz, Joseph. 1999. "Knowledge as a global public good." Available at www.worldbank .org/knowledge/chiefecon/articles/undpk2/.

Strevens, Michael. 2006. "The role of the Matthew effect in science." *Studies in History and Philosophy of Science* 37:159–70.

Van den Belt, Henk. 1989. "Action at a distance." In *Expert evidence: Interpreting science in the law*, ed. R. Smith and B. Wynne, 184–209. London: Routledge, 1989.

———. 1997. *Spirochaetes, serology, and salvarsan: Ludwik Fleck and the construction of medical knowledge about syphilis*. Ph.D. diss.

Verkade, Feer. 1997. *Intellectuele eigendom: Wetenschaps-stimulator?* Amsterdam: Koninklijke Academie van Wetenschappen.

Walterscheid, Edward C. 1999. "The use and abuse of history: The Supreme Court's interpretation of Thomas Jefferson's influence on the patent law." *IDEA: The Journal of Law and Technology* 39:195–223.

Wassermann, August von. 1921. "Neue experimentelle Forschungen über Syphilis." *Berliner Klinische Wochenschrift* 58:193–97.

Weingart, Peter. 1978. "The relation between science and technology—A sociological explanation." In *The Dynamics of Science and Technology*, ed. W. Krohn, E. T. Layton, and P. Weingart, 251–86. Dordrecht: Reidel.

Wiener, Norbert. 1948. *Cybernetics: Control and communication in the animal and the machine*. Cambridge, MA: MIT Press, 1961.

Williams, Raymond. 1983. *Keywords: A vocabulary of culture and society*. London: Flamingo.

Woodmansee, Martha. 1984. "The genius and the copyright: Economic and legal conditions of the emergence of the 'author.'" *Eighteenth-Century Studies* 17 (4): 425–48.

Zilsel, Edgar. 1942. "The sociological roots of science." *American Journal of Sociology* 47:544–62.

Zuckerman, Harriet, Jonathan R. Cole, and John T. Bruer, eds. 1991. *The outer circle: Women in the scientific community*. New York: W. W. Norton.

CHAPTER 10

Mertonian Values, Scientific Norms, and the Commodification of Academic Research

Hans Radder

1. Introduction

IN THE COURSE of the past decade, the commodification—and more specifically the commercialization—of academic science since the 1980s has been explored and a variety of studies of this phenomenon have become available.[1] To be sure, science at large has always included research primarily carried out for its economic benefit, especially since the second half of the nineteenth century. Just think of the many scientific laboratories of smaller and larger industrial firms. The substantial commodification of academic science is a more recent phenomenon, however, even if it surely occurred to some extent in earlier times. This chapter addresses the recent commodification of academic science and focuses on its normative dimensions. Assessments of the rise of entrepreneurial academia differ sharply. On the one hand, it is welcomed and sometimes even seen as a necessary step in the history of academic institutions (see, e.g., Gibbons et al. 1994; Etzkowitz 2004). On the other hand, the problematic consequences of commodified academic science are also widely discussed and increasingly acknowledged.[2]

In response to these problems, universities, research institutes, and science policy organizations have composed (or updated) various normative codes of good scientific conduct. At present, such codes have been adopted by both national and international scientific organizations in many disciplines. Almost invariably, these codes are based on, or derived from, the social ethos of science formulated by Robert K. Merton in 1942. In the 1970s, however, this Mertonian ethos and, more generally, the entire notion of a normative structure of science, was being strongly criticized by the then rising sociology of scientific knowledge. In this chapter, I analyze and assess this dispute. My purpose is to find out to what extent a Mertonian approach can still be useful in the present context of heavily commodified science, in particular regarding the issue of the patenting of the results of academic research. The approach is philosophical in nature, which involves presenting an intentional mixture of theoretical, normative, and reflexive considerations without losing sight of empirical and historical issues.[3]

Following the definitions in chapter 1, I use "university" primarily to mean a wholly or largely publicly funded institution of higher education (though in a broader sense it may also include private but nonprofit research and teaching institutes). "Academic science" involves not only teaching and research at universities but also research and scholarship in independent, publicly funded institutions. Although the commodification of university teaching, management, and administration is an equally important subject of study, my focus is on academic research.

The structure of the chapter is as follows. In section 2, I set out Merton's views on the ethos of science. Section 3 reviews the criticism by sociologists of scientific knowledge and concludes that it is only partly right. Some recent codifications of Mertonian standards for good scientific conduct are discussed in section 4. Section 5, then, explains in which sense and to what extent a Mertonian approach is still valuable, and even badly needed, in the current context of strongly commodified academic research. My claim is that Merton's notions of universalism, communism, disinterestedness, and organized skepticism (or similar "Mertonian" notions) are best interpreted as overarching values that may be realized by following more specific scientific norms (or better, phrased as a matter of degree: norms that may bring those values closer to realization). In section 6, I focus the discussion on the issue of the patenting of results of academic science, and I demonstrate the significance of Mertonian values and scientific norms for this issue. An important conclusion is that a Mertonian approach can be effective if it is not limited to an after-the-event assessment of the behavior of individual scientists, but also constructively employed in crafting and implementing more structural science policies. The concluding section briefly addresses some questions regarding the scope, presuppositions, and implications of what I call a deflationary, neo-Mertonian critique of commodified science.

2. Merton's Ethos of Science

In 1942 Robert K. Merton published his well-known article on the normative structure of science, originally and significantly entitled "A Note on Science and Democracy." At the time science was, or was perceived to be, threatened by anti-intellectual criticisms, nationalist ideologies, and racist politics.[4] For Merton, this context defined the broader goal of his article: "an institution under attack must reexamine its foundations, restate its objectives, seek out its rationale. Crisis invites self-appraisal" (Merton 1942/1973, 267). Thus right from the start his approach is partial, in defense of science as *the* exemplar of a democratic social institution. The qualification "social" is important for Merton. He emphasizes that his account of science is sociological in nature and claims that it does not aim to include methodological criteria and that it is not based on substantive findings of the sciences. In this spirit, he then proposes his four famous norms of science (also called "institutional imperatives") as the backbone of the ethos of science: universalism, communism, disinterestedness, and organized skepticism. The claim is that the existence and operation of this ethos, even if it has not been explicitly formulated and codified, can be inferred from the practices, behaviors, and verbal expressions of the scientists.

Merton explains his four norms as follows. "Universalism" means that the acceptance or rejection of scientific claims should be based on impersonal criteria. Put negatively, nationality, ethnicity, religion, sex, and any other personal qualities of a scientist should be irrelevant to the evaluation of scientific truth-claims. Quoting historical studies of national scientific styles, Merton admits that discoveries may depend on the particularities of a given sociocultural situation. Yet (what is now called) the context of justification is characterized by universalism, and hence "sooner or later, competing claims to validity are settled by universalistic criteria" (Merton 1942/1973, 271n6). In a broader sense, the notion of universalism includes the norm that science should be open to anyone who is sufficiently talented. Thus, access to science should be universal and not be blocked on the basis of nationality, ethnicity, sex, religion, and the like.

The second element of the scientific ethos is "communism" or the common ownership of goods.[5] For science this means that its fruits should not be privately owned, because they result from an essentially collective effort. "The substantive findings of science are a product of social collaboration and are assigned to the community" (Merton 1942/1973, 273). Priority claims by scientists regarding specific discoveries are compatible with the norm of communism, because they do not lead to ownership of the discovery but merely to general recognition and esteem as a result of having made the discovery. Secrecy and patenting, however, do contradict the idea of common ownership of the results of scientific research, as Merton explicitly states.

"Disinterestedness" constitutes the third norm of good scientific practice. Merton emphasizes that this should not be mistaken for a lack of individual motivation. Individual scientists may have a variety of motivations for practicing science in the way they do, ranging from a craving for fame and wealth to a concern for the well-being of humanity. The point of the norm of disinterestedness, however, lies at the institutional level or, in philosophical jargon, in the context of justification. Through the presence of institutional controls, such as peer review, publication, and replication of research results, the potential distortion by individual motivations is being filtered out. Conversely, if the accountability of scientists to their peers is diminished or eroded by ideological or economic forces, a real and damaging loss of scientific integrity and objectivity will result.

The fourth and last element of Merton's scientific ethos is "organized skepticism." This is akin to Karl Popper's idea of the critical attitude. It requires the "temporary suspension of judgment and the detached scrutiny of beliefs in terms of empirical and logical criteria" (Merton 1942/1973, 277). The reference to empirical and logical criteria implies that this norm is not purely institutional but has a methodological aspect as well. The qualification "organized" means that the locus of this norm is again institutional: individual scientists may be committed to their cherished theories, models, or methods, but it is the task of the scientific community as a whole to practice a temporary suspension of judgment. The opposite of organized skepticism is institutionalized dogmatism. Of course, science itself should be antidogmatic. In addition, Merton advocates the Enlightenment vision more generally, which implies that "uncritical doctrines" in the areas of religion, economy, or politics should give way to views based on critical scientific research.

3. "Deviant Viewpoints" and Their Assessment

Merton's account of the ethos of science has been both influential and controversial. Since the aim of this contribution is to discuss the significance of a Mertonian approach in the present situation of an increasing commodification of academic research, I will not provide a comprehensive review of the impact and critiques of this approach (see, e.g., Sismondo 2004, 20–32). Yet the criticisms proffered by advocates of the sociology of scientific knowledge (SSK) are directly relevant to my purposes, hence I will address those criticisms here. My focus is on the "deviant viewpoints" advocated during the 1970s by S. B. Barnes and R. G. A. Dolby and by Michael Mulkay. From a broadly Kuhnian perspective, these authors formulate several points of criticism of Merton's claims about the normative structure of science.

First, these critics claim that empirically there is no such thing as a uniquely institutionalized set of scientific norms. Historical and sociological studies of scientific practice refute the claimed existence of a homogeneous scientific ethos. Thus, Barnes and Dolby argue that Merton's four norms were almost totally irrelevant to seventeenth- and eighteenth-century amateur science and mostly irrelevant to twentieth-century big science with its dependence on large-scale national and military interests. And even during the stage of professional academic science (roughly, from the middle of the nineteenth century until the First World War) Merton's account is claimed to apply, at best, only partially. Mulkay (1976, 638–39) draws the following general conclusion.

> In recent years there has been much criticism of this kind of functional analysis of science. One reason for such criticism is that detailed study by historians and sociologists has shown that in practice scientists deviate from some at least of these putative norms with a frequency which is remarkable if we presume that the latter are firmly institutionalized. Another reason is that none of the empirical studies designed to discover how far defined samples of scientists express agreement with verbal formulations of the norms has produced evidence of any strong general commitment.

In addition to historical criticism like that put forward by Barnes and Dolby, Mulkay discusses sociological work that claims to demonstrate the existence of "counternorms" (such as particularism, secrecy, interestedness, and dogmatism), which are the very opposite of Merton's norms.

A second point of the SSK critique is that Merton's norms are far too abstract. For this reason, in as far as they do apply to science, they do not demarcate it from other social practices. Thus, regarding the norm of universalism, Barnes and Dolby claim that all societies (including societies that do not have a well-developed, institutionalized science) possess certain impersonal criteria of truth.[6] Hence this norm does not demarcate science from nonscience. Another important issue stemming from the abstract nature of these norms is that they are too vague to guide concrete research. In this respect, they differ from the more local, "technical" norms that are incorporated in specific research practices. For example, in contrast to the phlogiston tradition, Lavoisier's new chemical paradigm (developed during the last decades of the eighteenth century) demanded an accurate quantitative determination of the weight of the substances involved in chemical reactions by means of the balance (see Levere 1990). Mulkay concludes that Merton's abstract ethos of science lacks any content as compared to these more local and substantive norms.

Finally, Barnes and Dolby emphasize that it is important to distinguish between norms that can be shown to be operative in actual practice and norms that are merely professed in tracts or speeches for broader or nonscientific audiences. Similarly, Mulkay contrasts the norms that guide informal interactions between scientists with the norms that are followed in formal communications such as journal articles or textbooks. The claim is that (to the extent that their presence can be substantiated at all) only the operative and informal norms really count, since the professed and formal norms merely function as a legitimation, or even as an ideology, to protect the interests of either particular groups of scientists (in the case of controversies) or of science as a whole (when its autonomy is under attack).[7] The point of this claim with respect to Merton is that, in as far as he does adduce empirical evidence for his views, this evidence mostly pertains to professed and formal norms, which are not relevant to science as it is actually practiced.

For the purpose of this chapter, this brief summary of the main points of criticism of Merton's ethos by these early proponents of the sociology of scientific knowledge should suffice.[8] Hence, let us proceed to evaluate these criticisms. The first point—that actual scientists do not always, and oftentimes hardly ever, live up to Merton's ethos of science—seems hard to deny. In addition to the evidence already adduced, just consider the simple fact that until the late nineteenth century (in the Netherlands until 1871) female students were structurally, and sometimes even legally, excluded from the university system. Moreover, many studies have convincingly shown that not only the admission to academic science but also the evaluation of scientific claims has been influenced by contextual, and hence by nonuniversal, interests and values (see, among many others, Longino 1990).

Nonetheless, the fact that norms are not (always) being followed neither implies that they do not exist nor that they are inconsequential in practice. Although I will say more on this below, to appreciate the plausibility of this point it is enough to change one of the phrases in the above quotation from Mulkay into the claim that "detailed study by historians and sociologists has shown that in practice people frequently deviate from the norm that they should not kill other people." Clearly, we do not conclude from this that the norm of not killing is not "firmly institutionalized." Moreover, if we take into account more recent developments (as I will do in section 4), there is more to say about the issue of the actual institutionalization of the Merton norms.

An additional problem is that Mulkay (along with some of the Mertonians) assumes that "social norms are to be regarded as institutionalised when they are positively linked to the distribution of rewards" (Mulkay 1976, 641). However, a scientist who follows Merton's norms and writes a great article will be rewarded for the content of this article, not for following the norms. Similarly, somebody who follows the common norms of politeness will usually not be rewarded for that reason. In fact, rewards for following norms are primarily given during learning or socialization stages (for instance, to a novice or a small child). Thus while it is true that nonconformity to prevailing norms may engender sanctions, "normal" conformity is usually taken for granted rather than rewarded.

Assessing the second point of the SSK criticism is less straightforward. It is correct that each single norm will not demarcate science from nonscience. Yet it might well be true that the four norms taken together entail a nonlocal pattern of behaviors that can be found significantly more frequently within science than outside of it. The fact that there are no hard and fast demarcation criteria does not mean that Merton's norms might not pattern scientific activities in ways that contrast with typical religious or artistic activities. Hence this part of the SSK criticism is too quick. Apart from this, however, Merton's ethos of science may be deemed significant and worth defending even if it is equally applicable to both science and other human practices. That is to say, even if this ethos does not demarcate science from nonscience, it may be useful in assessing the value of present-day commodified science. That is the view I take in this chapter.

More important than the demarcation issue is the complaint that Merton's norms are too abstract to guide scientific practice. If this means that these norms need to be complemented—instead of replaced, as Mulkay (1976, 643) recommends—by more specific scientific norms, the point is well taken. Hence I will return to it in the following sections.

Third, there is the claim that only informal norms, that can be shown to be actually followed in scientific practice, count as evidence for the existence of an institutionalized ethos, while professed and formal norms do not count in this respect. This criticism is highly problematic for two reasons. The first is that it presupposes a Kuhnian separation between the internal, front-line research of "real" practitioners and the "merely" justificatory and ideological activities of other scientists (or of front-line scientists in external, "nonscientific" contexts). However, this internalist account of science postulates an artificial and unempirical rift in the range of activities that are being practiced by scientists. In contrast to the notion of justification used by Barnes and Dolby, both a specialist argument for a technical scientific claim (for instance, that it is supported by a particular test) and a general argument for that claim (for instance, that it has withstood prolonged organized skepticism) can be said to be justificatory, albeit, of course, at different levels of generality. That is to say, professed norms are not necessarily "merely professed": they can be equally operative, namely in activities (such as the writing of textbooks or funding applications) that Barnes and Dolby have unjustly excluded from the practice of science. Mulkay (1976, 642) constructs a similar "divergence between the formal procedures of communication and the social realities of scientific research." But again, this claim presupposes a Kuhnian "one-pass model" of scientific development (Nickles 1992). Once we discard this model as inadequate, formal procedures of communication (in this case, the impersonal style of scientific writing) are as much a "genuine reality" of scientific practice as the laboratory practices on which they are based. As Thomas Nickles convincingly argues, published articles are not a "misrepresentation" of real scientific practice but a reconstructed continuation of that practice (Nickles 1992; see also Gooding 1990; Radder 1997).

Underlying this issue, however, is another, deeper problem with the SSK position. This has to do with the fact that its proponents do not see, or do not wish to acknowledge, that Merton's account itself constitutes an interested position. As mentioned in the previous section, this account is explicitly designed to defend science against strong and prolonged assaults.[9] In this respect, the postulation of the four norms is itself a normative act. As such, it cannot be refuted by empirical counterexamples but instead requires a normative assessment: is promoting these norms a good thing to do? The SSK critics, however, exclude this question from their discourse, implicitly (in the case of Mulkay) or explicitly (in the case of Barnes and Dolby).[10] Thus the latter note that one of Merton's reasons for positing the norms is that "they are theoretically necessary by virtue of their functional relationship to the institutional goal of science," but they go on to state that they will not discuss this claim because "it rests upon the theory of functionalism which has achieved no consensus within sociology."[11] I agree that functionalism as a general sociological framework possesses several questionable features. For my purposes, however, a discussion and assessment of functionalism can be left aside. Indeed, one can go beyond the narrow confines of the SSK account by including an ethical-political perspective from which to address the normative question of whether or not Merton's ethos of science is still valuable in an age of pervasive commodification of academic research. From the point of view of philosophy as primarily theoretical, normative, and reflexive, asking (and trying to answer) this normative question makes full sense, as I have argued elsewhere (see Radder 1996, chap. 8).

4. Recent Codifications of an Ethos of Science

As we have seen, one important point of contention between Merton and his SSK critics is the claim of the actual institutionalization of a normative ethos of science. In the previous section, I sided with Barnes/Dolby and Mulkay in that, generally speaking, the historical study of scientific development entails a challenge to Merton's claim. In this chapter, however, the focus is on the contemporary situation, in particular the situation after the mid-1970s. A remarkable feature of this period is the strong increase of codifications of desirable scientific conduct. Three main reasons account for this. First, some codes have arisen out of concern for the negative social or moral consequences of (the uses of) science. A second reason was the high-profile exposure of several major cases of fraud and scientific misconduct. Third (and somewhat later), there has been the documentation and acknowledgment of the downsides of the commercialization of academic science. While the first kind of codes emphasize the social responsibility of scientists, the codes adopted for the latter two reasons stress the significance of their professional integrity. Typically, concerned scientists, investigative journalists, and science administrators have played, and still play, a substantial role in raising awareness of these problems,[12] while the scholarly study of science lagged behind and has only recently begun to catch up.

Janet Kourany (2008) usefully discusses the many research ethics codes that have been devised (or updated) and adopted over the past decades, including the international Uppsala Code of Ethics for Scientists (1984), the U.S. Chemist's Code of Conduct (1994), and the U.S. Ethical Principles of Psychologists and Code of Conduct (2002), among many others.[13] There has also been extensive debate on the ethical issues of research in the Netherlands, in part induced by cases of misconduct and fraud, and in part by the increasing commodification of academic research (see, e.g., Heilbron 2005). As a result, Dutch universities and other scientific organizations have devised an ethical code of teaching and research, and institutionalized a policy to sanction violations of this code. The *Vereniging voor Samenwerkende Nederlandse Universiteiten* (VSNU, or Association of Universities in the Netherlands) has adopted a Code of Conduct for Scientific Practice that provides a codification of principles of good scientific teaching and research (VSNU 2004). Furthermore, in 2003 the Koninklijke Nederlandse Akademie van Wetenschappen (KNAW, or Royal Netherlands Academy of Arts and Sciences) institutionalized the Landelijk Orgaan Wetenschappelijke Integriteit (LOWI, or National Organization for Scientific Integrity). Thus, while the VSNU code describes and discusses desirable scientific conduct, the task of the LOWI is to handle formal complaints about scientific misconduct.

Leaving aside the issues of misconduct and its sanctions, I will briefly describe the main ideas of the VSNU (2004) code. First, it lists five primary values, to wit, scrupulousness, reliability, verifiability, impartiality, and independence. Since these values—similar to those of other codes—are clearly inspired by Merton's work, I suggest referring to them as Mertonian values and a Mertonian ethos of science.[14] Next, these primary values are specified in two steps. First, by adding principles (in my terminology, norms) which all academic scientists should observe, and second by describing best practices in which these principles are applied. For instance, connected to the value of verifiability is the principle that "Whenever research results are publicized, it is made clear what the data and the conclusions are based on, where they were derived from and how they can be verified"; furthermore, in the case of this principle, best practice includes the claim that "Research must be replicable in order to verify its accuracy. The choice of research question, the research set-up, the choice of method and the reference to sources studied is accurately documented."[15] As to the value of impartiality, the corresponding principle reads: "in his scientific activities, the scientific practitioner heeds no other interests than the scientific interest. In this respect, he is always prepared to account for his actions." And here best practice includes the norm that "The choice of methods and criteria is guided solely by the goal of truth-finding, and not by external goals such as commercial success or political influence." Finally, the code discusses several examples of the dilemmas and gray areas that may, and will, be found in actual scientific practice. In doing so, it rightly shows an awareness of the ambivalences that can be expected to arise in the application of ethical codes.

Thus the present situation is rather different from both that in 1942 and that in the 1970s. Because there were no (or very few) explicitly institutionalized codes of conduct in 1942, Merton had to infer the existence of such codes from the practice and writings of scientists. Because the situation in the 1970s had not yet changed as dramatically as it has during the last three decades, Barnes/Dolby and Mulkay found a relatively easy target for their criticism of the claimed institutionalization of Merton's ethos in actual practice. At present, however, this criticism has lost its plausibility (see also Montgomery and Oliver 2009, 141ff).

However, while this part of the SSK position has been displaced by recent historical events, the problem of the abstract nature of the Mertonian ethos and its lack of applicability to concrete scientific practices still persists. Thus Kourany rightly observes that many of the ethical codes are unhelpfully vague or ambiguous. Yet she concludes that the existence of vagueness and ambiguity do not make such codes superfluous or meaningless. Instead, this situation presents a novel challenge to the philosophy of science.

> Helping to make the ethics codes in the sciences adequate is thus an important project—an important *normative* project, one that looks deeply into not only the aims and attendant responsibilities that scientists do set for themselves, both individually and collectively, but also the aims and responsibilities scientists ought to set for themselves. It is, moreover, an important epistemic as well as ethical project: helping to make the ethics codes adequate responds to needs that are both epistemic and ethical. (Kourany 2008, 776)

In the remaining sections of this chapter, I try to meet this challenge by showing how a Mertonian approach may be honed to become more specific and effective. In the next section, I develop a theoretically more satisfactory account of the nature and function of Mertonian values and scientific norms. In section 6, this approach is applied in a discussion of a number of normative, socioepistemic issues surrounding the patenting of the results of academic research. Furthermore, this section points to another crucial limitation of the present use of ethical codes, namely the fact that they are almost invariably aimed at individual scientists and are not systematically exploited in designing and implementing more structural science policies.

To avoid misunderstanding I should add that this approach does not imply the endorsement of the general interpretations of science that frequently underlie Mertonian codes of ethical scientific conduct. From a philosophical point of view, these general interpretations are often rather questionable. Thus, on the basis of Michael Polanyi's or Thomas Kuhn's views, one could easily argue that impartiality, in the VSNU (2004) sense of being fully unprejudiced, would make practicing science impossible.[16] However, criticisms like this one do not rule out that (what I will call in section 7) a deflationary, neo-Mertonian approach can be useful for the more limited purposes of this chapter which, after all, does not aspire to provide a comprehensive philosophical interpretation of science.

5. Mertonian Values and Scientific Norms

Having discussed and assessed the SSK criticisms of Merton's ethos of science, I will now add several critical comments of my own that are important in the context of this chapter. For a start, Merton's terminology and his explanations are not always clear and convincing. One may, for example, question the accuracy of the term "universalism" if this is meant to refer to the impersonal nature of evaluation criteria of scientific claims. In this case, a more appropriate alternative would seem to be "(epistemic) objectivity."[17] Merton's term "universalism" may easily lead to confusion, as is for instance the case with those authors who connect it closely to the idea of a universal *scope* of scientific claims. However, there is no necessary connection between impersonal judgment and universal scope, since the norm in question is meant to apply to the evaluation of both singular statements (e.g., "this piece of copper conducts electricity") and universal statements (e.g., "all copper conducts electricity"). Another issue is the independence of the four norms. In this respect, one might ask whether disinterestedness is not already implied by universalism. When all scientific claims are assessed on the basis of impersonal criteria, any impact of the particular interests of individual scientists on the processes through which scientific claims are justified will have been prevented. Finally, one may question the completeness of the set of four norms. Do they cover the entire normative structure of science, as Merton claims, or do we need additional values, such as "scrupulousness" or "reliability" (which are included in the code of conduct of the Association of Universities in the Netherlands discussed in the previous section)?

These questionable features of Merton's terminology and explanations provide another reason for a terminological shift from Merton's ethos to a Mertonian ethos. By making this shift, I assume that the above problems can in principle be solved by providing a more finely honed terminology and a better analysis, so that "something like" Merton's ethos makes sense.[18] However, this is not the place to carry out such an analysis. Instead, I will argue that a Mertonian ethos should preferably be phrased in terms of values, while—in line with the discussion in section 3—it should be complemented by an account of more specific scientific norms.

Although Merton himself uses the terms "norms," "imperatives," "mores," and "values" more or less indiscriminately, in scholarly practice the phrase "Merton's norms" has become the established usage. However, if we define a norm, as I suggest, as "a socially embedded directive about what people should, or should not, do or say," in a purely terminological sense universalism, communism, disinterestedness, and organized skepticism are values rather than norms. Of course, it is trivially possible to derive norms that correspond to given values. Thus, given a value v, one may construct the trivially corresponding norm "one should strive to realize value v." However, as compared to the value this norm does not give us any further information about what (not) to do or say. For these reasons, I think it preferable to see an element of a Mertonian ethos as primarily a value, that is, a quality of things, states of affair, events, activities, and the like, that renders them useful or estimable.[19] The idea, then, is that general Mertonian values should be specified through adding more concrete norms about how to realize these values. In this way, we may also bridge Merton's artificial gap between institutional and methodological or social and epistemic norms.

Often, values denote rather general or even vague qualities of things. There is a positive and a negative side to this. In positive terms, due to their generality and vagueness, values can be relatively easily shared, while such shared values can serve to promote a sense of community. Who would not endorse the value of scientific integrity, for instance? More negatively, however, merely endorsing general and vague values "as such" may be vacuous. Hence, in order to know what is meant by a value, further interpretation is needed. A first step in this interpretation is to devise more specific norms that may enable or facilitate the realization of said value. A second step involves the clarification of what it means to apply these norms in concrete situations. Making these two steps entails that adopting a certain value may be a matter of argued judgment rather than mere taste (see Kuhn 1977, 336–37). At the same time, this interpretation and clarification may also lead to disagreement among people who do share the same value. Thus, some scientists may interpret a project funded by a national research council as a form of contract research, while others may see this project as a case of independent inquiry. Furthermore, some scientists may think that any contract research will jeopardize their scientific integrity, while others may hold that the value of scientific integrity does not exclude all forms of contract research. Hence, while general values connect people, the more specific norms and their applications may divide them again. Yet the translation of values into norms, of course, does not necessarily lead to disagreement. In specific situations it may well be possible to reach agreement on the interpretation and application of particular norms. In this spirit, the following section argues for the adoption of certain norms in the context of the commodification of academic research and advocates their application to the issue of the patenting of the results of this research.

As we have seen in section 3, the suggestion of the SSK critics is simply to get rid of Merton's general values in favor of the more localized, technical norms. I do not think this is advisable. In spite of their rather general or vague nature, Mertonian values are important for two reasons. First, they serve to promote a sense of community, which is conducive to the maintenance of an appropriate measure of trust, both among scientists themselves and between science and the wider public. Second, like all (general) concepts Mertonian values possess a nonlocal meaning (Radder 2006), which may be exploited as a heuristic resource for the articulation of novel scientific norms that can be fruitfully applied in new situations.

Finally, it is important to see that neither values nor norms fully determine each and every aspect of the behavior of scientists. Yet they do guide scientists in certain directions. The norm that scientific claims should be open to critical discussion, which can be derived from the value of organized skepticism, patterns scientific publications in ways that distinguish the typical scientific article from the typical work of literature. Moreover, in a given situation, the norm of writing argumentative discourse directs the way scientists report on their research. In the science studies literature (e.g., Mulkay 1976, 643–45; Sismondo 2004, 29–30), one often finds the weaker claim that norms constitute flexible resources from which scientists pick and choose whatever they see fit with respect to their locally situated construction work. However, even if it is right to assume that norms do not determine practices, this constructivist claim is much too voluntaristic, and as such it fails to appreciate the fact that norms also constrain practices.[20]

6. Mertonian Values, Scientific Norms, and the Patenting of Academic Research

The commodification of academic research is a multifaceted phenomenon (see my opening chapter in this volume). Here I focus on one of its aspects, to wit the practice of patenting the results of academic research and the concomitant pressure on university scientists to engage in patent applications. In view of this practice and pressure, the question of whether or not the patenting of academic research conforms to Mertonian values and norms is pertinent. The fact that a problem exists has been noted by quite a few authors, mostly with reference to biomedical research. Thus Krimsky (2003, 84) states that "the norm of communalism . . . has become secondary to the norm of private appropriation of one's intellectual labor." The challenge is how to proceed from such statements to a more general account that is philosophically sophisticated, and normatively and practically useful. It is this challenge that I attempt to meet in this section.

To this end I first review some basic features of the patenting system.[21] A patent is an intellectual property right to exploit a particular technological invention. More precisely, it is the right of the patent holder(s) to exclude all other people or institutions from reaping the economic fruits of this invention. A patent has a restricted temporal scope, since its validity is limited, usually to twenty years. The three main criteria for patentability (in the United States' judiciary phrasing) are that the invention should be "novel," have "utility" and be "nonobvious to some-one skilled in the art." Furthermore, the invention should be reproducible by competent peers of the inventor. In return for the granting of the patent, the invention needs to be disclosed, that is, made publicly available through submitting a description of it to the relevant patent office. Over the last twenty-five years, the number of patent applications and grants has increased dramatically, in particular in the areas of biotechnology, information, communication technology, and pharmaceuticals. By way of general justification, patent law and regulation is often claimed to constitute a legitimate social arrangement because it stimulates innovation by rewarding inventors for making socially beneficial, new technology available to society as a whole.[22]

Of course, patenting takes place primarily in industry and, more generally, in commercial business. However, since the rise of the "entrepreneurial university" during the last quarter of the twentieth century, patenting is also increasingly practiced within academic science, first in the United States and, somewhat later, also in Europe (Slaughter and Rhoades 2004, chaps. 3 and 4; Etzkowitz 2004; Sterckx, this volume, chap. 3). In light of decreasing public funding, university administrators promote patenting as one of the novel ways of financing academic research. Academic researchers are pressed to engage in patent applications and the exploitation or licensing of acquired patents. At the same time, granted patents tend to be judged as equally important and valuable results of academic research as journal publications or books. Thus, a recent policy paper in my university, VU University Amsterdam, includes "acquired patents and sales of intellectual property" as a legitimate indicator of academic achievement. Another policy paper states that a researcher who thinks that his results may be patentable is even "obliged to cooperate in exploiting this knowledge." Similarly, for those areas where patents can be acquired, the European Research Council lists "five granted patents in the last ten years" as one of the benchmarks for being eligible for its prestigious Advanced Grant Scheme.[23]

But can this practice be justified? Can the practices of patenting conform to the same Mertonian values and norms as the practices of "ordinary" academic research? Or better still (since this is not a matter of all-or-nothing), phrased as a matter of degree: does the introduction of patenting contribute to, or does it detract from, the realization of Mertonian values? To answer these questions I will consider Merton's four values in the context of the patenting of the results of academic research. The aim of this section is to analyze and assess the consequences of the introduction of academic patenting as compared to the same situation without this patenting. Of course, this analysis and assessment is not about purely logical consequences, but about consequences that can be plausibly inferred in view of the actual situation and context of present-day academic institutions. As in this chapter as a whole, I refer primarily to those universities and institutes that are largely or fully funded by public money.

Consider first the value of universalism. As we have seen, for Merton universalism means that scientific knowledge claims should be assessed on the basis of impersonal criteria and that access to science should be open to anyone, independent of his or her personal identity or private situation. In line with my analysis in section 5, we may interpret these two claims as two different normative specifications of the value of universalism. As far as I can see, the introduction of patenting does not make an immediate difference regarding the impersonal assessment of scientific knowledge claims. However, on the basis of the connection between universalism and disinterestedness (see section 5), one may argue that patenting makes an indirect difference: since patenting decreases the measure of disinterestedness, as we will see further on, it will also contradict the norm of impersonal judgment.

The impact of patenting on the ideal of open access is more straightforward (see also Sterckx, this volume, chap. 3, sections 3.4 and 3.5). After all, patents—for instance on research tools or software—introduce an additional barrier to the financially weaker researchers or institutions who aspire to enter a certain field of research. Furthermore, the vast majority of licenses by universities are exclusive licenses. In this sense, patents decrease the accessibility of the results of academic research. To be sure, in theory the "experimental use" of a patented subject matter (such as the clinical testing of patented drugs for noncommercial purposes) may be exempted from protection. In the present situation, however, this exemption is by no means sufficient to guarantee the accessibility of academic research. First, this exemption holds true in Europe but not in the United States; second, the exemption does not apply to patented research tools used in experimentation, and the interpretation of the experimental use clause has become ever more restrictive; third, when universities define themselves as entrepreneurial organizations, it becomes very difficult to vindicate claims that university experimentation is "noncommercial." To offset the negative impact of patents on public research the Danish Board of Technology (2005, 49) recommends "to clarify and strengthen the experimental use exception so researchers may conduct unhampered research based on existing patents, as long as there is no commercial exploitation." In principle, this is a sensible recommendation. At the same time, it will be very hard to realize. For the reasons stated above, under the present circumstances, patenting constitutes a barrier to the open access of science.

Merton's second value, communism or the common ownership of scientific "goods," acknowledges that the fruits of science are the result of an essentially collective effort. In the case of publicly subsidized universities and research institutes, we should add that this effort has been financed through public tax funds. A natural normative specification of this value is that the results of academic research at wholly or largely publicly funded universities should not be privately appropriated through the acquisition of patents, neither by the university as an institution nor by individual researchers or research groups. Hence, the practice of patenting the results of academic research detracts from the realization of this part of the Mertonian ethos of science, as was already mentioned by Merton himself in the case of medicine (Merton 1942/1973, 274n12).

To appreciate the weight of this point, it is important to see that patent *protection* is not limited to the original process through which the invention has been actually produced, but can be extended by adding further claims "on the basis of" this invention. It is these claims that define the scope of the monopoly. In the case of broad patents, the protection granted includes claims that far transcend the original invention. During the past decades the significance of broad patents has strongly increased, in particular because of developments in the area of biotechnology and genomics (Sterckx 2000; Bostyn 2001; Calvert 2007). A well-known example is the U.S. OncoMouse patent, which is not limited to the mice actually modified, but claims all exploitation of the invention for all transgenic, nonhuman, mammalian onco-animals. Product patents constitute an even stronger form of broad patent. In the case of product patents protection is granted for *any* use of *any* process that *might* be realized to produce this product. Thus, granted product patents imply a particularly strong type of intellectual property, and something similar applies to the wider category of broad patents.[24]

One might reply to the argument that patenting goes against the value of communism by claiming that, if patents are acquired by public universities or university researchers, we do not have a case of private appropriation, since the profits will be returned to a public institution. This reply will not do, however. First, to allocate the fruits of science to one particular university, research group, or researcher is a far cry from assigning them to the collective of scientists on whose prior achievements the inventor built. This argument is even more compelling when a substantial part of the revenues are awarded to individual researchers for their private use. Although regulations may vary, in current practice these revenues are substantial: in the United States, researchers are given up to 50 percent of royalties or licensing income (Slaughter and Rhoades 2004, 103); in my own university, individual researchers acquire one-third of the net revenues that result from exploiting or licensing a patented invention. Furthermore, a patent confers to its owner an exclusive right, a monopoly. That is to say, the appropriation includes the right of patent holders to exclude potential users (for instance, their scientific rivals) from exploiting the patented invention.[25] Hence, the impact of patenting by far exceeds its direct financial consequences through licensing. Privatizing the results of academic research through patenting also prevents other scientists from freely developing these results through their own research.

Next, consider the value of disinterestedness. An obvious normative specification of this value is this: scientists should not have a *direct* commercial interest in a *specific* outcome of their research.[26] This norm applies to the case of patenting in a quite straightforward way. A patentable technology should work in the way explained in its public description and be reproducible by contemporary peers. However, in scientific and technological practice, whether a certain invention really works, or really works well, is often contested.[27] When commercial interests play a role, inventors will tend to be biased, and inclined to overstate the merits of their invention.[28] After all, if they can get away with their claims, they will be immediately rewarded through acquiring the patent.

As we have seen in section 2, Mertonian disinterestedness applies, primarily, to the context of justification. Hence, can we not assume that biased and overstated claims by the patentees will be exposed and corrected in critical follow-up debate? Analogous to the cases of "one-shot science" discussed by James Brown (this volume, chap. 5), a negative answer to this question is the most plausible. The reason for this is that the primary criteria for patenting (reproducibility, novelty, utility, and nonobviousness) do not entail explicit standards of epistemic, methodological, experimental, or technological quality. In the case of product patents, the patentees even have the legal right to block the realization of higher-quality (e.g., more reliable, more efficient, more sustainable, or safer) processes to produce the same product.[29] What is lacking in patent law is an institutional basis for critical debate aimed at improving the epistemic, methodological, experimental, or technological quality of the results obtained by the original inventors.

Thus the practice of academic patenting will tend to hamper the realization of a disinterested science. Again, however, one might object to this conclusion by pointing to the fact that the prospect of gaining scientific credit may just as well incline scientists to publish immature results or overestimate their significance. How different is the system of rewarding scientists by giving them professional credit from the practice of commercially rewarding them through patents?[30] A first response to this objection is a "so what?" Why would the fact that parallel problems may occur in noncommodified science be a reason not to confront the problems of commodified science? That is to say, the objection is better seen as an incentive to tackle both types of problems, rather than despondently giving in to them. Furthermore, these two cases are not as similar as suggested by the objection. In general, in scientific research the relationship between achievement and professional reward is less direct than in business, including the patenting business. Obtaining professional recognition often requires a variety of different achievements in different contexts. This mechanism decreases the chances of unjustly awarded credit and discourages the making of immature or overstated claims for one's work.

Merton's last value is organized skepticism, the attitude of open and critical reflection and debate for the purpose of improving the quality of the scientific claims in question. This value may be specified by the norm that scientific claims should be critically scrutinized from different perspectives. Such a norm can only become operative, however, if it has a solid social and material basis. As Steve Fuller (2000, 11) rightly remarks, "when Michael Polanyi . . . famously articulated the 'republic of science' as an ideal in the 1950s, he crucially failed to specify the relevant background conditions needed to realize this ideal." In this respect, the practice of patenting the results of academic research is problematic, since it structurally favors patentable over nonpatentable approaches. For instance, under these circumstances medical research into the social causes of illness will be disadvantaged as compared to the study of the physical causes of diseases. Hence, in cases like this, scientific debate will be one-sided, and the scope for organized skepticism will be limited.

In addition to these structural problems, there are some further issues concerning the opportunities for practicing organized skepticism. One is that applying for a patent will normally delay publication of the results (usually for a period between three and twelve months). Another issue is that, under the present circumstances, patent offices are hardly up to the task of critically examining the justifiability of the claims made by applicants. Indeed, these institutes are often claimed to be understaffed and poorly functioning (Shulman 1999; Danish Board of Technology 2005, 41; Paradise, Andrews, and Holbrook 2005). To be sure, the peer review system certainly does not function perfectly. In spite of this, it is vastly superior to the present system of reviewing patent applications. Although these practical issues may also undermine the extent and quality of critical academic debate, from the perspective of this chapter I should like to emphasize the more principled, structural problems.

The conclusion of the discussion thus far must be that patenting the results of academic research does not conform to the specific norms derived from the more general Mertonian values. Put differently, the introduction of academic patenting directs science away from, rather than bringing it closer to, the realization of these values. Since these Mertonian values are at the root of many of the recently adopted codes of good scientific conduct, they can be expected to garner wide-ranging support. The same applies to the more specific scientific norms employed in the above argumentation. Hence, given this widespread commitment to Mertonian codes of scientific conduct, the recent patenting practices of public universities and research institutes should be seen as unjustified, and ought to be stopped.

But can this critique become practically effective? Can universities and other academic research institutes realistically stop patenting practices? In view of the fact that the commodification of academic research is part of a widespread pattern of profound social and economic developments (in particular, the rise of neoliberalist doctrines and politics), this question does not have an easy answer.[31] But whatever other reasons may prevent the implementation of a noncommodified science, paradoxically enough the ethical codes themselves constitute a major obstacle to the practical effectiveness of a Mertonian critique (Radder 2009). The problem is that, almost invariably, these codes are aimed at the behavior of individual scientists. Thus, the Dutch code of conduct for scientific practice states that it "is intended for the individual scientific practitioner," and it explicitly adds that it "does not aim to provide guidelines for university administration" (VSNU 2004, 3). Such qualifications, however, severely limit the appropriateness and effectiveness of these codes. They unjustly separate the ethics of science from its politics and policies. Commodification, however, should not merely be analyzed and assessed in terms of individual corruption but also, or even primarily, in terms of structural coercion, to use the illuminating notions discussed in Mark Brown's contribution to this volume. As we have seen in this chapter in the case of patenting, many of the problems of a commodified academic science are structural in nature. As long as academic patenting is encouraged or even required through structurally imposed procedures, individual scientists cannot help but violate the ethical codes. Hence the current limitation of ethical codes of conduct to individuals, whose behavior is largely governed by structural science policies, is unjustifiable.

However, if the ethical codes were also applied to universities and science policy organizations, they could be an instrument for substantial change.[32] Moreover, science policy organizations, such as the Association of Universities in the Netherlands and similar organizations in other countries, have the means and the power to implement structural changes. If such organizations were to take their own ethical codes seriously, my university would be obliged to discard "acquired patents and sales of intellectual property" as a legitimate indicator of academic achievement, and the European Research Council would similarly be required to remove "five granted patents in the last ten years" from their list of criteria for eligibility to its Advanced Grant Scheme.

7. Concluding Observations

In this chapter, I have developed an account of Mertonian values and scientific norms and applied it to the patenting of the results of academic research. The conclusion is that academic patenting is, normatively speaking, undesirable. This account of Mertonian values and scientific norms could also be applied to other aspects of the commodification of science, such as the rise of contract research, the increasing entanglement of universities and small or large businesses, and so on. This extension will be a matter of further research, though. I conclude this chapter with some observations on the nature and implications of my approach.

To stave off the criticism that Merton's, or Mertonian, norms are too vague and too abstract to be of any help in practical matters, I have reinterpreted these norms as general values and proposed to look for more specific scientific norms that may contribute to realizing those values. In the context of the patenting of academic research, the following four norms have been formulated:[33] first, access to science should be open to any sufficiently talented person and should not be hampered by financial monopolies; second, the results of academic research at publicly funded universities should not be privately appropriated through the acquisition of patents; third, scientists should not have a direct commercial interest in a specific outcome of their research; and fourth, scientific claims should be critically scrutinized from different perspectives. The claim is that these norms can be expected to find widespread support.

But can any further reasons be given for adopting an ethos that includes these four norms, or is its adoption as arbitrary as the entrepreneurial ethos it opposes? With Harry Kunneman (this volume, chap. 13), this question can be interpreted as pertaining to the wider cognitive, social, and moral resources to which these norms owe their plausibility. Although much more could be said in response to this question, within the framework of this chapter I have to restrict myself to the following, short answer: first, open access implies that a society and its science fully exploit the available talents; second, public money should be used to increase the common good; third, because of its coercive and corruptive effects, mixing public responsibilities with private interests ought to be as undesirable among scientists as it is among judges, politicians or journalists; finally, it is an amply supported experiential fact that people learn from critical feedback concerning what they say or do.

As can be seen from the phrasing and explanation of these four norms, my analysis does not presuppose strong epistemological interpretations of the results of science, for instance in the sense of a correspondence theory of scientific truth, or a universal notion of objectivity, or a watertight demarcation between science and nonscience.[34] Similarly, the analysis does not depend on specific sociological notions, such as the idea that scientific knowledge is a public, that is, a nonexcludable and nonrival, good. I myself think that the dependence of scientific knowledge on skillful practices and realization contexts should at least entail a qualification of the claim that scientific knowledge constitutes a public good, but the analysis in terms of Mertonian values and scientific norms does not presuppose a specific view on this issue. Furthermore, as I have emphasized repeatedly, my analysis does not amount to "Mertonianism," with its problematic sociological functionalism, in which there is neither place for the interpretations of individual actors nor for a critical attitude toward a taken-for-granted, "well-functioning" social system. Finally, the analyses and assessments in this chapter do not presuppose or imply the questionable notion of the autonomy of science. In fact, they are compatible with a broad range of "public interest science." Spelling out this compatibility, however, would require a detailed account of the notions of autonomous and public-interest science, which I will leave for another occasion.

For these reasons, the position defended in this chapter may be labeled a *deflationary, neo-Mertonian* approach to the commodification of academic research. The approach is deflationary because its norms and values do not require particularly strong and specific commitments. Hence, it may be expected to be acceptable to scientists, philosophers, and policy makers with a variety of epistemological, sociological, and normative background views. It seems, for instance, compatible with both Henk van den Belt's and Steve Fuller's approaches, which are very different in all kinds of other respects (see van den Belt, this volume, chap. 9; Fuller, this volume, chap. 12). That is to say, this deflationary approach exploits the fact that human beings, including philosophers, are "differentially situated" (see Radder 1996, 183–87): although substantive or even unbridgeable disagreement may exist on certain issues, usually there will also be issues on which there is broad agreement. Finally, the conclusions drawn in this section suggest a shift from a Mertonian to a neo-Mertonian approach. On the one hand (the "neo"), this approach emphasizes its own normativity and is, accordingly, more careful about the implied empirical claims concerning the historical development of the sciences. On the other hand, it still is "Mertonian" because it argues for an institutionalized normative structure of science that is not limited to a moral appeal to individual scientists.

NOTES

The first draft of this chapter was prepared for the workshop "The Commodification of Academic Research: Analyses, Assessments, Alternatives" (Amsterdam, June 21–23, 2007). It is a pleasure to thank the participants of this workshop for a fruitful discussion of this draft. In particular, I would like to acknowledge detailed comments and suggestions by

Jeroen de Ridder, Julian Cockbain, Henk van den Belt, and Peter Kirschenmann. Additional feedback has been provided by audiences at meetings in Bielefeld, Amsterdam, and Madrid by the members of the research group Philosophy of Science and Technology at the Faculty of Philosophy of VU University Amsterdam, and by an anonymous reviewer of the University of Pittsburgh Press.

1. For the distinction between commercialization and commodification, see my introductory chapter to this volume. Here I will employ the broader notion of commodification.

2. See, for instance, Köbben and Tromp (1999); Shulman (1999); Mirowski and Sent (2002); Bok (2003); Krimsky (2003); Radder (2003); Healy (2006); Resnik (2007).

3. See Radder (1996); see also Fuller (2000); Pels (2003).

4. For an explanation of the political and intellectual background of Merton's article, see Turner (2007); for a broad and illuminating account of the historical roots and contemporary significance of Mertonian thinking, see van den Belt (this volume, chap. 9).

5. Some recent commentators speak of "communalism" (perhaps out of present-day political correctness), but the term "communism" expresses Merton's idea of common ownership more accurately.

6. Although they do not provide evidence for this claim, they presumably mean criteria for commonsense truths, such as "the sun is shining, at this moment and in this place."

7. Remarkably enough, Barnes characterizes his own approach to the sociology of scientific knowledge as disinterested. In an article defending the virtues of relativism, he and his coauthor write, "If relativism has any appeal at all, it will be to those who wish to engage in that eccentric activity called 'disinterested research'" (Barnes and Bloor 1982, 47). Whether or not Barnes intends this as merely a professed norm, or even an ideology, in this respect his position shows a significant lack of reflexivity.

8. Clearly, an important aspect of the debate concerns the nature of the sociology of science. In contrast to the sociology of scientific knowledge, Merton's sociology of science is limited to the social dimensions of the behavior of scientists and scientific institutions, and thus it explicitly aims to exclude social explanations of specific cognitive procedures and epistemic achievements.

9. In this context, Pels (2003, chap. 2) aptly speaks of the "self-interest" of the advocates of the autonomy of science. See also Turner, who concludes that "Merton's language . . . was political: governance by an ethos rather than central control is 'liberal.' . . . Thus did Merton produce a liberal argument for the autonomy of science, in the rhetorical clothing of the Left, but opposed both to Bernal and to Dewey" (2007, 175).

10. For a detailed, critical discussion of both the (implicit) presence and the (explicit) absence of normativity in science and technology studies, including the sociology of scientific knowledge, see Radder (1996, chap. 5).

11. Barnes and Dolby (1970, 7). In a recent article, with the telling title "Catching Up with Robert Merton: Scientific Collectives as Status Groups," Barnes seems to have made a sharp turn. He is far less critical and even outright positive about the significance of Merton's contribution to the sociology of science. In particular, he does not mention his 1970 article and its criticism at all, states that "the pseudo-aristocratic science [Merton's] historical sociology described was no fantasy" (Barnes 2007, 191), defends the approach to science as a functionally differentiated social subsystem (189), and concludes that Merton's work should be taken up to "remedy some of the weaknesses in our current patterns of thought" (186). However, if Olga Amsterdamska's judgment is correct, current work in STS on scientific institutions has not (yet) followed Barnes in making his Mertonian turn (see Amsterdamska 2008, 631–32).

12. See, e.g., Broad and Wade (1983); Drenth, Fenstad, and Schiereck (1999); Shulman (1999); Bok (2003); and Healy (2006).

13. See also Montgomery and Oliver (2009), who provide an institutional analysis of the developments in the United States from 1975 to the present. However, they do not discuss the broader issues of social responsibility and critique (such as, for instance, included in the 1984 Uppsala code, which states, among other things, that scientists should not engage in research that "causes significant ecological damage" or that "aims at applications or skills for use in war or oppression"). For a detailed discussion of the problems and prospects of professional codes in preventing warfare, in particular biological warfare, see Rappert (2004).

14. But note that—significantly (and unfortunately), in view of the strongly increased privatization of academic research—a notion similar to the value of communism is lacking from the Dutch code of good scientific conduct.

15. Sabina Leonelli (this volume, 146) writes, "There are no *general* rules in science about how researchers should treat the data that they produce. . . . [They] can still choose to discard specific datasets when they do not fit their interests or goals, so that no one will be able to see them again." The Dutch code, however, does include a clause against discarding scientific data: "Raw research data are stored for at least five years. These data are made available to other scientific practitioners at request" (VSNU 2004, 7).

16. See Polanyi (1958); Kuhn (1970). See also Leonelli's recent account of the significance of theoretical, performative and social commitments for achieving scientific understanding in biology (Leonelli 2007, chap. 8).

17. In fact, the term "objectivity" is occasionally used by Merton in this context (e.g., 1942/1973, 270).

18. For instance, Helen Longino's four social norms for social knowledge ("venues," "uptake," and "public standards" of critical debate, and "tempered equality" of intellectual authority) can be seen as constituting a broadly Mertonian ethos (Longino 2002, 128–35).

19. I will not enter here into the debate about whether or not there are intrinsic, in addition to instrumental, values (for this, see Kirschenmann 2001). For more about different kinds of values and their significance in science, see Lacey (1999, chaps. 2 and 3).

20. See for instance Radder (1996, chap. 2) for the case of the norm that scientific experiments should be reproducible. See also Tuunainen and Knuuttila, who conclude from their empirical study of the clashes between a Mertonian and an entrepreneurial ethos that "the entrepreneurial researchers in our study were not able to recreate the norms and rules *at will*" (2008, 157; emphasis added).

21. See, e.g., Sterckx 2000; Bostyn 2001, chaps. 1, 2; Danish Board of Technology 2005; van den Belt 2009, section 3. In addition to more general reviews, it is important to study the details of concrete patenting practices; see, for instance, Myers 1995; Biagoli 2006; Calvert 2007.

22. Whether patenting in fact benefits society is contested, however (see Bostyn 2001, chap. 2; Danish Board of Technology 2005, chap. 3; see also the views of Thomas Jefferson, discussed in van den Belt, this volume, chap. 9, section 3.3). Moreover, the usual accounts of this subject employ a crude notion of benefit as "rate of economic innovation" (see, e.g., Etzkowitz 2004; Hellström and Jacob 2005). If we would add considerations based on broader notions of human well-being and justice, in particular in view of the interests of poor and developing countries (see Lea 2008), skepticism about the benefits of the global

patenting system could only increase. See also Irzik (2007, 141–42), who rightly insists on not identifying "social utility" with "commercial and corporate interests."

23. As Sigrid Sterckx shows (this volume, chap. 3, section 5.2), thus far for most universities, academic patenting and licensing has not been very profitable in financial terms. However, because commodification is not merely a matter of money but tends to induce pervasive changes in academic culture (see Kleinman, this volume, chap. 2), the limited economic success of academic patenting by no means implies that the subject might just as well be ignored.

24. The justifiability of granting these strong monopolies is a different matter. See Radder (2004; 2006) for a detailed criticism of the concept and practice of broad and product patenting.

25. For this reason, patents differ substantially from other forms of intellectual property rights, in particular copyrights.

26. See, for instance, the "Declaration of Scientific Independence" by the Royal Netherlands Academy of Arts and Sciences (available at http://www.knaw.nl/nieuws/pers_pdf/wetenschappelijke_onafhankelijkheid.pdf), which states that "rewards and other signs of appreciation should never depend upon the outcome or interpretation of the research."

27. Just think of the many controversial pharmaceuticals; see also the chapters in this volume by J. Brown and by Musschenga, van der Steen, and Ho.

28. See the many shocking illustrations of this tendency in Shulman (1999); compare also with Resnik (2000; 2007).

29. Note also the direct contradiction between the criterion of utility (or, in its European phrasing, industrial applicability) and the VSNU norm, quoted in section 4, that the choice of criteria should not be guided by the external goal of commercial success.

30. As we have seen in section 2, the distinction between professional recognition and financial reward is a major characteristic of Merton's theory of science (see also the detailed discussion by van den Belt, this volume, chap. 9). Against what is sometimes claimed (for instance by Kieff 2001, 694), scientific recognition and esteem are *not* like forms of ordinary property. The basic distinction is that ordinary property can be bought by oneself, while acquiring esteem depends on others. In spite of PR campaigns and other promotional activities, the decisive point is ultimately whether other scientists see reason for, and are willing to grant, the recognition.

31. However, the recent, strongly increased criticisms of neoliberalism may be a sign of forthcoming change.

32. In describing his "mode-3" approach (a specific kind of humanized mode-2 social science), Kunneman also emphasizes the importance of taking the organizational context into account (this volume, 333): "From 1989 to about 1995, on the level of practical activities we were oriented almost exclusively to the questions and challenges connected with the counseling of individuals and groups with regard to existential questions and moral dilemmas, in relative *isolation* from the organizational context in which these questions occurred. More and more, however, we were confronted with the necessity to address this context itself."

33. Of course, in other contexts additional values and norms may be included.

34. Here, my strategy differs from the approach advocated by Gürol Irzik, who assumes that science is "curiosity-driven" and that scientific knowledge can be defined as "justified and true (or approximately true) belief" (Irzik 2007, 137).

REFERENCES

Amsterdamska, O. 2008. "Institutions and economics." In *Handbook of science and technology studies*, 3rd ed., ed. E. J. Hackett, O. Amsterdamska, M. Lynch, and J. Wajcman, 631–34. Cambridge, MA: MIT Press.

Barnes, B. 2007. "Catching up with Robert Merton: Scientific collectives as status groups." *Journal of Classical Sociology* 7 (2): 179–92.

Barnes, B., and D. Bloor. 1982. "Relativism, rationalism and the sociology of knowledge." In *Rationality and relativism,* ed. M. Hollis and S. Lukes, 21–47. Oxford: Blackwell.

Barnes, S. B., and R. G. A. Dolby. 1970. "The scientific ethos: A deviant viewpoint." *Archives Européennes de Sociologie* 11 (1): 3–25.

Biagoli, M. 2006. "Patent republic: Representing inventions, constructing rights and authors." *Social Research* 73 (4): 1129–72.

Bok, D. 2003. *Universities in the marketplace.* Princeton, NJ: Princeton University Press.

Bostyn, S. J. R. 2001. *Enabling biotechnological inventions in Europe and the United States.* Munich: European Patent Office.

Broad, W., and N. Wade. 1983. *Betrayers of the truth.* London: Century Publishing.

Calvert, J. 2007. "Patenting genomic objects: Genes, genomes, function and information." *Science as Culture* 16 (2): 207–23.

Danish Board of Technology. 2005. *Recommendations for a patent system of the future.* Copenhagen: The Danish Board of Technology. Available at www.tekno.dk.

Drenth, P. J. D., J. E. Fenstad, and J. D. Schiereck, eds. 1999. *European science and scientists between freedom and responsibility.* Luxembourg: Office for Official Publications of the European Communities.

Etzkowitz, H. 2004. "The triple helix and the rise of the entrepreneurial university." In *The science-industry nexus: History, policy, implications,* ed. K. Grandin, N. Wormbs, and S. Widmalm, 69–91. Sagamore Beach, MA: Science History Publications.

Fuller, S. 2000. *The governance of science.* Buckingham: Open University Press.

Gibbons, M., C. Limoges, H. Nowotny, S. Schwartzman, P. Scott, and M. Trow. 1994. *The new production of knowledge.* London: Sage.

Gooding, D. 1990. *Experiment and the making of meaning.* Dordrecht: Kluwer.

Healy, D. 2006. *Let them eat Prozac: The unhealthy relationship between the pharmaceutical industry and depression.* New York: New York University Press.

Heilbron, J. 2005. *Wetenschappelijk onderzoek: Dilemma's en verleidingen.* Amsterdam: Koninklijke Nederlandse Akademie van Wetenschappen.

Hellström, T., and M. Jacob. 2005. "Taming unruly science and saving national competitiveness: Discourses on science by Sweden's strategic research bodies." *Science, Technology and Human Values* 30 (4): 443–67.

Irzik, G. 2007. "Commercialization of science in a neoliberal world." In *Reading Karl Polanyi for the twenty-first century: Market economy as a political project,* ed. A. Bugra and K. Agartan, 135–53. New York: Palgrave Macmillan.

Kieff, F. S. 2001. "Facilitating scientific research: Intellectual property rights and the norms of science—a response to Rai and Eisenberg." *Northwestern University Law Review* 95 (2): 691–705.

Kirschenmann, P. P. 2001. "'Intrinsically' or just 'instrumentally' valuable? On structural types of values of scientific knowledge." *Journal for General Philosophy of Science* 32 (2): 237–56.

Köbben, A. J. F., and H. Tromp. 1999. *De onwelkome boodschap, of Hoe de vrijheid van wetenschap bedreigd wordt*. Amsterdam: Mets.

Kourany, J. 2008. "Philosophy of science: A subject with a great future." *Philosophy of Science* 75 (5): 767–78.

Krimsky, S. 2003. *Science in the private interest*. Lanham, MD: Rowman and Littlefield.

Kuhn, T. S. 1970. *The structure of scientific revolutions*. 2nd ed. Chicago: University of Chicago Press.

———. 1977. "Objectivity, value judgment, and theory choice." *The essential tension*, 320–39. Chicago: University of Chicago Press.

Lacey, H. 1999. *Is science value free?* London: Routledge.

Lea, D. 2008. "The expansion and restructuring of intellectual property and its implications for the developing world." *Ethical Theory and Moral Practice* 11 (1): 37–60.

Leonelli, S. 2007. *Weed for thought: Using Arabidopsis thaliana to understand plant biology*. Ph.D. diss., VU University Amsterdam. Also available at http://dare.ubvu.vu.nl/handle/1871/10703.

Levere, T. H. 1990. "Lavoisier: Language, instruments, and the chemical revolution." In *Nature, experiment, and the sciences*, ed. T. H. Levere and W. R. Shea, 207–23. Dordrecht: Kluwer.

Longino, H. E. 1990. *Science as social knowledge: Values and objectivity in scientific inquiry*. Princeton, NJ: Princeton University Press.

———. 2002. *The fate of knowledge*. Princeton, NJ: Princeton University Press.

Merton, R. K. 1942/1973. "The normative structure of science." In R. K. Merton, *The sociology of science*, ed. N. W. Storer, 267–78. Chicago: University of Chicago Press.

Mirowski, P., and E.-M. Sent, eds. 2002. *Science bought and sold: Essays in the economics of science*. Chicago: University of Chicago Press.

Montgomery, K., and A. L. Oliver. 2009. "Shifts in guidelines for ethical scientific conduct: How public and private organizations create and change norms of research integrity." *Social Studies of Science* 39 (1): 137–55.

Mulkay, M. 1976. "Norms and ideology in science." *Social Science Information* 15 (4–5): 637–56.

Myers, G. 1995. "From discovery to invention: The writing and rewriting of two patents." *Social Studies of Science* 25 (1): 57–105.

Nickles, T. 1992. "Good science as bad history: From order of knowing to order of being." In *The social dimensions of science*, ed. E. McMullin, 85–129. Notre Dame, IN: University of Notre Dame Press.

Paradise, J., L. Andrews, and T. Holbrook. 2005. "Patents on human genes: An analysis of scope and claims." *Science* 307 (March 11): 1566–67.

Pels, D. 2003. *Unhastening science: Autonomy and reflexivity in the social theory of science*. Liverpool: Liverpool University Press.

Polanyi, M. 1958. *Personal knowledge: Towards a post-critical philosophy*. London: Routledge and Kegan Paul.

Radder, H. 1996. *In and about the world*. Albany: State University of New York Press.

———. 1997. "Philosophy and history of science: Beyond the Kuhnian paradigm." *Studies in History and Philosophy of Science* 28 (4): 633–55.

———. 2003. *Wetenschap als koopwaar? Een filosofische kritiek*. Amsterdam: VU Boekhandel/Uitgeverij.

———. 2004. "Exploiting abstract possibilities: A critique of the concept and practice of product patenting." *Journal of Agricultural and Environmental Ethics* 17 (3): 275–91.

————. 2006. *The world observed/The world conceived*. Pittsburgh: University of Pittsburgh Press.

————. 2009. "Hoe herwin je 'de ziel van de wetenschap'? Academisch onderzoek en universitaire kenniseconomie." *Academische Boekengids,* no. 75 (July): 8–13. Also available at http://www.academischeboekengids.nl/do.php?a=show_visitor_artikel&id=836.

Rappert, B. 2004. "Responsibility in the life sciences: Assessing the role of professional codes." *Biosecurity and Bioterrorism: Biodefense Strategy, Practice, and Science* 2 (3): 164–74.

Resnik, D. B. 2000. "Research bias." *Perspectives on Science* 8 (3): 255–85.

————. 2007. *The price of truth: How money affects the norms of science.* New York: Oxford University Press.

Shulman, S. 1999. *Owning the future.* Boston: Houghton Mifflin.

Sismondo, S. 2004. *An introduction to science and technology studies.* Malden, MA: Blackwell.

Slaughter, S., and G. Rhoades. 2004. *Academic capitalism and the new economy: Markets, state, and higher education.* Baltimore: Johns Hopkins University Press.

Sterckx, S. 2000. "European patent law and biotechnological inventions." In *Biotechnology, patents and morality,* 2nd ed., ed. S. Sterckx, 1–112. Aldershot: Ashgate.

Turner, S. 2007. "Merton's 'norms' in political and intellectual context." *Journal of Classical Sociology* 7 (2): 161–78.

Tuunainen, J., and T. Knuuttila. 2008. "Determining the norms of science: From epistemological criteria to local struggle on organizational rules?" In *Cultural perspectives on higher education,* ed. J. Välimaa and O.-H. Ylijoki, 143–58. Berlin: Springer.

van den Belt, H. 2009. "Philosophy of biotechnology." In *Philosophy of technology and engineering sciences,* ed. A. W. M. Meijers, 1301–40. Amsterdam: Elsevier.

VSNU. 2004. *The Netherlands code of conduct for scientific practice.* Amsterdam: VSNU. Available at http://www.vsnu.nl/web/show/id=75803/langid=42/contentid=1095.

CHAPTER 11

Coercion, Corruption, and Politics in the Commodification of Academic Science

Mark B. Brown

1. Introduction

COMMERCIAL VENTURES BETWEEN university researchers and private companies have become a matter of widespread debate. Advocates of such ventures usually present university-industry partnerships as benefiting the general public. They promise new technologies and consumer products that will stimulate the economy, and thus eventually benefit everyone. Even a prominent critic of commercialization notes that market forces have caused universities "to become less stodgy and elitist and more vigorous in their efforts to aid economic growth" (Bok 2003, 15–16). Indeed, some recent studies of scientific practice reveal an emerging "spiral model of innovation," in which laboratory research and its commercial applications mutually inform each other (Etzkowitz and Webster 1995, 481; Nowotny et al. 2001).

Unfortunately, much evidence suggests that university-industry partnerships fail to generate widespread public benefits.[1] They tend to focus on innovations that either concern very few people or lead to trivial consumer products (Greenberg 2007; Slaughter and Rhoades 2004, 332). Other frequently voiced concerns include both direct and indirect pressures on faculty to design research projects in light of their commercial potential, patent restrictions on open scientific communication, the use of publicly funded research to generate private profits, private consulting by university faculty on matters in which they have a personal financial stake, and the commercialization of educational materials (Krimsky 2003; Slaughter and Rhoades 2004; Washburn 2005). These and other concerns are sometimes captured under the rubric of "commodified" research.

What does it mean for academic research to become a commodity? As I use the term here, drawing on Margaret Radin (1996), commodification refers to the social process whereby a person or thing becomes understood as a "mere thing," as entirely separate from the people and relations that give it meaning. Commodities are seen as commensurable with each other through the medium of money. When academic research becomes a commodity, it loses any explicit association with either particular scientific communities or society as a whole, and it becomes reduced to a possession of individual agents that can be exchanged on the market.

Objections to commodification can be usefully grouped into two basic categories: coercion and corruption (Sandel 1998, 94ff). Coercion arguments focus on how money, power, and other resources are socially distributed, and whether uneven distribution enables some people to exercise undue power over others. Corruption arguments focus on what money can buy, and whether some things should not be for sale (Walzer 1983). Coercion arguments are motivated by the concern that commodification may limit the freedom of scientists, students, and others associated with academic research, in particular by hindering open scientific communication or putting pressure on scientists to commercialize their research. Corruption arguments focus on the threat that commodification poses for the shared meanings associated with particular goods or spheres of life, including scientific knowledge, public education, and democratic citizenship. The coercion and corruption arguments are frequently intertwined, but it is helpful to consider them separately. Both sorts of arguments raise valid concerns, a few of which I briefly outline in the first half of this chapter. Ultimately, however, neither argument captures the full impact of commodification on the distinctive institutional features of academic science. The second half of the chapter considers an alternative way of thinking about the commodification of academic research, associated with a republican view of university governance as a way to reach collective decisions regarding the economic dimensions of academic research.

2. Commodification as Coercion

The coercion argument against commodification focuses on the way unequal distributions of power and wealth cause economic markets to affect people in different ways. Those with less power are more likely to be forced to buy and sell things they would rather not. Proposals to establish regulated markets in human organs, for example, may create markets that are formally voluntary, but most of those who choose to sell a kidney will probably be relatively poor, and those who purchase one relatively rich. Similar concerns surround the growing market in human eggs for use in both assisted reproduction and stem cell research. The U.S. National Academies recommend against payment, and several U.S. states are moving to ban or restrict payment for human eggs.[2] The problem is not only that a market in human eggs or organs may effectively create a transfer program of body parts from the poor to the rich. It is that those who sell their body parts may face strong economic, social, and psychological pressures to engage in market exchanges to which, for whatever reason, they are opposed—or would be opposed, if they had the resources to fully consider their options. Such concerns need not rely on exaggerated claims regarding the "false consciousness" of disadvantaged groups. They merely assert quite plausibly that people's perceived options are shaped by their social context. The same might be said of academic scientists who reluctantly enter into commercial arrangements with private corporations, either in response to direct instructions from department chairs or deans, or due to more subtle modes of power that shape the types of research questions they deem worth pursuing (Kleinman 2003; Kleinman, this volume). At the same time, however, as I discuss briefly in what follows, bans on commodification may hurt potential sellers more than buyers, by depriving them of a source of much needed money.

It seems clear that, in many respects, the commodification of academic research has been a response to the coercive effects of markets. Since the 1970s, repeated crises in public budgets for education and research have created new pressures on universities to replace declining government funding with increased student tuition and private research contracts (Bok 2003).[3] These crises have also pushed universities to look beyond the academy for managers with training in business and finance. It is ironic, therefore, that the coercive effects of commodification have the potential to destroy rather than create markets in academic research. People who exchange their money, labor, or knowledge out of desperation and necessity, with no real capacity to bargain, are not, strictly speaking, engaged in "free" market activity (Walzer 1983, 121). As universities become more deeply involved with industry, and public budgets become more constrained, the idea that universities enter into freely chosen collaborations with industry becomes less plausible.

The underlying ideal of the coercion argument is the liberal theory of consent. Commodification is seen as a problem to the extent it threatens individual freedom. From this perspective, if scientists freely consent to the commodification of their research, there is no coercion and, hence, little cause for concern. Indeed, the coercion argument often presupposes that scientists have a "right to research" that entitles them to contract with whomever they choose (Brown and Guston 2009). At the most general level, the coercion argument is framed in quantitative terms: the key question is whether there is a balance of power between the parties to the exchange. Like the "checks and balances" of liberal constitutionalism, the imagery of coercion arguments tends to be mechanistic. Coercion occurs where there is an imbalance of power, such that scientists are forced to market their research, women their eggs, or universities their faculty and facilities.

The coercion argument leads to a distinctive set of proposed reforms. Proponents of this view suggest that the coercive potential of commodification can be counteracted by regulations that both shield scientists from market pressures and establish fair bargaining conditions for them to participate in market exchanges in a truly voluntary manner. David Resnik (2007) thus outlines elements of a regulated market economy for science. The aim is to "establish an appropriate balance" between scientific norms of openness, public ownership, and public interest, on the one hand, and commercial norms of secrecy, private ownership, and private interest, on the other. To realize this aim, societies need to "develop standards and regulations for managing and monitoring financial incentives and pressures that affect science." The various public and private organizations involved in science should "adopt rules, policies, and guidelines for regulating the knowledge economy in order to promote economic fairness and to protect moral, social, political, and scientific values" (Resnik 2007, 33, 34).[4] Although such measures for establishing fair background conditions for the commercialization of research may limit coercion, they do little to respond to those who see the commodification of academic research as inherently objectionable on moral, political, and/or epistemic grounds. This concern leads to the corruption argument.

3. Commodification as Corruption

Another line of criticism sees commodification as a form of corruption. From this perspective, the commodification of academic research violates the distinctive ideals, habits of mind, and institutional purposes traditionally associated with science. Commodification corrupts science, according to this view, because exchanging scientific knowledge for money threatens the moral dignity, social purpose, and/or epistemic quality of science. Just as prostitution denigrates sex and bribery denigrates government, commercialized research denigrates science. Sheldon Krimsky echoes this perspective when he frames the question of commodification in terms of "whether universities should be turned into the instruments of wealth rather than protected enclaves whose primary roles are as sources of enlightenment" (2003, 2). He suggests that choosing the former option amounts to abandoning the ideals of science. "And what would the soul of academia be without the pure virtue of the pursuit of knowledge and the protection of that pursuit from commodification and distortion by the marketplace?" (2003, 52). Another writer sees the corporatization of the university as analogous to the 1956 science fiction horror film *Invasion of the Body Snatchers*, "a story of alien creatures who steal the soul and personality of individuals while retaining the identical and pleasant and amiable exterior" (Steck 2003, 68).

Exchanging scientific research for money, according to this view, violates a boundary between two spheres of human activity that should be kept distinct. The problem is not merely that scientists face various commercial pressures; it is that money and science are incommensurable goods. In this respect, corruption results not only from selling something that should not be sold but also from bartering incommensurable goods. Selling a baby is wrong, but it is just as wrong to trade a baby for a car (Cohen 2003, 696). Different goods are associated with different spheres of activity, and justice requires that they be distributed according to different principles (Walzer 1983). Just as political office should not be allocated on the basis of friendship, the appointment, promotion, and funding of academic researchers should be determined by genuine scientific merit and not by their ability to acquire corporate research grants or to excel at scientifically trivial but commercially lucrative projects. Nor, for that matter, should admission to a university be determined by a student's athletic ability (and the potential to attract sports fans and corporate donors), which has become a prevalent form of academic commodification in the United States (Bok 2003, chap. 3).

From this perspective, regulating the commercialization of research to ensure that all exchanges are voluntary does little to remedy the fundamental problem. The problem with commodification is not merely that those with more money and power have more access to and control over the process and products of science. Rather, the problem is that the process and products of science should be governed by principles appropriate to science and not to some other sphere of human activity, such as commerce or politics. When things acquire monetary value, they become commensurable with other things and thus lose their uniqueness.

"When something is done for money, it is done for a different purpose than it otherwise is, and the change in purpose can change the nature of the action" (Andre 1992, 44, 45). If the coercion argument frames its critique in quantitative terms, as a matter of balancing the forces of public science and private commerce, the corruption argument focuses on the distinctive qualities of different social goods.

Whereas the coercion argument leads to regulations that ensure fair terms of exchange, the corruption argument generally leads to legal, institutional, or cultural bans on certain kinds of exchanges. Those opposed to such bans frequently argue that setting boundaries on markets will simply create a black market. And indeed, there are thriving black and gray markets in many goods currently banned from the open market: narcotics, stolen art, human organs, babies, wives, and prostitutes, to name a few (Ertman and Williams 2005). The common and, I think, largely persuasive response, however, is that the existence of murderers is not an argument for legalizing murder, and societies define themselves in part by setting moral and legal boundaries on market activity. A society where everything were for sale, a society of "universal commodification," would be a totalitarian society, pervaded by a single logic (Walzer 1983, 119–20; Radin 1996, 2–6). Of course, when criminalization of morally objectionable market exchanges (e.g., prostitution, recreational drugs) threatens *other* values of a particular society (e.g., public safety, assistance for the needy), legalization may be justified. But the reason for legalization is to uphold the society's values, not merely to prevent a black market.

A more important challenge to the corruption argument is that it depends on collective agreement on the meaning of social goods, which in contemporary societies is often lacking (Sandel 1998, 106–7). With regard to science, the corruption argument has often relied on an idealized image of science as a uniquely objective, authoritative, and value-free form of knowledge (see Proctor 1991). That image is becoming increasingly untenable, however, as both scholars and laypeople adopt the view that science is inevitably shaped to some extent by economic, social, and political factors. Although philosophers have long sought to specify "demarcation criteria" that would distinguish scientific from nonscientific modes of thought and activity, none of these efforts has proven successful. Philosophers have not been able to reach consensus on the essential nature of science and what distinguishes it from nonscientific practices, institutions, or beliefs. Indeed, it seems impossible to establish a list of necessary and sufficient conditions for calling something "scientific." Many of the attributes typically associated with science can also be found in nonscientific activities, and no single list of attributes is shared by all the fields of study typically deemed part of science (Laudan 1996).

This does not mean, however, that there is nothing distinctive about science, nor that efforts to articulate what it is have lost importance. Indeed, the fact that science is shaped by social values and political decisions does not mean it lacks institutional specificity. As Dick Pels puts it, "the claim that science is social or political acquires its full significance precisely when it is *specified:* the scientific field is a field similar to others, and similarly subject to laws of capital formation and competition, but it is simultaneously a 'world apart' that obeys its own specific logic of functioning" (Pels 2003, 147; original italics). Pels conceives the specificity of science with reference to its "timescape." Laboratories provide a partially estranged, provisionally detached social setting from which to develop an autonomous perspective on reality (Pels 2003, 149). From this perspective, the autonomy of science does not rest on a philosophical commitment to value-freedom or particular methodological rules but rather on institutional features that slow things down and create the time required for research. This view of science highlights a feature of commodification not emphasized by either the coercion or corruption arguments: commodification speeds things up. Corporate sponsors, university administrators, patient advocacy groups, and the general public frequently pressure scientists to get new technologies and medical remedies to market as fast as possible. Such pressures, compounded by personal ambition, arguably pose a major threat to the institutional culture of university science.

There are other ways to conceive the distinctive qualities of scientific institutions that, like Pels's approach, do not rely on precise demarcation criteria. For example, some have understood science as a "gift economy" (Bollier 2002; Ziman 2002, 331; Hyde 1979, 78; Hagstrom 1965). For these authors, the reputational market of academic science is like the *potlatch* of certain indigenous cultures: a public ceremony in which the highest honors go to those who give away the most goods. Gift economies generate new wealth just like market economies, but the excess wealth remains in circulation within the community rather than being privatized as profit. In a related vein, Hans Radder's essay in this volume reconstructs Robert K. Merton's famous argument regarding the norms of science as itself a normative project, rather than a disinterested assessment of scientific practice. Merton's norms, from Radder's perspective, advance the normative project of generating community among scientists, guiding their work, and protecting them from undue interference from commerce or politics.

This is not the place to compare different conceptions of the institutional specificity of science, but it seems clear that such efforts capture something important about how science produces practical and authoritative knowledge. In this respect, they underwrite the corruption argument against the commodification of academic research. Nonetheless, I want to mention three shortcomings of many such efforts, and by extension, of the corruption argument.

First, such efforts tend to focus on the institutional features of science, usually the natural sciences, rather than universities as a whole. There are many different kinds of universities today, of course, but most have important tasks other than research. Many universities provide some combination of vocational training, civic education, political advice, and community service. And all universities provide an institutional context in which students, faculty, staff, and administrators potentially engage in some sort of collective self-governance. Analyses of the appropriate relationship between science and commerce need to consider how scientific research relates to any given university's other goals.

Second, as Radin (1996) has argued, erecting a wall between market and nonmarket relations obscures both the economic dimensions of nonmarket relations and the moral dimensions of market relations. Although many scientists dislike the idea that economics shapes their work, "it is indisputable that someone, for some reason, has been picking up the tab" (Mirowski and Sent 2002, 1; see also Kleinman 2003, 35–44; Resnik 2007, 32–33). Science and other gift economies are usually intertwined with monetary economies. This point should not be understood as an attack on the integrity of science. When giving someone a gift, it is indeed "the thought that counts," but expressing that thought by purchasing a gift with money need not denigrate the thought. Similarly, most people must work for pay, and yet most hope to have jobs they would enjoy doing for free. And anyone who takes pride in "a job well done" does the job in a manner that is not fully captured by its market price (Radin 1996, 102–14; Waldron 1995, 165). Rather than simply banning certain things from being sold, society might resist universal commodification by finding ways of protecting and promoting the nonmarket dimensions of things exchanged on the market. From this perspective, the point of regulation is not simply to ensure free choice, as the coercion argument suggests, but to reflect societal understandings about the meaning of particular activities. For me to sell my teaching services or research products does not by itself make them into commodities. They become commodities only when the nonmarket dimensions of those exchanges are suppressed (Cohen 2003).[5] The challenge, therefore, is not merely to protect or expand gift economies, because that effectively abandons everything else to naked market forces. Rather, the larger challenge is to find ways of structuring market transactions such that they preserve the nonmarket dimensions of those transactions.

Third, philosophers, sociologists, and other scholars concerned about commodification cannot, by themselves, establish societal consensus on the meanings of social goods, including academic research. They also lack political authority to dictate which exchanges should be blocked or allowed. Scholarly arguments regarding the appropriate relationship between science and commerce, therefore, are best understood as contributions to processes of public deliberation and decision making. They should not be used to shortcut such processes. This means that efforts to prevent academic research from being reduced to a commodity should not confine themselves to establishing codes of ethics, which tend to focus on individual behavior.[6] Instead, such efforts need to attend to the distinctive features of academic institutions, including their internal processes of deliberation and decision making. Assistance in this endeavor may be found in the republican tradition of political thought, which is distinguished in part by its emphasis on the institutional features of public life.

4. Republicanism and University Governance

Steve Fuller (2000, 2002) draws on republican political theory to generate proposals for the governance of contemporary science.[7] Where liberals focus on the "negative liberty" of noninterference, and communitarians on the "positive liberty" of self-mastery and civic participation, republicans see freedom in nondomination, that is, not being subject to arbitrary authority (Pettit 1997, 21ff, 51ff). A republican approach to the governance of science would thus focus not on commercial interference with academic research, as such, but on *arbitrary* interference, and not solely on actual interference but on the *power* to interfere in an arbitrary manner. For republicans, regardless of whether or not an act or decision constitutes interference with someone, it is considered arbitrary whenever "it is chosen or rejected without reference to the interests, or the opinions, of those affected" (Pettit 1997, 55, 63ff). So where liberals generally seek to minimize all societal restrictions on individual choice, republicans argue that as long as restrictions take account of citizens' ideas and interests, and remain open to effective public challenge, they are a necessary means of protecting citizens from domination by both government and society. From a republican perspective, regulation may cause more interference than it prevents, as long as it reduces people's subjection to arbitrary power (Pettit 2006, 145–46). In the case of academic research, republicanism highlights the possibility that corporations have sufficient power to impose terms of exchange unresponsive to faculty interests and concerns.

Against the "Platonic" republicanism of Michael Polanyi's "Republic of Science" (1962), Fuller aligns his version of republicanism with Karl Popper's open society, arguing that republicanism's central ideal is public deliberation, protected by the "right to be wrong" (Fuller 2000, 7, 13; Fuller 2002, 203–11).⁸ Fuller argues that science "has failed to apply the democratic spirit to itself," which is that of an "experimenting society" (2000, 135). He goes on to propose various institutional means of "constituting science as a democratic polity" (2000, 146–51). The basic goal of these measures is to equalize power among scientists and between scientists and lay citizens. Equalizing power promises to facilitate open deliberation and the free exchange of ideas. With regard to universities, Fuller suggests various ways to renew their corporate identity, equalize power between faculty and students, and assert independence from both nonacademic business interests and specialized disciplinary interests (Fuller 2002, 216–25).

Fuller's version of republicanism seems similar to what John Rawls (1993) calls a "comprehensive doctrine," a set of values and beliefs applicable to all areas of social life. That is, Fuller does not specify the type of democratization or the sort of republicanism appropriate to science policy making, university governance, and the polity as a whole, respectively. Fuller thus writes of the university, not as an institution *in* a republic, but as "the ultimate republican institution," and he seems to favor reviving the medieval system of "checks and balances" that equalized power (to some extent) between faculty and students (Fuller 2002, 216–20).⁹

Although democratizing university governance is a worthwhile goal, it should be considered in light of the distinctive institutional purposes of academic science, and of universities more generally, as described previously (see Thompson 1972, 159–60). By apparently not recognizing anything distinctive about the pursuit of republican principles within the specific institutional context of universities, Fuller echoes the coercion argument, which treats all coercion the same, regardless of where it occurs. The corruption argument, in contrast, acknowledges that different spheres of activity, and hence different associations centered around those spheres, have different social meanings and purposes, as well as different incentive structures.

To put the point somewhat differently, although every association in a democracy should respect certain basic human rights, not every association needs to be organized democratically (Rawls 1993, 40–43, 146n13; Rosenblum 1998, 56). This is true not merely for practical reasons, nor only for reasons of abstract right, but because democracy may benefit from associations that are nondemocratic or only partially democratic. Highly exclusive associations, including Marxist, feminist, and black separatist associations, for example, have been instrumental in increasing the inclusion of their constituencies in mainstream politics (Kohn 2002, 291). Moreover, different kinds of associations have different educational effects on those who participate in the association, as well as different effects on public discourse and public decision making. As a result, tradeoffs between different associational effects are inevitable (Warren 2001, 60–93, 142–205). A hierarchical association that represents its members primarily in a trustee sense, for example, requiring little input from its members, like most interest groups, will not foster its members' political skills and sense of political efficacy as much as one that represents in the delegate sense, requiring its members' active participation. Similarly, associations that cultivate political skills through internal dialogue and debate, such as universities, often lack a unified position on controversial public issues, and thus, may fail to effectively represent their members' views in the public sphere.[10] Because no single association can achieve every effect to an equal degree, it is important that citizens have access to a range of different types of associations. This point raises the question of what specific institutional features of universities are most threatened by commodification, and what the most promising institutional response to such threats might be.

Although many associations have a single dominant "constitutive good," universities have multiple constitutive goods, leading to enduring conflicts over their purposes. Generally speaking, as suggested previously, universities provide some combination of vocational goods, civic goods, and scholarly or scientific goods, with different universities weighing these goods very differently. In the United States—from Thomas Jefferson's founding of the country's first public university, the University of Virginia, to the Morrill Act of 1862, which created the system of land-grant colleges focused on agriculture and engineering—public universities long framed the scholarly and vocational dimensions of university education as contributions to the civic dimension (Lustig 2005, 23–24). That began to change as early as the late nineteenth century, however, when Progressive Era fascination with expert administration, and the emergence of academic disciplinary organizations, led to an increase in the role of business and science in university priority setting that has continued ever since.

In recent years many scholars and activists have called for a reinvigoration of the university's civic and educational goals. This requires, among other things, conceiving of academic freedom and the autonomy of science in public rather than only private terms. Conceived in a liberal mode, along the lines of the coercion argument, academic freedom is a private right that guarantees protection against outside intrusion. This appears to be the orientation of most university faculty, who tend to view participation in university governance as a burden not linked to their professional identity. Conceived in a republican mode, in contrast, academic freedom is "a collective right to self-governance" (Lustig 2005, 26, 40–41).

Put differently, the private autonomy of university faculty depends on their public autonomy of collective self-governance (see Habermas 1996, 84–104, 313–14). From this perspective, university faculty should conceive of their professions not merely in terms of their particular research programs, departments, or disciplines. They should understand "that public action is necessary to their identity as professionals, and understand that their calling is fundamentally collective in its character" (Lustig 2005, 45).[11] Derek Bok articulates a similar view when he states that engaging faculty in university governance is "the principal challenge" facing universities seeking to benefit from the commercial marketplace without sacrificing academic integrity (Bok 2003, 189).

To be sure, many faculty governance bodies are inefficient and lack relevant competence. And many university faculty have little time or interest to participate. But the situation is not improved by turning over decision making to trustees and administrators. The latter are often appointed, not for their appreciation of the university's mission, but for their managerial expertise or ability to attract wealthy donors, or sometimes merely to reward political supporters. It is thus not surprising that administrative efforts to foster collaboration with industry have often led to hasty profit-seeking ventures with few long-term benefits (Bok 2003, 192).

One possible response is to require that all university administrators have previous experience as faculty members. The idea would be to ensure that administrators have a sufficient commitment to academic values (Duderstadt 2004, 151). Although this approach is often presented as a "realistic" alternative to directly engaging faculty in decision making on commercial ventures, it relies on considerable idealism regarding the persistence of academic values among those who have left the classroom behind for administrative careers. Indeed, it seems that "universities will do a better job of upholding essential values if faculty members help design and oversee all profit-making or commercial activities that affect the academic life of the university" (Bok 2003, 193). The current trend toward dual-track modes of governance—with faculty relegated to academic hiring, promotion, and curricular decisions and administrators in charge of budgetary matters—does not offer faculty, students, and staff sufficient opportunity to shape decisions regarding university-industry partnerships. In areas where faculty have professional interests but may lack relevant expertise (e.g., funding priorities), they might be given increased advisory authority. Such authority might be linked with accountability requirements aimed at preventing faculty governance bodies from becoming irrelevant debating societies (cf. Duderstadt 2004, 148–50). A republican approach to university governance fosters widespread participation, not for its own sake, but as a means of holding university governance bodies accountable for promoting the distinctive aims of their particular institution.

In sum, republicanism suggests that the distinctive features of academic institutions include not only the production of scientific knowledge, as proponents of the corruption argument tend to assume, but the provision of knowledge, education, and other social goods in a context of collective self-governance. The republican perspective on commodification is not merely an abstract ideal, but captures key elements of the efforts by some universities to regulate university-industry partnerships. Greenberg thus notes that, in contrast to ten years ago, recent university-industry partnerships face "public and academic scrutiny and the specter of embarrassment of disgrace for ethical shortcomings." Such scrutiny generates "academic insistence on shared governance over use of industrial money; quick, if not immediate, publication of the results; and adherence to academe's concept of the rules of the game" (Greenberg 2007, 48; see also 283–85). From the republican perspective, collective self-governance is an intrinsic feature of the institutional purpose of universities, and efforts to protect academic research against corruption by market forces should take this feature into account. The corruption at issue is not only the corruption of research but also of academic self-governance.

This republican perspective on the corruption argument raises a dilemma: What if faculty governance bodies decide to allow university-industry partnerships that undermine the integrity of faculty research? What if faculty collectively fail to promote their long-term collective interests? Conversely, why not impose administrative or legal bans on problematic entrepreneurial endeavors, regardless of what faculty say, thus preventing faculty from undermining their collective purpose? These questions highlight a dilemma that Radin (1996, 123–30) calls the double bind: compromising ideals may delay the realization of an ideally just society, but refusing to compromise ideals may prevent one from pursuing those ideals at all. Allowing the sale of body parts may create a new means of exploiting the poor, but a ban may be an elite luxury that deprives the poor of both income and personal autonomy. By the same token, university-industry partnerships might provide much needed funds for faculty research, and yet also threaten the institutional norms that make research possible. Similarly, administrative or legal bans on university-industry partnerships might restrict faculty self-governance, but not doing so might allow faculty to undermine the integrity of their own profession.

Although Radin does not discuss university-industry partnerships, her analysis suggests that such dilemmas can only be resolved on a case-by-case basis. There is no philosophical answer to the question of when the benefits of university-industry partnerships outweigh the costs. Her analysis also suggests, however, that efforts to respond to such dilemmas should take account of how the dilemma arose in the first place (Radin 1996, 46–53). Even if critics of commodification persuade decision-making bodies to ban problematic university-industry ventures, such bans would not address the underlying social and political conditions that create incentives for scientists to pursue such ventures. Just as preventing poor people from selling their kidneys does nothing to alleviate their poverty, banning university-industry partnerships does not address the crisis in public funding and confidence that many universities now face.

A satisfying response to this dilemma is beyond the bounds of this chapter. It is not inconceivable, however, that profits from university-industry partnerships, undertaken with extensive faculty input, could be directed into efforts to determine, articulate, and institutionalize a particular university's purpose. With a clear sense of the university's purpose, profits from university-industry partnerships could be creatively employed to make such partnerships economically unnecessary, and thus, more fully a matter of choice. Scholars who then still choose to work with industry could do so on terms that preserve academic values. The corruption argument's emphasis on the social meaning of academic activities would serve the coercion argument's emphasis on academic freedom.

5. Conclusion

The coercion and corruption arguments each capture important dimensions of commodification, but taken by themselves, their responses seem inadequate. Efforts to mitigate the risk of coercion by establishing fair terms of trade easily neglect the social meanings at stake in exchanging, say, the collective work of a university research team for a corporate contract that provides large monetary rewards but requires keeping results secret from other scientists, or more subtly, robs scientists of the sense of civic purpose traditionally associated with academic work. At the same time, however, simply banning certain exchanges based on the presumed meaning of social goods neglects the difficulty of establishing consensus on such meanings, as well as the way meanings change over time.

Additionally, conceiving the commodification of academic research in terms of a simple opposition between "science" and "commerce" neglects the specific risks that commodification poses for the many features of university life that have little to do with research. It also neglects the possibility of conceptualizing academic freedom in terms of public rather than private autonomy, such that the relationship between science and commerce becomes a matter for deliberation and debate among all members of the university. It seems clear that academic norms are shifting, and that academic scientists are becoming increasingly comfortable with the commercialization of their research (Etzkowitz and Webster 1995). But unless university faculty have effective means of deliberating about and, if they deem it necessary, blocking or shaping such changes, they will not know whether their newfound comfort is justified.

NOTES

For helpful comments many thanks to Marvin Brown, Jeff Lustig, Hans Radder, Jan van der Stoep, and the participants at the June 2007 workshop on the commodification of academic research at Vrije Universiteit Amsterdam.

1. It has been over twenty-five years since the Bayh-Dole Act of 1980 facilitated increased academic-industrial collaborations in the United States. The economic effects are difficult to measure, but there seems to be little evidence that the increase in university patenting and licensing has had the intended effect of increasing universities' overall contribution to economic growth beyond what it would be without the incentive of private profit (Sampat 2006). Very few of the several hundred technology transfer offices established on American campuses have actually made a profit, and many have lost money (Slaughter and Rhoades 2004, 330–31; Washburn 2005, 230; Greenberg 2007, 62–81). Industry's share of total university R&D funding is disputed; according to National Science Foundation statistics, it reached only 7.4 percent in 1999 and has remained below that ever since, although it is considerably higher at some universities (Greenberg 2007, chap. 2).

2. Information available from the Center for Genetics and Society Web site: http://www.genetics-and-society.org. For an argument in favor of regulated commercialization of human eggs, see Resnik 2001.

3. Mirowski and Sent (2002, 26–32) note an undercurrent of xenophobia in declining public support for higher education in the United States, due to the perception that foreign nationals are being trained at U.S. taxpayer expense, and then going back to home countries and competing with U.S. workers. Moreover, the end of the cold war led to a large reduction in defense R&D, and other areas have not made up the difference.

4. Resnik is also concerned about the corrupting effects of commercialization on academic norms, but his focus seems to be on regulating rather than banning the commodification of academic research. He writes, "The most prudent and realistic response to this situation is to try to mitigate the corrupting effects of private interests and to establish policies and procedures to safeguard the norms of science" (Resnik 2007, 33). For a similar endorsement of a "balance" between private and public claims on research, see Anderson (2001, 237–43).

5. This line of thinking suggests one way to get beyond what Steve Fuller (2002, 227) calls the "Myth of the Modes": the assumption that contract-based research ("mode-2") and what is taken to be the traditional role of the university as pure science ("mode-1") are the only available possibilities.

6. A similar point appears in Biddle (2007, 27, 30) and Radder (this volume, chap. 10). Indeed, because processes of exchange do not simply reflect the meanings of social goods but often transform those meanings, people may have to try out new forms of exchange before they can reach agreement on what sorts of exchanges to allow (Waldron 1995, 158–59).

7. Parts of this section draw on Brown (2009, chap. 9).

8. By reading republicanism through Popper's critical rationalism, and despite the nondeliberative elements of some of his reform proposals, Fuller arguably overemphasizes the deliberative component of republicanism (Radder 2000, 523).

9. As Fuller rightly notes, students today exercise little or no influence over the university curriculum, whereas in medieval universities, and in Germany until the early twentieth century, students influenced the curriculum indirectly by the fees they paid to lecturers (Fuller 2002, 217). Fuller does not say to what extent he thinks such "checks and balances" might be reintroduced today.

10. Universities also have difficulty campaigning for their own interests in the public sphere, because their legitimacy is taken to rest on remaining politically neutral. As Warren puts it, "their public neutrality is a studied strategy that enables them to provide institutional shelter for multiple public sphere activities built around classroom debates, conferences and speakers, journals and newspapers, student and faculty associations, and research" (Warren 2001, 120). Holding a "vested" position in society, universities are reluctant to take strong public stands for fear of losing their aura of neutrality. They tend instead to lobby legislatures and businesses behind the scenes (Warren 2001, 169–70).

11. In its 1940 Statement of Principles on Academic Freedom and Tenure, the American Association of University Professors asserted that university faculty are "entitled to full freedom in research and in the publication of the results, subject to the adequate performance of their other academic duties," and that "college and university teachers are citizens, members of a learned profession, and officers of an educational institution." Available at http://www.aaup.org/AAUP/pubsres/policydocs/contents/1940statement.htm.

REFERENCES

Anderson, Melissa S. 2001. "The complex relations between the academy and industry: Views from the literature." *The Journal of Higher Education* 72 (2): 226–46.

Andre, Judith. 1992. "Blocked exchanges: A taxonomy." *Ethics* 103 (1): 29–47.

Biddle, Justin. 2007. "Lessons from the Vioxx debacle: What the privatization of science can teach us about social epistemology." *Social Epistemology* 21 (1): 21–39.

Bok, Derek. 2003. *Universities in the marketplace: The commercialization of higher education.* Princeton, NJ: Princeton University Press.

Bollier, David. 2002. *Silent theft: The private plunder of our common wealth.* New York: Routledge.

Brown, Mark B. 2009. *Science in democracy: Expertise, institutions, and representation.* Cambridge, MA: MIT Press.

Brown, Mark B., and David H. Guston. 2009. "Science, democracy, and the right to research." *Science and Engineering Ethics* 15 (3): 351–66.

Cohen, I. Glenn. 2003. "The price of everything, the value of nothing: Reframing the commodification debate." *Harvard Law Review* 117:689. Available at http://ssrn.com/abstract=479321.

Duderstadt, James J. 2004. "Governing the twenty-first-century university: A view from the bridge." In *Competing conceptions of academic governance: Negotiating the perfect storm,* ed. William G. Tierney, 137–57. Baltimore: Johns Hopkins University Press.

Ertman, Martha, and Joan Williams, eds. 2005. *Rethinking commodification: Cases and readings in law and culture.* New York: New York University Press.

Etzkowitz, H., and A. Webster. 1995. "Science as intellectual property." In *Handbook of science and technology studies,* ed. S. Jasanoff, G. E. Markle, J. C. Petersen, and T. Pinch, 480–505. Thousand Oaks, CA: Sage Publications.

Fuller, Steve. 2000. *The governance of science.* Buckingham: Open University Press.

———. 2002. *Knowledge management foundations.* Boston: Butterworth-Heinemann.

Greenberg, Daniel S. 2007. *Science for Sale: The perils, rewards, and delusions of campus capitalism.* Chicago: University of Chicago Press.

Habermas, Jürgen. 1996. *Between facts and norms: Contributions to a discourse theory of law and democracy.* Trans. by William Rehg. Cambridge, MA: MIT Press.

Hagstrom, Warren O. 1965. *The scientific community.* New York: Basic Books.

Hyde, Lewis. 1979. *The gift: Imagination and the erotic life of poetry.* New York: Random House.

Kleinman, Daniel Lee. 2003. *Impure cultures: University biology and the world of commerce.* Madison: University of Wisconsin Press.

Kohn, Margaret. 2002. "Panacea or privilege? New approaches to democracy and association." *Political Theory* 30 (2): 289–98.

Krimsky, Sheldon. 2003. *Science in the private interest: Has the lure of profits corrupted biomedical research?* Lanham, MD: Rowman and Littlefield.

Laudan, Larry. 1996. "The demise of the demarcation problem." In *Beyond positivism and relativism: Theory, method, and evidence,* 210–22. Boulder: Westview Press.

Lustig, Jeff. 2005. "The university revisioned: The alternative to corporate mis-education." *The Review of Education, Pedagogy, and Cultural Studies* 27:17–52.

Mirowski, Philip, and Esther-Mirjam Sent. 2002. Introduction. In *Science bought and sold: Essays in the economics of science,* ed. Mirowski and Sent, 1–66. Chicago: University of Chicago Press.

Nowotny, Helga, Peter Scott, and Michael Gibbons. 2001. *Re-thinking science: Knowledge and the public in an age of uncertainty.* London: Polity Press.

Pels, Dick. 2003. *Unhastening science: Autonomy and reflexivity in the social theory of knowledge.* Liverpool: Liverpool University Press.

Pettit, Philip. 1997. *Republicanism: A theory of freedom and government.* Oxford: Oxford University Press.

———. 2006. "Freedom in the market." *Politics, Philosophy and Economics* 5 (2): 131–49.

Polanyi, Michael. 1962. "The republic of science: Its political and economic theory." *Minerva* 1 (1): 54–73.

Proctor, Robert N. 1991. *Value-free science? Purity and power in modern knowledge.* Cambridge, MA: Harvard University Press.

Radder, H. 2000. "The governance of science." *Science, Technology and Human Values* 25:520–27.

Radin, Margaret Jane. 1996. *Contested commodities*. Cambridge, MA: Harvard University Press.

Rawls, John. 1993. *Political liberalism*. New York: Columbia University Press.

Resnik, David B. 2001. "Regulating the market for human eggs." *Bioethics* 15:1–25.

———. 2007. *The price of truth: How money affects the norms of science*. Oxford: Oxford University Press.

Rosenblum, Nancy. 1998. *Membership and morals: The personal uses of pluralism in America*. Princeton: Princeton University Press.

Sampat, Bhaven. 2006. "Universities and intellectual property: Shaping a new patent policy for government funded academic research." In *Shaping science and technology policy: The next generation of research,* ed. D. Guston and D. Sarewitz, 55–76. Madison: University of Wisconsin Press.

Sandel, Michael J. 1998. "What money can't buy: The moral limits of markets." The Tanner Lectures on Human Values. Available at http://www.tannerlectures.utah.edu/lectures.

Slaughter, Sheila, and Gary Rhoades. 2004. *Academic capitalism and the new economy: Markets, state, and higher education*. Baltimore: Johns Hopkins University Press.

Steck, Henry. 2003. "Corporatization of the university: Seeking conceptual clarity." *Annals of the American Academy of Political and Social Science* 585:66–83.

Thompson, Dennis F. 1972. "Democracy and the governing of the university." *Annals of the American Academy of Political and Social Science* 404 (1): 157–69.

Waldron, Jeremy. 1995. "Money and complex equality." In *Pluralism, justice, and equality,* ed. David Miller and Michael Walzer, 144–71. Oxford: Oxford University Press.

Walzer, Michael. 1983. *Spheres of justice: A defense of pluralism and equality*. New York: Basic Books.

Warren, Mark E. 2001. *Democracy and association*. Princeton, NJ: Princeton University Press.

Washburn, Jennifer. 2005. *University, Inc.: The corporate corruption of higher education*. New York: Basic Books.

Ziman, John. 2002. "The microeconomics of academic science." In *Science bought and sold: Essays in the economics of science,* ed. Philip Mirowski and Esther-Mirjam Sent, 318–40. Chicago: University of Chicago Press.

CHAPTER 12

Capitalism and Knowledge

THE UNIVERSITY BETWEEN COMMODIFICATION

AND ENTREPRENEURSHIP

Steve Fuller

CRITIQUES OF CAPITALISM come in two kinds. I shall begin by presenting them in the spirit in which they are normally discussed. One kind attacks capitalism *in practice*. It is associated with Joseph Schumpeter, who targeted the monopolization of capital for stifling the entrepreneurial spirit, capitalism's very soul. The other critique is older and goes deeper, attacking capitalism *in principle*. It is associated with Karl Marx, who targeted the commodification of labor for alienating us from our common humanity. Whereas Schumpeter was worried about capitalism's practical tendency to concentrate wealth and thereby arrest the economy's natural dynamism, Marx objected to capitalism's principled tendency to evaporate the solid core of our "species being" through the dynamics of the price mechanism.

I believe that both critiques continue to have merit, though to a large extent they cut against each other: after all, Schumpeter's entrepreneurs and Marx's commodifiers are equally interested in the fact that people will pay for things they had not paid for before. The difference lies simply in the positive and the negative spin, respectively, that is given to this moment. Here Marx appears clearly as the secular heir of natural law theory, with his rather strict, metaphysically inspired ideas about what is and is not properly bought and sold. For him, our freedom lies in our capacity to remain unchanged despite changing circumstances, such as fluctuating prices. This also captures Kant's sense of autonomy as principled resistance to external pressure. In contrast, Schumpeterian liberty is the freedom to change our minds—and even ourselves. (I shall return to this attitude as characteristic of the relatively relaxed attitude that Austrian economics has had toward commodification.) If Marx worried about our regressing to animals, Schumpeter was concerned that we might instead turn into robots: the one too sensitive, the other too oblivious to what happens outside oneself. In this respect, the entrepreneur thus regularly reminds us of the other sorts of lives we might lead, especially the one she would like to sell us now. The permanent openness to change is also the feature of the Austrian stance that Popper imported into his critique of irreversible social engineering (Hacohen 2000, chaps. 3, 10).

At the ontological level, the difference between Marx and Schumpeter can be understood as capturing the economic dimension of both sides of the "carbon-silicon divide" that increasingly draws human identity in countervailing directions (Fuller 2006b, 202–5; Fuller 2007a, 44–52): are we "moral animals" who should rejoin our fellow carbon-based creatures in promoting a common sustainable ecology, à la Peter Singer (1999), or "spiritual machines" who should create as much distance as possible from our animal past, à la Ray Kurzweil (1999)? On the one hand, like Marx, though on different grounds, Singer wants to establish a nonnegotiable source of value. On the other, like Schumpeter, though again on different grounds, Kurzweil wants to maximize our capacity for "shapeshifting," to use the preferred term for transformations that one's identity can undergo in virtual reality.

My own considered view is that in today's knowledge economy, a dose of Schumpeter's original concern to maintain capitalism's entrepreneurial spirit is needed to prevent Marx's critique of commodification from turning into a defense of an unholy alliance of the labor theory of value and a strong proprietary sense of intellectual life that I call "epistemic racism," whereby identity comes to be associated with a nonnegotiable, indeed, hereditary sense of knowledge, understood in the broad nineteenth century sense of "inheritance" in which genetic and cultural modes of transfer are blended into an economic conception of property, in this case "intellectual property."

At the same time, as Schumpeter came to realize later in his career, entrepreneurship is not an unmitigated good, especially as it puts increasing numbers of people and resources at risk. In that case, something is needed to contain these destabilizing effects—the so-called boom and bust phases of the business cycle. Schumpeter (1942/1950) famously predicted that socialism would fill this need but only by strangling entrepreneurship altogether in its determination to bring the economy to a state of general equilibrium. However, as I shall argue, the university provides an alternative model of an institution capable of not only containing entrepreneurship but also channeling it so that it has the maximum positive effect on society as a force for change. In some respects, this justification of the university recalls the Marquis de Condorcet's rather optimistic view of markets, whereby commodification appears as a political device for disciplining the passions so as to facilitate the intellectual and material growth of society.

The chapter begins with a somewhat revisionist take on commodification, stressing its capacity for freeing people from essentialist links, including to their own culture and biology, as everything becomes in principle subject to exchange relations. Moreover, knowledge is no different from any other property that might be alienated from its original possessor and undergo commodification. This point is not more apparent due to the somewhat mystified views of knowledge that continue to surround discussions of intellectual property. Nevertheless, just as Marx held, commodification remains a dangerous process, one exemplified in the promotion of market-based thinking from a means to get more people to think more expansively about themselves and the world to an end pursued for its own sake, which serves to enslave people, understood as both producers and consumers. Once again, epistemic practices are equally susceptible to this insidious process, which is perhaps most dramatically registered in the conflicting pressures nowadays placed on the institutional autonomy of the university by the global "knowledge economy." In particular, market-based thinking has fostered increasing segmentation of the university's teaching and research functions, the interrelatedness of which had been at the heart of its mission in the modern era. However, in the concluding section I explore the eighteenth-century precedents for what amounts to a return to the elitism of many of the original Enlightenment *philosophes,* who wanted to sharply distinguish knowledge "as a public good" and "for the public good." The former is the ideology that is taught to the general public, the latter the technology that is provided exclusively to the rulers, based on the latest research. Threatened to be lost in this revisitation of the eighteenth century is the civic republican ethic that Wilhelm von Humboldt forged for academia that would integrate teaching and research in a unified conception of knowledge as a public good.

1. Commodification as the Friend of Universalism and the Enemy of Racism

In the Marxist tradition, commodification is the process by which the use value of things is replaced by their exchange value. In principle, everything is up for sale. *Worth* is reduced to *price,* to recall a distinction in the concept of value that is central to Kantian ethics. While we should not reject this critique out of hand, let us begin with the conceptual obstacles that our neoliberal times place in the way of accepting it. In particular, complaints about commodification have come to appear old-fashioned, reflecting a mystified view of human activity that ideally resists all efforts at comparative evaluation. If nothing else, the great advantage of demanding a price for everything is that it forces us to consider explicitly the cost we are willing to bear for the benefit we would like to receive. After all, is there an activity so inherently valuable that any improvements, let alone a radical transformation, if not outright replacement, would *always* violate what is worth preserving about the activity? It would seem that to complain about the alienation of labor today is to risk sounding like an enemy of efficiency and, worse, a rent-seeking protector of guild privileges. The decline in the political power of organized labor over the past three decades speaks to this now widespread perception.

From the neoliberal standpoint, starting with Eugen Böhm-Bawerk's original critique of labor theory of value and continuing to Ludwig Mises and Friedrich Hayek, what Marx called "commodification" was simply a metaphysically prejudiced way of talking about something rather positive, namely, the basic freedom to exchange my own activities and products for those of others in order to satisfy my wants as I see fit. On this view, there is no principled difference whether I satisfy my hunger for bread by working a certain amount of time or paying a certain amount of money for it or, for that matter, buying something cheaper that satisfies my hunger equally well or even financing a surgical procedure that inhibits my hunger altogether. All of these transactions, if agreed freely by the traders concerned, constitute valid exchanges. Indeed, as Nozick (1974) notoriously advised, if in doubt, turn to the terms entitled by the original contract: any outcome permitted by a freely negotiated contract is legitimate. To be sure, at the end of a sufficiently long sequence of exchanges negotiated by such contracts, the traders may have been transformed beyond all recognition, so as to have "sold their souls" —at least in the eyes of some, including Marxists. However, that prospect by itself causes no problems for the neoliberal, who differs from the Marxist in holding a resolutely antiessentialist view of humanity.

This point raises an interesting presupposition of commodification, which has equally interesting consequences. Capitalism as secular heir of the Protestant ethic has historically retained a residue of humanist essentialism. As Randall Collins (1999, 206–7) has observed, capitalism broke with earlier forms of political economy in its principled refusal to treat people as outright property, say, through marriage or slave markets. Of course, this did not prevent people from engaging in transactions that severely disadvantaged them, even to the point of compromising their effective freedom. Indeed, this is where, first, civic republicanism and, later, socialism departed from classical liberalism (Fuller 2000, 7–27). But all of these transactions presupposed, however unrealistically, a distinction between the trading agent and whatever goods or services she might wish to sell: in capitalism, everything potentially has a price except oneself, the ultimate source of value. This moment of "transcendental subjectivity," as Kant might say, casts a new, albeit unflattering, light on the increasing insistence on the intellectual property rights by native peoples (Brown 2003). Such "indigenization" of knowledge assumes an intimacy between modes of knowing and being that recalls precapitalist, if not racialized, forms of identity.

Take the case of transnational agribusinesses that contract with Indian peasants to gain access to their traditional knowledge of the land, which the firms then treat as raw material to convert into patentable life-forms, teachable skills, and commercial products. Most accounts of this instance of commodification are critical (e.g., Gupta 2007). Even though the peasants might enjoy short-term windfalls from the transactions, they are presented as having sold their birthright and compromised their political position in the wider society where they must continue to live. However, this negative appraisal of commodification makes two interrelated and problematic assumptions, which are explored below. To make my own position clear: I am much less troubled by the prospect of indigenous peoples buying and selling their distinctive forms of knowledge, including their genomes, than by the idea that they might enjoy a natural monopoly over the disposition of such knowledge simply because it forms part of their cultural or biological inheritance.

The first problematic assumption is that the natives are spontaneously inclined to share their knowledge, on the basis of which claims to intellectual property for techniques used to extract the relevant knowledge are largely exaggerated. The second is that the preservation and extension of indigenous knowledge requires promoting the welfare of the people who are currently the main possessors of that knowledge. These two assumptions are interconnected when the appropriation of indigenous knowledge is treated as a potential restriction, if not violation, of human rights. However, it is possible to grant that the human rights of indigenous peoples should be protected and that the integrity of the knowledge traditionally possessed by such peoples should be maintained, yet also hold that these are matters best handled as two separate legal issues. *Contra* the defenders of indigenous knowledge, knowing and being are *not* identical, and hence knowledge policy is *not* reducible to identity politics.

Put bluntly, indigenous peoples deserve to be respected as human beings even if they are not best placed to continue the forms of knowledge native to them. For example, the future of a minority language may be in safer hands at a world-class university linguistics department specifically dedicated to its preservation than in the last remaining community of native speakers who are forever tempted to abandon the language for the sorts of social and economic reasons they share with majority language users. Similarly, the harvesting of DNA from near-extinct biological species may provide a more secure route to species survival than the much more costly and less certain maintenance of living species members in their natural ecologies. This point is evaded by presuming that the indigenous impulse to share knowledge amounts to making it universally available. However, such spontaneous impulses are not sufficient to constitute an active policy of universalization, just as the sheer removal of restrictions to knowledge access does not *ipso facto* turn knowledge into a public good. Contrary to those still in the sway of the Scottish Enlightenment like Hume and Adam Smith, freedom and benevolence cannot make up for a lack of incentive and material resources. Whatever their ultimate motives, commercial firms and scientific disciplines are well designed to globalize knowledge in a way well-meaning indigenous peoples are not.

Behind the neoliberal resistance to the prerogatives of indigenous knowledge lies a more general point about human evolution, namely, the fundamentally contingent character of the specific assortment of genes that enables a relatively enclosed population to survive in a given region over a long period, during which they may develop distinctive forms of knowledge as part of what Richard Dawkins (1982) calls their "extended phenotype" (aka culture). This is not only a theoretical point about population biology, but it also reflects the fact that indigenous peoples can successfully transfer both their knowledge and their genes to other humans in other places: they can commodify their "biocapital" (Rajan 2006). In short, defenders of indigenous knowledge fail to recognize the degree of "positive racism" embedded in their claims to intellectual property. As we shall now see, regardless of whether one believes that the laws of nature are fixed or known, an implication of knowledge's universality is its resistance to *all* proprietary restrictions. If progress in the law in the modern era has been marked by the removal of hereditary privilege, then the prospect of indigenous intellectual property rights may constitute the final challenge that needs to be overcome.

2. Commodification as the Friend of Knowledge and the Enemy of Power

Through the neoliberal lens, then, commodification appears as a mechanism by which the integrity of knowledge is not compromised but, on the contrary, actively maintained. An interesting argument to this effect was made by the U.S. legal theorist Edmund Kitch (1981), partly to justify five centuries of judicial precedent in the Anglo-American common law tradition to favor the free mobility of labor, even when the employer had invested heavily in the laborer's training. In effect, judges have been undermining the rationale for such investments by making it easy for workers to take what they have learned to another employer. That the old employer might suffer competitively from her local secrets being divulged to the new one has failed to sway judges in most cases. On the contrary, judges have been more interested in ensuring the overall competitiveness of the market, which means removing bottlenecks in the transmission of knowledge, especially of the sort that would maintain the advantage currently enjoyed by one competitor.

Moreover, judicial reasoning ran afoul of a distinction drawn in human capital theory in economics, namely, between *general* and *specific* human capital, for which Gary Becker (1964) had won the 1992 Nobel Prize in Economics. The former refers to knowledge that is of use to the worker regardless of the firm that employs her services, the latter to knowledge that has value only in the context of a specific firm. The difference between the knowledge imparted in an academic degree course and on-the-job training captures the spirit of Becker's distinction. More abstractly, human capital in its general and specific forms corresponds, respectively, to the distinction between "knowledge" and "information," as clarified by the Shannon-Weaver theory of communication, according to which it is in the nature of information to resolve the uncertainty that its receiver experiences about a decision she must take. On this definition, what is informative for one receiver—in this case, a firm—may not be so for another if the two receivers possess different background knowledge and action contexts.

Thus, information can be easily subject to a proprietary regime, once specific receivers are targeted for whom possession of the information would clarify their action context. For everyone else, the same information would offer little or no specific advantage vis-à-vis potential competitors. However, judges realize that the public's interest in the protection of markets pertains primarily not to the interests of particular traders but to the overall dynamism in the system of exchange —that is, the ability for information to circulate freely so as to enable agents to be as informed as possible when making choices in line with their respective interests. While we have seen that this concern inclines judges to remove blockages resulting from the knowledge-hoarding attempts of employers, it equally inclines judges to allow employers to undermine the attempts by individual workers to gain power within a firm by commissioning "knowledge engineering" projects that involve the construction of "expert systems" that attempt to make explicit, however imperfectly, workers' so-called tacit knowledge (Fuller 2002, 116–67).

Kitch traces the wisdom of these equilibrating moves to a realization that knowledge lacks some of the basic qualities that would enable its literal treatment as property. In particular, knowledge is not really "divisible": The fact that you know something does not exclude me from knowing it. All that happens in that case is that the value of your knowledge diminishes because you lose whatever advantage you hold over me in my prior state of ignorance. In effect, knowledge is a pure "positional good" in Hirsch's (1976) sense, the value of which is tied exclusively to its scarcity. In that respect, the burgeoning field of "knowledge management" is in the business of maintaining the scarcity of knowledge, upholding its value as "information" in the sense noted above (Fuller 2002, 2–36).

Kitch characterizes the negative consequences of knowledge as a positional good in terms of its "self-protective" character: whatever positional advantage a solitary knower might have is dissipated as more people come to know the same thing. Thus, the "power" that philosophers from Plato and Bacon onward have associated with knowledge pertains to the fact that *at first* only a few possess it. However, it is not in the nature of knowledge to remain contained in this fashion. In this respect, Kitch's turn-of-phrase "self-protective" is a personification. He is reifying knowledge as something whose nature is not to be captured by anyone—but "itself." But of course, knowledge cannot be captured—at least not permanently—only because at least some of those who do not currently possess a given piece of knowledge have the (intellectual and material) means at their disposal either to create the same knowledge for themselves or to provide an adequate substitute by more or less efficient means.

Kitch justifies the self-protective character of knowledge solely on empirical grounds, noting the difficulty in maintaining trade secrets, both at the level of business practice and formal legislation. In the latter case, the key feature of intellectual property legislation is not the assignment of rights *per se* but the limits imposed on them. Any legal incentive to invention founded on property rights always recognizes the necessarily artificial restrictions they pose to the free flow of knowledge. Were we to generalize this approach to cover all intellectual activity, then a statute of limitations would be placed on charges of plagiarism: someone would be required to receive financial or citational credit for an idea for only a fixed amount of time, after which the idea might be appropriated by others for their own purposes under their own names. The fact that plagiarism looms as such a large normative problem in academic life these days reveals the extent to which academics have mutated from knowledge seekers to information managers —or, more precisely, text managers.

Finally, Kitch leaves open the possibility of a more philosophically principled reason for knowledge's so-called self-protectiveness. One such reason might be that the metaphysics presupposed by the very idea of intellectual property is wrong. Patent law is an outgrowth of the eighteenth-century Enlightenment view that, courtesy of Newtonian mechanics, science had nearly completed human comprehension of nature. In this frame of mind, it made sense to speak of fixed—and known— "laws of nature" that were an intellectual legacy of all human beings, as equal products of the same divine creator. Thus, intellectual property would be a temporary right based on a demonstrated ability to work over a determinate part of that commons so as to benefit oneself in the short term but everyone in the long term. This line of thought, famously enshrined in article 1, section 8 of the U.S. Constitution, assumes easy analogical transfers between "conceptual space" and "physical space." Thus, an application of the laws of nature is like the application of labor to a plot of land. In this context, a property right is meant to provide an incentive for perhaps otherwise lazy people not simply to live off the work of others.

However, the analogy between conceptual and physical space does not make sense if the laws of nature are still thought to be up for grabs. It suggests that the fundamental principles that were originally used to assign a patent to an invention may be later shown false. Taking such fallibility seriously, as is routinely done by historians, philosophers, and sociologists of science and technology, casts doubt on the very need to create a specially regulated domain of "intellectual property" beyond the ordinary regulation of market transactions. The arguments for a distinct category of intellectual property would then have to be restricted to the purported socioeconomic benefits of innovation, regardless of the epistemic security of the principles on which it might be based. To be sure, these revised arguments might work, but they would be no different from the arguments the state uses to justify financial incentives for any risky private investments.

Notwithstanding the lip service that continues to be paid to well-established Newton-style "laws of nature," of which a claim to intellectual property is supposed to be an application, intellectual property legislation has adapted to their fallible character. I refer here to the increasing willingness of judges to follow the precedent set by the U.S. Supreme Court in *Diamond v. Chakrabarty* (1980) to grant patents for biological species (and later mathematical proofs), typically on the basis of some unique codification that permits the species to be created (or the proof to be demonstrated). Such "codification" requires a specially equipped laboratory (or computer) through which the patented object can be presented as the product of a step-by-step process. It matters that the species (or proof) can be reliably produced by this process, *not* that it represents or instantiates one or more laws of nature. Indeed, the state of our knowledge of such laws is irrelevant for purposes of making the legal point about property rights *per se*. Thus, it does not matter whether the oil-eating bacterium at dispute in *Diamond* was genetically engineered from a species that arose as a result of Darwinian natural selection or divinely inspired intelligent design, as long as the bacterium successfully removes oil spills.

In short, the fugitive character of knowledge—what Kitch dubs "self-protective"—is entirely explicable in terms of the normal types of property regimes associated with commodification, which together create both an incentive and an opportunity for creative destruction, without requiring any special epistemic access to the "laws of nature."

3. Motivating the Marxist Critique: The Market from Teacher to Tyrant

We have seen that the neoliberal account of commodification drives a wedge between knowledge and property sufficiently deep to obviate the need for a distinct legal category of intellectual property. So far, so good. Nevertheless, we should not rush to abandon the Marxist critique. At the very least, we should understand how Marx came to it, which might give us a clue as to its continuing relevance. To understand how the commodification of alienated labor became the basis for a profound critique of capitalism, we need to look at the spirit in which the "free market" was first proposed in the eighteenth century as a panacea for a variety of problems associated with the emergence of the nation-state, a social formation that forced unprecedented numbers of previously unrelated people to see themselves as sharing a common fate, which over the next two centuries was elaborated as "civic duty" and "national identity." The sense of discipline required the sublimation of instinctive loyalties and passionate impulses into a refined conception of "self-interest" that could be rationally ascertained and calculated from an impartial standpoint (Hirschman 1977).

To be sure, there were skeptics that any such fundamental transformation of human nature was possible. Most notable of such skeptics was the Anglo-Dutch physician Bernard Mandeville, who regarded the project of instilling good motives —moral instruction—as little more than psychic quackery peddled by the priestly classes. His legacy to the discussion is the 1714 satirical poem and commentary, *The Fable of the Bees,* which coined the phrase much beloved by free market theorists, "Private vices make for public benefits" (Mandeville 1970). However, in its day, Mandeville's *Fable* was meant as a contribution to the literature Voltaire later immortalized in the novella *Candide*—what may be called "antitheodicy," that is, a perverse understanding of divine justice that undermines ordinary human comprehension.

And Mandeville's understanding was especially perverse. He was driven to verse in response to parliamentary complaints that a politician was promoting war for personal reasons, as if the value of his actions could be determined by their motives. Mandeville found this critique at once naïve and hypocritical (Runciman 2008, 45–73). *Of course* people act out of self-interest, but, so argued Mandeville, the point of good government is to get them to channel this selfishness into acts that ultimately benefit everyone. Here it is worth recalling Mandeville's original expression of this sentiment: "Private vices by the dextrous management of a skillful politician may be turned into public benefits." The interesting point here is that the only thing "invisible" about this "invisible hand" is that people remain as self-interested as ever but they are forced to behave in ways that do good for others. This view, now routinely discussed in terms of "incentivization," caused great offense in its day because it suggested that the most efficient way to get people to do good is *not* by getting them to want to do good but simply by structuring the environment so that their most likely actions turn out to be good.

Such was the context in which the "free market" was first socially constructed. To appreciate the controversial nature of Mandeville's perspective, we may liken it to the work of today's "knowledge engineer" who specializes in the design of "expert systems" and "smart environments" (Norman 1993; Fuller 2002, 116–67). The knowledge engineer deals with the various biases, prejudices, liabilities, and deficiencies in our cognitive powers that regularly compromise our judgment *not* by proposing rigorous training in formal logic and statistical inference to correct our faults but by capitalizing on the predictability of our errors. This enables her to design systems and environments that complement and compensate for those deficiencies, rendering the overall result of our decisions positive. However, the knowledge engineer is under no illusions that her schemes will alter our basic dispositions. While progress may be made in the construction of markets as smart environments, resulting in ever greater productivity, the human organism itself remains fundamentally unchanged, still tainted by a secular cognitive version of original sin.

Despite their mutual differences, Adam Smith and the Marquis de Condorcet were agreed in wanting to reinterpret the significance of free markets to overturn Mandeville's relatively gloomy prognosis for human improvement (Rothschild 2001). Their strategies moved in opposing directions—Smith retreating from Mandeville's nascent institutionalism, Condorcet pushing it to the limit.

For his part, Smith deemphasized Mandeville's institution-building implications, stressing a much more literal, "naturalistic" reading of Mandeville's apiary allegory. Thus, Smith left the impression that the removal of the monopoly privileges that the state bestowed on specific producers would enable the "private vices make for public benefits" principle to emerge as a spontaneously self-organizing process, as everyone reverts to their natural tendency to do whatever they can to survive, which includes producing the sorts of things that make them attractive trading partners. A biological version of this view would resurface in the late nineteenth century among anarchists and communists, notably Prince Piotr Kropotkin, who wished to derive scientific support for their political views from the symbiotic aspects of Spencer's and Darwin's theories of evolution. Although rarely acknowledged as such, perhaps the latest legacy of this trajectory from Mandeville's original account of the unsociably social hive is W. D. Hamilton's applications of game theory to capture the "reciprocally altruistic" behavior of organisms as they sustain a common gene pool, the basis of Richard Dawkins's image of the "selfish gene."

In contrast, Condorcet amplified Mandeville's institutionalism into a full-blown theory of social engineering that used markets as essentially an educational device to enable the emergence of reason through the gradual sublimation of the passions (Fuller 2006a). Condorcet's scenario for the educative function of markets can be rationally reconstructed as follows. Before free markets, state-protected producers act like vain gods, and their captive consumers act like base animals: producers give what they want in a "struggle for recognition," while consumers take what they are given in a "struggle for survival." Producers are thus governed by aesthetic self-expression ("avidity"), consumers by carnal self-gratification ("avarice"). However, neither state approximates the rationality exhibited by utility maximization, which requires the capacity to discriminate from among alternatives. This requires a proliferation of producers, which entails competition among products from which consumers must then select under cognitive, temporal, and fiscal resource constraints. This mutual disciplining removes both producer pretensions and consumer inertia, resulting in fully rational humans, at least in the sense of utility maximizers.

So, why are we not basking in the afterglow of Condorcet's educative markets? In a sense, producers and consumers did come to think of themselves in Condorcetian terms. They realized that they were disciplining each other, but they wanted the disciplining process to yield a profit beyond the intrinsic benefit of the process. Thus, consumption and production came to be treated as second-order processes. The market became "theorized" or "functionalized," subject to "semantic ascent" or underwent "self-observation," depending on whether one favors the jargon of analytic philosophy or systems theory. In short, producers aimed not to produce products but to reproduce demand in consumers, which their products then satisfy to varying degrees on a regular basis. It follows that knowledge itself enters as a third-order process that increases both the effectiveness of producers to reproduce demand and consumers to satisfy it by heightening powers of discrimination all round.

In short, all traders become more sophisticated in the "economy of signs," the sense in which Max Weber's great rival, Werner Sombart, first used "capitalism" in the title of a book in 1902 (Grundmann and Stehr 2001). The phenomenon was marked by a shift in the locus of market activity from manufacturing to advertising (or, in Thorstein Veblen's terms, from "industry" to "business"). Thus, wealth comes more from the possession of knowledge (of how to discriminate goods) than from the goods themselves, whose value waxes and wanes in trade. This development forces consumers to become educated in reading the signs needed to navigate through the multiple levels of choice in the marketplace. In effect, consumers assume personal responsibility—and generate corresponding forms of knowledge and accounting (from Ralph Nader's *Consumer Reports* to online tutorials and Weblogs)—that in the past would have been provided for them through state-based licensing and regulation of markets.

The historical logic of the above developments may be formally represented in the following scheme:

Levels of Commodification

First Order: The Ideal Market

Producers and consumers trade actual goods, often face-to-face, with character transformation as a possible unintended benefit, as traders become more sensitive to their own and each other's capacities and needs (eighteenth century).

Second Order: Industrial Capitalism

Producers and consumers trade what the goods stand for, insofar as actual goods are seen as providing utilities that may someday be provided more efficiently by other goods. An intended benefit of this shift in perspective is entrepreneurship, which spurs growth in the supply and demand of goods (early nineteenth century).

Third Order: Semiotic Capitalism

Producers and consumers trade signs of what the goods stand for, such as trademarks, which are primarily indicators of ideational associations. A growth in the need for trading competence—including the rise of marketing as a distinct profession—is an unintended consequence (late nineteenth to early twentieth century).

We now face a situation in which knowledge does not merely accelerate commodification but is itself subject to commodification:

Fourth Order: Epistemic Capitalism

Producers and consumers trade what competence stands for, so that the value of, say, knowledge of physics lies less in the access to physical reality that it provides than in its effectiveness as a credential for employment. A growth in the supply and demand for knowledge goods is an unintended harm (late twentieth to early twenty-first century).

4. Interim Conclusion: Commodification Is Still Evil Even if Necessary

A subtle shift occurs between Marx's *die Ware* and its English translation, *commodity,* itself derived from the French *la commodité* (Borgmann 2006). The original German *die Ware* focuses on the idea of a thing whose value is negotiated as a price (as opposed to something whose value is intrinsic and hence nonnegotiable, or *Wert,* as in Max Weber's *Wertrationalität*), whereas the Latin root of the English translation focuses on the conceptual space that needs to be made for something to enter the market that would otherwise have no place there, as in "accommodation."

The shift in semantic focus is subtle but significant. Austrian economists like Mises and Hayek, who remain close to the spirit of classical political economy, stress the fluctuating nature of prices as literally whatever the particular traders happen to negotiate (Steele 1992). From that standpoint, the value of a commodity is inherently indeterminate, as its price is determined from transaction to transaction. A social constructivist would be quite comfortable with this conceptualization. However, once Latinized as *commodity*, *Ware* comes to stand for a determinate place in the thinking of both buyers and sellers. Take a clear case of something that shifted from a nonmarket to a market existence: (clean) water. Whereas the original German stresses that the price of water depends on what actual traders decide, the Latinized English draws attention to the stable niche that water occupies as a locus of trade: suppliers regularly make money from water, as consumers budget water among the other goods they require to lead a satisfactory existence.

The shift in emphasis raises an interesting conceptual—and political—question: Which feature of commodification is worse? Is it that something previously treated as intrinsically valuable is now subject to the vicissitudes of the marketplace? Or, is it that something previously taken for granted about one's life-world is now regularly problematized? In other words, does the evil of commodified water lie mainly in what it does to water or what it does to those who now "need" water? Of course, commodification involves both transformations, but the difference in emphasis matters. At a conceptual level, one notes the difference between the inconstancy of price and the constancy of need—neither of which obtained before water was brought into the marketplace. But the political implications arguably matter more. How are states likely to respond to the commodification of water: Will they retrieve it from the market and convert it into a public good—that is, making it free at the point of delivery—by a taxation on wealth according to the principle of "Each according to his ability to each according to his need"? Or rather, will they stabilize the price of water to affordable levels so that (virtually) everyone can purchase the amount they need? Certainly in these neoliberal times—if not all times—the latter is politically more plausible. Notice that this political solution seems to express a greater concern for the variability of water prices than the very fact that people are being forced to pay for it.

The starkness of this contrast is not so evident if one focuses mainly on goods like education that did not have a taken-for-granted status in people's lives until they were explicitly made into public goods. I raise this point because many, especially in the Marcusean strand of neo-Marxism (e.g., Borgmann 2006), operate with the historically misleading assumption that "in the beginning" there were public goods like education, which over time, through the inexorable march of capitalism, have become commodified. Strictly speaking, water was not a public good before the rise of capitalism. But it was not a commodity either. Those are not the only alternatives. Just because water has been always a part of our natural existence, it does not follow that societies have felt collectively responsible—let alone implemented the relevant irrigation and sewage systems—for ensuring that everyone in a given region has adequate access to this necessary substance.

What historians and anthropologists used to call our "primitive" or "subsistent" state consisted precisely of people spending most of their days locating the stuff they need to maintain their existence. People literally lived to find water, which they did sufficiently well to spend thirty or forty years alive. To call this state "primitive communism" may be to romanticize the brute fact that everyone was subject to a common fate. Once primitive life is suitably demystified, the commodification of water appears as a *progressive* development, since it meant that the substance could be regularly supplied at a price, freeing up time for people to do other things. Of course, as Marx would quickly point out, that time would be spent doing things that would enable one to purchase the water! From a global evolutionary perspective, it has been argued that *even today* the commodification of water would represent a step in the right direction for most parts of the world (Seabright 2004, 123–36). In particular, it would help to remove the ideological stigma of "handouts" associated with redistribution that has impeded agreement on water as a public good worldwide. Sympathy for the poor in remote parts of the world is unlikely to be translated into sustained action, if it is not part of a general strategy for raising the poor to the status of players in the global economy.

The idea of water as a public good involves further considerations of efficiency based on economies of scale and long-term socioeconomic projections, specifically, the multiplier effect to the general welfare of a region if everyone has ample access to free clean water. In that respect, public goods are just as "manufactured" as commodities, reflecting a sensibility that *presupposes,* not opposes, capitalism. Indeed, the welfare state was always sold as a means of increasing society's productivity by allowing more people to work and spend the fruits of their labors.

But in the end, there is no denying that, given the spiraling senses of market reflexivity over the past 250 years, commodification has resulted in two complementary harms, each associated with the two major linguistic sources of the English "commodity" that contributed to Marx's original conceptualization:

- *Harm to the producer:* This is based on the German, *die Ware.* The value of the labor expended to produce a good is reduced to the value that the good can fetch in the market, which reflects more the good's relative advantage vis-à-vis rival goods in satisfying a common want or need than its intrinsic "front-loaded" qualities. Thus, the good's use value shifts along with the competitive field, rendering it potentially replaceable, and in that sense "useless," even though it may continue satisfying the original want or need.

- *Harm to the consumer:* This is based on the French, *la commodité*. A good is reified as something that satisfies a standing want or need. The good thus occupies—or perhaps more precisely "symbolizes"—a fixed place in the consumer's moral economy, regardless of whether the corresponding use value is genuinely sustained. In effect, consumer choice is reduced to which of a field of competing products satisfies something that consumers have come to expect will be provided for them, more out of habit than as a reflection of what is in their best interests.

One of the many forgotten insights of cold war mathematician and cybernetics pioneer Norbert Wiener was his understanding of Satan's *modus operandi* in terms of positive feedback loops (Wiener 1950, 51). In other words, Satan does not introduce a distinctly evil element into an otherwise good situation but rather more insidiously reinforces tendencies that are good in the limited contexts in which they normally occur but become pathological when extended indefinitely. Commodification is "evil" precisely in this sense: it fails to know the limits of its own virtue. As suggested above, the results from both the producer and the consumer side are perverse to say the least: the increasing disposability of the former is matched by the increasing dependency of the latter, which together undermine autonomy and create addiction.

To mark the transition to the second phase of our argument, in which this general analysis of commodification and entrepreneurship is applied to the specific case of the university, consider how these complementary harms are exemplified in academic life in today's neoliberal knowledge society:

Harm to Knowledge Producer Integrity

People are paid according to the efficiency of their knowledge products, i.e., the capacity to accomplish the most with the least.
The consequence of this is that specific forms of knowledge are made more disposable (open question is the general form that defines the market within which specific forms must compete). For example,

1. Contract-based teachers and researchers replace tenured academics;
2. Automated technology replaces both explicit reasoning and tacit knowledge;
3. Summaries and syntheses replace original works;
4. Short-term product cycles replace long-term significance even in academic settings.

Harm to Knowledge Consumer Integrity

People are forced to purchase knowledge products as part of their overall survival strategy. As a consequence, general forms of knowledge are made less disposable (an open question is what specific form will satisfy the need/want represented by the general form). For example,

1. More academic certification is required for comparable levels of employment;
2. The sociocognitive division of labor implies that personal decision making is increasingly alienated from oneself to experts;
3. More gadgets are needed to mediate an ever-changing life-world;
4. The increasing reach of intellectual property law introduces tolls and rents as ad hoc costs to knowledge acquisition.

In short, as the need for knowledge as a mediator of social life grows, the disposability of specific forms of knowledge also grows. The former corrupts the consumer, the latter the producer. These complementary harms today especially challenge the institutional integrity of the university, which is supposed to be in the business of manufacturing knowledge as a public good. But the university is fast becoming a factory for intellectual property rights and job credentials as the products of research and teaching as functionally differentiated processes, both designed for obsolescence in tow to the endless circulation of capital. To reiterate, the problem here is not commodification *per se* but its unlimited extension. To say that certain products or processes should not be commodified is to deny them access to entrepreneurship. By examining the ways in which entrepreneurship has been contained in the history of capitalism, we can begin to understand the sense in which the university ideally—that is, in its Humboldtian guise—operates as an expressly entrepreneurial institution dedicated to "creatively destroying" social capital in order to manufacture knowledge as a public good (Fuller 2003).

5. The Promise and Perils of Epistemic Entrepreneurship

The second major critique of capitalism after Marx's turns on the system's failure to live up to its own ideal. This ideal was most vividly captured by Joseph Schumpeter (1912/1982), now nearly a hundred years ago, as the "entrepreneur," the agent who "creatively destroys" the market by introducing a new product that not only attracts consumers but also changes how consumers conceptualize their demand of products of that sort. Schumpeter's paradigm case of entrepreneurship was Henry Ford's revolutionary transformation of the transport market with the mass-produced automobile. Critics in the Schumpeterian vein bemoan the obstacles that capitalists themselves, often with the help of government, have placed in the way of future Fords, such as overly restrictive intellectual property regimes or excessively lenient inheritance and corporate taxes. However, some believe—as Schumpeter (1942/1950) himself ultimately did—that such obstacles to the free flow of capital are an inevitable, and largely justified, response to the scaling up of capitalist activity, which requires containment of the market volatility normally generated by entrepreneurship. This need to minimize risk is shared by those at the helm of both business and government: the former wanting to maintain high profit margins for shareholders and the latter wanting to maintain social security for citizens.

Not surprisingly, the Schumpeterian critic often ends up saying that pure capitalism is self-defeating. However, this judgment is typically delivered in the spirit of ambivalence. In other words, the following restrictions in the flow of innovation into the marketplace, which might be heinous if administered by the dominant capitalists to their own advantage, could actually be quite salutary from a more general societal standpoint, if administered by government or some other agency—such as the university—expressly dedicated to promoting the public good:

1. *Restrict the domain of legitimate producers and consumers by requiring prior licensing.* This was the feature of mercantilism that Adam Smith decried as holding back the full productive use of capital and labor. Prima facie the requirement of state licenses for production and consumption looks like nepotism and paternalism, respectively, whereby forms of family life are inappropriately imported into the public sphere. However, a potential advantage of such protectionism is the capacity to regulate the growth and spread of markets. In the case of innovations, that allows for the containment of risk: after all, the state stands to lose credibility if it authorizes the manufacturers of unreliable products or fails to check or correct consumer ignorance by, say, requiring a level of competence for driving a car (Fuller 2002, 81–93).

2. *Outsource product research and development either to potential market competitors as a form of co-optation or—better still—to potential consumers.* In the latter case, consumers are motivated to purchase the product and feel guilty if it does not succeed, because they have assumed partial responsibility for the product's fate. This strategy has worked especially well in software design relating to human-computer interfaces, that is, so-called participatory design research. As canonized in Woolgar (1991), this process has become a paradigm case of the "coproduction" of science and society in STS. However, despite its democratic rhetoric, and STS's own

rhetoric of methodological symmetry, participatory design research usually harbors the same asymmetrical power relations between producers and consumers one expects from the business world (Fuller and Collier 2004, xvii–xx).

3. *Shift capital investment from production to marketing, since success in a crowded market requires informing consumers that your product not only can but should be bought.* This point is related to Werner Sombart's first use of "capitalism" to capture what is now routinely called "product placement" (Grundmann and Stehr 2001). In a world where traditional markers of social status have lost reliability, the burden is shifted to producers to promote their products by offering, beyond the product itself, a normative framework through which the product should be understood in order to be seen as superior. This explains the ingenious appeals to the imagination made in television commercials, which are increasingly used to sell degree programs and research enterprises.

4. *Purchase the rights to already existing products and rebrand them as one's own, thereby reducing the field of current competitors.* This anti-entrepreneurial phenomenon was first publicized by Thorstein Veblen a century ago as the transition from "industry" to "business," which he associated with the rise of monopoly capitalism. Recently Naomi Klein (2000) has reinvented the critique as part of her "no logo" campaign. The success of rebranding capitalizes on the profound information asymmetry between producers and consumers, such that consumers cannot judge product values for themselves but must rely on brands. However, branding hides the work of the dominant market players who have subsumed potential competitors, whose values might have been radically different. While Klein has in mind the activities of transnational corporations vis-à-vis third world native industries, the point equally applies to the role that the global spread of science has played vis-à-vis local indigenous forms of knowledge, the latest and most extreme phase of which was discussed in section 1 as "biocapital." In this respect, the corresponding term to "monopoly" in science might be "paradigm."

5. *Influence the direction of future market activity through heavy investment in anticipated products even before a single prototype has been produced.* This anti-entrepreneurial strategy may be seen as effectively creating the economic equivalent of a self-fulfilling prophecy. Economists have further mystified the situation with the concept of "path dependency," which when applied to funding streams deemed "scientific" (e.g., in laboratories and skilled knowledge workers) continue indefinitely to yield proportionally greater return on investments (Arthur 1994). It is as if the idea of "sunk costs," the economic principle behind cutting one's losses, did not exist in this context. A cynic might argue that such heightened expectations serve to motivate scientists and their investors to cast their nets more widely for "unintended" benefits of research whose stated goals may never be achieved.

This, in turn, contributes to the "halo effect" of investments deemed "scientific": Not only are they more productive but also, and more importantly, they inspire greater effort to ensure their productivity.

It is easy to imagine the university trying to maintain its advantage in an expanding knowledge system by arresting and channeling entrepreneurship in all of the above senses. In particular, universities need not outperform corporate R&D divisions or online diploma mills if they alone can reliably discriminate among their products and impart the relevant skills that are likely to work in the long term, an attractive prospect for any producer or consumer who values longevity in the marketplace. Indeed, this strategy has been used to good effect by universities to maintain their advantage in a rapidly changing knowledge economy. For example, instead of competing directly with the mechanics' colleges that were training aspiring industrialists of nineteenth-century Britain, Oxford and Cambridge decided to become accrediting agencies for college degrees by both standardizing the theoretical bases of their technical instruction and forcing the introduction of subjects that might otherwise not have received exposure because of their lack of immediate practical value. However, this "second-order" leverage depends on the university's ability to maintain the integrity of its own distinctive product, knowledge as a public good.

The idea of the university as an entrepreneurial institution that manufactures knowledge as a public good by creatively destroying social capital can be understood as a cyclical process that passes through the following phases. Let us start with a newly minted piece of research, published in a journal or a patent. The research investors—both researchers themselves and their funders—are the primary beneficiaries, who together constitute a relatively closed network of social capital. The knowledge they have produced becomes a source of advantage in the various markets where they operate—what I earlier called a "positional good." Rents, royalties, and fees are then charged to others to make that research more generally available but at a staggered pace, so as to prolong the innovator's market advantage. However, the academic obligation to translate research into teaching effectively removes the protections surrounding this form of social capital. "Creative destruction" in this sense involves the elimination of the financial and intellectual obstacles that impede access to the new knowledge. Such obstacles often come together, as in the cost of technical training required to understand the language of the original articles or patents in which the knowledge was introduced.

In contrast, the student body for the relevant curricular translations is likely to draw upon a wider range of society than those who form the social capital network for a given piece of research. This increases the likelihood that the research innovation will be applied or extended in directions that the originators had not anticipated, thereby further reducing their market advantage. To be sure, the process creates an incentive for the originators to develop new research networks that generate new social capital and hence market advantage, etc. But in the meanwhile the original innovation has been converted into a public good.

More specifically, two conditions need to be satisfied for knowledge to make the transition from social capital to public good. First, you need a dedicated site to translate specialist research into general education. Ideally you need a common liberal arts curriculum beyond professional and vocational training, but much the same effect may be captured in a well-structured, discipline-based major. Second, you need a compulsory policy of incorporating more people into education so that knowledge cannot be consolidated as the intellectual property of a class, race, culture, or gender. The heart of the modern university—that is, since its Humboldtian reinvention—has been the curriculum, especially as something that imparts a "liberal education" whose relevance to life extends beyond job qualifications, including qualifications in specialist academic jobs. The curriculum is the site of "education" in a rather specific sense, namely, the completion of the human being by preparing him (and later her) for "citizenship," whereby one identifies not merely with family or town or profession but the entire nation, which conceives of itself as an exemplar, if not vanguard, of all humanity. Not surprisingly, this has made the university the perennial site of "culture wars," as successive waves of excluded groups seek a transhistorical sense of social justice by writing themselves into—and others out of—the curriculum (Fuller 2000, 62–74). In true Hegelian fashion, the very idea of a "core curriculum" or "general education" naturally generates its own opposition, as its claims to universality are never literally redeemed. Nevertheless, states that pride themselves as being liberal democracies can ill afford to ignore these complaints, since they strike at the foundations of their own legitimacy.

But once we weaken the university's unique commitment to knowledge as a public good and move instead, as Mark Brown suggests in his essay in this volume, to the idea of knowledge as "multiple constitutive goods," commodification and entrepreneurship soon conspire to undermine the institution's integrity, as researchers and teachers become more responsive to extramural clients and constituencies than to each other. In particular, as detailed in section 4 above, research and education, understood as two of Brown's multiple constitutive goods need to be delivered in a quite targeted fashion over a short time frame. To be sure, this outcome is not necessary but it requires the will and canny of what I have called an "Academic Caesar" (Fuller 2008). Reflecting on the long-term consequences of the Bayh-Dole Act (1980), whereby the U.S. Congress for the first time allowed universities and other nonprofit institutions to seek intellectual property rights without seeking prior government approval, Greenberg (2007) provocatively argues that claims about the capitalist corruption of academia may be overblown. The problem may be the failure of academic leadership in taking control of the situation. Universities already provide an array of free or low-cost services for business with little or no complaint—from training potential employees to researching potentially lucrative fields. Moreover, such activities are bound to increase in the coming years. In that case, it might be in academia's own interest to cultivate more explicit ties with the commercial sector, if only to ensure that business pays its own way.

6. Whither Academic Republicanism?

Henk van den Belt presents the founder of modern chemistry, Antoine Lavoisier, in a sympathetic light, begging the French Jacobin regime in 1793 not to dismantle the Academy of Sciences. Lavoisier appears as a proto-Mertonian who recognizes that the intellectual property of a scientist (i.e., an elite member of the academy) is tied to his willingness to share with others, whereas that of a technologist (i.e., an ordinary member of a craft guild) is tied to his ability to keep trade secrets. Van den Belt wants us to draw the conclusion that the scientist's spontaneous epistemic generosity reflects his disinterestedness, unlike the craftsman who always wants to make a profit.

The problem with this pretty picture, also shared by contemporary economists (e.g., Dasgupta and David 1994), is that it assumes that knowledge is *automatically* public if it is not deliberately kept secret. However, knowledge becomes truly public only once a mechanism is in place to make it available to everyone, at least in principle. By its very nature, an innovation (or "invention," in Schumpeter's strict sense) is esoteric because it is initially known only to its creators and funders, hence, the paradoxes associated with "predicting progress" that liberals have used against socialist planners since the end of the first World War (Steele 1992). To publish in an academic journal is merely to stake a claim to knowledge in terms of one's peers. If the knowledge process ends there, all that such "sharing" has accomplished is to increase the relative knowledge (and presumably power) of the academic peer group vis-à-vis the rest of society who still lacks it.

Craftsmen are not so driven to publication because they do not regard sheer epistemic priority as inherently virtuous—on the contrary, as suggested above, strategically limited publication could end up realizing George Bernard Shaw's quip that every profession is a conspiracy against the public. "Ye shall know them by their fruits" is closer to the craftsman's norm. In other words, it matters less that you get there first than you get the most out of it. This typically means subjecting the innovation to a market test: Can people use it? Do they buy it? While this orientation also falls short of full publicity, it comes closer to it than the sort of practice defended by Lavoisier. In this respect, tendencies in capitalism like commodification and entrepreneurship—as long as they do *not* result in strong intellectual property claims—may be seen as going halfway between pure secrecy and pure publicity of knowledge.

What is clearly missing from Lavoisier's thinking—as well as Merton's, for that matter—is an institution like the university, a proactive universalizing agent explicitly dedicated to manufacturing knowledge as a public good. The university's mission to translate research into teaching is the key. New discoveries and inventions are thus not allowed to spread *laissez-faire* like a virus, perhaps widely but also haphazardly. Rather, they are incorporated into a regularly reproduced body of collective knowledge, as represented by the curriculum. In this context, the competitive spirit of scientists is oriented neither exclusively to their peers (à la Lavoisier) nor to the market (à la technologists) but to an intermediate category of "public recognition" that Condorcet emphasized. This means the public intellectual significance of one's work, which might be codified in popular books and media or, of course, inclusion in standard textbooks. Common to all these is the idea of *eponymy*—that one lives on in the memory of others by having one's name associated with a lasting achievement. This very Greek idea also emerges in Charles Sanders Peirce's conception of the competitive nature of scientific consensus formation.

However, *contra* van den Belt's suggestion (again taken from Merton), this sense of recognition is *not* reducible to citation counts, *especially* in the natural sciences, where the most highly cited people are often those who publish many pieces (typically with others) that provide canonical presentations of findings or ideas that began life in the work of someone else, who may or may not be cited in such pieces. By "canonical presentations," I mean that the argument, the research design, the data analysis, or something else is presented in a perspicuous manner without taking too much for granted or introducing diversionary assumptions or issues. Ironically perhaps, a closer fit between citation counts and the relevant sense of public recognition might be found in the humanities, where the most famous people do tend to be most highly cited.

I could imagine a good experiment in social psychology on the difference between how scientists process a pair of questions, "Who do you think are the most highly cited people in your field?" and "Who do you think are the most widely recognized people in your field?" Answers to the latter question are likely to correspond more closely to index entries in textbooks than to research citation counts. If correct, it would reveal the extent to which researchers, when left to their own devices in the peer environment, treat each other's work in purely instrumental terms—that is, as means for enabling them to stake their own claims to knowledge. To construct such a relationship as "the taking and giving of credit" mystifies a process that appears to be a straightforward case of people paying for what they find useful, while leaving on the shelf the more exotic luxury items, such as involved presentations of the same ideas and findings, including the original ones.

The larger lesson of these observations is that, *contra* Lavoisier and Merton, it is one thing to decouple the production of scientific knowledge from any need to prove itself in the ordinary consumer market but quite another for it then to be coupled with another practice—namely, formal university instruction—that genuinely converts the knowledge into a public good. The default, uncoupled position is that the knowledge producers simply constitute themselves as an internal market in which they become the primary consumers of each other's goods. The U.S. sociologist Harrison White (1981) has promoted this idea, with artisan guilds in mind, into a general account of the origin of markets. In this respect, knowledge produced in the manner that Lavoisier defended vis-à-vis the Academy of Sciences is potentially even *less* public than the guilds, whose agreed standards of craftsmanship at least had to be also tested against consumers (albeit often with the benefit of a hard-to-get royal license).

In other words, the knowledge so esteemed by Lavoisier was "disinterested" and "public" only in the backhanded sense of being *indifferent* to the uses made by others not directly involved in the knowledge production process. On the one hand, if someone manages to acquire the relevant technical expertise, they are free to draw whatever benefits from the knowledge that they can. On the other hand, it is unlikely that all but the most diligent and/or wealthy would ever find themselves in such a position. Rather, and truer to the actual history, the knowledge produced by the Academy of Sciences would be used mainly by the ministries of state who pay the salaries of the academicians, who would then be obliged to provide them personal instruction about potential applications.

Here we see the Achilles heel of what has been the trademark feature of knowledge production *à la mode Française* in the modern period: a sharp institutional differentiation of research and teaching, each with its own tasks and requirements, though academics might aspire to be involved in both. The former would be allowed to produce knowledge under autonomous conditions for the state to use as it sees fit, while the latter would be entrusted with educating the next generation of elites. Neither would make demands on the other. This division had been generally promoted by the Enlightenment *philosophes* and was enthusiastically embraced by Napoleon, which in turn triggered Humboldt's nation-building reinvention of the university as the site for the unification of teaching and research (Collins 1998, 618–87).

While some academics under the dual French regime might take it upon themselves to render new knowledge a public good, that would not be especially encouraged by the system's division of labor. Rather, the autonomy of research institutes implied that researchers would be responsible for the consequences of the knowledge they produced *only* within the peer community but not outside it. Under the circumstances, research fraud becomes a much more serious normative infraction. This is because an autonomous research community is presumed to work with a common understanding of what is unknown and known, as well as the procedure for demonstrating the transition from the former to the latter state. In contrast, research fields that lack such complete control over their conditions of inquiry—such as the humanities and the social sciences and perhaps even medicine —tend to operate with much less determinate sense of the known/unknown distinction, such that even controversial accounts of phenomena (e.g., psychoanalysis, Marxism) may have quite substantial real world effects, simply if enough people act as if they were true.

Therefore, implied in the social epistemology of the French system is a strict distinction between the contexts of testing (within the peer community) and application (outside the peer community). The purported virtues of this system would be undermined if the research community were to become hostage to the wishes of their political paymasters to reach certain conclusions. Yet arguably this is precisely what happened in the Soviet Union, whose knowledge policy copied the French approach—that is, insulated from all external pressures except those coming from the state. (Under the circumstances, it is easy to appreciate the neoliberal "dirty hands" attitude, which appears, slightly sanitized, in actor-network theory: if research is always tainted by external interests, then the worst possible world is where there is only *one* such interest.)

The most obvious consequence of the dual French regime is an updated version of Plato's theory of multiple truths, each appropriate to a given mode of governance, where the researchers function as philosopher-kings in training (most of whom will never see public practice) and the teachers as guardians of vis-à-vis the socioepistemic order. Absent here is any obvious means for expanding the overall domain of knowers as new knowledge increases—what I describe above as the "creatively destructive" tendency of the modern university, whose teaching function redistributes the advantage that researchers gain with an innovation. Plato himself presumed the need for hard class distinctions that corresponded to the functions that a society must fulfill to survive. In his mind, the only room for maneuvering was in terms of individual membership in a given class in a given generation. Although Plato notoriously advocated the promulgation of a eugenic mythology to ensure social stability, his preferred selection process was closer to an examination system—or at least a talent-spotting agency focused on the young.

But of course, over time even if new knowledge does not serve to expand the sphere of knowers, it may nevertheless alter both what one takes to be relevant knowledge and how it is examined. This applies no less to knowledge of the human condition relevant for the execution of Plato's political project. Thus, Kuhn's mentor, Harvard President James Bryant Conant, spent the final years of his career (into the 1960s) arguing that America's protracted racial disharmony was the result of (mostly) African Americans lacking the opportunity to demonstrate their exact talents, as a result of the egalitarian pretense of early schooling, which assumes that in principle anything worth knowing is knowable by everyone (Conant 1959). The prototype for Conant's proposed "streaming" of students was Alfred Binet's introduction of intelligence testing at the end of the nineteenth century to place French students into appropriate classes. Arguably Pierre Bourdieu's entire career as a sociologist might be explained as one long argument against the persistence of this Platonic legacy, whereby "being in the know" serves to stratify a market environment.

The French model of social epistemology, with its strong functional differentiation of research and teaching, implies a clear distinction between *knowledge for the public good* and *knowledge as a public good* that has been absent so far in our discussion. In this updated version of Plato's elite republicanism, knowledge need not—perhaps even should not—itself be a public good in order to be for the public good. From this follows a politics of paternalism or, as the Enlightenment *philosophes* preferred to call it, "benevolent despotism"—in any case, a regime where the idea of public good implies nothing democratic about either its construction or its validation. Such an undemocratic conception of the public good, by virtue of its strict separation of research and teaching, destroys science as an autonomous form of knowledge. In its place are two distinct processes: technologies of governance (for the state, aka research) and ideologies of governance (for the public, aka teaching).

The volatile history of republicanism as a political ideal can be told as one long attempt to make good on the idea that knowledge cannot be for the public good unless it is itself a public good: we can do more than simply update Plato's elite republicanism—we can decisively break with it (Fuller 2000). There are at least three ways to characterize this historical tendency, which I have identified with the open society's narrative of epistemic progress (Fuller 2007a, 48–52): (1) toward more inclusive participation in the knowledge production process; (2) toward a redistribution of power from the knowledgeable to the ignorant; and (3) toward reflexive consistency in the accountability of goods that are deemed to be public. Already by the time of the American and French revolutions, the Enlightenment had moved decisively in this direction with the emergence of the hybrid role of the "citizen scientist," whose intellectual autonomy licensed claims of political independence. Jacobin science policy, as negatively portrayed by van den Belt, falls under this category, but even earlier were the likes of Benjamin Franklin, Thomas Jefferson, and their mutual friend, Joseph Priestley (Fuller 2006c, 171–73). However, these were exemplary individuals. The university in its modern Humboldtian guise—as the site for unifying research and teaching—has been the primary institutional vehicle for reproducing this ideal.

Let me conclude by addressing van den Belt's puzzlement with Mirowski and Sent (2002), who appear to damn the very idea of knowledge as a public good by virtue of its historic association with the cold war political economy, the manufacture of the so-called welfare-warfare state. Van den Belt argues, in a way that recalls the old positivist distinction between the contexts of discovery and justification in science, that the idea of public good may still be desirable and feasible in spite of this specific origin. However, this is to miss the depth of Mirowski and Sent's critique: the cold war itself may not be needed to motivate the kind of political economy needed to produce public goods. However, what may be needed is the sense of some sustained external threat to which all members of a given society are equally vulnerable. The great university expansion projects—be it nineteenth-century Germany or twentieth-century America—flew under the flag of national security (in wartime) or national competitiveness (in peacetime). Without this sense of impending crisis, it becomes hard to see why people from quite diverse backgrounds and interests would feel compelled to produce a common body of knowledge that may well appear highly ideological to outsiders. This is not so different from motivating a strong ongoing commitment to the maintenance of a republican polity that in so many other respects encourages freedom and individuality. In this respect, it is interesting that the prospect of universities as sites for producing "global public goods" (Stiglitz 1999) rests on attending to aspects of nature—e.g., pandemics and climate change—that might threaten the longevity of humanity as an entire species.

REFERENCES

Arthur, W. Brian. 1994. *Increasing returns and path dependence in the economy*. Ann Arbor: University of Michigan Press.

Becker, Gary S. 1964. *Human capital: A theoretical and empirical analysis, with special reference to education*. Chicago: University of Chicago Press.

Borgmann, Albert. 2006. "A moral conception of commodification." In *The moralization of the market,* ed. N. Stehr, C. Henning, and B. Weiler, 193–211. New Brunswick, NJ: Transaction Books.

Brown, Michael F. 2003. *Who owns native culture?* Cambridge, MA: Harvard University Press.

Collins, Randall. 1998. *The sociology of philosophies: A global theory of intellectual change*. Cambridge, MA: Harvard University Press.

———. 1999. *Macrohistory: Essays in sociology of the long run*. Palo Alto, CA: Stanford University Press.

Conant, James Bryant. 1959. *The american high school today: A first report to interested citizens*. New York: McGraw Hill.

Dasgupta, Partha, and Paul David. 1994. "Towards a new economics of science." *Research Policy* 23:487–521.

Dawkins, Richard. 1982. *The extended phenotype*. Oxford: Oxford University Press.

Fuller, Steve. 2000. *The governance of science*. Milton Keynes, UK: Open University Press.

———. 2002. *Knowledge management foundations*. Woburn, MA: Butterworth-Heinemann.

———. 2003. "In search of vehicles for knowledge governance: On the need for institutions that creatively destroy social capital." In *The governance of knowledge,* ed. N. Stehr, 41–76. New Brunswick, NJ: Transaction Books.

———. 2006a. "The market: Source or target of morality?" In *The moralization of the market,* ed. N. Stehr, C. Henning, and B. Weiler, 129–53. New Brunswick, NJ: Transaction Books.

———. 2006b. *The new sociological imagination*. London: Sage.

———. 2006c. *The philosophy of science and technology studies*. London: Routledge.

———. 2007a. *New frontiers in science and technology studies*. Cambridge: Polity.

———. 2007b. *Science vs. religion? Intelligent design and the problem of evolution*. Cambridge: Polity.

———. 2008. "Academic leadership in the twenty-first century: The case for academic caesarism." In *Geographies of knowledge, geometries of power: Higher education in the twenty-first century, world year book of education 2008,* ed. D. Epstein, R. Boden, R. Deem, F. Rizvi, and S. Wright, 50–66. London: Routledge.

Fuller, Steve, and James Collier. 2004. *Philosophy, rhetoric and the end of knowledge*. 2nd ed. Hillsdale, NJ: Lawrence Erlbaum Associates. (Originally by Fuller only, 1993).

Greenberg, Daniel S. 2007. *Science for sale: The perils, rewards, and delusions of campus capitalism*. Chicago: University of Chicago Press.

Grundmann, Reiner, and Nico Stehr. 2001. "Why is Werner Sombart not part of the core of classical sociology?" *Journal of Classical Sociology* 1:257–87.

Gupta, Anil. 2007. "Is a just system also fair? Traversing the domain of knowledge, institutions, culture and ethics." In *Who owns knowledge? Knowledge and the law,* ed. N. Stehr and B. Weiler, 87–98. New Brunswick, NJ: Transaction Books.

Hacohen, Malachi. 2000. *Karl Popper: The formative years, 1902–1945*. Cambridge: Cambridge University Press.

Hirsch, Fred. 1976. *The social limits to growth*. London: Routledge and Kegan Paul.

Hirschman, Albert. 1977. *The passions and the interests*. Princeton, NJ: Princeton University Press.

Kitch, Edmund. 1981. "The law and economics of rights in valuable information." *Journal of Legal Studies* 9:683–723.

Klein, Naomi. 2000. *No logo*. New York: Alfred Knopf.

Kurzweil, Ray. 1999. *The age of spiritual machines*. New York: Random House.

Mandeville, Bernard. 1970. *The fable of the bees*. Harmondsworth, UK: Penguin.

Mirowski, Philip, and Esther-Mirjam Sent, eds. 2002. *Science bought and sold: Essays in the economics of science*. Chicago: University of Chicago Press.

Norman, Donald. 1993. *Things that make us smart*. Reading, MA: Addison-Wesley.

Nozick, Robert. 1974. *Anarchy, state and utopia*. New York: Basic Books.

Rajan, Kaushik Sunder. 2006. *Biocapital: The constitution of postgenomic life*. Durham, NC: Duke University Press.

Rothschild, Emma. 2001. *Economic sentiments: Adam Smith, Condorcet, and the enlightenment*. Cambridge, MA: Harvard University Press.

Runciman, David. 2008. *Political hypocrisy*. Princeton, NJ: Princeton University Press.

Schumpeter, Joseph. 1942/1950. *Capitalism, socialism, and democracy*. 2nd ed. New York: Harper & Row.

———. 1912/1982. *The theory of economic development*. New Brunswick, NJ: Transaction Books.

Seabright, Paul. 2004. *The company of strangers: A natural history of economic life*. Princeton, NJ: Princeton University Press.

Singer, Peter. 1999. *A darwinian left*. London: Weidenfeld & Nicolson.

Steele, David Ramsey. 1992. *From Marx to Mises: Post-capitalist society and the challenge of economic calculation*. La Salle, IL: Open Court Press.

Stiglitz, Joseph. 1999. "Knowledge as a global public good." In *Global public goods: International cooperation in the twenty-first century,* ed. I. Kaul, I. Grunberg, and M. Stern, 308–25. Oxford: Oxford University Press.

White, Harrison. 1981. "Where do markets come from?" *American Journal of Sociology* 87:517–47.

Wiener, Norbert. 1950. *The human use of human beings*. Boston: Houghton Mifflin.

Woolgar, Steve. 1991. "Configuring the user: The case of usability trials." In *A sociology of monsters: Essays on power, technology and domination,* ed. J. Law, 58–97. London: Routledge.

CHAPTER 13

Viable Alternatives for Commercialized Science

THE CASE OF HUMANISTICS

Harry Kunneman

1. Introduction

IN THIS CHAPTER I try to heed Hans Radder's suggestion, formulated in the introduction to this book, to address "viable alternatives for commercialized science." To this end I focus on humanistics as a new discipline, situated at the crossroads of the social sciences and the humanities. This discipline tries to connect two different types of questions. On the one hand questions in the domain of existential meaning and the "art of living," on the other questions concerning the humanization of institutions and organizations. I will argue that the case of humanistics is highly interesting for the central theme of this book, because this new discipline tries to *combine* different forms of knowledge and insight, both cognitive and moral, on the level of concrete practices. To illustrate the wider relevance of this local effort, I will first address the question why alternatives are needed anyway. What's wrong with the commercialization of the sciences?

From the contributions to this book three different answers to this question can be distilled. In the first place the commercialization of science is perceived as a threat to the *epistemic autonomy* of science. When this autonomy is undermined by commercial influences, both the agenda of scientific research threatens to be dominated by themes and avenues promising economic benefit, and the methodological standards of science run the risk of being corrupted by commercial interests. In the second place, the commercialization of science is perceived as a threat to *academic culture*. The growing influence of an "entrepreneurial ethos" within the academy entails the marginalization of "critical voices." This poses not only a threat to the Mertonian value of "organized skepticism" within academia, but also contributes to the curtailment of critical voices on the level of public debate: "instead of educating for citizenship, we will educate for the market" as Daniel Kleinman says. Finally, the commercialization of science threatens to undermine the *social responsibility* of modern science, its responsibility for the alleviation of human suffering by addressing themes of *general* social interest, irrespective of commercial gain.

These different perceptions of the main threats connected with the commercialization of science, show an interesting common characteristic. Almost all of the contributions to this book focus on the natural sciences, including biology and medicine, as the main areas where the commercialization of science and the concomitant risks are manifesting themselves. At the same time they draw primarily on the social sciences and the humanities (especially sociology, political economy, philosophy, and ethics) as the main *resources* for critical analysis. This focus on the natural sciences is, of course, not accidental. Historically, the values jeopardized by the three different risks outlined above, are primarily embodied by the natural sciences. Both the high standards and the high hopes of Enlightenment thinkers with regard to the autonomy of the sciences and their beneficial potential for humankind at large, are anchored in the example of Newtonian mechanics, and the greatest part of modern philosophy of science, from Russell and Whitehead, to Carnap, Popper, Hempel, Kuhn, and Lakatos, focuses first and foremost on the natural sciences as the primary embodiment of scientific rationality. The same goes for the extensive debates within the social sciences and the humanities—from the nineteenth century until the present day—on the appropriateness of the example of the natural sciences for the specific questions and problems at stake in the human sciences. It is no exaggeration to state that all attempts to develop an *alternative* view of scientific rationality deviating in important respects from the example of the natural sciences but claiming equal scientific status have failed dramatically. Neither the "dialectical method," nor the hermeneutic approach, nor Habermas's communicative model of rationality—to cite but a few important examples—has ever reached a status and influence within the human sciences comparable to the great example of modern science "proper."

Seen in this light, most contributions to this book show an interesting inner tension. On one hand they try to defend the autonomy of science, the academic culture of modern universities and the social responsibility of science against the general background of Enlightenment thinking; on the other hand they take recourse to values that are deemed to be *embodied* by modern science before it got to be thoroughly commercialized, but that cannot be *upheld* by these sciences on their own. The chapters by Kleinman, Resnik, Radder, and van den Belt, for instance, explicitly refer to values and norms embodied by the ideal of autonomous and socially responsible science, which *should* be upheld, but they fail to specify the moral resources upon which we could draw to accomplish this feat.

This inner tension points to an important lesson to be drawn from their critical analyses and to one of the central theses of this chapter: the commercialization of the sciences cannot be effectively combated with the help of scientific rationality itself; "viable alternatives" for commercialized science will remain in the dark as long as the natural sciences keep providing the (explicit or implicit) *standard* for valid knowledge. Stated otherwise, the lack of effective resistance from the side of the academy against the commercialization of science, its *defenselessness* against the undermining of its time-honored values, signals in my eyes the need to embed these values in a *wider* moral, and epistemic, framework beyond the central premises of Enlightenment thinking.

2. The Millennium-Goals and Mode-2 Science

2.1. The Example of China

As a first step toward the elucidation of these theses, I want to point to the recent economic success of China, which seems to be based on the combination of widely available cheap labor, a state-controlled market economy, and massive investments in higher education, market-oriented scientific research, and technological innovation. The commercialization of science within the framework of a capitalist economy, as analyzed in most contributions to this book, finds its counterpart here in a state-controlled instrumentalization of science and technology for economic and political goals.

Remarkable about this instrumentalization is the fact that it is so successful. To take but one example: in the field of biotechnology and genomics, Chinese scientists operate at the frontier of international research. In a situation where, to a great extent, research agendas are steered "from above" in directions that promise to lead to economically profitable results, nevertheless "real scientific progress" seems to be possible, in the sense specified, for instance, by Imre Lakatos (Lakatos and Musgrave 1970). Thus, at first sight the example of China seems to corroborate the thesis formulated in Martin Carrier's contribution to this book. According to Carrier, commercialized science "need not suffer from a methodological decline. . . . Technological intervention is achieved best by relying on knowledge that has passed tough standards of quality control." In the light not only of the undemocratic and authoritarian character of the Chinese one-party system and the concomitant violation of central human rights but also in the light of the massive contribution of China to worldwide environmental problems, it seems clear that in the case of China, this "tough quality control" is limited to epistemic progress and technological applications and does not extend to the critical potential of the sciences nor to their contribution to themes of *general* social interest, irrespective of commercial gain.

Formulated in terms of the three risks connected with the commercialization of science, this suggests an important difference between the first risk, the undermining of the epistemic autonomy of science, and the two other risks. The commercialization and instrumentalization of the sciences, which seems to be the rule in all developed and developing countries, does not necessarily threaten what we could call the *epistemic productiveness* of science, because—as Carrier rightly argues, in my eyes—the realization of commercial goals remains dependent up to a point upon more "fundamental," Lakatosian research programs and the concomitant "internal" forms of scientific quality control. But the contribution of science to the alleviation of human suffering, irrespective of commercial goals, and responsible citizenship surely are undermined and marginalized by the commercialization and instrumentalization of scientific research.

This implies, in my view, that Carrier's more or less optimistic conclusion with regard to the commercialization of science does not hold. Carrier not only ignores the second risk—the undermining of "academic culture" and the marginalization of critical voices in academia—but also trivializes the third risk by presenting state-financed and state-monitored research with regard to themes of more general social interest as the solution for this problem. His reliance on the state, or on cooperative efforts by different states, to finance and monitor scientific research with regard to central causes of human suffering appears to be quite naïve, as transpires for instance from the example of the millennium goals and the sorry state these goals find themselves in halfway to the pivotal date of 2015. In a recent interview Kemal Dervis (who is in charge of the UN organization responsible for the realization of the millennium goals, the UNDP) comments on the fact that world leaders pledged in 2005 to double their efforts with regard to these goals, while in 2006 the investments were in fact even less than in 2005: "I really do not understand why they spend ten times as much on weapons as on the millennium goals. How can 300 more military airplanes help to alleviate the great threats of our times? This is not rational" (Dervis 2007). The same could be said about the massive investments in scientific research directed at the prolongation of the life of the rich minority in our world and the comparatively modest investments into research aiming to ameliorate the chances of the majority of the citizens of the present-day world society to survive their early days.

2.2. Mode-1 and Mode-2 Knowledge

This situation can be further clarified with the help of the well-known distinction between mode-1 and mode-2 knowledge, introduced by Gibbons et al. (1994). This distinction articulates a far-reaching change in the mode of production of scientific knowledge, which has been analyzed under different headings by many contemporary philosophers and sociologists of science such as Lyotard (1984), Latour (1987), Collins and Pinch (1998), Grint and Woolgar (1997), and Nowotny, Scott, and Gibbons (2001). The common focus of these different analyses is the social embedment of scientific knowledge, which is analyzed from different but related angles. In the first place, according to these authors, scientific research is embedded in cultural frameworks, or "grand narratives," as Lyotard has it, providing a legitimation for its importance and social significance. In the second place, scientific research is dependent upon forms of financial support which are connected with economic and political power structures and which heavily influence the agenda of scientific communities. In the third place, in present-day postindustrial societies, scientific research is intertwined with, and furthers the spread of, a technological culture characterized by a high level of trust in the possibility of controlling ever more aspects of daily life and a concomitant focus on permanent technological innovation. By focusing on the social embedment of science and the complex web of interactions between scientific and technological developments, cultural frameworks, and economic and political interests, most of these analyses tend to blur the classic distinction between the context of discovery and the context of justification and interpret scientific knowledge not as a representation of an objective reality, but as a historically situated social construction. Thus they raise serious doubts as to the epistemic autonomy of scientific research.

In my view these doubts are justified up to a point, but they also run the risk of throwing away the baby with the bathwater. To save the baby it is necessary to do justice both to the social embedment of scientific research and to the possibility and importance of a certain measure of epistemic autonomy of the sciences.

The distinction between different modes of production of scientific knowledge introduced by Gibbons et al. (1994) makes this possible. Mode-1 science refers to kinds of scientific research regulated by procedures for quality control that are under the direction of a specific scientific community. Gibbons et al. define the relative autonomy characterizing mode-1 research primarily in terms of sociological criteria, especially the monopolization of quality control by "academic" communities by way of peer reviewing. In this way, however, the *epistemic* grounds for the specific "productiveness" of mode-1 research, as underlined by Carrier, tend to fade into the background. These epistemic grounds are connected with the focus on deep structures underlying perceived phenomena and on the articulation of universal principles characterizing mode-1 research. This focus differs markedly from the central concerns of another type of socially embedded scientific research, designated by Gibbons et al. as mode-2 science, which in their view has become the dominant way of production of scientific knowledge in the last decades of the twentieth century. Mode-2 science is characterized by mixed forms of agenda setting and hybrid, "transdisciplinary" forms of quality control: apart from the different scientific communities involved, other parties have a *legitimate* stake in the agenda and the outcome of research efforts and thus openly influence the course of scientific research and the evaluation of its results. Thus we could say that whereas mode-1 is characterized by a high degree of epistemic autonomy of scientific research, mode-2 is characterized by a certain degree of epistemic heteronomy. This epistemic heteronomy hinges upon the *practical aims* of mode-2 science: this mode of production of scientific knowledge is geared to the solution of practical problems and is thus intimately bound up with technological construction and innovation. Gibbons et al. correctly stress, however, that mode-2 science should not be understood in terms of the *application* of mode-1 theories or insights. Although mode-2 science is in many ways dependent upon insights stemming from mode-1, it involves the development of *new* knowledge, which can also be fed back into mode-1. The epistemic heteronomy of mode-2 science not only goes back to the influence exerted on agenda setting and evaluation by third parties, such as pharmaceutical companies, or religious groups and NGOs in the field of genomics; the heteronomy characterizing mode-2 in comparison with the relative epistemic autonomy of mode-1 science is also related to the multi- and interdisciplinary character of mode-2 science and to the construction of new, hybrid fields of research and technological innovation: different conceptual traditions, different research agendas, and different criteria for evaluation stemming from different disciplinary traditions are interconnected in the production of mode-2 knowledge against the horizon of their contribution to the solution of specific practical problems.

2.3. Mixed Forms of Quality Control

Against this background I can now return to the contribution of Carrier to this book, especially to his thesis that commercialized science "need not suffer from a methodological decline. . . . Technological intervention is achieved best by relying on knowledge that has passed tough standards of quality control." In terms of the distinction between mode-1 and mode-2, both the merits and the limitations of this thesis can now be analyzed more precisely. In view of the *dependence* of mode-2 on mode-1 insights, "tough standards of quality control" certainly play a role in the context of mode-2 science. This form of science is characterized, however, by *mixed* forms of quality control, among which short-term expectations of financial return on investments take a prominent part. As a consequence, the "toughness" of the quality control in the domain of mode-2 science is considerably "softened" by considerations rooted in commercial and political interests. These considerations introduce a *different* kind of "tough quality control," by blocking or discontinuing lines of scientific research, which could be very interesting and worthwhile on the basis of a mode-1 agenda but are not pursued because they do not promise to yield interesting results for the military or commercial purposes, or only in the very long run. The same goes for the influence of religious beliefs, for instance, in the case of stem cell research in the United States, or for the moral and political perspectives of radical NGOs opposing genetic manipulation of crops. Thus, these religious beliefs and political perspectives introduce "tough" forms of control of scientific research on the basis of evaluative criteria differing markedly from those envisaged by Carrier.

With the help of the distinction between mode-1 and mode-2, also a second, more severe limitation of Carrier's perspective can be elucidated. This limitation concerns the other two risks connected with the commercialization of the sciences. These risks pertain to the undermining of academic culture, to the curtailing of critical voices, and to the neglect of themes of general social interest, irrespective of commercial gain. These two risks are clearly enhanced by the spread of mode-2 forms of science and the concomitant changes on the level of academic culture. Students can be trained effectively in a mixture of mode-1 and mode-2 science *without* being educated for responsible citizenship, as the example of China testifies; furthermore, mode-2 science can be, and is in fact, massively steered toward specific commercial and military goals, while largely ignoring questions of more general interest, as exemplified by the sorry state of the millennium goals.

2.4. Complexity

Here we reach the heart of the problem. As long as mode-1 forms of research and the epistemic quality criteria connected with them are—explicitly or implicitly—considered as the ultimate standard for "proper science," the risks connected with the rise of mode-2 science and the concomitant commercialization and instrumentalization of scientific knowledge can only be combated by subjugating mode-2 science some way or other to the standards for mode-1 science. Such a project is not only unpromising on empirical grounds, but also for principle reasons, especially the fact that mode-2 science is characterized by a different *ontological* framework. The search for deep structures underlying perceived phenomena and the articulation of universal principles that characterize mode-1 research, has only a limited significance here, because most of the problems addressed by mode-2 research pertain to *complex* systems and complex phenomena.

Following Cilliers (1998, 2005) and Morin (2008), I define complex systems as open, situated systems consisting of many components and displaying *emergent* behavior, that is, "behavior that results from the *interaction* between components and not from characteristics inherent to the components themselves" (Cilliers 1998, 5). Due to this last characteristic, relations between the components and between subsystems of complex systems are nonlinear and can only be partially modeled with the help of laws and algorithms. Thus, in the case of complex systems, the search for deep structures and for universal principles encounters *ontological* limits. Because complex systems are open and dynamic and develop in interaction with dynamic environments, they exhibit both "robustness," as Cilliers says, and emergent forms of renewal and innovation, which interact with, and potentially change, the robust parts of the system. The emergence of modern science itself and its interaction with deep-seated religious belief systems during the last centuries provides a good example of this dynamic. The same goes for the expansion of the universe we live in. This expansion certainly results from the fundamental laws governing it, but within contemporary astrophysics it is an open question whether this expansion will go on indefinitely, or at some point a "big crunch" will occur as a kind of inverse of the "big bang" giving birth to the universe.

As this example illustrates, my characterization of complex systems does not exclude the possibility that complex systems also exhibit deep structures, nor the possibility to describe those in terms of universal principles. It does imply, however, the *partial* character of such descriptions. Because of their openness and their ability to develop new characteristics and new forms of emergent behavior—because of their "historicity"—complex systems always contain a potential for *exceeding* the "fundamental" characteristics contained in their "deep structures."

Following a suggestion by Morin, Cilliers has tried to elucidate this important point by distinguishing between "restricted complexity" and "general complexity." The notion of restricted complexity designates those approaches to complex systems that developed primarily from chaos theory and fractal mathematics and aim to uncover underlying patterns or deep structures and formulate universal principles regulating the behavior and development of all complex systems. The work of Stuart Kauffman and other members of the Santa Fe Institute provides the most influential example of this approach (Kauffmann 1995, 2000). According to Morin and Cilliers, this approach remains bound to the "reductive paradigm" characterizing classical science. As Morin has it, "Restricted complexity made . . . possible important advances in formalization, in the possibility of modeling. . . . But one still remains within the epistemology of classical science. When one searches for the 'laws of complexity,' one still attaches complexity as a kind of wagon behind the truth locomotive, that which produces laws" (Morin 2008, 10). Over and against this restricted form of modeling the complexity of complex systems, Morin and Cilliers define "general complexity" as an approach that accepts that all models of complex systems are limited *in principle:* the only "model" which would adequately represent the complexity of a complex system would be the system itself. All models of complex systems decompose them in specific ways, dependent upon the position and perspective of the observer. As Cilliers puts it,

> the knowledge gained by any description is always relative to the perspective from which the description was made. This does not imply that any description is as good as any other. It is merely the result of the fact that only a limited number of characteristics of the system can be taken into account by any specific description. Although there is no *a priori* procedure for deciding which description is correct, some descriptions will deliver more interesting results than others. (Cilliers 2005, 6; see also Cilliers 1998, passim)

This difference between restricted and general complexity sheds more light on an important characteristic of mode-2 science, distinguishing it from mode-1. Gibbons et al. (1994) state that mode-2 is characterized by the fact that different *stakeholders* are involved in the evaluation of the results of scientific research. Following Cilliers we can now add that mode-2 science in most cases concerns complex systems and complex problems, allowing for different forms of modeling and different descriptions, some of which "will deliver more *interesting* results than others." Seen in this way, mode-2 science is characterized by the concurrence of different legitimate descriptions of the problems involved, connected with different interests and values. That is to say, the notion of a "true" description has only a limited significance here, because other legitimate descriptions are possible, which do not focus on a true description of underlying deep structures, but reflect all kinds of pragmatic interests. In other words, the complexity of the problems taking central stage in mode-2 science is internally connected with the fact that the realities involved are *modeled* in different ways at the same time. Thus, the ontological complexity involved also goes back to the fact that the "mode of being" of the complex systems and complex problems at stake is characterized by self-modeling or self-interpretation. Within contemporary sociology this problem is designated as the "double hermeneutics" involved in the validation of sociological theories and concepts: on the one hand is the validation within the scientific community of sociologists, a process that is dependent upon hermeneutic forms of understanding; on the other hand is the reinterpretation by social scientists of concepts stemming from concrete, historically situated life-worlds: "Sociology deals with a universe which is already constituted within frames of meaning by social actors themselves. . . . This double hermeneutic is of considerable complexity, since the connection is not merely a one-way one . . . there is continual 'slippage' of the concepts constructed in sociology" (Giddens 1976, 162; Habermas 1981; Kunneman and de Vries 1991). Transplanted to mode-2 science in general, this line of thought would imply the complex interplay of at least three different forms of modeling of practical problems and the realities involved: the search for deep structures, economic and political interests, and hermeneutical frameworks involving values and meaning.

2.5. The Example of Psychiatry

A good example of this complexity is provided by contemporary psychiatry, a discipline exhibiting very clearly the dynamics and dilemmas of mode-2 science. During the last decades psychiatry has clearly benefited from mode-1 advances in neurobiology and the development of new pharmaceutical means for treating mental illness. The new "biological" psychiatry has been severely criticized, however, for disregarding the social embedding of psychiatric problems and all questions concerning possibilities for a meaning-full life and the maintenance of self-respect confronted by patients suffering from mental illness. Moreover, pharmaceutical research in this field is heavily influenced by commercial interests.

The concurrence of, and conflicts between, these different forms of modeling psychic problems and ways to deal with them are reflected very clearly in contemporary debates concerning *DSM-IV,* the *Diagnostic and Statistical Manual of Mental Disorders,* providing the dominant standard for psychiatric diagnoses all over the world. In an interesting analysis of the scientific status of psychiatry as a mode-2 oriented discipline, the Dutch psychiatrist Kortmann distinguishes five different types of diagnosis to be found in this manual (Kortmann 2007):

- Type 1 diagnoses refer to psychiatric problems with an undisputed somatic background, characterized by symptoms for which reliable and valid measuring instruments are available with a high sensitivity and a high specificity.

- Type 2 diagnoses are characterized by Kortmann as "patho-physiological diagnoses," which are based on physiological parameters. A characteristic for this type of diagnosis is a fleeting transition from illness to health, for instance, a delirium caused by abstention from a drug or from alcohol.

- Type 3 diagnoses are made on the basis of the presence of characteristic symptoms, such as lack of energy, concentration difficulties, loss of appetite, and sleeplessness, together pointing toward a depression. In contrast with the first two, this third type of diagnosis rests at least in part on experiences and interpretations from the side of patients and/or their surroundings.

- Type 4 diagnoses rest on a cluster of symptoms relating to different dimensions of experiencing and acting and thus having a complex character. Typical examples are schizophrenia, borderline personality disorders, and post-traumatic stress disorders.

- Type 5 diagnoses refer to problematic behavior with a psychosocial background. The characteristics are not sharply delineated, and there is no clear boundary separating problematic from "normal" behavior. A typical example would be an adjustment disorder accompanied by an anxious or depressive mood due to severe trouble at work or a crisis in a marriage.

Put in terms of mode-1 and mode-2 knowledge, the "mode-1 backing" of these different types of diagnoses diminishes when moving from type 1 to type 5; and their mode-2 character gets progressively stronger. An important transition point is situated between type 2 and type 3: at this point experiences and interpretations from the side of patients and/or their surroundings come into play and, in their wake, specific cultural frameworks, social relations, and interests informing these interpretations. The influence of these cultural frameworks and the interests connected with them are strongest in type 5 diagnoses. An interesting example of the interplay of different forms of mode-2 modeling, and of the risks connected with this interplay, is provided by the diagnostic category "passive-aggressive personality disorder," which figured prominently in the third edition of *DSM,* but was removed in the fourth edition under effective pressure of the feminist movement in the United States. This pressure was based on the remarkable fact that this diagnosis was "awarded" almost exclusively to women, while the classificatory system of *DSM* pretended to be gender neutral (Kortmann 2007, 61).

2.6. A Third Mode of Knowledge Acquisition

In the introduction I said that "viable alternatives for commercialized science" will remain in the dark as long as the natural sciences keep providing the (explicit or implicit) *standard* for valid knowledge. However, the complete rejection of the modern standards for rational knowledge by the different brands of social constructivism will not help either. In my view social constructivists rightly stress the massive incorporation of present-day scientific knowledge into processes of social and economic reproduction and its entanglement with relations of power. However, instead of doing away with the notion of truth and epistemic progress altogether, distinguishing between different modes of scientific knowledge as illustrated above offers the opportunity to do justice both to the social embedding of all forms of scientific knowledge and to the epistemic productivity of the *specific* form of social embedding exemplified by mode-1 science. This specific mode of "production" of scientific knowledge is also dependent upon power relations, financial resources, and forms of cultural and political legitimation. But the strict limitation of the stakeholders legitimately involved in the evaluation of knowledge claims, in combination with the search for underlying patterns and deep structures from a perspective of "restricted complexity," results in a specific, very valuable form of epistemic productivity. However, this "classical" epistemological perspective, so dear to many Enlightenment thinkers, becomes ideological and even dangerous when it is installed as the overriding standard for all forms and modes of science or for all forms of knowledge in general. As documented in most chapters of this book, the majority of scientific work in our time no longer corresponds to the classical mode-1 perspective but is characterized instead by mixed forms of quality control, connected with (often) conflicting interests and with different forms of modeling the complex systems and complex problems addressed in mode-2 scientific research. This development clearly entails new risks: not only the risk that short-term economic and political interests will progressively diminish the space and support for mode-1 research, but also the curtailment of critical voices under influence of market-oriented research and the undermining of the social responsibility of modern science.

Against this background, it is my central contention that, in order to alleviate these risks and to develop viable alternatives for commercialized science, we can no longer fall back on the standards for rational knowledge embodied in modern science and articulated in Enlightenment thought. Instead of vainly trying to purify mode-2 science from interests and values, we should acknowledge the complexity of the practical problems confronted by present-day scientists, engineers, and professionals. This complexity stems from the *interplay* between emergent properties of complex systems and situations and the role of interests and values in "defining" the principal characteristics of these systems and situations. Because of this interplay, advocating a reductionist research program with regard to complex systems becomes *itself* an interested, value-laden position. When interests and values cannot be separated from cognitive models of complex systems, as is the case in all forms of mode-2 science, the only responsible way to deal with conflicting claims with regard to the problems at hand is to try and maximize knowledge and insight in *both respects:* not only with regard to the cognitive models involved, but also with regard to the interests and values at stake. This implies that the development of viable alternatives to commercialized science asks for two different but complementary forms of learning and insight: (1) cognitive learning processes after the model of mode-1 science, and (2) existential and moral learning processes with regard to the interests and values at stake in the definition of problems and possible solutions in the context of mode-2 science. I have dubbed the results of such existential and moral learning processes in the context of mode-2 science "mode-3 knowledge" (Kunneman 2005; 2007). The development of viable alternatives to commercialized science thus asks in my view for a combination of mode-1 and mode-3 knowledge within mode-2 practices. To elucidate the specific characteristics, possibilities, and pitfalls of mode-3 knowledge, I turn to the example of humanistics.

3. Mode 3 Knowledge Illustrated with the Example of Humanistics

3.1. Humane Values

To elucidate the notion of mode-3 knowledge and its relevance for the development of alternatives for commercialized science, I now turn to humanistics as an instructive example of a new discipline in which mode-3 knowledge development plays an important role. To forego possible misunderstandings, I add that I could equally well have used other examples to illustrate the characteristics of mode-3 knowledge, such as ecology or psychiatry or colonial studies. I use humanistics as an example, however, because due to its peculiar history, central characteristics of mode-3 knowledge are exemplified in humanistics with great clarity.

The University for Humanistics (located in Utrecht) is a small, independent, state-financed university which is fully integrated into the Dutch university system, including the procedures monitored by the Dutch Ministry of Education for scientific quality control. It was founded in 1990 to provide a six-year academic training for humanist counselors and to conduct scientific research in the domains of existential meaning and the humanization of society. The fact that this humanist university is financed by the state goes back to the peculiarities of the Dutch "pillar system." The metaphor of the "pillar system"—coined by the Dutch social scientist A. Lijphart (1968)—designates the specific social and political arrangement that took shape in Dutch society from the beginning of the twentieth century onward and reached its height after the Second World War. The main characteristic of this pillar system was the concurrence of a high degree of segregation between different religious and political groups, the different "pillars," and a high degree of political integration of these groups in a jointly supported political arrangement, which secured financial state support for all of them in a broad range of domains. The most important of these was the domain of education, where the main religious traditions within Dutch society secured the right to state-financed "special education" from the level of basic school up to universities, where (within general educational frameworks laid down by the Ministry of Education) their own religious belief informed, up to a point, both the form and the content of the educational programs. After the Second World War, the growing group of nonreligious people within Dutch society organized themselves within the Humanistisch Verbond and started a long struggle to secure official recognition for humanism as a worldview in its own right, on a par with religious worldviews. The first domain where this struggle had any success was the Dutch army, where in the 1950s a few humanist counselors were commissioned to support the growing number of nonreligiously affiliated military with respect to existential and ethical questions. In the course of time the number of humanist counselors grew steadily and the emerging profession spread to other domains, especially prisons, hospitals, and homes for the elderly. This process of professionalization was supported and enhanced by special training courses, first on a voluntary basis, from the 1970s onward in the form of a state-supported, three-year educational course. Within the different domains where humanist counselors were employed, they collaborated mainly with religious counselors who had received academic training at a theological faculty within one of the state-financed Catholic or Protestant universities. On the basis of the principle of equal rights for religious and nonreligious worldviews, finally in 1989 the (Christian!) Minister of Education decided to finance a small, independent humanist university dedicated to the academic and practical training of humanist counselors and to conduct research in existential questions and the humanization of society, against the background of humanist traditions in philosophy, the social sciences, and the humanities.

This peculiar history provided a unique opportunity for the interdisciplinary group of researchers and teachers involved (totaling some fifty staff members at the start) to develop a new, practically oriented discipline at the crossroads of the social sciences and the humanities. In terms of the distinction between mode-1 and mode-2 knowledge, humanistics was conceived from the start as a discipline devoted to the development of mode-2 knowledge, building on mode-1 insights from the social sciences and the humanities. Instead of being oriented toward commercial interests, however, research at the University for Humanistics is explicitly guided by "humane values," as articulated within humanist philosophical and scientific traditions, but also within literary traditions and within the great religious and spiritual traditions. Because we specialize in the academic and practical training of humanist counselors, our research is also informed by the *practice* of humanist counseling, especially by the values embodied in this practice and the experiences and feedback from the clients involved in domains such as hospitals, prisons, homes for the elderly, education, and the army.

3.2. Slow Questions

These practical experiences and the concomitant values provide a good starting point for the elucidation of a first, very important characteristic of mode-3 knowledge. These values are internally connected with the type of questions humanist counselors are confronted with from the side of their clients. These can be metaphorically characterized as "slow questions" (Kunneman 2005). These types of questions are grouped around two focal points. In the first place they are connected with the *fragility* and *finitude* of human bodies and of human persons. This fragility manifests itself primarily in experiences of loss and powerlessness. Such experiences are often connected with serious injuries and illness or with the prospect of death of oneself or beloved others. They can also stem from relational domains, however, for instance, in the form of deep conflicts between children and parents, or between siblings, or a relationship or marriage going wrong notwithstanding sincere efforts to keep it going, or problems at work resulting in burnout. In many cases such problems can be remedied up to a point with the help of "fast" technical means, such as medical interventions, cognitive therapies, or psychopharmaceutical means. Such "fast" remedies often leave an "existential residue," however, which cannot be completely absorbed with the help of objective knowledge and technical means. An example would be a diagnosis of breast cancer and the decision to amputate a breast and to apply chemotherapeutic treatment of the cancer. Even if this would lead to a fast healing process in the somatic register, it would nevertheless engender slow questions, connected, for instance, with the risk of return of the cancer and the mourning of lost beauty. An important characteristic of slow questions is thus the confrontation with the limits of fast, technical solutions and the necessity to "muddle through," to apply oneself to the "labor of mourning," to try and rewrite to a certain extent one's life history and envisage alternative ways to lead a meaningful life.

The confrontation with slow questions also brings moral questions into play, related primarily to questions of dependence, help and care, or indifference and desertion coming from one's surroundings. Slow questions of one person, we could say, always imply moral challenges and dilemmas for others. Here we touch upon the second focal point around which slow questions are grouped, apart from the confrontation with finitude, namely the confrontation with our own moral limitations and moral possibilities (and those of others around us) manifesting themselves, for instance, in indifference for the fate and suffering of others or in outright hostile and violent actions toward them, or again in forms of care, support, and commitment. Humanist counselors are confronted with these types of slow questions, for instance, in the form of loneliness in homes for the elderly and concomitant existential questions and moral dilemmas of the children or relatives of the elderly people involved; or in the form of repressed or acknowledged feelings of guilt and remorse of prisoners; or of the moral doubts and existential bewilderment of soldiers with incisive combat experiences and the inability of their friends and family to understand their bewilderment and underlying existential questions.

Against this background, the most important value-laden premise of humanist counseling concerns the ability of human beings to engage in forms of "narrative self-exploration" when confronted with slow questions (Hoogeveen 1996; Jorna 1997; Mooren 1999; Kunneman 2005). As the combination of the notions "narrative" and "self" indicates already, this exploration concerns a "territory" consisting of different, dynamically interacting layers comprising both past and present-day experiences of individuals and possible causal chains connected with them, cultural frameworks providing an interpretative foil for these experiences, and the "interpretative identity-work" of the people involved. Generally speaking, the confrontation with slow questions also involves a confrontation with the interpretative *limits* of the cultural frameworks articulating the contents of a "normal" meaningful life: one is confronted with a change in the course of one's life history, which seriously threatens its "narratability" as a normal, worthwhile, and meaningful life, both to oneself and to others. Confronted with slow questions, one has to reconsider one's taken-for-granted identity and reconfigure the further course of one's life history without much help from the dominant cultural frameworks, or even in opposition to them. This goes especially for all the images of control—success, self-sufficiency, and "existential speed"—connected with present-day consumer society and neoliberal individualism. The confrontation with slow questions thus involves a confrontation with the existential and moral limits of modernism, especially the limits of the scientific worldview projecting our world as a field of unlimited technological control in the service of freely defined values of autonomous individuals. Thus, this confrontation entails the painful realization that one cannot choose freely, that one's world cannot be controlled with technological means and, moreover, that one is *dependent upon others* to wrestle new meaning from the situation one finds oneself in.

Against this background, I deem it very significant that the professional quality of the support given by humanist counselors in such situations is not primarily guided by a horizon of true knowledge and the search for deep structures of reality, but by a horizon of *moral values* and concomitant existential and moral insights. Central among these values are *respect* for the other as a unique individual, sincere *emotional involvement* with the questions clients struggle with, a clear *awareness* of processes of transference and countertransference, and *trust* in the possibility of narrative self-exploration. These values are not so much espoused as *enacted* by humanist counselors. In a reflection on her work as a humanist counselor in a big hospital, Elly Hoogeveen formulates the bottom line of humanist counseling as follows:

> You should not abandon a client; not even when the other communicates that everybody should go away. As counselor you can feel desperate with someone like this, because you receive nothing back. Still, it is important also in this situation to perform the quality of staying with the other—right through your own fear of being rejected. The other can then feel my relating to the total impasse she finds herself in, where I could also be. This form of relating can possibly help the other. (Hoogeveen, in Jorna 1997, 38–39)

This not-walking-away from insoluble suffering, but staying with the other also when nothing meaningful can be said, and sharing "the total impasse" up to a point, can be considered as the bottom line of humanist counseling. In many cases, however, the confrontation with slow questions does not involve the apparent loss of all meaning, but the necessity to reconsider and reevaluate taken-for-granted meanings and search for a new horizon and for words, metaphors, and ideas pointing toward such a horizon.

Marion Ragetlie, a humanist counselor also working in a hospital setting, describes the way in which she supports the process of narrative self-exploration:

> By telling stories, people construct meaningful relations in the here and now. The art of humanist counseling consists among other things in the ability to shape conversations in such a way that clients are helped to experience these meanings in the act of relating stories, to "find" these meanings among the multitude of anecdotes, feelings and evaluations contained in their stories. To this end I point to relations between elements from their stories; if need be I articulate underlying emotions; I reinforce emergent ideas with regard to which clients feel hesitant or shy away from; I bring questions to the fore, in order to help the client to check what she says with the reality as she experiences it; I bring dilemmas and contradictions into the spotlight, especially when they seem to refer to unresolved conflicts or stagnating decisions, and I focus on giving words to specific elements of their frame of reference. (Ragetlie, in Jorna 1997, 69–70)

In some (but certainly not all, or even most, cases) such processes of narrative self-exploration can lead to self-clarification, to a deepening of insight of clients into their own life histories, and to a richer vision on the possible ingredients of a meaningful life. Hoogeveen describes this emergence of deeper self-insight and new meaning as follows: "To my surprise, with wonder and admiration, I see how people suddenly admit something to themselves, that life also has another side to it than only this grotesque and disgusting side they are confronted with in their situation. And then you see the emergence of a certain healing. Every time you see this, it is almost art" (Hoogeveen, in Jorna 1997, 37).

3.3. Co-Creation as a Central Characteristic of Mode-3 Knowledge

These descriptions not only illuminate central characteristics of humanist counseling, but also contain important clues for the elucidation of mode-3 knowledge. The insights that can emerge in humanist counseling and in related forms of psychotherapy are not derived from mode-1 knowledge to which the professionals involved have a privileged access. Instead they are the result of a process of *co-creation,* made possible by the *moral quality* of the relation between the people involved. Research into experiences of clients with humanist counseling and related forms of professional support reveals that values such as respect, involvement, and trust take central stage in their evaluation of the quality of counseling (Hoogeveen 1996; Baart 2004). These findings are consonant with the results of recent research into the effectiveness of different psychotherapeutic models. The quality of the therapeutic relation as experienced by clients ("alliance") and their belief in the specific model or paradigm used by therapists ("allegiance"), are more important for the outcome than the model itself. The same goes for the personal characteristics of therapists, their general or a-specific "healing capacity": these characteristics have much more influence on the outcome of therapies than the disciplinary or paradigmatic background and the experience of therapists. According to the results of recent research, the most important contribution to the successful outcome of psychotherapy is provided by the resources of the clients themselves, their "self-healing capacity" and the ability of therapists to respect and support these capacities (Miller, Duncan, and Hubble 2004).

Kortmann's analysis of the different types of diagnosis involved in *DSM-IV,* referred to above, can help to elucidate further the specific type of knowledge and insight involved in humanist counseling and dialogically structured forms of psychotherapy. To be sure, just like psychiatrists, counselors also make use of knowledge and insights with a relatively strong mode-1 backing, for instance, concerning psychopathological symptoms that would necessitate cooperation with a psychiatrist; or sociological insights into the individual consequences of the unequal distribution of cultural capital among different social groups in Dutch society; or feminist insights concerning the possible consequences of the "double burden" confronting many women in present-day postindustrial societies: both work and care for children and partners. But the main thrust of their professional expertise lies in other registers: in the first place in the register of *embodied* and enacted moral qualities, and in the second place in the register of *existential* and *moral* insights, based on the interplay between, on the one hand, their own, unfolding life histories and their past confrontations with slow questions and, on the other, the insights concerning meaningful ways to confront slow questions and moral dilemmas embodied in philosophical and literary traditions, in the great religious and spiritual traditions, and within the broad range of humanist traditions (Said 2004).

3.4. The Seductive Power of Modern Technology

Of course, seen from the perspective of modern science "proper," such insights belong to the domain of subjective convictions and irrational opinions. "Proper" science can only flourish when it is shielded as best as possible from such influences and radically purified from them when they infiltrate the domain of scientific research. However, maybe we have to face the disconcerting fact that this "purifying perspective" has only a limited value nowadays, because it stems from a bygone era in which modern science had to secure its own "free space" within specific social and cultural surroundings dominated by bitter fights and oppositions between religious worldviews with absolutist pretensions, as Stephen Toulmin has argued in his book *Cosmopolis* (Toulmin 1990). Without doubt such bitter fights and the concomitant absolutist pretensions are still very much with us in present-day world society. But as this book testifies, in our days the main risks confronting scientific rationality and the values connected with it no longer stem from absolutist religious worldviews but are connected with the commercialization and instrumentalization of science by "worldly powers."

It is important to realize that these worldly powers not only include the powers exerted by the financial interests of big corporations and shareholders and the political interests of powerful nations, but also the *seductive power* exerted by modern technology itself, especially its promise to do away completely with slow questions, to secure unlimited economic growth for everyone, and to solve all our problems in the domain of health and personal happiness with the help of technical means and professional expertise. It is this seductive power which in my view provides the main energetic thrust for the commercialization and instrumentalization of science. This thrust cannot be countered by trying to purify science from the different form of instrumentalization characterizing mode-2, because this thrust gets its energy from deep existential sources: from the phantasm of doing away with all slow questions and exerting unlimited control over our lives and our happiness.

So I suggest that instead of vainly trying to reduce the influence of commercial interests on the level of mode-2 science, we should delve deeper and directly address the existential and moral questions underlying the seductive power of commercialized science and technology. As I suggested in the introduction to this chapter, the commercialization of the sciences cannot be combated with the help of scientific rationality alone, as embodied in mode-1 knowledge acquisition. Viable alternatives for commercialized science will remain in the dark as long as the natural sciences keep providing the (explicit or implicit) *standard* for valid knowledge. Such alternatives, I can now add, also require other forms of knowledge and insight. They require the *combination* of mode-1 and mode-3 knowledge, not on the level of abstract worldviews, but on the level of concrete mode-2 practices of knowledge production. That is to say, within the knowledge-intensive organizations where the production of mode-2 knowledge takes place on a day-to-day basis.

In the remainder of this chapter I will try to answer two of the many urgent questions prompted by such a perspective. The first question concerns the supposedly irrational character of existential and moral perspectives. I will try to answer this question by elaborating upon a second important characteristic of mode-3 knowledge development, apart from co-creation, which could be designated as "dialogical friction." The second question concerns the room or space for mode-3 knowledge development within organizations that, *ex hypothesi,* are dominated by commercial interests and political priorities.

4. Hypergoods and Horizontal Transcendence

4.1. Substantive Objectivity and Surface Objectivity

I have stated that mode-3 knowledge development concerns existential and moral insights in the context of knowledge-intensive organizations. But does it make any sense to speak of knowledge and insight in this domain? Do moral values and existential perspectives not belong to the domain of subjective convictions and irrational opinions? This question has of course a very long history within philosophy and ethics, from Greek philosophy up to Kant, Nietzsche, Habermas, and Rawls. It clearly has a new significance and urgency in relation to the commercialization and instrumentalization of science and the concomitant social and political problems. I want to argue that the modern opposition between objective knowledge and subjective values and opinions is still relevant with regard to mode-1 knowledge, but leads in the wrong direction when used in the context of mode-2 science. With regard to the results of mode-1 science, we can speak about what I call "substantive objectivity." Of central importance here is the possibility of reproduction of the results of experiments or clinical trials. According to Hans Radder, it is a central tenet of scientific enquiry that experimental processes should be reproducible, not only by the scientists involved but also by other members of relevant scientific communities (Radder 1996). The importance of this substantive objectivity is vividly illustrated by Sabina Leonelli in this book. Leonelli points to the different ways biological data are handled and cared for in mode-1 and mode-2, respectively. In mode-1, or "process-driven," databases, general, long-term accessibility is the norm, whereas in "project-driven," mode-2 databases, "the access skills needed to retrieve data from such a database are specific to the field in question." As this example illustrates, in the domain of mode-2 science substantive objectivity changes into what we could call "surface objectivity." Here, at the surface, the norms of "proper science" seem to be satisfied, but if we dig deeper we encounter all kinds of *context-specific* elements and influences that are entangled with the "results." As a consequence it might be possible to reproduce these results *within* this context, but for various reasons they cannot be reproduced nor judged by "peers" outside this context. The standard procedures for mode-1 quality control are not applicable, or only up to a point.

At this point the modern opposition between objective knowledge on the one hand and subjective values and opinions on the other starts losing its usefulness, because it allows only one remedy: chastising the contextual elements and influences as value-laden, subjective, and irrational and trying to purify the results in the direction of substantive objectivity. The problem is, of course, that this remedy kills the patient. The predominance of context-bound and interest-ridden forms of mode-2 knowledge is not only the result of overpowering commercial and political influences colonizing science for private interests. It is also bound up with the rise of "technoculture" and the steady "scientification" of everyday life. The predominance of mode-2 knowledge also rests on the belief in the possibility of *technical* solutions for an ever-widening range of practical questions and problems.

The critical analysis of the "business of drug research" by Musschenga, van der Steen, and Ho (this volume) provides a good example of this development. "Pharmaceutical companies continuously try to induce doctors to prescribe their drugs, and the public to ask for their drugs," they write. This is of course true, and it clearly illustrates the complex mix of factors influencing the choice of pharmaceutical (instead of, for instance, psychoanalytical or lifestyle oriented) therapies to deal with psychiatric disorders and mental problems. But the great success of these strategies cannot be explained exclusively on the basis of the clever manipulation by all-powerful international companies. Such explanations have been extensively discussed within the social sciences, notably in the wake of the Frankfurt School perspective on the "Dialectic of Enlightenment" and on "One-Dimensional Society," but have been justly abandoned as much too simplistic (Habermas 1981; Dews 1987; Giddens 1991; Kunneman and de Vries 1991). As argued above, apart from specific economic and political power structures, we also have to reckon with the *seductive power* exerted by modern technology itself, especially its promise to do away completely with slow questions. We have to reckon, that is, not only with undemocratic power relations, but also with heavy emotional and *existential* investments from the side of consumers/clients and their surroundings in the power of modern technology—for instance, investments into the promise of solving psychiatric problems completely with the help of pharmaceutical means, or the promise of securing peace and safety by a "completely automated shield" of defensive missiles.

The contextual factors involved under the surface of mode-2 science thus not only entail different forms of relaxation or perversion of the scientific norms securing substantive objectivity; they also entail a complex constellation of cultural values and interpretations, dominant visions of the content of a good, meaningful life, and morally acceptable and unacceptable ways to realize such a life. The first type of influences can be combated up to a point in the name of substantive objectivity and the concomitant opposition between objective knowledge and subjective values, but the second type of influence, the massive role of cultural values and underlying interpretative frameworks, cannot be dealt with in the same way. Kourany (cited by Hans Radder, this volume, chap. 10) rightly stresses this point in the context of the role of ethics codes in the sciences: "Helping to make the ethics codes in the sciences adequate . . . is an epistemic as well as an ethical project."

Most of the contributions to this book explicitly or implicitly endorse the double character of this challenge, as testified by the many moral imperatives contained in the different chapters. James R. Brown, for instance, writes, "Theory testing . . . *must* pass into independent hands." According to Leonelli, research *should* be based on a long-term vision. Musschenga, van der Steen, and Ho argue that the system of funding medical research *should* be revised, and Resnik adds that "Scientists and society *should* adopt strategies for managing financial interests and minimizing their impact on the norms of academic science" (italics added). The same goes, of course, for the advocates of Mertonian-type norms, such as Helen Longino and Radder and van den Belt.

What holds for the ethics codes in the sciences and for all related exhortations just cited, also goes, and even more, for the cultural values and interpretative frameworks co-determining the contextual character of mode-2 science; for instance, all the values, emotions, and existential dilemmas connected with gender relations in postmodern societies, which heavily inform psychiatric diagnoses and therapies. To enhance the moral quality of the social processes involved, we surely need epistemic means and penetrating cognitive analyses, but these are *not enough* by far. Mode-2 science production is a mix of substantive objectivity, economic and political interests, and cultural frameworks articulating existential and moral values. To deal responsibly with this mixture, we also need moral resources, and thus a notion of knowledge and learning which is wider and more inclusive than the notion of rationality embodied in modern epistemology. A central stumbling block for the development of a more inclusive notion of knowledge and learning is the modern divide between facts and values, the deep cleft between objective knowledge and subjective values and emotions.

4.2. The Relation between Facts and Values

In this respect the example of humanistics could be of some help again. In our discussion of the central premises and the scientific status of humanistics, as a discipline that explicitly orients itself to humane values, we encountered the problem that humanism itself does not supply a clear-cut and unified set of values, but instead comprises a loosely coupled set of different traditions, ranging from Hellenistic thought and Renaissance thinking to nineteenth-century, "*Bildung*-centered" hermeneutic perspectives, Kantian universalism, liberal individualism, secularism, and science-oriented rationalism. We also encountered the problem of the tense relation between this pluralistic humanism on the one hand and other worldviews, especially religious worldviews, on the other. We encountered, in other words, precisely the state of affairs that famously prompted Max Weber to plead for a very strict separation between facts and values, arguing that different value-laden moral and existential perspectives in the last resort stand in a relation of unbridgeable opposition to each other: "Hier streiten eben auch verschiedene Götter miteinander, und zwar für alle Zeit" (Weber, 1949/1968, 604; "We have to face that different Gods are combating each other here, and this for ever"). However, as present-day sociological theory shows, ongoing modernization during the twentieth century resulted not only in *Entzauberung* (disenchantment) in the ongoing march of instrumental reason and in the barbarities of Nazism and Communism, but also in new perspectives in the domain of human rights and individual emancipation and—most importantly for the development of mode-3 knowledge—in a profound transformation with respect to the status and justification of transcendent perspectives and transcendent values. This transformation was prepared especially within hermeneutic and postmodern philosophy and by feminist thinkers, and it can be designated as a shift from *vertical* to *horizontal* transcendence. This shift is of crucial importance for the development of "viable alternatives for commercialized science," because it points beyond the bitter and insoluble struggle between different "gods" referred to by Max Weber, and by many other modern thinkers, as the underlying reason for the necessity to safeguard a strict separation between "subjective" values and "objective" scientific knowledge. In my eyes, this bitter struggle, and the concomitant absence of mutual learning, are internally connected with *vertical* articulations of transcendent values and transcendent entities, but not with the *horizontal* articulations of transcendent values emerging in our times.

4.3. Hypergoods and Transcendent Values

The meaning of these concepts can be elucidated with the help of the idea of hypergoods, as developed by Charles Taylor in his book *Sources of the Self* (1989). Following Taylor, I interpret transcendent values as "hypergoods," that is, orienting values that are articulated within specific cultural frameworks and that provide a horizon of meaning and standards to evaluate and judge one's own actions and those of others: "To think, feel, judge within such a framework is to function with the sense that some action, or mode of life, or mode of feeling is incomparably higher than the others, which are more readily available to us" (Taylor 1989, 19). The incomparability of these "hypergoods" hinges for Taylor on the fact "that these ends or goods stand independently of our own desires, inclinations, or choices, that they represent standards by which these desires and choices are judged" (Taylor 1989, 20). In our discussions at the University for Humanistics, we followed this lead of Taylor (and of related thinkers such as Gadamer, Ricoeur, Said, and Nussbaum), especially his thesis that such a horizon of *articulated* hypergoods, such a horizon of transcendent values, is a prerequisite for a meaningful life. Such a vision makes understandable both the importance of *experiences* of transcendence at the level of individuals—in whatever form—and the importance of shared stories, rituals, and all forms of association and congregation enabling people to heighten their *sensitivity* for such experiences and the values connected with them, and to share their meaningfulness. But Taylor's analysis is not very precise about the exact status of the *independence* of transcendent values with regard to "our own desires, inclinations, or choices," as he says. Here, of course, Weber's dictum on the irreconcilability of "ultimate values" looms very large. At this point, we profited from the distinction between vertical and horizontal articulations of transcendence, as introduced and provisionally developed by the feminist philosopher Luce Irigaray (Irigaray 1992; Halsema 2008).

Generally speaking, vertical articulations of transcendence have two main characteristics: in the first place they refer to an *absolute source* of meaning and value, whether this be God, Ideas, Nature, or Reason; in the second place they picture the transcendent values stemming from (and guaranteed by) this absolute source as universal *imperatives* that have to be obeyed without discussion or critique. Horizontal articulations of transcendence, however, are characterized by the distinction between the *horizon* of transcendent values and their source (whether this be a God, Platonic Ideas, or "humanity") on the one hand and specific *articulations* of these values and their possible source on the other. It is precisely the transcendent character of these values and their possible source, which implies that each and any articulation of them within a specific tradition and within a specific (linguistic or esthetic) medium of expression can only point to them and "evoke" them but can never adequately characterize or describe them "as they really are." Thus, horizontal articulations of transcendent values acknowledge and to a certain extent welcome their dependence upon "dialogical friction" with other articulations of transcendence. They acknowledge that the horizon of transcendent values to which they point can only be kept open on the basis of dialogical frictions between a *plurality* of articulations of the values involved and of possible transcendent sources of these values. In terms of Jessica Benjamin's analysis of aggression, omnipotence, and recognition on the level of personal relations, we could say that horizontal transcendence hinges on mutual *peaceful containment*. This containment involves a relation in which a plurality of different articulations of transcendent values serves as each other's "surviving other," containing the omnipotence of the other and creating space for difference and mutual recognition (Benjamin 1988; Kunneman 2007). Seen in this light, a transition from vertical to horizontal articulations of transcendence hinges upon the insight that the transcendence purportedly shining through in the different frameworks at stake can only be a source of illumination and inspiration, on the condition that none of them can *monopolize* the source and nature of this "light" and its supposed meaning for human life in general.

Looking back at the confrontations of the last centuries between secular humanism and religious worldviews, the conclusion is justified that from both sides aggression and the desire for omnipotence have been more dominant than the fruitful friction associated by Benjamin with intersubjective containment. From the side of secular humanists, for instance, religion has been associated consistently with vertical articulations of transcendence and with concomitant forms of dogmatism, whereas the scientistic dogmatism of secular humanism has been ignored by them with equal consistency. During the last decades, however, vertical articulations of transcendence have been criticized from *both* sides, and "weak" articulations of religious belief, as Gianni Vattimo has it, and critical, open, and democratic forms of humanism have come to the fore, as advocated among others by Edward Said (Vattimo 2002; Said 2004).

This emergent shift from vertical articulations of transcendent values to horizontal articulations oriented toward fruitful friction provides a provisional basis for humanistics as a value-laden, practice-oriented scientific discipline. It combines mode-1 insights from relevant scientific disciplines with a *plurality* of moral traditions and existential perspectives to shed light on *practical* problems and dilemmas encountered by professionals and customers, students or clients in the context of knowledge-intensive organizations which provide the context for mode-2 knowledge development. From the practice of humanist counseling and from contemporary articulations of horizontal transcendence, we distill the hope *and* the experience that in our times new, pluralistic forms of dealing with cultural differences and with frictions between the underlying transcendent values are becoming visible and "practicable." The disenchantment of the world as analyzed by Weber and the concomitant dominance of instrumental forms of rationality have resulted in the individualization and privatization of moral values and existential perspectives. But they have also led to the *re-emergence* of moral and existential questions in the heart of late-modern societies, more specifically, within the knowledge-intensive organizations in which the economic, technological, and governmental activities responsible for the inner dynamic of these societies are concentrated.

5. Meaning and Values in Knowledge-Intensive Organizations

This thesis brings me to a second complex question connected with the idea of mode-3 knowledge development and also to the last part of my argument. The question at stake concerns the *space* for mode-3 knowledge development on the basis of a plurality of moral perspectives, within organizations that are dominated as before by commercial interests and political priorities. Here for the last time the example of humanistics could be of help, especially with our discipline's development at the turn of the twenty-first century. From 1989 to about 1995, on the level of practical activities, we were oriented almost exclusively to the questions and challenges connected with the counseling of individuals and groups with regard to existential questions and moral dilemmas, in relative *isolation* from the organizational context in which these questions occurred. More and more, however, we were confronted with the necessity to address this context itself. On the one hand, this organizational context and its dominant strategic force fields acted as a prime source of existential and moral problems for clients. On the other hand, the organizations where humanist counselors were employed showed an increasing *need* for moral and existential insights in order to develop more adequate solutions for the practical problems defined within the professional language games dominating these organizations. A good example of this need for mode-3 insights is provided by the wish of the Dutch army to support the development of a certain measure of ethical sensitivity and ethical responsibility on the part of young soldiers being sent on UN missions.

In my view, present-day postindustrial capitalism shows a deep ambivalence in this respect. The strategic logic of short-term economic power, profit for shareholders, and geopolitical power clearly dominates, with all the concomitant negative effects for people and the planet. This dominant constellation is not completely homogeneous, however: it is perturbed and at times counteracted by other developments and undercurrents—for example, by the need for open communication and trust between professionals as a prerequisite for creative cooperation and innovation, but also by the movement toward new forms of corporate social responsibility, deeply ambivalent in itself but nevertheless pointing toward a long-term, more inclusive perspective on economic progress and the necessary social conditions for competitive firms to safeguard their own position in the long run.

The most important countertendency, however, concerns the limited possibilities for a meaningful existence provided by a life dominated by the necessity to produce, to be competitive, and to "enjoy" ever more sophisticated consumptive possibilities (Sennett 1998). Production, competition, and consumption refer to the logic of control and predictability and to strategic relations with other people. But they are of little use in dealing with central moral dilemmas and existential questions confronting present-day individuals not only within their personal lifeworld, but increasingly also on the level of their work and in their relation to an instable and insecure world-society. In these domains they are also in need of inspiration and of moral and existential insights that can help them find more adequate ways of dealing with the complex mixtures of technical, strategic, and moral questions confronting them. It is here that the importance of mode-3 learning processes becomes visible. They provide *a link* between the existential questions and moral dilemmas of present-day individuals on the one hand and questions concerning productivity, innovation, and efficiency within knowledge-intensive organizations on the other. The existential questions and moral dilemmas involved not only stem from individuals' personal lives and relations, but are increasingly entangled with experiences and dilemmas connected with the organizations in which they work. Moreover, the large-scale waste of people, scarce resources, and money due to escalating conflicts, miscommunication, and simplistic power games within present-day organizations clearly indicates that moral and existential questions are not *external* to questions of efficiency and productivity, but are, on the contrary, very much intertwined with them. Neither mode-1 objectifying learning processes, nor mode-2 knowledge, focused primarily on strategic goals and interests, can provide the inspiration, the existential insights, and the creative friction between alternative evocations of a meaningful life and of enriching moral relations among people, which are necessary for learning processes in this crucial respect.

Thus, I conclude, with Radder, Kourany, and many others, that the development of viable alternatives for commercialized science not only involves an epistemic but also and even primarily an ethical and moral project. The ethics at stake here, however, do not primarily concern the conduct of proper science, although they do so too, but hinge upon visions and experiences of a good, meaningful life in the context of, and in contact with, knowledge-intensive organizations. In short, they concern appropriate *combinations* of mode-1 knowledge and mode-3 insights in the context of the knowledge-intensive organizations where the development of valid and socially responsible knowledge is concentrated in our times.

REFERENCES

Baart, A. 2004. *Aandacht: Etudes in presentie.* Utrecht: Lemma.

Benjamin, J. 1988. *The bonds of love.* New York: Pantheon.

Cilliers, P. 1998. *Complexity and postmodernism: Understanding complex systems.* London: Routledge.

———. 2005. "Complexity, deconstruction and relativism." *Theory, Culture, Society* 22 (5): 255–67.

Collins, H. M., and T. Pinch. 1998. *The golem: What you should know about science.* 2nd ed. Cambridge: Canto.

Dervis, K. 2007. Interview. *De Volkskrant,* June 14.

Dews, P. 1987. *Logics of disintegration.* London: Verso Books.

Gadamer, H.-G. 1972. *Wahrheit und Methode.* 3rd ed. Tübingen: J. C. B. Mohr.

Gibbons, M., C. Limoges, H. Nowotny, S. Schwartzmann, P. Scott, and M. Trow. 1994. *The new production of knowledge: The dynamics of science and research in contemporary societies.* London: Sage Publications.

Giddens, A. 1976. *New rules of sociological method.* London: Hutchinson.

———. 1991. *Modernity and self-identity.* Cambridge: Polity Press.

Grint, K., and S. Woolgar. 1997. *The machine at work.* Cambridge: Polity Press.

Habermas, J. 1981. *Theorie des kommunikativen Handelns.* Frankfurt a.M.: Suhrkamp.

Halsema, A. 2008. "Horizontal transcendence: Irigaray's religion after ontotheology." In *Religion: Beyond a concept,* ed. H. de Vries, 813–25. New York: Fordham University Press.

Hoogeveen, E. 1985. "Methodiek van de geestelijke verzorging." *Rekenschap* 32:150–57.

———. 1996. *Verbondenheid: Opstellen over humanistische geestelijke verzorging.* Utrecht: Universiteit voor Humanistiek.

Irigaray, L. 1992. *J'aime à toi: Esquisse d'une félicité dans l'histoire.* Paris: Grasset.

Jorna, T., ed. 1997. *Door eenheid verbonden.* Utrecht: Uitg. Kwadraat.

Kauffman, S. 1995. *At home in the universe.* Oxford: Oxford University Press.

———. 2000. *Investigations.* Oxford: Oxford University Press.

Kortmann, F. 2007. *Transculturele psychiatrie.* Assen, Netherlands: Van Gorcum.

Kunneman, H. 2005. *Voorbij het dikke-ik: Bouwstenen voor een kritisch humanisme.* Amsterdam: Humanistics University Press/SWP.

———. 2007. "Critical humanism and the problem of evil: From vertical to horizontal transcendence." In *Probing the depths of evil and good: Multireligious views and case studies,* ed. J. D. Gort, H. Jansen, and H. M. Vroom, 319–42. Amsterdam: Rodopi.

Kunneman, H., and H. de Vries, eds. 1991. *Enlightenments: Encounters between critical theory and contemporary French thought.* Kampen, Netherlands: Kok Agora.

Lakatos, I., and A. Musgrave, eds. 1970. *Criticism and the growth of knowledge.* Cambridge: Cambridge University Press.

Latour, B. 1987. *Science in action.* Cambridge, MA: Harvard University Press.

Lijphart, A. 1968. *The politics of accommodation: Pluralism and democracy in the Netherlands.* Berkeley and Los Angeles: University of California Press.

Longino, H. 2002. *The fate of knowledge.* Princeton, NJ: Princeton University Press.

Lyotard, J.-F. 1984. *The postmodern condition: A report on knowledge.* Minneapolis: University of Minnesota Press.

Miller, S. D., B. L. Duncan, and M. A. Hubble. 2004. "Beyond integration: The triumph of outcome over process in clinical practice." *Psychotherapy in Australia* 10 (2): 2–19.

Mooren, J. H. M., ed. 1999. *Bakens in de stroom: Naar een methodiek van het humanistisch geestelijk werk.* Utrecht: SWP.

Morin, E. 2008. *On complexity.* Cresskill, NY: Hampton Press.

Nowotny, H., P. Scott, and M. Gibbons. 2001. *Re-thinking science.* Cambridge: Polity Press.

Radder, H. 1996. *In and about the world.* Albany: State University of New York Press.

Said, E. W. 2004. *Humanism and democratic criticism.* New York: Palgrave/Macmillan.

Sennett, R. 1998. *The corrosion of character: The personal consequences of work in the new capitalism.* New York: W. W. Norton.

Taylor, C. 1989. *Sources of the self: The making of the modern identity.* Cambridge: Cambridge University Press.

Toulmin, S. 1990. *Cosmopolis: The hidden agenda of modernity.* Chicago: University of Chicago Press.

Vattimo, G. 2002. *After Christianity.* New York: Columbia University Press.

Weber, M. 1949/1968. *Gesammelte Aufsätze zur Wissenschaftslehre.* 3rd ed. Tübingen: J. C. B. Mohr. Originally published as *The methodology of the social sciences,* ed. and trans. E. A. Shils and H. A. Finch. New York: Free Press.

Contributors

James Robert Brown is professor of philosophy at the University of Toronto in Canada. His interests include a number of topics within the philosophy of science and mathematics, such as thought experiments, realism, visual reasoning in mathematics, and the relation between science and society, which is the subject of his article in this volume. He is the author of *The Rational and the Social; The Laboratory of the Mind: Thought Experiments in the Natural Sciences; Smoke and Mirrors: How Science Reflects Reality; Philosophy of Mathematics: An Introduction to the World of Proofs and Pictures;* and *Who Rules in Science? An Opinionated Guide to the Wars.* Several works will appear soon, including a new edition of his book on thought experiments, a joint-authored book on foundational issues in seismology, and a book on Platonism and naturalism in the philosophy of mathematics.

Mark B. Brown is associate professor in the Department of Government at California State University, Sacramento. He was previously a postdoctoral fellow at the Institute for Science and Technology Studies, Bielefeld University. He studied at the University of California–Santa Cruz and the University of Göttingen, and received a Ph.D. in political science from Rutgers University. Brown's research draws on science and technology studies, democratic theory, and the history of political thought to explore various dilemmas associated with public participation and representation in the politics of science. He is the author of *Science in Democracy: Expertise, Institutions, and Representation,* as well as a book co-authored with Justus Lentsch and Peter Weingart, *Politikberatung und Parlament* (Political advice and parliament), and several book chapters and journal articles.

Martin Carrier is professor of philosophy at Bielefeld University and member of the Institute of Science and Technology Studies (IWT). His chief area of work is the philosophy of science, in particular, historical changes in science and scientific method, theory-ladenness and empirical testability, intertheoretic relations and reductionism, and currently, the methodology of applied research. He is a member of the German Academy of Science Leopoldina and the Mainz Academy of Sciences, Humanities and Literature. He was codirector of a research group on "science in the context of application" at the Center for Interdisciplinary Research (ZiF) at Bielefeld University 2006–2007, and was awarded the Leibniz Prize of the German Research Association (DFG) for 2008. His publications include *Mind, Brain, Behavior: The Mind-Body Problem and the Philosophy of Psychology* (coauthored with Jürgen Mittelstrass); *The Completeness of Scientific*

337

Theories: On the Derivation of Empirical Indicators within a Theoretical Framework: The Case of Physical Geometry; Nikolaus Kopernikus; Wissenschaftstheorie: Zur Einführung (Introduction to the Philosophy of Science); and *Raum-Zeit (Space-Time).*

Steve Fuller is professor of sociology at the University of Warwick. Originally trained in history and philosophy of science, Fuller is best known for his work in the field of "social epistemology," which addresses normative philosophical questions about organized knowledge by historical and social scientific means. He has recently been working on the future of the public intellectual and the university, as well as the biological challenge to the social sciences, especially in its bearing on the future of "humanity" as a normative and empirical category. He has published sixteen books and his work has been translated into nearly twenty languages. Relevant recent works include *The Knowledge Book: Key Concepts in Philosophy, Science and Culture; New Frontiers in Science and Technology Studies;* and *The Sociology of Intellectual Life.* Fuller was awarded a "higher doctorate" (D.Litt.) in 2007 by Warwick for long-term major contributions to scholarship.

V. K. Y. (Vincent) Ho holds an M.Sc. in medical biology and in epidemiology from VU University Amsterdam. He currently works at the Netherlands Cancer Registry as a cancer epidemiologist focusing on breast cancer, lung cancer, soft tissue tumors, and quality of care analysis. He is also a researcher with the Faculty of Behavioural and Social Sciences at the University of Groningen, where he is writing his dissertation on the limitations of evidence-based medicine. Together with Wim van der Steen, he has published several articles and two textbooks that reflect on the cultural forces that shape medicine, including the role played by the pharmaceutical industry.

Daniel Lee Kleinman is professor (2008–2009 Buttel-Sewell professor) and chair at the Department of Community and Environmental Sociology at the University of Wisconsin–Madison, where he is also the director of the Robert F. and Jean E. Holtz Center for Science and Technology Studies. Over the past decade, his research has focused on three central areas: the commercialization of the university, the politics of agricultural biotechnology policy, and the relationship between democracy and expertise. He is the author of three books: *Politics on the Endless Frontier: Postwar Research Policy in the United States; Impure Cultures: University Biology and the World of Commerce;* and *Science and Technology in Society: From Biotechnology to the Internet.* Among Kleinman's edited volumes is *Controversies in Science and Technology,* vol. 2, *From Climate to Chromosomes* (with Karen Cloud-Hansen, Christina Matta, and Jo Handelsman). He has recently initiated a project on the intersection of discipline formation and state building.

Harry Kunneman received his M.A. in sociology and his Ph.D. in philosophy from the University of Amsterdam. Since 1990 he has occupied the chair for Social and Political Theory at the University for Humanistics in Utrecht. From 2000 to 2004 he was vice-chancellor of this university. His main research interests lie in the fields of critical theory, the philosophy of the social sciences, complexity thinking, and sustainability. He has published six books and many articles in Dutch. His latest book, *Voorbij het dikke-ik: Bouwstenen voor een kritisch humanisme* (Beyond the swollen ego: Materials for a critical humanism), offers a critical analysis of the autocatalytic loop between consumerism, the urge to be competitive in all domains of life, and the moral indifference toward the fate of others, and explores ways to advance beyond this loop.

Sabina Leonelli is a research fellow of the ESRC Centre for Genomics in Society (Egenis) based at the Department of Sociology and Philosophy of the University of Exeter. She was trained in the history, philosophy, and social studies of science in London and Amsterdam. Her research focuses on the interplay between scientific practices (such as modeling, understanding, abstracting, and labeling) and the governance of science. She has published several articles on the relations between regulatory and classificatory practices within the biomedical sciences, paying particular attention to the role played by bioinformatic tools for data sharing. She is also writing a monograph on the history of research on the model organism *Arabidopsis thaliana*.

A. W. (Bert) Musschenga is professor of philosophical ethics at VU University Amsterdam. From 1999 to 2003 he was the director of the Netherlands School for Research in Practical Philosophy. He is editor-in-chief of *Ethical Theory and Moral Practice*. He has written many articles and edited many volumes (both in Dutch and English) on practical ethical topics, as well as on more fundamental theoretical questions such as the relation between religion and morality, moral reasoning, and personal and moral identity. He has published monographs on quality of life and on integrity. In recent years he has written several articles on the relation between psychological processes, intuitive moral judgments, and epistemological intuitions.

Hans Radder is professor of philosophy of science and technology at VU University Amsterdam. He holds degrees in physics (B.A. and M.Sc.) and in philosophy (B.A., M.A., and Ph.D.). Principal themes in his work are: scientific observation and experimentation; the historical, epistemological, and ontological significance of concepts; scientific realism; and the normative and political significance of science and technology. He has published numerous articles and several books, including *The Material Realization of Science, In and about the World, The World Observed / The World Conceived*, and, as editor, *The Philosophy of Scientific Experimentation*. As associate editor he contributed to the volume *Philosophy of Technology and Engineering Sciences*, edited by A. W. M. Meijers.

David B. Resnik is a bioethicist at the National Institute of Environmental Health Sciences (NIEHS), National Institutes of Health (NIH). He is also the chair of the Institutional Review Board for Human Subjects Research at the NIEHS and an adjunct professor of philosophy at North Carolina State University. He has published seven books and over 150 articles on philosophical, ethical, and legal issues in science, technology, and medicine. Resnik is associate editor of *Accountability in Research* and is on the editorial boards of several journals. Prior to joining the NIEHS, he was a professor of medical humanities at the Brody School of Medicine at East Carolina University and associate director of the Bioethics Center at University Health Systems of East Carolina. Resnik has a B.A. (philosophy) from Davidson College, a Ph.D. (philosophy) from the University of North Carolina, and a J.D. (law) from Concord University.

Sigrid Sterckx is professor of ethics and senior research fellow of the Fund for Scientific Research, Flanders, associated with the Department of Philosophy and Moral Science of Ghent University, Belgium. She is also a professor of ethics at the Vrije Universiteit Brussels's Faculty of Medicine and Pharmaceutical Sciences and Faculty of Arts and Philosophy. She obtained a master of moral sciences (1994) and a Ph.D. (2000) in moral sciences at Ghent University. She teaches courses in ethics, bioethics, and medical ethics. Sterckx serves on several advisory committees, including the Belgian National Advisory Council on Bioethics. Her publications include the book *Biotechnology, Patents and Morality*, numerous book chapters and articles in international legal and (bio)ethics journals on issues such as the impact of patents on access to medicines and the patentability of human embryonic stem cells. She has recently started preparing a book aimed at an ethical, historical, and legal analysis of the various categories and fields that are excluded from patentability under European patent law.

Henk van den Belt works at the Department of Applied Philosophy of Wageningen University, the Netherlands. His interests include science and technology studies, consumer and food ethics, and the ethics of intellectual property in modern life sciences. He has published on social constructivism, the work of Ludwik Fleck, the justification of the precautionary principle, biotechnology, synthetic biology, and biofuels.

Wim van der Steen is emeritus professor of biology and philosophy at VU University Amsterdam. He has published many books and articles in these disciplines. His research concerns the foundations and ethics of medicine and psychiatry, particularly that many areas of biology are disregarded in medicine and psychiatry, with unfortunate consequences for research and practice. Circadian rhythms and nutrition are salient examples. As a researcher, van der Steen has always worked as a generalist. In the current atmosphere of superspecialization, bridges between specialisms are often lacking. The areas of biology that are disregarded in medicine and psychiatry illustrate this. The problems of the occurrence of these lacunae are aggravated by the way the pharmaceutical industry determines research agendas. Van der Steen has attempted to help ensure more independence for science through contacts with highly placed officials in the political arena. In most cases, the response has been that the officials in question could not even attempt to get the matter on the political agenda, since such an attempt could cost them their job. Still, the hope is that a new, independent science may emerge in the future.

Index

Note: *Figures and tables are indicated by "f" or "t," respectively, following a page number.*

academic, conceptualization of, 5
academic culture. *See* commercialization of academic culture
academic research: as basic research, 29, 169; economic instrumentalization of, 4–5; indirect effects of commercial interests on, 31–34; industrial research in cooperation with, 165–66; as an ivory tower, 25–28; knowledge exchange in, 139; long-term vs. short-term, 14, 142–45, 152; norms of, 26–27, 67–72; patenting of, 7, 8, 14, 15, 46, 244–50; synthesis of specialized research needed for, 126. *See also* commodification of academic research; medical research; research agendas; research results; science
Academy of Sciences (France), 62n27, 187–90, 197, 198, 203, 220n2, 221n3, 299, 301
access skills, 149
Actor-Network Theory (ANT), 210, 302
Affymetrix, 139, 206
agricultural disease control, 33–34
alternatives to commodified science, 18–20, 307–35
American Association of University Professors, 274n11
American Chemical Society (ACS), 73
American Competitiveness Initiative, 30
American Intellectual Property Law Association, 192
American Medical Association (AMA), 73
American Patent Law Association, 192
American Psychiatric Association (APA), 122
American Psychological Association (APA), 122
American Sociological Association, 28
Analatos, A. A., 123–24
Animal, Plant, and Inspection Service, U.S. Department of Agriculture, 31–32
antidepressants, 99–100, 118
antiessentialism, 280
antitheodicy, 287
application innovation, 172–74
applied research: basic research deriving from, 172–74; cascade model and, 170–75; commodification not coincident with, 5; and emergentism, 168–69; industrial science as, 29; linear model and, 169–71; NSF and, 29–30; standards of, 180; theory's role in, 175–79. *See also* industrial science; technology

The Arabidopsis Information Resource (TAIR), 137, 153
Aristotle, 159, 168, 170
Arrow, Kenneth, 206–9
Association of Universities in the Netherlands, 16, 239
AstraZeneca, 100
authorship, 82–84; and censorship, 223n17; "famous name" dilemma concerning, 215–16; ghost, 84, 105, 114, 123; honorary, 84, 214; importance of, 82–83; journal guidelines for, 83–84, 105; problems related to, 84; responsibility attached to, 83
autonomous science, 18–19; characteristics of, 265; Fuller's challenge to, 212; movement away from, 26; norms of, 26–27; reasons for, 156n26; threats to, 308; values of, 152

Bacon, Francis, 92, 160, 170, 202–3, 284
Bagley, Margo, 47
Barber, Bernard, 226n39
Barnes, S. B. (Barry), 203–4, 235–36, 238–40, 253n7, 253n11
Barton, J. H., 125
basic research: academic research as, 29; applied research as source of, 172–74; cascade model and, 170–74; linear model and, 169–71; and patent infringement suits, 49–50
Bayer, 100
Bayh-Dole Act (1980), 28, 30–31, 35, 45, 54–55, 61n21, 101, 273n1, 299
Becker, Gary, 283
Behring, Emil, 191
Benjamin, Jessica, 332
Berman, Elizabeth Popp, 30
Bernal, John Desmond, 194, 212
Bessen, J., *Patent Failure*, 58–59
bias in research, 17, 106, 115–16, 124, 162–64, 179–81
Binnig, Gerd, 173
BioBricks Foundation, 220
biocontrol agents, 33–34
bioinformatics, 137–40
biological research, profit motive in, 138–39
biology: data exchange in, 138; diversity of approaches based on, 118–22; and psychiatry, 117–18, 126. *See also* biomedical research
biomedical research, disseminating data in, 134–38. *See also* medical research

biotechnology: green vs. red, 139; and patenting boom, 45; and university-industry relationships, 24, 26, 28
Biotechnology and Biological Sciences Research Council (BBSRC), 140
blue sky research, 57
Board of Arts (U.S.), 199
Board of Technology (Denmark), 246
Bogen, J., 134
Böhm-Bawerk, Eugen, 280
Bok, Derek, 14, 270
Boots Pharmaceutical, 26, 80–81
Bordet, Jules, 223n21
BP, 24
branding, 296
Bristol-Myers Squibb, 103, 219
British Medical Journal, 97
Brody, H., 123
Brown, James, 8, 10, 12, 15, 248, 329
Brown, Mark, 6, 8, 13, 18, 19, 250, 298
Brown, N., 154n8
Brown University, 26
Bruck, Carl, 223n21, 224n23
Burawoy, Michael, 28
Bush, George W., 29–30, 215
Bush, Vannevar, 29, 194; *Science: The Endless Frontier*, 169, 194
businesses. *See* commercial interests

Callon, Michel, 208, 210–12
CAMBIA, 220
Campbell, Eric G., 27
Canadian Medical Association Journal, 100
cancer, Nixon's war on, 171
capitalism: ambivalence of, 334; critiques of, 277; and humanist essentialism, 281
captopril, 176
Carnap, Rudolf, 308
Carnot, Sadi, 172
Carrier, Martin, 6, 10, 12, 15, 17, 310, 313
Cartwright, Nancy, 167
Cascade model of research, 170–75
case-controlled studies, 97
Cassells, A., 113
catatonia, 114–15
Celebrex, 99, 105
Celera, 140–41
censorship, 223n17
chairs: external funding for, 7, 16; personal ties associated with, 8
chaos theory, 315
China, 309–10
chromosomes, 135f
Ciba-Geigy, 34
Cilliers, P., 314–15
ciprofloxacin, 177
circadian rhythms, 120–22
citation indices, 7, 214, 300–301
civic republicanism. *See* republicanism
clinical trial registry, 76, 86, 105

clinical trials: recruitment for, 100–101, 105–6; unwitting enrollment in, 100. *See also* randomized clinical trials
clozapine, 114
codes of conduct/ethics, 17, 232, 239–41, 250, 254nn13–14, 267, 329
coercion, in academic research, 250, 260–62
Colbert, Jean-Baptiste, 62n27
cold war, 208–9, 212, 224n29, 304
Collegiate Research Council (CRC), 124–25
Collins, Francis, 140–41
Collins, Randall, 281
commercial funding: of academic research, 7; benefits of, 13, 182; corrupting effect of, 98–103, 105–6, 115–16, 263, 266; extent of, 9, 24, 85; of medical research, 98–103; of pharmaceutical research, 8, 115–16; and research agendas, 31–34, 75, 101, 162–64; of scientific research, 65. *See also* commercial interests; financial interests
commercial interests: chairs or professorships funded by, 7, 16; corrupting effect of, 66; impact of, on academic research, 14, 15; indirect effects of, on academic research, 31–34; and knowledge exchange, 142–43; 151–53; and socially relevant research, 110–11; strategic alliances with, 7. *See also* commercial funding; financial interests; university-industry relationships
commercialization. *See* economic instrumentalization
commercialization of academic culture, 34–39, 218; in administration, 37–39; inattention to, 26, 31; and scientists' commercial orientation, 35–37; significance of, 25, 308
commodification: competition as influence on, 141–45; defined, 4–5, 260; forms of, 6–8; as freedom, 280; German vs. English senses of, 290–93; and knowledge, 283–86; levels of, 289–90; private vs. public perspectives on, 141–42; and universalism, 280–83; of water, 291–92
commodification of academic research: advantages of, 13; applied science not coincident with, 5; assessments of, 10–16; as coercion, 260–62; conceptualizations of, 4–5; as corruption, 260, 262–67; by country, 9; critiques of, 13–16, 25–26, 40, 160–62, 244–50, 259–73, 307–8; defined, 4–5, 260; by discipline, 9; extent of, 10, 24; four levels of, 6; growth of, 8–9, 160; Mertonian approach to, 231–52; multidisciplinary approach to, 1–2; novelty of, 9–10; practical issues in assessment of, 13–16; rejection of critical analysis of, 11; research questions on, 3–4; restrictions on, 295–97; theoretical issues in assessment of, 10–13. *See also* academic research; alternatives to commodified science; commercialization of academic culture

communication. *See* knowledge exchange
communism (communalism): characteristics of, 164, 190–91, 195, 233–34; choice of term, 226n39, 253n5; criticisms of, 213–14; in Enlightenment science, 188–89; patenting and, 246–48
community databases, 148–49
competition: knowledge exchange influenced by, 141–45, 149–53; objectivity arising from, 181; science as, 202–5, 223n20
competitiveness, crisis of U.S., 30, 31
complex systems, 314–16
Compton, Arthur, 194
Conant, James Bryant, 212, 303
Condorcet, Marquis de, 188, 195–98, 200, 279, 288–89, 300
conferences, commercial influence on, 113, 123
conflicts of interest, 16; data interpretation influenced by, 82; defined, 115; proper response to, 17
consent: forms, 100; theory of free, 262
contract for science, 29
contributors, to scientific articles, 83–84
cooking data, 77–78
cooperation, science as, 202–5
copyright, 195–200
Copyright and Patent Clause, U.S. Constitution, 197–98
corporations. *See* commercial interests
corruption: in academic research, 260, 262–67; commercial funding as source of, 98–103, 105–6, 115–16, 263, 266; financial interests as source of, 66–67, 73–84, 116; responses to, 264; of scientists, 66–67
craft, vs. science, 187–88, 220n2, 299–300
creative destruction, 294, 297, 303
credit, giving due, 68, 213–14, 216, 248–49, 301. *See also* Matthew effect
cumulative advantage, principle of, 205, 214–17
curators, of database, 138–39, 144–45, 148–51
Cyberinfrastructure, 140

Daddario-Kennedy Amendment (1968), 29
Darwin, Charles, 288
Dasgupta, Partha, 189, 207–8
data: analysis of, 80–81; circulation of, 148–49, 254n15; cooking, 77–78; discarding, 254n15; disclosure of, 146–48; dissemination of, in biomedical research, 134–38; donation of, 143–44, 147–48; fabrication of, 78; falsification of, 78; formatting of, 147–48; for grant applications, 79; independence of, 134, 136; interpretation of, 81–82, 105; local, 134, 136, 150; misconduct/fraud regarding, 76; primary, secondary, and tertiary, 87n8; problems in circulating, 137; in product-driven competition, 142–43, 149, 151–53; in resource-driven competition, 143–45, 149–50, 152–53; retrieval of, 149–51; spinning,

80–82; trust in, 138; withholding of, 98, 105. *See also* knowledge exchange; research results
data production, contrasting goals of, 146
databases: community, 148–49; curators of, 138–39, 144–45, 148–51; for data circulation, 137–38; interrelationship of, 144; project-directed, 142, 149; public, 143–45, 147–49; resource-directed, 152–53, 155n15; in resource-driven competition, 143–45, 149–50; user needs concerning, 144–45
David, Paul, 189, 208
Davidson, Richard, 98
Dawkins, Richard, 282, 288
deflationary neo-Mertonian approach, to commodification, 156n27, 252
democracy: science and, 19, 217, 233; university governance and, 268
depression, medicalization of, 114, 117–18, 317
Dervis, Kemal, 310–11
Descartes, René, 92, 170
developing countries, research not geared toward, 19
Diagnostic and Statistic Manual of Mental Disorders (DSM), 115, 317–18
dialogical friction, 332
Diamond v. Chakrabarty (1980), 28, 45, 286
Diderot, Denis, 195–97
diet, 101, 119–20
disclosure of data, 146–48
discoveries, exclusion from patentability of, 57–58
discovery: effects of commercial funding on, 91; heroic vs. social determination theories of, 196; justification vs., 90–93; logic of, 92–96; mathematical examples of, 93–96; sources of error in, 94–95
disinterestedness, 27, 183n7, 188–89, 213, 234, 242, 248–49
Doctors without Borders, 219
Dolby, R.G.A. (Alex), 203–4, 235–36, 238–40
donation of data, 143–44, 147–48
Dong, Betty, 26, 80–81
drugs: commercial impact on testing, 66, 98–99, 179; as favored treatment option, 113; patenting of, 125; pricing of, 125; sales promotion of, 113–15, 122–23
Duhem, Pierre, 81
Dutch Advisory Council for Science and Technology Policy, 9
Dutch Patent Office, 192

EBM. *See* evidence-based medicine
economic instrumentalization: of academic research, 4–5, 33; in China, 309–10; existential foundation of, 326; justifiability of, 14–15; and mode-3 knowledge, 334–35; patenting and, 245; personal ties as form of, 7–8; research agendas affected by, 14, 15, 162–64; of university administration, 4–5, 8

economic liberalism, 201
economics of science, 205–11
E-Data, 58–59
education: Dutch system of, 320; markets as
    means of, 288–89; of psychiatrists, 126; and
    research-teaching relationship, 301–3;
    significance of curriculum in, 298
Einstein, Albert, 176, 194
elitism, of science, 212–17, 303
Emanuel, E. J., 125
emergentism, 168–69, 175
Enebakk, Vidar, 226n39
Engel, G. L., 118
Engineering Experiment Station, at Georgia Tech
    University, 29
Enlightenment, 195–97, 279, 285, 302–4, 308–9
entrepreneurialism: epistemic, 294–99; features
    of, 18; humanity and, 277–79; as logical
    development, 11; in universities, 38–39,
    245, 279
epistemic autonomy, 308, 311
epistemic entrepreneurship, 294–99
epistemic racism, 278
eponymy, 300
ethics: codes of, 15, 17, 232, 239–41, 250, 329;
    gifts as violation of, 123; and misconduct
    involving data, 78–80; norms of science
    involving, 70–71
Etzkowitz, Henry, 11, 18
European Research Council, 245, 250
European Union: and bioinformatics, 140; dis-
    coveries and patentability in, 57–58; pat-
    enting in, 45–46
Evans, Oliver, 199
evidence-based medicine (EBM): hierarchy of
    evidence in, 96–97; overview of, 96–97;
    shortcomings in actual practice of, 98–103,
    119–22
exchange value, 280
experimental use exception, 49–50, 246
expert opinion, 97
expert skills, 149–50
external funding, 7–8. *See also* commercial fund-
    ing; government funding

fact-value relation, 330
Federal Technology Transfer Act (1986), 28
fichte, Johann Gottlieb, 200
financial interests, 72–84; corrupting effect of,
    66–67, 73–84, 116; norms of science af-
    fected by, 73–84; of organizations, 72; of
    scientists, 72; strategies for managing im-
    pact of, 85–86; types of organizations with,
    72–73. *See also* commercial funding; com-
    mercial interests; government funding
finder's fees, 100–101, 106
fleck, Ludwik, 169, 224n23; *Genesis and Devel-
    opment of a Scientific Fact*, 204–5
fluoxetine (Prozac), 99
Food and Drug Act (1938), 119

Ford, Henry, 168, 295
fractal mathematics, 315
Frankfurt School, 328
Franklin, Benjamin, 198, 304
fraud, 78–79, 87n6, 100
Free and Open Source Software (FOSS), 220
free market, 286–87
French Revolution, and intellectual property,
    188–89, 196–97
Friedberg, M., 66, 98
Fuller, Steve, 6, 10, 12, 15–16, 19, 189–90, 212–18,
    249, 252, 267–68
fundamental research. *See* basic research

Gadamer, Hans-Georg, 331
Galileo Galilei, 170
Gauß, Carl Friedrich, 172
Gayler v. Wilder (1850), 49–50
general complexity, 315
generalization, in applied research, 176–78
genes, 135f
genetic fallacy, 90
Georgia Tech University, 29
ghost authorship, 84, 105, 114, 123
Gibbons, M., 311–12, 315
gift economies, 265–66
GlaxoSmithKline, 100, 139
Glenna, Leland, 31–32
Goethe, Johann Wolfgang, 201
good science: conceptualizations of, 12, 68; pub-
    lic vs. private conceptions of, 142, 145, 152
government: applied research promoted by, 29–30;
    and bioinformatics, 140; and knowledge
    exchange, 153; and ownership of inventions,
    61n21. *See also* government funding
government funding: of academic research, 7; of
    basic research as a public good, 206–7;
    counterbalancing of privately-funded re-
    search by, 124; problems with, 85; of science
    research, 65. *See also* financial interests
grace periods, for patent research, 56
grant applications, 79
Greenberg, Daniel S., 271, 299

Habermas, Jürgen, 308, 327
Hahn, Roger, 221n3
Hamilton, W. D., 288
Handelsman, Jo, 33, 36
Hanson, Russell, 92–93
Harvard University, 5
Hayek, Friedrich, 280, 290
Healy, D., 114
Hedfors, Eva, 224n23
Heemskerk, Jan, 201
Hegel, G. W. F., 200
Hempel, Carl, 308
Hesse, Carla, 196–97
Hirsch, Fred, 284
Ho, Vincent, 8, 10, 12, 15, 17, 328, 329
Hofmann, August Wilhelm, 222n15

honesty, 68
honorary authorship, 84, 214
Hoogeveen, Elly, 323, 324
hospitals, financial interests of, 73
human capital, 283
Human Genome Project, 66, 140–41
human rights, 281–82, 310
humanist counseling, 320–25
Humanistich Verbond, 320
humanistics: defined, 307; development of,
 320–21; mode-3 knowledge and, 319–27; in
 organizational contexts, 333–35; and slow
 questions, 321–24
humanities scholars, entrepreneurialism among,
 38–39
humanity: antiessentialist view of, 280; entrepreneurialism and, 277–79; fragility and
 finitude of, 321–22
Humboldt, Wilhelm von, 279, 302
Hwang, Woo Suk, 78–79, 87n4
hypergoods, 331–32

IBM, 58–59
indigenous knowledge, 281–83
industrial property, 192
industrial science: academic research in cooperation with, 165–66; as applied science, 29;
 complexity of, 167; methodological features of, 158–83; misconduct involving data
 in, 79–80; openness in, 165–66; pragmatic
 criteria employed in, 167–69; secrecy surrounding, 80, 164–66. *See also* applied
 research; technology
industry. *See* commercial interests
infections, 119–20
informatics. *See* bioinformatics
innovation: application, 172–74; incentives for,
 54–55; in linear model of research, 169;
 private benefit from, 103; public funding
 of, 102–3
The Institute for Genomic Research (TIGR),
 137–38
Institutional Patent Agreements, 61n21
Integra v. Merck, 50–51
integrity, compromise of scientific, 66, 80, 111–12,
 115–16, 243
intellectual property: paradoxical character of,
 189; conceptualizations of, 6; contemporary meaning of, 191–93, 201–2; Enlightenment and, 195–96, 285; fallibility of
 knowledge and, 285–86; French Revolution
 and, 188–89, 196–97; indigenous peoples
 and, 281–83; Jefferson and, 197–200;
 meanings of, 190–93; Merton's concept of,
 190–91, 221n6, 222n9; and secrecy in research, 164. *See also* licensing; patenting
interactive view of theory-experience relationship, 175
International Committee for Medical Journal
 Editors (ICMJE), 83, 105

inventions: heroic vs. social determination theories of, 196; incentives for, 54; in linear
 model of research, 169; ownership of,
 61n21
Ioannidis, J. P., 123–24
Irigaray, Luce, 331

Jacobins, 187, 189, 190, 304
Jacoby, Russell, 28
Jaffe, A., 50
Jefferson, Thomas, 197–200, 219, 269, 304
Jensen, R., 53
Jonge, Marinus de, 215
*Journal of the American Medical Association
 (JAMA)*, 99, 105
journals, on research integrity, 14, 83, 105
justification: adversarial approach to, 104; broad
 vs. narrow criterion of, 95–96; costs of, 96,
 103–4, 104t; discovery vs., 90–93; effects of
 commercial funding on, 91; independent,
 91; Mertonian norms and context of, 233,
 234, 248

Kant, Immanuel, 278, 280, 327
Kassirer, Jerome, 123
Kauffman, Stuart, 315
Kern, David, 26
Kilgore, Harley, 29
Kitch, Edmund, 54, 283–86
Kitcher, Philip, 19, 162, 183n1
Klein, Naomi, 296
Kleinman, Daniel, 6, 8, 10, 218, 308, 309
KNAW. *See* Koninklijke Nederlandse Akademie
 van Wetenschappen
knowledge: commodification as aid to, 283–86;
 indigenous, 281–83; as a positional good,
 284; power of, 284; as a public good,
 205–11, 218, 297–300, 303–4; for the public
 good, 303–4; self-protectiveness of, 284–86;
 universality of, 281–82
knowledge engineers, 287–88
knowledge exchange, 132–53; in biomedical
 research, 134–38; changing conditions for,
 132–33; competition as factor in, 141–45;
 copyright and, 195; and indigenous knowledge, 281–82; Merton's communalism
 and, 164; in public vs. private sectors, 133,
 138–45, 151–53, 154n8; in science vs. craft,
 299–300; stages of, 133–34, 145–51; synthesis of specialized research needed for, 126
knowledge transfer, 44–45, 52
Koninklijke Nederlandse Akademie van Wetenschappen (KNAW, Royal Netherlands Academy of Arts and Sciences), 116, 239
Kortmann, F., 317–18, 325
Kourany, Janet, 239, 240–41, 329, 335
Krimsky, Sheldon, 111, 244, 263; *Science in the
 Private Interest*, 25–28
Kropotkin, Piotr, 288
Kuhn, Thomas, 204, 212, 217, 241, 308

Index

Kunneman, Harry, 6, 8, 10, 13, 15, 20, 251, 255n32
Kurzweil, Ray, 278

Lakanal, Joseph, 188, 196–97
Lakatos, Imre, 181, 308, 309; *Proofs and Refutations*, 93
Lam, C. W. H., 94–95
Lancet (journal), 98
Landelijk Orgaan Wetenschappelijke Integriteit (LOWI, National Organization for Scientific Integrity), 240
Langmuir, Irving, 194
Latker, Norman, 30
Latour, Bruno, 210
Lavoisier, Antoine-Laurent, 187–89, 196–97, 221n6, 236, 299–301
Lemelson, Jerome, 62n24
Lemley, Mark, 49, 202
Leonelli, Sabina, 8, 10, 12, 15, 327, 329
Lerner, J., 50
licensing: of academic research, 219; defined, 48; exclusive, 49; justifications for, 52–55; profitability of, 53–54; and social return, 48–49; suggestions concerning, 55–60. *See also* intellectual property; patenting
light therapy, 120–21
Lijphart, A., 320
linear model of research, 209; cascade model superior to, 170–74; principles of, 169–70
local data, 134, 136, 150
Longino, Helen, 116, 254n18, 329
lorazepam, 114
Lyotard, Jean-François, 311

Madey v. Duke, 49–51
Madison, James, 198
Mandeville, Bernard, 287–88
Martinson, B., 78
Marx, Karl, 11, 277–78, 280, 286, 290, 292
material transfer agreements (MTAs), 47–48, 60n7, 226n40
mathematics, and logic of discovery, 93–96
Matthew effect, 205, 214–16, 226n43
McMaster University Medical School, 96
McPherson, Isaac, 199
"me too" drugs, 102
medical centers, financial interests of, 73
medical research: effects of commercial funding on, 98–103; government funding of, 124; pharmaceutical industry's influence on, 101, 112–15, 123–24; scandal of, 98–103; synthesis of specialized research needed for, 126. *See also* biomedical research, disseminating data in; pharmaceutical industry
medicalization, 114
melatonin, 120–21
mental disorders: biological approaches to, 112, 117–18, 126; nutrition and, 119–20
mercantilism, 295
Merck, 75, 98, 105

meritocratic science, 212–18
Merton, Robert K., 18, 20, 26, 67, 87n3, 164, 183n7, 188–95, 201–5, 207–8, 212–18, 220, 232–52, 265, 300; *Science, Technology and Society in Seventeenth-Century England*, 192
methodology, commercialization's effect on, 158–83
Meurer, M., *Patent Failure*, 58–59
microarrays, 135f, 136, 173
microbiology, 172
millennium goals, 310–11
Millikan, Robert, 194
Ministry of Education, Research, and Technology (Germany), 140
Ministry of Education, Science, Sport, and Culture (Japan), 140
Mirowski, Philip, 11, 201, 208–9, 212, 224n29, 304
Mises, Ludwig, 280, 290
Mitroff, I. I., 26
mode-1 knowledge, 311; in combination with mode-3, 319, 326, 332–33; dangers of, 318; defined, 20n7, 312; mode-2 in relation to, 11; and objectivity, 327; psychiatry and, 317; quality control in, 312
mode-2 knowledge, 311; and complexity, 315–16; dangers of, 313–14; defined, 20n7, 312; epistemic heteronomy of, 312; existential foundation of, 328–29; mode-1 in relation to, 11; and objectivity, 327–28; psychiatry and, 317; quality control in, 313
mode-3 knowledge: co-creation as characteristic of, 324–25; in combination with mode-1, 319, 326; and cultural limits, 322–23; defined, 13, 318; and fragility/finitude of human existence, 321–22; and humanistics, 319–27; and morality, 322; and narrative self-exploration, 322–24; in organizational contexts, 255n32, 333–35
model debate, in philosophy of science, 174
model organisms, 137
models, as mediators between theory and experience, 174
Monsanto, 139, 153
morality: mode-2 knowledge and, 329; mode-3 knowledge and, 322; in organizational contexts, 334–35; in postindustrial capitalism, 334
Morin, E., 314–15
Morrill Act (1862), 269
Mowery, David, 30, 54–55
Moynihan, R., 113
MTAs. *See* material transfer agreements
Mulkay, Michael, 26, 235–40
Munich Information Protein Service (MIPS), 137
Musschenga, Albert, 8, 10, 12, 15, 17, 328, 329

Nader, Ralph, 289
Nanoscale Science and Engineering Centers, 30
Napoleon, 302
naproxen, 98

narrative self-exploration, 322–24
National Academies (U.S.), 261
National Cancer Institute (NCI), 103
National Heart, Lung, and Blood Institute, 102
National Institute of Mental Health, 121
National Institutes of Health (NIH), 82, 113, 140
National Science Foundation (NSF), 29–30, 140
nature: laws of, 285–86; scientific control of, 159–60, 170; universal laws inadequate for explaining, 167–68, 174, 178
Nature (journal), 141
Nelson, B., 117
Nelson, R., 54–55
Nelson, Richard, 206–10
neoliberalism, 39, 218, 250, 280, 282, 283
neopopulism, 212
Netherlands, 9, 16, 118, 201, 219, 239–40, 320–21
Netherlands Environmental Assessment Agency, 5
New Deal, 212, 217
New England Journal of Medicine, 98, 105
New York Times (newspaper), 37
Newman (judge), 50–51
Newton, Isaac, 92
Nickles, Thomas, 92, 238
Nietzsche, Friedrich, 327
Nixon, Richard, 171
nonexcludability, 199, 206–7, 252
nonobviousness, patent criterion of, 47, 245
nonrivalry, 199, 206–7, 252
norms of science, 26–27, 67–72; codes of conduct and, 232, 239–41; and conduct of science, 68–69; conflicts between, 71–72; descriptive vs. prescriptive, 67, 74; epistemic, 70; ethical, 70–71; financial interests' effects on, 73–84; informal, 236–38; interrelationship of, 71–72; Mertonian, 240–52; Merton's formulation of, 193, 212–14, 232–38, 241–42, 265; "norms" defined, 67, 242; patenting and, 245–50; and scientific practice, 235–37, 240–41; social enforcement of, 67–68; social epistemology and, 69; social norms in conflict with, 72; sociology of scientific knowledge perspective on, 235–39; teleological character of, 68; values in relation to, 242–44; VSNU code and, 240
Novartis, 24–26
novelty, patent criterion of, 47, 56, 193, 222n11, 222n15, 245
Nozick, Robert, 280
NSF. *See* National Science Foundation
Nussbaum, Martha, 331

objectivity, 70, 159, 180–81, 242, 327–29
observations, 81, 87n8
Observer (newspaper), 100
Office of Corporate Relations, University of Wisconsin, 35
Office of University-Industry Relations, University of Wisconsin, 35
Oken, Lorenz, 201

Okruhlik, Kathleen, 93
olefin metathesis, 177
omega-3 PUFAs, 119–20
OncoMouse, 247
O'Neill, J., 110–11
one-shot science, 95, 96, 103
open science, 188, 218–20
organized skepticism, 213, 234, 249

paclitaxel (Taxol), 102–3
Paramacia, 99
paroxetine (Paxil, Seroxat), 99–100
participatory design research, 295–96
Pasteur, Louis, 172, 194
Patent Act (France, 1791), 62n27
Patent Act (U.S., 1790), 198, 199
Patent Act (U.S., 1793), 199
patenting, 44–60; of academic research, 7, 8, 14, 15, 244–50; and communism (communalism), 246–48; criticisms of, 219–20, 245–52; and disinterestedness, 248–49; of drugs, 125; economic liberalism and, 201; in Europe, 45–46; growth in, 30–31, 44–45, 245; and infringement suits, 49–51, 57; Jefferson and, 197–200, 219; justifications for, 52–55; knowledge transfer through, 44–45, 52; Mertonian values and norms applied to, 245–50; nonobviousness criterion, 47, 245; novelty criterion, 47, 56, 245; overview of, 244–45; person skilled in the art criterion, 59; prior art criterion, 56; profitability of, 53–54; reorientation of, 55–60; review process for, 249; scope of, 58–59, 247; and organized skepticism, 249; social contribution of, 245, 254n22; trends in, 45–46; undesirable and paradoxical consequences of, 46–51; and universalism, 246; university policies regarding, proposals for, 59–60; and upstream research, 51–52; utility criterion, 245; Wisconsin Alumni Research Foundation and, 35–36. *See also* intellectual property; licensing
patient organizations, 123
Patsopoulos, N. A., 123–24
Paxil, 99
Peirce, Charles Sanders, 300
Pels, Dick, 152, 156n26, 265
Perkin-Elmer Corporation, 140
Perkins, John, 33–34
Pfizer, 99
pharmaceutical industry, 110–27; funding of academic/medical research for, 101, 112–13, 115–16, 123–24; ghost authorship in, 84, 114, 123; gifts from, 113, 123; profits in, 101; proposals for controlling, 122–27; psychiatric profession's relations with, 117–18; and sales promotion of approved drugs, 113–15. *See also* medical research
Philips, 219
philosophes, 279, 302, 303
Physics Today (journal), 215

placebo effects, 97, 102
plagiarism, 78, 285
Platform for Psychotherapy and Psychiatry, Dutch
   Society for Psychiaatry and Neurology, 126
Plato, 284, 303
Platonism, 170, 174
pluralism: horizontal transcendence and, 332;
   and objectivity, 181
Poehlman, Eric, 87n4
Polanyi, Michael, 241, 249, 267
polymerase chain reaction (PCR), 173
polyunsaturated fatty acids (PUFAs), 119–20
Popper, Karl, 92, 180, 234, 267, 278, 308
population biology, 282
postacademic science, 18
power, of knowledge, 284
power relations, and commodified science, 13,
   250, 260–62, 296, 318, 326
price, in relation to value, 280, 290–91
Priestley, Joseph, 304
principle of cumulative advantage, 205, 214–17
priority claims, 191–93, 201, 203–5, 234, 299
product-driven competition, 142–43, 147, 151–53
professorships. *See* special professorships
profit motive, its effect on biological research,
   138–39
project-directed databases, 142, 149, 151–53, 327
prospect theory of patents, 54
Prozac, 99–100
psychiatry: as complex system, 316–18; declining
   professional population in, 117; mind vs.
   body in, 117–18, 125–26; pharmaceutical
   industry's relations with, 117–18
psychosocial approaches, 118, 317
public databases, 143–45, 147–49
public goods, 110–11, 199–200, 205–11, 218,
   291–92, 297–300, 303–4
public information, and transparency, 16–17
Public Intellectual Property Resource for Agriculture, 219
public interest: defining, 19; and knowledge
   exchange, 143–45; research in service of,
   28, 182–83. *See also* socially relevant
   research
public interest science, 19
public sociology, 28
public trust, 14, 15, 107, 153, 243. *See also* trust
publication: disclosure of data through, 147–48;
   influence of financial interests on, 75–76,
   76t, 105
PUFAs. *See* polyunsaturated fatty acids
pure science. *See* basic research

Quine, W. V., 81
Quine-Duhem thesis, 81

Radder, Hans, 92, 218, 225n36, 265, 307, 309,
   327, 329, 335
Radin, Margaret, 260, 266, 271–72
Ragetlie, Marion, 324

randomized clinical trials (RCTs), 119–22; and
   cost of justification, 103–4; criticisms of,
   97, 119, 121–22, 179; not research per se,
   179–80; overview of, 96–97, 119; pharmaceutical industry funding of, 124, 179;
   public control of, 106–7, 124–25; significance of, 97, 119. *See also* clinical trials
Rappert, B., 154n8
Ravetz, Jerry, 194
Rawls, John, 268, 327
RCTs. *See* randomized clinical trials
recruitment, of patients for clinical trials, 100–
   101, 105–6
regulation, 16–18, 102, 124, 262
Reichenbach, Hans, 91–92
republicanism, 279, 303–4
republicanism, and university governance, 267–72
research. *See* academic research; medical
   research
research agendas: commercialization's effect on,
   14, 75, 116, 162–64, 182; government setting of, 101, 309; patenting's, 249; pharmaceutical industry's influence on, 123–24;
   societal needs as source of, 110, 183n1
research design, review of, 78
research results: accessibility of, 246;
   commodification of, 138; cooking the data,
   77; fraud involving, 76, 78–80; misconduct
   involving, 78–80; patent-friendly, 46–47;
   responsibility for, 83; sharing of, 47–48;
   skewing of publication record, 75–76, 76t;
   suppression of, 75, 105
research tool patents, 52
researchers, business ownership by, 8
Resnik, David, 8, 10, 13, 15, 17, 115–16, 124, 125,
   223n20, 262, 309, 329
resource-directed databases, 152–53, 155n15
resource-driven competition, 143–45, 149, 152–53,
   155n15
restricted complexity, 315
revolutionary technologies, 172–73
rewards, for scientists, 68, 82–83, 202, 207, 237
Ricoeuer, Paul, 331
Ridker, P., 66
rofecoxib, 98
Rohrer, Heinrich, 173
Royal Netherlands Academy of Arts and Sciences, 5, 116, 239. *See also* Koninklijke
   Nederlandse Akademie van
   Wetenschappen
Royal Society (London), 203
Rules of the European Patent Convention, 58
Russell, Bertrand, 308

Said, Edward, 331, 332
Sampat, B., 54–55
SARS virus, 206
Sawyer, Richard, 34
scanning tunneling microscope (STM), 172–73
Scheler, Max, 222n9

Scherer, Frederic, 191
schizophrenia, 114, 317
Schön, Jan Hendrick, 87n4
Schopenhauer, Arthur, 200
Schumpeter, Joseph, 277–79, 294–95
Schweber, Sylvan, 161
science: adversarial approach in, 104; autonomous, 18–19, 26–27, 152, 156n27, 212, 252, 265, 308; codes of conduct/ethics for, 17, 232, 239–41, 250; as competitive cooperation, 202–5, 223n20; costs of, 66; craft vs., 187–88, 220n2, 299–300; and democracy, 19, 162, 217, 233, 268; discovery-justification distinction in, 90–93; distinctiveness of, 264–66; economics of, 205–11; epistemic autonomy of, 308, 311–12; integrity of, 66, 80, 111–12, 115–16; meritocratic, 212–18; money invested in, 65; norms of, 67–72; open, 188, 218–20; postacademic, 18; practical purposes of, 159–62; public trust in, 14, 15, 107, 153, 243; public-interest, 19; in relation to technology, 168–75, 189, 193–94, 222n15; "self-interested," 152, 156n27; social embedment of, 311–12; social epistemology perspective on, 69; social sciences and humanities vs., 9, 308. *See also* academic research
Science (journal), 78–79, 141
science and technology studies (STS), 212, 253n11, 295
Science Citation Index (SCI), 202, 214
scientists: codes of conduct/ethics aimed at, 250; corrupt, 66–67; earnings of, 66; financial interests of, 72; rewards gained by, 68, 82–83, 202, 207, 237
scientometric databases, 7
scientometric indicators, 7
secrecy, 14, 15; of commercial research, 56, 80, 164–66; prevalence of, 27; reasons for, 27
selective serotonin reuptake inhibitors (SSRIs), 99–100, 114, 118
self-governing science. *See* autonomous science
self-interest, 287
Sent, Esther-Mirjam, 11, 201, 208–9, 212, 224n29, 304
serotonin-norepinephrine reuptake inhibitors (SNRIs), 118
Seroxat, 99–100
sertraline (Zoloft), 99, 114
Shaw, George Bernard, 300
Simon, Herbert, 92
Singer, Peter, 278
Sismondo, S., 114
skepticism. *See* organized skepticism
slow questions, 321–24
Smith, Adam, 288, 295
social constructivism, 318
social epistemology, 69, 183n7
social responsibility, 68, 254n13, 308

social return, licensing as cause of diminishing, 48–49
socially relevant research, 110–11. *See also* public interest
sociology of science, 253n8
sociology of scientific knowledge (SSK), 232, 235–39
Soleto, J., 124–25
Solla Price, Derek de, 214
Sombart, Werner, 289, 296
South Korea, 78–79
Space Station Freedom, 66
special professorships: external funding for, 7, 16; personal ties associated with, 8
Spencer, Herbert, 288
spinning data, 80–82
SSK. *See* sociology of scientific knowledge
Stallman, Richard, 201–2
Stanford University, 60n7
statins, 82
Stelfox, H. T., 99
Stephan, Paula, 205, 208
Sterckx, Sigrid, 8, 10, 15, 17, 41n6, 255n23
Stevens Institute of Technology, 37
Story, Joseph, 49
strategic alliances, 7
Strevens, Michael, 226n43
STS. *See* science and technology studies
substantive objectivity, 327–29
surface objectivity, 327–28
Syngenta, 139

Taxol, 102–3
taxpayers, patents' effect on, 46
Taylor, Charles, 331
technology: in relation to science, 168–75, 189, 193–94, 222n15; seductive power of modern, 325–28. *See also* applied research; industrial science
technology transfer offices, 35, 47–49, 53, 163, 219, 273n1
thalidomide, 119
theory: in cascade model, 170–74; emergentist view of, 168–69, 175; in interactive model, 175; limitations of, 178; in linear model, 169–70; role of, in applied research, 175–79
thermal efficiency, 172
thermodynamic cycle, 172
thermodynamic theory, 172
Thomas, Dorothy Swaine, 216
Thomas, William I., 216
Thomson Reuters, 7
Thursby, J., 49, 53–54
Thursby, M., 49, 53–54
Torres, J., 66
tragedy of the anticommons, 52, 218
transcendence: and hypergoods, 331–32; vertical vs. horizontal, 330–32
transgenic crop research, 31–32

trust: in data, 136, 138; among scientists, 69, 99, 243. *See also* public trust
type II error, 77

understanding, applied research role of, 175–79
United Nations, 191, 310; Genomics Working Group, 206
universalism, 213, 233, 242, 246, 280–83
universities: and entrepreneurship, 38–39, 279, 294–99; financial interests of, 73; political neutrality of, 274n10; profit-seeking activities of, 7; transformation of American, 28–31. *See also* university administration; university-industry relationships
Universities and Small Business Patent Procedures Act (1980), 61n21
university administration: business model of, 37–39; economic instrumentalization of, 4–5, 8; faculty participation in, 269–71, 274n11; republicanism and, 267–72; technology transfer offices in, 35, 47–49, 163, 219, 273n1
University for Humanistics, 320–21, 331
University of California at Berkeley, 24–26
University of Minnesota, 38
University of Twente, 8
University of Virginia, 269
University of Wisconsin–Madison, 30, 33, 35–38, 218
university-industry relationships (UIRs): benefits of, 259; criticisms of, 24–25; and declining public orientation of scientists, 28; economic factors in, 261–62; factors behind, 28; history of, 29–30; as minor problem, 40; republican perspective on, 271–72; societal input on, 267
Uppsala Code of Ethics for Scientists, 239, 254n13
upstream patents, 52
U.S. Chemist's Code of Conduct, 239
U.S. Court of Appeals for the Federal Circuit (CAFC), 49–50
U.S. Department of Agriculture, Animal, Plant, and Inspection Service, 31–32
U.S. Ethical Principles of Psychologists and Code of Conduct, 239
U.S. Food and Drug Administration (FDA), 98, 102
U.S. National Institute of Health, 101, 140
U.S. Supreme Court, 28, 45, 50–51, 286
use value, 280
utility, patent criterion of, 245, 248

Vallas, Steven, 35, 37–38
values: of autonomous science, 152; community-promoting function of, 243; defined, 242–43; facts in relation to, 330; generality/vagueness of, 243–44; Mertonian, 242–52; norms in relation to, 243; patenting and, 245–50
Van den Belt, Henk, 6, 12, 15, 20, 252, 299–300, 304, 309, 329
Van der Steen, Wim, 8, 10, 12, 15, 17, 328, 329
Vattimo, Gianni, 332
Veblen, Thorstein, 289, 296
Venter, Craig, 140–41
Vereniging voor Samenwerkende Nederlandse Universiteiten (VSNU, Association of Universities in the Netherlands), 239–41, 255n29
Vicq d'Azyr, Félix, 201
VIGOR study, 98
Vioxx, 75, 98, 105
Voltaire, *Candide*, 287
VSNU. *See* Vereniging voor Samenwerkende Nederlandse Universiteiten
VU University Amsterdam, 4–5, 245

Washburn, Jennifer, *University, Inc.*, 25–27
Wassermann, August, 204, 223n21, 224n23
Wassermann reaction, 204–5, 223n21, 224n23
water, commodification of, 291–92
Weber, Max, 289, 290, 330, 331, 333
Weil, Eduard, 223n21
Welsh, Rick, 31–32
Western countries, research geared toward, 19
White, Harrison, 301
Whitehead, Alfred North, 308
Whittemore v. Cutter (1813), 49
Whittington, Craig, 99
Wiener, Norbert, 293
Wisconsin Alumni Research Foundation (WARF), 35–37, 218
Woodward, J., 134
World Intellectual Property Organization (WIPO), 191

Yale University, 219

Ziedonis, A., 54–55
Zilsel, Edgar, 202–3
Ziman, John, 18, 161
Zoloft, 99
Zuckerman, Harriet, 67, 215–16